THE HARVILL BOOK OF TWENTIETH-CENTURY POETRY IN ENGLISH

Edited by Michael Schmidt

THE HARVILL PRESS

LONDON

for
Joan McAllister
with love

First published in Great Britain in 1999 by
The Harvill Press
2 Aztec Row
Berners Road
London N1 0PW

1 3 5 7 9 8 6 4 2

www.harvill-press.com

Preface and Introduction copyright © Michael Schmidt, 1999

A CIP catalogue record for this book
is available from the British Library

ISBN 1 86046 351 7

Designed and typeset in Bembo at
Libanus Press, Marlborough, Wiltshire

Printed and bound in Great Britain by Mackays of Chatham

CONTENTS

PREFACE

Thom Gunn is one of the most conservative and at the same time one of the most radical British poets of his generation. He has made himself at home on the American West Coast, with its disparate cultures and languages, without losing his original bearings. He argues for a "spectrum" approach to modern American poetry. There can be spectrums of colour, of sound – and of language. Although remote from one another in conception and intent, the experimentalism of the L=A=N=G=U=A=G=E poets, and the inventive traditionalism of the old and new formalists, share a medium. It has rules that one can observe or break, rhythms one can regularise or disrupt. Gunn's "spectrum" approach acknowledges this diversity, yet also this inescapable commonality of resource. It can apply beyond America, to all English-language poetries.

This alert tolerance is of value to anyone trying to make sense of modern poetry. It insists not on plurality but continuity, it suggests a republic of poetry rather than an irreconcilable anarchy of factions or a severe state of canonical closures. Factions inevitably come about when poets are finding their feet in a difficult "culture of reception". Such factions are points of redefinition, but the critical factions that sometimes grow up in their wake can prove reductive and impoverishing.

Gunn's approach has little to do with subject-matter, ideology, ethnicity or gender, and everything to do with the development of poetic language and form, the extension of the realm of the expressible, and the way poets depend on one another and upon the poets of the past. It proposes definable points of departure, whatever the variety of destination.

The Harvill Book of Twentieth-Century Poetry in English takes as its province a whole century and the whole of the English-speaking world. It features work by over a hundred writers. In general it presents poems which, however rooted in a locality and a particular "speech", survive the crossing of decades, seas and continents.

The century provides no coherent pattern. Its contradictory beginnings are with the poems of Thomas Hardy and Ezra Pound, W. B. Yeats and T. S. Eliot (initial poets in two senses), Wallace Stevens and William Carlos Williams. It can be a pitiless and forgetful age, abandoning important writers like H. D., Isaac Rosenberg, Charlotte Mew, Ivor Gurney, David Jones, Basil Bunting, Laura Riding, Sorley MacLean, and only later trying to make amends. It piously honours, say, Carl Sandburg and Cecil Day-Lewis, Rupert Brooke and Edith Sitwell, but at last dumps them at the roadside, alongside substantial figures like Edwin Muir and George Barker.

Such seeming fickleness is inevitable: poets never know when their hour will come. George Herbert and John Donne were dusted down after long neglect in the nineteenth and twentieth centuries respectively; Emily Dickinson and Gerard Manley Hopkins are – ironically – twentieth-century phenomena. What crowded them out was a fashion that did not relish their difficult originality, any more than the eighteenth century could properly value Christopher Smart or Thomas Chatterton.

Of the many younger poets who have a claim to be included in a book of this kind, I can only say that their century will be the twenty-first, their best work (one hopes) is yet to come. Every anthology proposes a canon and the canonisation of the young can be damaging. It damaged W. H. Auden and has damaged others. Had a book like this been published in 1899 featuring the work of Hardy, Kipling and Yeats, it would have done itself and them no service.

Hardy comes first in this anthology: where else does the century's poetry start if not with his paradoxically unmelancholy thrush? And how better to end than with a poem which, a hundred years on, celebrates and parodies the forms and tones of that resourceful piece? Sophie Hannah is in no danger of being canonised in this book: the twenty-first will certainly be her century. But she has written at my request a new poem, "The Norbert Dentressangle Van", to show how the formal resources that Hardy possessed survive, but also illustrating how Modernist elements inform and extend them, so that they can deal with new subject matter, the new velocities, joys and sorrows of a different *fin de siècle*. The Thrush and the Van are, equally, harbingers.

I am grateful to Christopher MacLehose for entertaining this unlikely project, to Ian Pindar for readying the book for press and tackling editorial and technical challenges with skilful equanimity, and to Harvill *tout court*. I am much indebted to Penny Jones who helped me assemble the text, and to my Carcanet colleagues Pamela Heaton, Joyce Nield, Chris Gribble and Gaynor Hodgson. The incomparable Dennis Enright may have sown a seed of this book years ago with his *Oxford Book of Contemporary Verse 1945–80*, and I was introduced to many of these poems by Peter Jones, with whom I set up Carcanet Press in 1969.

INTRODUCTION

Modernism in its various forms is the defining movement of the twentieth century: a call-to-arms, to *make it new*. Modernism – but also reactions to it. In order to appreciate what "new" means in modern poetry, we should briefly sketch in the context of the old, not forgetting that poets have been "making it new" in one way or another from the very beginning. After all, Modernist renewal did not happen *ex nihilo*: it involved finding energies and resources from the past and from alien cultures. Ezra Pound, who loudly voiced the call-to-arms, later declared: "If we never write anything save what is already understood, the field of understanding will never be extended. One demands the right, now and again, to write for a few people with special interests and whose curiosity reaches into greater detail." If it works, in following generations those "few people" will become the many – perhaps, for a time . . .

On the day that Oscar Wilde was sentenced to two years' hard labour in 1895, Richard Garnett, editor of the British Museum Catalogue, predicted that British poetry would be dead for fifty years. Respectability and real poetry – poetry that makes a difference to the language, to tradition and to the reader – are seldom comfortable bedfellows. Poetry in Britain was doomed to be what it had already largely become, a minor art: the Rhymers and then the Georgians, with only Hardy and Kipling to suggest that it might be something more. (Yeats gave quality time to the experimentalists, but he had declared himself Irish.)

As the century progressed, poets in English got busy doing all sorts of things they had never done before. At the same time, many of them were busy forgetting things their predecessors had done incomparably well. The century's poetic revolutions begin in polemical experiment and end in polemic plain and simple. Imagism is first a discipline and then a repetitive school; New Formalism an articulate reaction and then a prescriptive orthodoxy. Those young poets who stand aside from revolution maintain a wary distance: they group together for the treacherous journey to Parnassus, draw their wagons round in a circle at night and guard the perimeters. But the scouts – who are often the best poets – move off ahead of the wagon train, sometimes out of sight.

The century's poetry is not set characteristically in the big outdoors of Thomas Hardy, Edward Thomas and Robert Frost, or even the literary outdoors of A. E. Housman, populated by common men and women. If there is a landscape, it is often unpeopled. Then there is the thronging city – the real city of Roy Fisher and Frank O'Hara, the unreal city of T. S. Eliot's *The Waste Land* and H. D.'s *Trilogy* and the surreal city of Hart

Crane and John Ashbery. Modernism, cosmopolitan in its origins, remains
metropolitan in its aftermaths.

Also common is a poetry concerned with itself, poetry about poetry,
and poetry that is so wedded to the paradoxes of its medium that it stops in
language. The decadent, experimental legacy of the last *fin de siècle*, "Art for
Art's sake" (deflected by the Wilde affair and the philistinism it licensed)
eventually re-emerged, without the taint of decadence. It came back with
larger philosophical and political pretensions. Yeats made no bones about
it: poetry was not primarily a civic activity. Art can initiate a process of
understanding only by understanding itself. This can involve singling
out one or two resources or techniques (metre, syntax, metaphor, image)
and foregrounding them, experimenting. Among the *fin de siècle* artists,
Swinburne (whose legacy is still underestimated) was obsessed with the
properties of metre and rhythm. He is as Modern as the early Modernists.
Poets were not alone, however, in feeling the need to reinvent their
medium. Aubrey Beardsley was fascinated with line, and not only with line
but with line on varied textures of paper. He never allows the viewer to
forget the mediums employed, even while an image struggles in its louche
web of ink. Henry James perfected an increasingly nuanced syntax, each
extension reaching into deeper crannies of character and motive, where
action declines into a patient catalepsy before such discriminating exactness.

Experimental poetry was not intended to foreground the poet, but
because they exaggerated some elements and excluded others, and con-
trived to reveal the contrivance, they became objects of curiosity. After the
Modernist revolution, experiments were received by consumers (the age
of the consumer arrived with the decline of literary journalism) without
new understanding: less "What is being done?" than "What sort of crack-
pot is doing it?" (Among those "crackpots" were a number of Americans.)
Journalistic opprobrium gave radical new work a kind of notoriety, but
the poet was denied that initial (Coleridgean) critical courtesy, which
inquires after intention, appraises the work's success within the terms it
proposes, and then appraises the validity of the intention. The new work
didn't sell. While in the century's teens, Georgian anthologies sold in
their tens of thousands, Imagist anthologies sold in their dozens. In *The
New Poetic*, C. K. Stead demonstrates how criticism sometimes tried not
to extend but to limit understanding: the word "no" replaced "how" and
"why". What the poet meant literally was interpreted in outdated ways.
The weird lyric narratives of Hardy, Frost and Eliot were taken up in
the same spirit as the narratives of Crabbe or Wordsworth and found
morally obnoxious – or ambiguous – and put down again. Was not the
inspiration for such things often foreign, in particular American, or French?
And those "schools": Imagists, Vorticists and the rest of them, with their
Bohemian lives – Bohemian, a deplorable middle-European model,
generally imported via Paris? Was there not rather too much of the love
that dares not speak its name in those circles, too little respect for the

hierarchy and mechanisms of transmission and appraisal? When Edward Thomas had the temerity to praise Pound's early work, he was dragged over the coals by Gordon Bottomley and others who controlled the economy of literary journalism. A free-minded critic could face unemployment if he bet on the long shot.

Established critics, some of them astute and eloquent men (all of them men) missed the jokes and misunderstood the radical investigations that were under way. For them art and morality were indissoluble, and poetry for poetry's sake was irresponsible. The unconventional was *per se* unpalatable. Change and renewal had to insinuate themselves subtly, quietly, minutely, from unexpected places and undefended flanks. A Trojan horse was required, and one arrived, carrying in its belly a Cambridge philosopher-mathematician, a working-class Midlands lad, a gang of Americans and some Irish.

The horse's first droppings were hard and curious:

> I was bound
> Motionless and faint of breath
> By loveliness that is her own eunuch.

It is unpromising minor poetry, self-parodying in its absence of tone. The poet, Thomas Ernest Hulme, is an enigma. For T. S. Eliot he was a talisman, "the author of two or three of the most beautiful short poems in the language". Michael Roberts (the best modern verse anthologist) admired Hulme's critical work and adopted many of his ideas. If modern readers know Hulme at all, it is usually as a philosopher rather than a poet. Like Coleridge he teased his ideas out of other writers, in this case Henri Bergson, Remy de Gourmont and Théophile de Gaultier. Nevertheless British poetry (and British culture more widely) needed a clear-headed outsider to begin diagnosing its infirmities, to prescribe remedies, and to encourage debate between British and non-British writers of English. Ezra Pound, Wyndham Lewis, D. H. Lawrence, H. D., T. S. Eliot, Edgell Rickword and several others are in his debt.

Hulme reacted against the facility and self-indulgence of the 1890s poets and was equally unfriendly to the popular "new" Georgian verse of the day. He discussed oriental forms with young writers: tanka and haiku, *vers libre* ("free" or unmetered verse), French poetry of the immediate past and present, and "poems in a sacred Hebrew form". He preferred precise brevity to what he saw as prolixity, and rejected the "vacuity" of his contemporaries in favour of vivid, tightly phrased imagery. He insisted on "absolutely accurate representation and no verbiage". At first his attitude to language and reality seemed refreshingly naive, but his conviction that our very sense of the world is inferred through language proved to be genuinely radical.

Although he was killed in action in 1917, Hulme's influence on the century's risk-taking poets cannot be overestimated. Where common sense ignores the jumps and gaps in perception, he affirmed *dis*continuity, the possibility of making unexpected connections that would hold, and hold true. This altered perception of the world led to the possibility – indeed, the necessity – of new forms. In this context "image" implies that objects and feelings not usually associated with each other can be significantly juxtaposed. Hulme calls for a neoclassical poetry, free to find or to forge associations, without reference to "continuous contexts": accurate, hard, intellectual, precise and pessimistic (for man is small, displaced from the centre of the world, no longer underwritten by religious certitudes).

Hulme argues against metre: "It enables people to write verse with no poetic inspiration, and whose mind [*sic*] is not stored with new images." At first the word "inspiration" might seem an unpurged residue from the ideologies he rejected, but not if we redefine it from within the disciplines he proposes. What he says of metre is crucial. Metre is a facilitator, and poetry is not a facile art. Metre and the rhetorics that go with it can inflate a poem, can impose a lax diction and deform ideas if unskilfully handled. In a poem, if a thought is true it must cut its own path through language; the existing pathways, because sanctioned by convention, are already clichéd.

The unit of sense in a poem is not the word but the phrase or sentence; a poet should consider the effect of a whole poem, not local felicities. Here is the germ of William Carlos Williams's "variable foot", which instinct rather than rule legitimises, and of Charles Olson's "breath" theories which have proven so puzzling to critics who want to systematise a poetics that is repelled by system. If not the word, then the line becomes the crucial unit, a poem is a construction made less of words than of lines, each with a dynamic which harmonises or contrasts with those that precede and follow. Rhythm, in short and long measures, displaces metre; and the appraisal of rhythm becomes a matter of nice discrimination, not a standard measurement against a yardstick. "As regarding rhythm," Pound declares, "to compose in sequence of the musical phrase, not in sequence of the metronome." We must distinguish intellect from intuition. Intellect analyses and is the language of prose; intuition, the language of poetry, places the artist "back within the object by a kind of sympathy and breaking down . . . the barrier that space puts between him and his model". Pound gets his "Make It New" from Hulme, who takes from de Gourmont the notion that language is constantly shedding resonance and must be regularly reinvigorated through the creation of new metaphors.

Pound's idea of the *image* ("that which presents an intellectual and emotional complex in an instant of time") was not new, but it had never before become the basis of a poetic movement. Previously it had been one ingredient among many in the complex thing called poetry. Coleridge in his *Biographia Literaria* had written that images "have the effect of reducing multitude to unity, or succession to an instant". Despite the romantic implications, this defines better than Hulme or Pound what an image is and isn't, what it can and cannot do. It appears in the context of an argument about language and the scope of poetry that is much broader than Hulme ever envisaged.

That Hulme's and Pound's axioms could bring together an apprentice school of poets reveals how disorientated younger writers were at the time, how they hankered for liberation but also for rules, how some of the outstanding imaginations of the century lacked the broader perspectives that earlier poets took for granted. Their irrepressible imaginations and hunger for formality extended these early theories in a dozen directions. Pound, again, is exemplary: there is a coherence in his development; to the very end he retained the crucial lineaments of his early discipline, but he made them more capacious; the *Cantos*, although incomplete, are one of the defining works of the century.

Had we only the early, aesthetic work of the Modernists to set in the scales against Kipling's compelling rumbustiousness, Hardy's hard, traditional stanzas and the popular, accessible work of the Georgians, the whole movement would seem a thin, rarified digression, a footnote to the values of the decadents. Those Modernists who managed to develop survived, and Imagism, in retrospect, was an apprenticeship.

In Hulme's "Images" one poem reads in its entirety:

Old houses were scaffolding once and workmen whistling.

A past and a present are juxtaposed. The effect is more resonant than in much strictly Imagist verse because it has a chronology, it does not exist (as "I was bound" does) in a perpetual timeless present. William Empson, the subtlest of poet-critics, says that Imagist poetry is poetry that has lost the use of its legs – it does not move, it does not evoke time, existing only in space. This is one way in which it resists the tyranny of continuity, of cause-and-effect. Committed to the image alone, it strips it from its contexts.

The introvert passions of T. S. Eliot, the extrovert passions of Pound and the classical purity of H. D. characterise a generation of American writers who made it their business to create new spaces in English poetry. They thought that they might break through the conventional façade of the host literature to gain access to the empowering tradition behind.

One Englishman of genius, as much of an outsider in London as the Americans were, identified with their programme. David Herbert Lawrence was not a pure radical. He contributed verse to both Georgian and Imagist anthologies. Conflicting voices are heard in his early poems. The more popular is dramatic, telling stories, interposing moral comment, loosely formal in approach. The Georgians could hear such verse, though the presence of Lawrence's apprentice work in staid Georgian compilations only highlights its erotic power and the conventionality of much of the poetry that surrounds it.

Amy Lowell, for her Imagist anthology, chose terse, imagistic and – crucially – unmoral poems by Lawrence. The images are left to speak for themselves, though we can infer a narrative. These poems are less immediately appealing than those in the Georgian book. "Green" was published in 1915:

> The sky was apple-green.
> The sky was green wine held up in the sun.
> The moon was a golden petal between.

This verges *avant la lettre* on surrealism. In another poem Lawrence wrote: "The street-lamps in the twilight have suddenly started to bleed." He may have been writing to order for the Imagists but, as he gained confidence in his ability to create images to convey different shades of feeling, he moved towards a personal, and then a vatic, idiom. Eventually he came to sound like Nietzsche's Zarathustra: big-voiced, assertive, with less emphasis on delicacy but with abiding precision. He never settled for one particular style, but each poem bears his inimitable voice-print.

His letters and essays are full of arguments useful to other writers. In 1913 he wrote to Edward Marsh that he saw his poems more "as a matter of movements in space than footsteps hitting the earth". There is an emphasis on movement, away from the footfall of prescriptive metre towards expressive cadences and the stops and starts of natural speech; later it is the incantatory, often Biblical movement inspired by Walt Whitman. "It all depends on the pause," Lawrence wrote, "the lingering of the voice according to feeling – it is the hidden emotional pattern that makes poetry, not the obvious form."

He advocated a poetry of process, without goal, wedded to "the imme-diate present", where "there is no perfection, no consummation, nothing finished": open poetry. "Consummation" is a key word, suggesting that his poems deliberately defer or avoid dramatic climax. Such climaxes set the artist outside the artifact, casting him in the role of constructor or orchestrator. For Lawrence, Whitman is the master poet of the "present", whose *Leaves of Grass* (1855) has neither beginning nor conclusion – but this, Lawrence reminds us, does not mean he has no past or future. The voice of the "present" tends to be rhapsodic, celebrating "the urgent, insurgent Now".

Reading Lawrence's statements about poetry, we might have expected from him long poems like Whitman's or William Blake's, or, among his successors, Charles Olson's or Robert Duncan's. Though he learned from American poetry, his sensibility remained thoroughly English, he seldom outruns the lyric or lyric sequence. Long runs are found in the prose, and often the prose is truer to the spirit of his poetics than the poems.

For Lawrence, free verse is essential to poetic utterance. A poetry with-out preconceived metre, stress patterns or syllable count, which involves "the whole man", his passions, conflicts and contradictions, is a poetry of integrity. Nevertheless, for all his ambition to explore new spaces, his free verse is ultimately restricted by his "I". Subjectivity, the wilful attribution of personal meanings to certain words, images and rhythms, is his principal limitation. Yet unlike his imitators, who labour to achieve a voice unique to themselves, there is a Wordsworthian legacy still at work in Lawrence: a man speaking to men. What matters is not idiosyncrasy of voice but integrity and fidelity to the moment.

The impact of free verse on twentieth-century poetry can be felt as often in a poet's choice of diction as in his or her prosody. Formal traditional diction, tending towards archaism, available off-the-peg for a poet working at half-energy, sounds quite silly in free verse. (After free verse, conventional diction becomes less serviceable in traditional metrical verse as well.) The Modernist revolution in prosody revivified diction even for those writers – like Robert Frost or Philip Larkin – who stand aloof from it. Lawrence took this experiment further than Hulme and the Imagists. He wrote an accessible poetry which was immediately appealing and the product of authentic experience; a kind of poetry which, although with entirely different techniques, the Georgians were crafting in more conventional ways. He sloughs clichés like his famous snake sloughs skins, and makes a fresh language: new wine in new bottles. He tells us (in a characteristically eroticised phrase) that in free verse, "we look for the insurgent naked throb of the instant moment". We are to expect "no satisfying stability" because the "pure present" is a realm we have never conquered. And he, too, fails to conquer it, for there *is* a stability in his poems – though it is not always "satisfying". It is not the stable meaning of the moralist, though Lawrence is often intrusively didactic, delivering his message in a paraphrase alongside the images. In the end, it is his rhythmic phrasing that supplies stability, his free verse is rarely as free as he claims: in many poems a cadence pattern is repeated with minimal variation.

Lawrence identifies those elements in his work which conventional readers will note as faults, and champions them as necessary virtues. The poet James Reeves writes of Lawrence: "He had not the craftsman's sense of words as living things, as ends in themselves. Words were too much means to an end." And so they were. Lawrence would have said, and so they should be. This is why he sits uneasily alongside the Georgians. He was never "craftsmanly". Reeves adds: "He can seldom have conceived a poem as a whole before he sat down to write it. It grew under his pen." The same could be said of the poems of William Carlos Williams and – we may guess – some of Pound's. The freedom of free verse has something to do with tolerating surprise, inviting chance and randomness into the process of making.

After their deaths, writers suffer a revaluation. Since he died in 1965, T. S. Eliot's reputation has undergone a serious and excessive devaluation. His politics, usually presented in a form so simplified that he would not have recognised them, have been made to tell against him. There are shadowy areas in his biography, into which prurient critics have pointed their torches. The pre-*Four Quartets* poems and essays remain controversial in ways they were when they first appeared, as though the paint has not yet dried on them. Eliot created the critical space: he effected a radical change in the ways in which the intelligentsia thought about poetry and literature generally, but the impact in Britain is not as fundamental as it once seemed.

Eliot makes play of the poet's impersonality, yet it would be hard to confuse even his least-known lines with those of another poet. His images, cadences and tones are entirely his own. Why did he advocate "impersonality" and recoil at the idea of a biography? He may have wished to protect his poems from the higher gossip of biography, which tends to read each work as an act of self-disclosure. He was right to fear the worst. Biographical sensationalism is a modern vice.

Eliot insists that "the emotion of art is impersonal . . . The progress of an artist is a continual self-sacrifice, a continual extinction of personality". His language borders on the religious (the poet as martyr to his art), and these terms he employed before he became a committed Anglican. What occurs in his work is an extinction of biographical referents; but his personality, for all its reticence, is palpably present in every line. We might say the same of Elizabeth Bishop or Charles Tomlinson.

For Eliot, tradition is a kind of accretion. Each individual talent relates to and subtly alters the work that has come before. A writer acquires tradition through dedicated reading, application and a sharpening discrimination. Writers and readers develop an instinct for both the "pastness" and the presence of tradition. In this way, all literature remains contemporary and no poet can be judged outside the context of this living tradition. But some resources are no longer, or not immediately, serviceable; forms, registers and elements of diction can belong specifically to their period, and though the works still speak, their resources are not available today. This description of tradition has been satirised by his critics: Tradition as a carefully modulated, self-regulating system, like the stock exchange.

Eliot's later career took him into the thick of publishing. The task of editing other people's work, appraising manuscripts for publication and engaging in the actual trade, diverted him from his own writing. He became an influential member of the establishment. His forcefulness as a critic, the patrician authority of his style, defined one possible route for English literature this century; but when he became established, he began a recantation, manifested in his plays, his later poems and criticism, and in the poetry he published at Faber & Faber with its sins of omission and commission. He qualified and undermined the challenges he had thrown down in his early works. He changed ground on Milton and on Goethe, poets he had once criticised with severity. The later Eliot hardly diminishes the early firebrand. Prufrock may have grown into the Elder Statesman, but Prufrock remains our contemporary.

Eliot's poetry has a comparable importance within the tradition to Dryden's and Wordsworth's in earlier centuries. He effects a renewal in poetic language. "The Love Song of J. Alfred Prufrock" and *The Waste Land* remain more "contemporary" in feel than much work produced in the last decade, or last year. Like all great poems, they remain present and available, lodging in our aural memory. In the first half of the century, Eliot and Pound thoroughly unsettled our poetic and critical language, our sensibility. Against the rigour of Eliot's considerable body of work, the hectic fiddlings of postmodernism can appear facile and pointless. Much anti-Modernist polemic is earnest and reactionary by contrast: again the chilly hand of conventionality grips firmly. Even Eliot in his long last years breathed the same air as lesser poets.

But Ezra Pound didn't. His engagement with other languages is more important than the movements with which he associated himself. From Ernest Fenollosa he learned something of the dynamic of Chinese, a language entirely alien to English, its writing ideographic and in his view Imagistic. In his translations, Pound's Chinese-influenced measure is not the syllable or stress count, but the fulfilment of the grammatical movement of the sentence – a contained rhythm of syntax. "To break the pentameter, that was the first heave," he said.

In *Hugh Selwyn Mauberley* (1920), he managed to discard the remnants of the 1890s. Eliot read the poem as the "document of an epoch". The quatrains break down in the fourth section, and in *vers libre* Pound writes one of the great war poems, prefiguring the clarity and anger of his *Cantos*. *Mauberley* brings into focus the political, cultural and spiritual England after the war, the poverty of spirit, the coarse materialism and vacuity of those who make and those who promote "value". It is a poem of bankruptcy: it was only a matter of time before Pound abandoned England for good as irreparable. *Mauberley* is the last poem by Pound which a majority of Pound-tolerant English readers enjoy. Many part company with him after this point, seeing the later work as wildly aberrant in its form, language, allusiveness, and – of course – in its politics.

As Donald Davie remarks, for those who value the *Cantos*, the poetry "has to survive a self-evidently and perilously wrong understanding of history, and hence of politics". It also has to survive the huge wealth of reference, of apparently disparate traditions, which inform it – such as Chinese ideograms, quotes from Thomas Jefferson, from the Provençal, Italian, Greek, and a host of other cultural "zones". Pound's poetry illustrates the transformations of Tradition that occur when the centre no longer holds, when the English that was exported to the Colonies comes home with its own luggage.

After Pound we read poetry differently. Without him, it is hard to know how we could read Basil Bunting, Charles Olson, George Oppen, Robert Duncan and a host of others, including H. D., who was to some extent Ezra's own creation. Without Pound, much innovative poetry looks like nonsense. William Carlos Williams is not solid enough to bear the weight: Pound is our problematic, polyphiloprogenitive ancestor. Those who reject him, whether for his politics or for his poetry, build instead on a tradition he resolutely abandoned in 1920, when he left the "sinking island" for ever.

Zealous to remake poetry, to subtilise and extend it, the Modernists did not reconsider or reconstruct their understanding of what "the poet" is. In their polemical assurance and the occasional hauteur with which they regard the common reader, in their sense of the exclusive importance of their programmes, they have more in common with the Victorian sages and the Romantics than is generally acknowledged. The "selves" they "set back within the object" were not refigured selves. When contemporary readers recoil from the tone and manner of Modernist poetry, critical writing and polemic, it is often a response to the tone of voice, marked less by candour than by a kind of hubris. In our postmodern, ironic age, sarcasm looks coarse; in an era which insists on "the humility of the artist" and what one pair of anthologists celebrate as "the democratic voice", the over-confident manner grates.

It is possible to make too much of Pound and Eliot. But we cannot make too much of the various Modernisms they helped to generate – Wallace Stevens, Williams, Lawrence, Marianne Moore, H. D., Hugh MacDiarmid, Robert Graves, Laura Riding and others flourish in spaces which they first cleared. In one way or another Pound and Eliot touch even those poets who seem to dissent most eloquently from them. The impact of the Modernist Yeats – and of French symbolist poetry – on that curmudgeonly stick-in-the-mud Philip Larkin is a matter of record. Larkin read and was astounded by Laura Riding.

Each major Modernist stands free of his or her origins in the "movements" of the early part of the century. We read them because they are the few and generally isolated exceptions. Perhaps it is always so: we read, in the end, the exceptions, whether in the sixteenth, eighteenth or twentieth century. This is an anthology of exceptions. Some of them are popular writers. Popularity need not mean (as a Modernist might argue) that the poetry is compromised. Among British and Irish poets, Thomas Hardy and A. E. Housman, John Betjeman, Philip Larkin, Ted Hughes and Seamus Heaney, sold and sell well. But, apart from Hardy, they are not a true measure of their century. If we define its lineaments by them, we remain deaf, because we hear Heaney, to the merits of Thomas Kinsella and Eavan Boland; because we hear Larkin and his imitators, to the merits of C. H. Sisson, Roy Fisher and Geoffrey Hill. We will be tempted among the new writers to single out those who are in a familiar mould. "Where is the new Larkin/Hughes?" Where, in fact, are the old Larkin and the old Hughes? Each exceptional poet is his or her own changing prototype.

This Harvill anthology takes its bearings from Michael Roberts's *Faber Book of Modern Verse*. It is an attempt to do for the entire twentieth century what Roberts did for the period *entre deux guerres*. "I have included," he wrote, "only poems which seem to me to add to the resources of poetry, to be likely to influence the future development of poetry and language, and to please me for reasons neither personal nor idiosyncratic." I share his desire, with one difference of emphasis: instead of his "and please me" I must say "and/or please me". Taste is one function, judgement another; both have authority but they do not always operate in unison. It is possible (if taste is to develop) for it to be led by judgement; and there are poems in this book which puzzle me in a way that I believe will turn to pleasure in due course. I was puzzled by Basil Bunting, Donald Davie, John Ashbery and C. H. Sisson when I first read them. Coming to terms with that puzzlement has itself made this anthology more broadly-based than previous anthologies of its kind.

Anthologies of modern poetry often aim to be representative. By this editors or editorial teams mean that they have tried to include poets from every school and movement they can find, even work for which they feel little or no affinity. The net effect of such efforts is that nothing is represented. Instead, a suggestive and unresolved mass of material is presented. Such an approach is of value, not least because it is correct, democratic in purpose, politically unassailable, morally commendable. But it leaves the task of the anthologist to readers who must select, as a publisher or magazine editor would do from a pile of submissions, work that actually makes sense within the tradition and has earned its place. Philip Larkin's *Oxford Book of Twentieth-Century English Verse* was among the first anthologies to sacrifice robust discrimination for a more neutral approach. This anthology has no such aim. The inclusions and exclusions are generally deliberate. It has to be said, however, that one or two poets are absent by their own choice.

What is the purpose of this book? To insist that there is a continuity between the radical experimental poets and those who are usually presented as mainstream; to select poems which engage a reader solely because of what they do with language, regardless of subject matter or the orientation of the poet. It is a book of poems, not of poets. The perspective is one of a particularist, aware that particularism itself is regarded as a theory and ideology by theorists and ideologues.

It sometimes seems that the second half of this century has been lavishly preoccupied – when it claims to be preoccupied with poetry at all – with other things, with poetry's context, its usefulness, its witness and moral probity construed in the light of the age's shifting preferences and concerns. This may always have been in part the case, but it is hard to think of a period in which attention has so often been focussed on the ephemeral, in which critics have been so resolutely blind to inappropriate achievement or to radical imaginations – if by "radical" we mean those imaginations which refine and redefine poetry, whose work affirms traditions by innovation and extension, and which exist in a state of impatience with the fashions of the day. At last some eyes turn to such work, but eyes made partisan by a sense of perceived neglect, so that when claims are made they are made too shrilly. The emergence of Basil Bunting, of W. S. Graham and other writers who missed the boat of youth, can be valuable to readers and poets today, but their absence from their own period – as

Hopkins's absence from his or Emily Dickinson's from hers – deprive not only the author but the literature itself of crucial resources. It is possible for half a century to look in the wrong direction, or even to look for the wrong things in the right direction.

This book has a bias that ought to be declared. Since Gower and Langland were addressing their very different audiences in the fourteenth century, there have been at least two kinds of poetry and two kinds of audience. One poetry aims to elicit a collective response. Its origins are in the popular, Bible tradition, its loudest contemporary exponents are the performance poets. It is immediately political and deeply wedded to what it takes to be its community of concern. There is another poetry, also deriving from the Bible and the Prayer Book, which elicits what one critic calls a "communal" response, a poetry to which each reader responds in an individual way and which is sufficiently capacious to admit a variety of responses. The first kind of poetry engenders a solidarity of sorts, the second kind, communion. This is largely an anthology of the second kind of poetry. I am ill at ease with a poetry that has designs on me rather than on its subject and its medium. I take my editorial bearings from Modernism, though a love of Hardy and Frost, a taste for Les Murray and Wendy Cope, excuse me from being doctrinaire. An anthology that takes Modernist bearings is an anthology that believes it is possible to find coherence within so large a body of work, from so many corners of the world.

MICHAEL SCHMIDT

THE HARVILL BOOK OF
TWENTIETH-CENTURY
POETRY IN ENGLISH

THOMAS HARDY

The Darkling Thrush

I leant upon a coppice gate
  When Frost was spectre-gray,
And Winter's dregs made desolate
  The weakening eye of day.
The tangled bine-stems scored the sky
  Like strings of broken lyres,
And all mankind that haunted nigh
  Had sought their household fires.

The land's sharp features seemed to be
  The Century's corpse outleant,
His crypt the cloudy canopy,
  The wind his death-lament.
The ancient pulse of germ and birth
  Was shrunken hard and dry,
And every spirit upon earth
  Seemed fervourless as I.

At once a voice arose among
  The bleak twigs overhead
In a full-hearted evensong
  Of joy illimited;
An aged thrush, frail, gaunt, and small,
  In blast-beruffled plume,
Had chosen thus to fling his soul
  Upon the growing gloom.

So little cause for carolings
  Of such ecstatic sound
Was written on terrestrial things
  Afar or nigh around,
That I could think there trembled through
  His happy good-night air
Some blessed Hope, whereof he knew
  And I was unaware.

Thoughts of Phena

At News of her Death

Not a line of her writing have I,
    Not a thread of her hair,
No mark of her late time as dame in her dwelling, whereby
    I may picture her there;
    And in vain do I urge my unsight
      To conceive my lost prize
At her close, whom I knew when her dreams were upbrimming with
      light,
    And with laughter her eyes.

What scenes spread around her last days,
    Sad, shining, or dim?
Did her gifts and compassions enray and enarch her sweet ways
    With an aureate nimb?
    Or did life-light decline from her years,
      And mischances control
Her full day-star; unease, or regret, or forebodings, or fears
    Disennoble her soul?

Thus I do but the phantom retain
    Of the maiden of yore
As my relic; yet haply the best of her – fined in my brain
    It may be the more
    That no line of her writing have I,
      Nor a thread of her hair,
No mark of her late time as dame in her dwelling, whereby
    I may picture her there.

"I look into my glass"

I look into my glass,
And view my wasting skin,
And say, "Would God it came to pass
My heart had shrunk as thin!"

For then, I, undistrest
By hearts grown cold to me,
Could lonely wait my endless rest
With equanimity.

But Time, to make me grieve,
Part steals, lets part abide;
And shakes this fragile frame at eve
With throbbings of noontide.

Drummer Hodge

1

They throw in Drummer Hodge, to rest
    Uncoffined – just as found:
His landmark is a kopje-crest
    That breaks the veldt around;
And foreign constellations west
    Each night above his mound.

2

Young Hodge the Drummer never knew –
    Fresh from his Wessex home –
The meaning of the broad Karoo,
    The Bush, the dusty loam,
And why uprose to nightly view
    Strange stars amid the gloam.

3

Yet portion of that unknown plain
    Will Hodge for ever be;
His homely Northern breast and brain
    Grow to some Southern tree,
And strange-eyed constellations reign
    His stars eternally.

A Broken Appointment

    You did not come,
And marching Time drew on, and wore me numb. –
Yet less for loss of your dear presence there
Than that I thus found lacking in your make
That high compassion which can overbear
Reluctance for pure lovingkindness' sake
Grieved I, when, as the hope-hour stroked its sum,
    You did not come.

You love not me,
And love alone can lend you loyalty;
— I know and knew it. But, unto the store
Of human deeds divine in all but name,
Was it not worth a little hour or more
To add yet this: Once you, a woman, came
To soothe a time-torn man; even though it be
     You love not me?

In Tenebris (I)

Percussus sum sicut foenum, et artuit cor meum. — *Ps. ci.*

    Wintertime nighs;
But my bereavement-pain
It cannot bring again:
    Twice no one dies.

    Flower-petals flee;
But, since it once hath been,
No more that severing scene
    Can harrow me.

    Birds faint in dread:
I shall not lose old strength
In the lone frost's black length:
    Strength long since fled!

    Leaves freeze to dun;
But friends can not turn cold
This season as of old
    For him with none.

    Tempests may scath;
But love can not make smart
Again this year his heart
    Who no heart hath.

    Black is night's cope;
But death will not appal
One who, past doubtings all,
    Waits in unhope.

The Man He Killed

"Had he and I but met
    By some old ancient inn,
We should have sat us down to wet
    Right many a nipperkin!

"But ranged as infantry,
    And staring face to face,
I shot at him as he at me,
    And killed him in his place.

"I shot him dead because —
    Because he was my foe,
Just so: my foe of course he was;
    That's clear enough; although

"He thought he'd 'list, perhaps,
    Off-hand like — just as I —
Was out of work — had sold his traps —
    No other reason why.

"Yes; quaint and curious war is!
    You shoot a fellow down
You'd treat if met where any bar is,
    Or help to half-a-crown."

Channel Firing

That night your great guns, unawares,
Shook all our coffins as we lay,
And broke the chancel window-squares,
We thought it was the Judgement-day

And sat upright. While drearisome
Arose the howl of wakened hounds:
The mouse let fall the altar-crumb,
The worms drew back into the mounds,

The glebe cow drooled. Till God called, "No;
It's gunnery practice out at sea
Just as before you went below;
The world is as it used to be:

"All nations striving strong to make
Red war yet redder. Mad as hatters
They do no more for Christés sake
Than you who are helpless in such matters.

"That this is not the judgement-hour
For some of them's a blessed thing,
For if it were they'd have to scour
Hell's floor for so much threatening . . .

"Ha, ha. It will be warmer when
I blow the trumpet (if indeed
I ever do; for you are men,
And rest eternal sorely need)."

So down we lay again. "I wonder,
Will the world ever saner be,"
Said one, "than when He sent us under
In our indifferent century!"

And many a skeleton shook his head.
"Instead of preaching forty year,"
My neighbour Parson Thirdly said,
"I wish I had stuck to pipes and beer."

Again the guns disturbed the hour,
Roaring their readiness to avenge,
As far inland as Stourton Tower,
And Camelot, and starlit Stonehenge.

The Convergence of the Twain

(Lines on the loss of the Titanic)

I

In a solitude of the sea
Deep from human vanity,
And the Pride of Life that planned her, stilly couches she.

2

Steel chambers, late the pyres
Of her salamandrine fires,
Cold currents thrid, and turn to rhythmic tidal lyres.

3

Over the mirrors meant
To glass the opulent
The sea-worm crawls – grotesque, slimed, dumb, indifferent.

4

Jewels in joy designed
To ravish the sensuous mind
Lie lightless, all their sparkles bleared and black and blind.

5

Dim moon-eyed fishes near
Gaze at the gilded gear
And query: "What does this vaingloriousness down here?"

6

Well: while was fashioning
This creature of cleaving wing,
The Immanent Will that stirs and urges everything

7

Prepared a sinister mate
For her – so gaily great –
A Shape of Ice, for the time far and dissociate.

8

And as the smart ship grew
In stature, grace, and hue,
In shadowy silent distance grew the Iceberg too.

9

Alien they seemed to be:
No mortal eye could see
The intimate welding of their later history,

10

Or sign that they were bent
By paths coincident
On being anon twin halves of one august event,

11

Till the Spinner of the Years
Said "Now!" And each one hears,
And consummation comes, and jars two hemispheres.

The Going

Why did you give no hint that night
That quickly after the morrow's dawn,
And calmly, as if indifferent quite,
You would close your term here, up and be gone
  Where I could not follow
  With wing of swallow
To gain one glimpse of you ever anon!

  Never to bid good-bye,
  Or lip me the softest call,
Or utter a wish for a word, while I
Saw morning harden upon the wall,
  Unmoved, unknowing
  That your great going
Had place that moment, and altered all.

Why do you make me leave the house
And think for a breath it is you I see
At the end of the alley of bending boughs
Where so often at dusk you used to be;
  Till in darkening dankness
  The yawning blankness
Of the perspective sickens me!

  You were she who abode
  By those red-veined rocks far West,
You were the swan-necked one who rode
Along the beetling Beeny Crest,
  And, reining nigh me,
  Would muse and eye me,
While Life unrolled us its very best.

Why, then, latterly did we not speak,
Did we not think of those days long dead,
And ere your vanishing strive to seek
That time's renewal? We might have said,
  "In this bright spring weather
  We'll visit together
Those places that once we visited."

Well, well! All's past amend,
Unchangeable. It must go.
I seem but a dead man held on end
To sink down soon . . . . O you could not know
That such swift fleeing
No soul foreseeing –
Not even I – would undo me so!

The Voice

Woman much missed, how you call to me, call to me,
Saying that now you are not as you were
When you had changed from the one who was all to me,
But as at first, when our day was fair.

Can it be you that I hear? Let me view you, then,
Standing as when I drew near to the town
Where you would wait for me: yes, as I knew you then,
Even to the original air-blue gown!

Or is it only the breeze, in its listlessness
Travelling across the wet mead to me here,
You being ever dissolved to wan wistlessness,
Heard no more again far or near?

Thus I; faltering forward,
Leaves around me falling,
Wind oozing thin through the thorn from norward,
And the woman calling.

His Visitor

I come across from Mellstock while the moon wastes weaker
To behold where I lived with you for twenty years and more:
I shall go in the gray, at the passing of the mail-train,
And need no setting open of the long familiar door
As before.

The change I notice in my once own quarters!
A formal-fashioned border where the daisies used to be,
The rooms new painted, and the pictures altered,
And other cups and saucers, and no cosy nook for tea
As with me.

I discern the dim faces of the sleep-wrapt servants;
They are not those who tended me through feeble hours and strong,
But strangers quite, who never knew my rule here,
Who never saw me painting, never heard my softling song
    Float along.

So I don't want to linger in this re-decked dwelling,
I feel too uneasy at the contrasts I behold,
And I make again for Mellstock to return here never,
And rejoin the roomy silence, and the mute and manifold
    Souls of old.

After a Journey

Hereto I come to view a voiceless ghost;
    Whither, O whither will its whim now draw me?
Up the cliff, down, till I'm lonely, lost,
    And the unseen waters' ejaculations awe me.
Where you will next be there's no knowing,
    Facing round about me everywhere,
      With your nut-coloured hair,
And gray eyes, and rose-flush coming and going.

Yes: I have re-entered your olden haunts at last;
    Through the years, through the dead scenes I have tracked
      you;
What have you now found to say of our past –
    Scanned across the dark space wherein I have lacked you?
Summer gave us sweets, but autumn wrought division?
    Things were not lastly as firstly well
      With us twain, you tell?
But all's closed now, despite Time's derision.

I see what you are doing: you are leading me on
    To the spots we knew when we haunted here together,
The waterfall, above which the mist-bow shone
    At the then fair hour in the then fair weather,
And the cave just under, with a voice still so hollow
    That it seems to call out to me from forty years ago,
      When you were all aglow,
And not the thin ghost that I now fraily follow!

Ignorant of what there is flitting here to see,
   The waked birds preen and the seals flop lazily;
Soon you will have, Dear, to vanish from me,
   For the stars close their shutters and the dawn whitens
       hazily.
Trust me, I mind not, though Life lours,
   The bringing me here; nay, bring me here again!
    I am just the same as when
Our days were a joy, and our paths through flowers.

Places

Nobody says: Ah, that is the place
Where chanced, in the hollow of years ago,
What none of the Three Towns cared to know –
The birth of a little girl of grace –
The sweetest the house saw, first or last;
   Yet it was so
   On that day long past.

Nobody thinks: There, there she lay
In a room by the Hoe, like the bud of a flower,
And listened, just after the bedtime hour,
To the stammering chimes that used to play
The quaint Old Hundred-and-Thirteenth tune
   In Saint Andrew's tower
   Night, morn, and noon.

Nobody calls to mind that here
Upon Boterel Hill, where the waggoners skid,
With cheeks whose airy flush outbid
Fresh fruit in bloom, and free of fear,
She cantered down, as if she must fall
   (Though she never did),
   To the charm of all.

Nay: one there is to whom these things,
That nobody else's mind calls back,
Have a savour that scenes in being lack,
And a presence more than the actual brings;
To whom to-day is beneaped and stale,
   And its urgent clack
   But a vapid tale.

The Voice of Things

Forty Augusts – aye, and several more – ago,
    When I paced the headlands loosed from dull employ,
The waves huzza'd like a multitude below
    In the sway of an all-including joy
        Without cloy.

Blankly I walked there a double decade after,
    When thwarts had flung their toils in front of me,
And I heard the waters wagging in a long ironic laughter
    At the lot of men, and all the vapoury
        Things that be.

Wheeling change has set me again standing where
    Once I heard the waves huzza at Lammas-tide;
But they supplicate now – like a congregation there
    Who murmur the Confession – I outside,
        Prayer denied.

Heredity

I am the family face;
Flesh perishes, I live on,
Projecting trait and trace
Through time to times anon,
And leaping from place to place
Over oblivion.

The years-heired feature that can
In curve and voice and eye
Despise the human span
Of durance – that is I;
The eternal thing in man,
That heeds no call to die.

The Oxen

Christmas Eve, and twelve of the clock.
    "Now they are all on their knees,"
An elder said as we sat in a flock
    By the embers in hearthside ease.

We pictured the meek mild creatures where
    They dwelt in their strawy pen,
Nor did it occur to one of us there
    To doubt they were kneeling then.

So fair a fancy few would weave
    In these years! Yet, I feel,
If someone said on Christmas Eve,
    "Come; see the oxen kneel

"In the lonely barton by yonder coomb
    Our childhood used to know,"
I should go with him in the gloom,
    Hoping it might be so.

During Wind and Rain

They sing their dearest songs —
He, she, all of them — yea,
Treble and tenor and bass,
    And one to play;
With the candles mooning each face . . .
    Ah, no; the years O!
How the sick leaves reel down in throngs!

They clear the creeping moss —
Elders and juniors — aye,
Making the pathways neat
    And the garden gay;
And they build a shady seat . . .
    Ah, no; the years, the years;
See, the white storm-birds wing across!

They are blithely breakfasting all —
Men and maidens — yea,
Under the summer tree,
    With a glimpse of the bay,
While pet fowl come to the knee . . .
    Ah, no; the years O!
And the rotten rose is ript from the wall.

They change to a high new house,
He, she, all of them – aye,
Clocks and carpets and chairs
    On the lawn all day,
And brightest things that are theirs . . .
    Ah, no; the years, the years;
Down their carved names the rain-drop ploughs.

In Time of "The Breaking of Nations"

I

Only a man harrowing clods
    In a slow silent walk
With an old horse that stumbles and nods
    Half asleep as they stalk.

2

Only thin smoke without flame
    From the heaps of couch-grass;
Yet this will go onward the same
    Though Dynasties pass.

3

Yonder a maid and her wight
    Come whispering by:
War's annals will cloud into night
    Ere their story die.

Afterwards

When the Present has latched its postern behind my tremulous stay,
    And the May month flaps its glad green leaves like wings,
Delicate-filmed as new-spun silk, will the neighbours say,
    "He was a man who used to notice such things"?

If it be in the dusk when, like an eyelid's soundless blink,
    The dewfall-hawk comes crossing the shades to alight
Upon the wind-warped upland thorn, a gazer may think,
    "To him this must have been a familiar sight."

If I pass during some nocturnal blackness, mothy and warm,
    When the hedgehog travels furtively over the lawn,
One may say, "He strove that such innocent creatures should come to
        no harm,
    But he could do little for them; and now he is gone."

If, when hearing that I have been stilled at last, they stand at the door,
    Watching the full-starred heavens that winter sees,
Will this thought rise on those who will meet my face no more,
    "He was one who had an eye for such mysteries"?

And will any say when my bell of quittance is heard in the gloom,
    And a crossing breeze cuts a pause in its outrollings,
Till they rise again, as they were a new bell's boom,
    "He hears it not now, but used to notice such things"?

A. E. HOUSMAN

Reveille

Wake: the silver dusk returning
    Up the beach of darkness brims,
And the ship of sunrise burning
    Strands upon the eastern rims.

Wake: the vaulted shadow shatters,
    Trampled to the floor it spanned,
And the tent of night in tatters
    Straws the sky-pavilioned land.

Up, lad, up, 'tis late for lying:
    Hear the drums of morning play;
Hark, the empty highways crying
    "Who'll beyond the hills away?"

Towns and countries woo together,
    Forelands beacon, belfries call;
Never lad that trod on leather
    Lived to feast his heart with all.

Up, lad: thews that lie and cumber
   Sunlit pallets never thrive;
Morns abed and daylight slumber
   Were not meant for man alive.

Clay lies still, but blood's a rover;
   Breath's a ware that will not keep.
Up, lad: when the journey's over
   There'll be time enough to sleep.

"Farewell to barn and stack and tree"

"Farewell to barn and stack and tree,
   Farewell to Severn shore.
Terence, look your last at me,
   For I come home no more.

"The sun burns on the half-mown hill.
   By now the blood is dried;
And Maurice amongst the hay lies still
   And my knife is in his side.

"My mother thinks us long away;
   'Tis time the field were mown.
She had two sons at rising day,
   To-night she'll be alone.

"And here's a bloody hand to shake,
   And oh, man, here's good-bye;
We'll sweat no more on scythe and rake,
   My bloody hands and I.

"I wish you strength to bring you pride.
   And a love to keep you clean,
And I wish you luck, come Lammastide.
   At racing on the green.

"Long for me the rick will wait,
   And long will wait the fold,
And long will stand the empty plate,
   And dinner will be cold."

"When I watch the living meet"

When I watch the living meet,
  And the moving pageant file
Warm and breathing through the street
  Where I lodge a little while,

If the heats of hate and lust
  In the house of flesh are strong,
Let me mind the house of dust
  Where my sojourn shall be long.

In the nation that is not
  Nothing stands that stood before;
There revenges are forgot,
  And the hater hates no more;

Lovers lying two and two
  Ask not whom they sleep beside,
And the bridegroom all night through
  Never turns him to the bride.

"On Wenlock Edge the wood's in trouble"

On Wenlock Edge the wood's in trouble;
  His forest fleece the Wrekin heaves;
The gale, it plies the saplings double,
  And thick on Severn snow the leaves.

'Twould blow like this through holt and hanger
  When Uricon the city stood:
'Tis the old wind in the old anger,
  But then it threshed another wood.

Then, 'twas before my time, the Roman
  At yonder heaving hill would stare:
The blood that warms an English yeoman,
  The thoughts that hurt him, they were there.

There, like the wind through woods in riot,
  Through him the gale of life blew high;
The tree of man was never quiet:
  Then 'twas the Roman, now 'tis I.

The gale, it plies the saplings double,
    It blows so hard, 'twill soon be gone:
To-day the Roman and his trouble
    Are ashes under Uricon.

"Into my heart an air that kills"

Into my heart an air that kills
    From yon far country blows:
What are those blue remembered hills,
    What spires, what farms are those?

That is the land of lost content,
    I see it shining plain,
The happy highways where I went
    And cannot come again.

"Crossing alone the nighted ferry"

Crossing alone the nighted ferry
    With the one coin for fee,
Whom, on the wharf of Lethe waiting,
    Count you to find? Not me.

The brisk fond lackey to fetch and carry,
    The true, sick-hearted slave,
Expect him not in the just city
    And free land of the grave.

"Here dead lie we because we did not choose"

Here dead lie we because we did not choose
    To live and shame the land from which we sprung.
Life, to be sure, is nothing much to lose;
    But young men think it is, and we were young.

RUDYARD KIPLING

The Dykes

We have no heart for the fishing – we have no hand for the oar –
All that our fathers taught us of old pleases us now no more.
All that our own hearts bid us believe we doubt where we do not
    deny –
There is no proof in the bread we eat nor rest in the toil we ply.

Look you, our foreshore stretches far through sea-gate, dyke, and
    groin –
Made land all, that our fathers made, where the flats and the fairway
    join.
They forced the sea a sea-league back. They died, and their work
    stood fast.
We were born to peace in the lee of the dykes, but the time of our
    peace is past.

Far off, the full tide clambers and slips, mouthing and testing all,
Nipping the flanks of the water-gates, baying along the wall;
Turning the shingle, returning the shingle, changing the set of the
    sand . . .
We are too far from the beach, men say, to know how the outworks
    stand.

So we come down, uneasy, to look; uneasily pacing the beach.
These are the dykes our fathers made: we have never known a breach.
Time and again has the gale blown by and we were not afraid;
Now we come only to look at the dykes – at the dykes our fathers
    made.

O'er the marsh where the homesteads cower apart the harried sunlight
    flies,
Shifts and considers, wanes and recovers, scatters and sickens and dies –
An evil ember bedded in ash – a spark blown west by the wind . . .
We are surrendered to night and the sea – the gale and the tide
    behind!

At the bridge of the lower saltings the cattle gather and blare,
Roused by the feet of running men, dazed by the lantern-glare.
Unbar and let them away for their lives – the levels drown as they
    stand,
Where the flood-wash forces the sluices aback and the ditches deliver
    inland.

Ninefold deep to the top of the dykes the galloping breakers stride,
And their overcarried spray is a sea – a sea on the landward side.
Coming, like stallions they paw with their hooves, going they snatch
    with their teeth,
Till the bents and the furze and the sand are dragged out, and the
    old-time hurdles beneath.

Bid men gather fuel for fire, the tar, the oil, and the tow –
Flame we shall need, not smoke, in the dark if the riddled sea-banks
    go.
Bid the ringers watch in the tower (who knows how the dawn shall
    prove?)
Each with his rope between his feet and the trembling bells above.

Now we can only wait till the day, wait and apportion our shame.
These are the dykes our fathers left, but we would not look to the
    same.
Time and again were we warned of the dykes, time and again we
    delayed:
Now, it may fall, we have slain our sons, as our fathers we have
    betrayed.

*   *   *

Walking along the wreck of the dykes, watching the work of the seas!
These were the dykes our fathers made to our great profit and ease.
But the peace is gone and the profit is gone, with the old sure days
    withdrawn . . .
That our own houses show as strange when we come back in the
    dawn!

The Broken Men

For things we never mention,
    For Art misunderstood –
For excellent intention
    That did not turn to good;
From ancient tales' renewing,
    From clouds we would not clear –
Beyond the Law's pursuing
    We fled, and settled here.

We took no tearful leaving,
    We bade no long good-byes.
Men talked of crime and thieving,
    Men wrote of fraud and lies.

To save our injured feelings
    'Twas time and time to go –
Behind was dock and Dartmoor,
    Ahead lay Callao!

The widow and the orphan
    That pray for ten per cent,
They clapped their trailers on us
    To spy the road we went.
They watched the foreign sailings
    (They scan the shipping still),
And that's your Christian people
    Returning good for ill!

God bless the thoughtful islands
    Where never warrants come;
God bless the just Republics
    That give a man a home,
That ask no foolish questions,
    But set him on his feet;
And save his wife and daughters
    From the workhouse and the street.

On church and square and market
    The noonday silence falls;
You'll hear the drowsy mutter
    Of the fountain in our halls.
Asleep amid the yuccas
    The city takes her ease –
Till twilight brings the land-wind
    To the clicking jalousies.

Day long the diamond weather,
    The high, unaltered blue –
The smell of goats and incense
    And the mule-bells tinkling through.
Day long the warder ocean
    That keeps us from our kin,
And once a month our levée
    When the English mail comes in.

You'll find us up and waiting
    To treat you at the bar;
You'll find us less exclusive
    Than the average English are.

We'll meet you with a carriage,
    Too glad to show you round,
But – we do not lunch on steamers,
    For they are English ground.

We sail o' nights to England
    And join our smiling Boards –
Our wives go in with Viscounts
    And our daughters dance with Lords,
But behind our princely doings,
    And behind each coup we make,
We feel there's Something Waiting,
    And – we meet It when we wake.

Ah, God! One sniff of England –
    To greet our flesh and blood –
To hear the traffic slurring
    Once more through London mud!
Our towns of wasted honour –
    Our streets of lost delight!
How stands the old Lord Warden?
    Are Dover's cliffs still white?

Mesopotamia

They shall not return to us, the resolute, the young,
    The eager and whole-hearted whom we gave:
But the men who left them thriftily to die in their own dung,
    Shall they come with years and honour to the grave?

They shall not return to us, the strong men coldly slain
    In sight of help denied from day to day:
But the men who edged their agonies and chid them in their pain,
    Are they too strong and wise to put away?

Our dead shall not return to us while Day and Night divide –
    Never while the bars of sunset hold.
But the idle-minded overlings who quibbled while they died,
    Shall they thrust for high employments as of old?

Shall we only threaten and be angry for an hour?
    When the storm is ended shall we find
How softly but how swiftly they have sidled back to power
    By the favour and contrivance of their kind?

Even while they soothe us, while they promise large amends,
    Even while they make a show of fear,
Do they call upon their debtors, and take counsel with their friends,
    To confirm and re-establish each career?

Their lives cannot repay us – their death could not undo –
    The shame that they have laid upon our race.
But the slothfulness that wasted and the arrogance that slew,
    Shall we leave it unabated in its place?

from *Epitaphs of the War 1914–18*

A Servant

We were together since the War began.
He was my servant – and the better man.

Ex-Clerk

Pity not! The Army gave
Freedom to a timid slave:
In which Freedom did he find
Strength of body, will, and mind:
By which strength he came to prove
Mirth, Companionship, and Love:
For which Love to Death he went:
In which Death he lies content.

The Coward

I could not look on Death, which being known,
Men led me to him, blindfold and alone.

Common Form

If any question why we died,
Tell them, because our fathers lied.

Journalists

On a Panel in the Hall of the Institute of Journalists

We have served our day.

Mandalay

By the old Moulmein Pagoda, lookin' lazy at the sea,
There's a Burma girl a-settin', and I know she thinks o' me;
For the wind is in the palm-trees, and the temple-bells they say:
"Come you back, you British soldier; come you back to Mandalay!"
        Come you back to Mandalay,
        Where the old Flotilla lay:
        Can't you 'ear their paddles chunkin' from Rangoon to
           Mandalay?
        On the road to Mandalay,
        Where the flyin'-fishes play,
        An' the dawn comes up like thunder outer China
           'crost the Bay!

'Er petticoat was yaller an' 'er little cap was green,
An' 'er name was Supi-yaw-lat – jes' the same as Theebaw's Queen,
An' I seed her first a-smokin' of a whackin' white cheroot,
An' a-wastin' Christian kisses on an 'eathen idol's foot:
        Bloomin' idol made o' mud –
        Wot they called the Great Gawd Budd –
        Plucky lot she cared for idols when I kissed 'er where
           she stud!
        On the road to Mandalay . . .

When the mist was on the rice-fields an' the sun was droppin' slow,
She'd git 'er little banjo an' she'd sing "Kulla-lo-lo!".
With 'er arm upon my shoulder an' 'er cheek agin my cheek
We useter watch the steamers an' the hathis pilin' teak.
        Elephints a-pilin' teak
        In the sludgy, squdgy creek,
        Where the silence 'ung that 'eavy you was 'arf afraid
           to speak!
        On the road to Mandalay . . .

But that's all shove be'ind me – long ago an' fur away,
An' there ain't no 'buses runnin' from the Bank to Mandalay;
An' I'm learnin' 'ere in London what the ten-year soldier tells:
"If you've 'eard the East a-callin', you won't never 'eed naught else."
        No! you won't 'eed nothin' else
        But them spicy garlic smells,
        An' the sunshine an' the palm-trees an' the tinkly
           temple-bells;
        On the road to Mandalay . . .

I am sick o' wastin' leather on these gritty pavin'-stones,
An' the blasted English drizzle wakes the fever in my bones;
Tho' I walks with fifty 'ousemaids outer Chelsea to the Strand,
An' they talks a lot o' lovin', but wot do they understand?
  Beefy face an' grubby 'and –
  Law! wot do they understand?
  I've a neater, sweeter maiden in a cleaner, greener land!
  On the road to Mandalay . . .

Ship me somewheres east of Suez, where the best is like the worst,
Where there aren't no Ten Commandments an' a man can raise a
  thirst;
For the temple-bells are callin', an' it's there that I would be –
By the old Moulmein Pagoda, looking lazy at the sea;
  On the road to Mandalay,
  Where the old Flotilla lay,
  With our sick beneath the awnings when we went
   to Mandalay!
  On the road to Mandalay,
  Where the flyin'-fishes play,
  An' the dawn comes up like thunder outer China
   'crost the Bay!

The Way through the Woods

("Marklake Witches" – *Rewards and Fairies*)

They shut the road through the woods
Seventy years ago.
Weather and rain have undone it again,
And now you would never know
There was once a road through the woods
Before they planted the trees.
It is underneath the coppice and heath
And the thin anemones.
Only the keeper sees
That, where the ring-dove broods,
And the badgers roll at ease,
There was once a road through the woods.

Yet, if you enter the woods
Of a summer evening late,
When the night-air cools on the trout-ringed pools
Where the otter whistles his mate,
(They fear not men in the woods,
Because they see so few.)
You will hear the beat of a horse's feet,
And the swish of a skirt in the dew,
Steadily cantering through
The misty solitudes,
As though they perfectly knew
The old lost road through the woods . . .
But there is no road through the woods.

Harp Song of the Dane Women

("The Knights of the Joyous Venture" – *Puck of Pook's Hill*)

What is a woman that you forsake her,
And the hearth-fire and the home-acre,
To go with the old grey Widow-maker?

She has no house to lay a guest in –
But one chill bed for all to rest in,
That the pale suns and the stray bergs nest in.

She has no strong white arms to fold you,
But the ten-times-fingering weed to hold you –
Out on the rocks where the tide has rolled you.

Yet, when the signs of summer thicken,
And the ice breaks, and the birch-buds quicken,
Yearly you turn from our side, and sicken –

Sicken again for the shouts and the slaughters.
You steal away to the lapping waters,
And look at your ship in her winter-quarters.

You forget our mirth, and talk at the tables,
The kine in the shed and the horse in the stables –
To pitch her sides and go over her cables.

Then you drive out where the storm-clouds swallow,
And the sound of your oar-blades, falling hollow,
Is all we have left through the months to follow.

Ah, what is Woman that you forsake her,
And the hearth-fire and the home-acre,
To go with the old grey Widow-maker?

W. B. YEATS

No Second Troy

Why should I blame her that she filled my days
With misery, or that she would of late
Have taught to ignorant men most violent ways,
Or hurled the little streets upon the great,
Had they but courage equal to desire?
What could have made her peaceful with a mind
That nobleness made simple as a fire,
With beauty like a tightened bow, a kind
That is not natural in an age like this,
Being high and solitary and most stern?
Why, what could she have done, being what she is?
Was there another Troy for her to burn?

The Coming of Wisdom with Time

Though leaves are many, the root is one;
Through all the lying days of my youth
I swayed my leaves and flowers in the sun;
Now I may wither into the truth.

September 1913

What need you, being come to sense,
But fumble in a greasy till
And add the halfpence to the pence
And prayer to shivering prayer, until

You have dried the marrow from the bone?
For men were born to pray and save:
Romantic Ireland's dead and gone,
It's with O'Leary in the grave.

Yet they were of a different kind,
The names that stilled your childish play,
They have gone about the world like wind,
But little time had they to pray
For whom the hangman's rope was spun,
And what, God help us, could they save?
Romantic Ireland's dead and gone,
It's with O'Leary in the grave.

Was it for this the wild geese spread
The grey wing upon every tide;
For this that all that blood was shed,
For this Edward Fitzgerald died,
And Robert Emmet and Wolfe Tone,
All that delirium of the brave?
Romantic Ireland's dead and gone,
It's with O'Leary in the grave.

Yet could we turn the years again,
And call those exiles as they were
In all their loneliness and pain,
You'd cry, "Some woman's yellow hair
Has maddened every mother's son":
They weighed so lightly what they gave.
But let them be, they're dead and gone,
They're with O'Leary in the grave.

The Magi

Now as at all times I can see in the mind's eye,
In their stiff, painted clothes, the pale unsatisfied ones
Appear and disappear in the blue depth of the sky
With all their ancient faces like rain-beaten stones,
And all their helms of silver hovering side by side,
And all their eyes still fixed, hoping to find once more,
Being by Calvary's turbulence unsatisfied,
The uncontrollable mystery on the bestial floor.

An Irish Airman Foresees His Death

I know that I shall meet my fate
Somewhere among the clouds above;
Those that I fight I do not hate,
Those that I guard I do not love;
My country is Kiltartan Cross,
My countrymen Kiltartan's poor,
No likely end could bring them loss
Or leave them happier than before.
Nor law, nor duty bade me fight,
Nor public men, nor cheering crowds,
A lonely impulse of delight
Drove to this tumult in the clouds;
I balanced all, brought all to mind,
The years to come seemed waste of breath,
A waste of breath the years behind,
In balance with this life, this death.

The Cat and the Moon

The cat went here and there
And the moon spun round like a top,
And the nearest kin of the moon,
The creeping cat, looked up.
Black Minnaloushe stared at the moon,
For, wander and wail as he would,
The pure cold light in the sky
Troubled his animal blood.
Minnaloushe runs in the grass
Lifting his delicate feet.
Do you dance, Minnaloushe, do you dance?
When two close kindred meet,
What better than call a dance?
Maybe the moon may learn,
Tired of that courtly fashion,
A new dance turn.
Minnaloushe creeps through the grass
From moonlit place to place,
The sacred moon overhead
Has taken a new phase.
Does Minnaloushe know that his pupils
Will pass from change to change,

And that from round to crescent,
From crescent to round they range?
Minnaloushe creeps through the grass
Alone, important and wise,
And lifts to the changing moon
His changing eyes.

Easter 1916

I have met them at close of day
Coming with vivid faces
From counter or desk among grey
Eighteenth-century houses.
I have passed with a nod of the head
Or polite meaningless words,
Or have lingered awhile and said
Polite meaningless words,
And thought before I had done
Of a mocking tale or a gibe
To please a companion
Around the fire at the club,
Being certain that they and I
But lived where motley is worn:
All changed, changed utterly:
A terrible beauty is born.

That woman's days were spent
In ignorant good-will,
Her nights in argument
Until her voice grew shrill.
What voice more sweet than hers
When, young and beautiful,
She rode to harriers?
This man had kept a school
And rode our wingèd horse;
This other his helper and friend
Was coming into his force;
He might have won fame in the end,
So sensitive his nature seemed,
So daring and sweet his thought.
This other man I had dreamed
A drunken, vainglorious lout.

He had done most bitter wrong
To some who are near my heart,
Yet I number him in the song;
He, too, has resigned his part
In the casual comedy;
He, too, has been changed in his turn,
Transformed utterly:
A terrible beauty is born.

Hearts with one purpose alone
Through summer and winter seem
Enchanted to a stone
To trouble the living stream.
The horse that comes from the road,
The rider, the birds that range
From cloud to tumbling cloud,
Minute by minute they change;
A shadow of cloud on the stream
Changes minute by minute;
A horse-hoof slides on the brim,
And a horse plashes within it;
The long-legged moor-hens dive,
And hens to moor-cocks call;
Minute by minute they live:
The stone's in the midst of all.

Too long a sacrifice
Can make a stone of the heart.
O when may it suffice?
That is Heaven's part, our part
To murmur name upon name,
As a mother names her child
When sleep at last has come
On limbs that had run wild.
What is it but nightfall?
No, no, not night but death;
Was it needless death after all?
For England may keep faith
For all that is done and said.
We know their dream; enough
To know they dreamed and are dead;
And what if excess of love
Bewildered them till they died?
I write it out in a verse —

MacDonagh and MacBride
And Connolly and Pearse
Now and in time to be,
Wherever green is worn,
Are changed, changed utterly:
A terrible beauty is born.

The Second Coming

Turning and turning in the widening gyre
The falcon cannot hear the falconer;
Things fall apart; the centre cannot hold;
Mere anarchy is loosed upon the world,
The blood-dimmed tide is loosed, and everywhere
The ceremony of innocence is drowned;
The best lack all conviction, while the worst
Are full of passionate intensity.

Surely some revelation is at hand;
Surely the Second Coming is at hand.
The Second Coming! Hardly are those words out
When a vast image out of *Spiritus Mundi*
Troubles my sight: somewhere in sands of the desert
A shape with lion body and the head of a man,
A gaze blank and pitiless as the sun,
Is moving its slow thighs, while all about it
Reel shadows of the indignant desert birds.
The darkness drops again; but now I know
That twenty centuries of stony sleep
Were vexed to nightmare by a rocking cradle,
And what rough beast, its hour come round at last,
Slouches towards Bethlehem to be born?

Sailing to Byzantium

I

That is no country for old men. The young
In one another's arms, birds in the trees
– Those dying generations – at their song,
The salmon-falls, the mackerel-crowded seas,

Fish, flesh, or fowl, commend all summer long
Whatever is begotten, born, and dies.
Caught in that sensual music all neglect
Monuments of unageing intellect.

2

An aged man is but a paltry thing,
A tattered coat upon a stick, unless
Soul clap its hands and sing, and louder sing
For every tatter in its mortal dress,
Nor is there singing school but studying
Monuments of its own magnificence;
And therefore I have sailed the seas and come
To the holy city of Byzantium.

3

O sages standing in God's holy fire
As in the gold mosaic of a wall,
Come from the holy fire, perne in a gyre,
And be the singing-masters of my soul.
Consume my heart away; sick with desire
And fastened to a dying animal
It knows not what it is; and gather me
Into the artifice of eternity.

4

Once out of nature I shall never take
My bodily form from any natural thing,
But such a form as Grecian goldsmiths make
Of hammered gold and gold enamelling
To keep a drowsy Emperor awake;
Or set upon a golden bough to sing
To lords and ladies of Byzantium
Of what is past, or passing, or to come.

Leda and the Swan

A sudden blow: the great wings beating still
Above the staggering girl, her thighs caressed
By the dark webs, her nape caught in his bill,
He holds her helpless breast upon his breast.

How can those terrified vague fingers push
The feathered glory from her loosening thighs?
And how can body, laid in that white rush,
But feel the strange heart beating where it lies?

A shudder in the loins engenders there
The broken wall, the burning roof and tower
And Agamemnon dead.
                   Being so caught up,
So mastered by the brute blood of the air,
Did she put on his knowledge with his power
Before the indifferent beak could let her drop?

Among School Children

I

I walk through the long schoolroom questioning;
A kind old nun in a white hood replies;
The children learn to cipher and to sing,
To study reading-books and history,
To cut and sew, be neat in everything
In the best modern way – the children's eyes
In momentary wonder stare upon
A sixty-year-old smiling public man.

2

I dream of a Ledaean body, bent
Above a sinking fire, a tale that she
Told of a harsh reproof, or trivial event
That changed some childish day to tragedy –
Told, and it seemed that our two natures blent
Into a sphere from youthful sympathy,
Or else, to alter Plato's parable,
Into the yolk and white of the one shell.

3

And thinking of that fit of grief or rage
I look upon one child or t'other there
And wonder if she stood so at that age –
For even daughters of the swan can share
Something of every paddler's heritage –
And had that colour upon cheek or hair,
And thereupon my heart is driven wild:
She stands before me as a living child.

4

Her present image floats into the mind –
Did Quattrocento finger fashion it
Hollow of cheek as though it drank the wind
And took a mess of shadows for its meat?
And I though never of Ledaean kind
Had pretty plumage once – enough of that,
Better to smile on all that smile, and show
There is a comfortable kind of old scarecrow.

5

What youthful mother, a shape upon her lap
Honey of generation had betrayed,
And that must sleep, shriek, struggle to escape
As recollection or the drug decide,
Would think her son, did she but see that shape
With sixty or more winters on its head,
A compensation for the pang of his birth,
Or the uncertainty of his setting forth?

6

Plato thought nature but a spume that plays
Upon a ghostly paradigm of things;
Solider Aristotle played the taws
Upon the bottom of a king of kings;
World-famous golden-thighed Pythagoras
Fingered upon a fiddle-stick or strings
What a star sang and careless Muses heard:
Old clothes upon old sticks to scare a bird.

7

Both nuns and mothers worship images,
But those the candles light are not as those
That animate a mother's reveries,
But keep a marble or a bronze repose.
And yet they too break hearts – O Presences
That passion, piety or affection knows,
And that all heavenly glory symbolise –
O self-born mockers of man's enterprise;

8

Labour is blossoming or dancing where
The body is not bruised to pleasure soul,
Nor beauty born out of its own despair,
Nor blear-eyed wisdom out of midnight oil.

O chestnut-tree, great-rooted blossomer,
Are you the leaf, the blossom or the bole?
O body swayed to music, O brightening glance,
How can we know the dancer from the dance?

Byzantium

The unpurged images of day recede;
The Emperor's drunken soldiery are abed;
Night resonance recedes, night-walkers' song
After great cathedral gong;
A starlit or a moonlit dome disdains
All that man is,
All mere complexities,
The fury and the mire of human veins.

Before me floats an image, man or shade;
Shade more than man, more image than a shade;
For Hades' bobbin bound in mummy-cloth
May unwind the winding path;
A mouth that has no moisture and no breath
Breathless mouths may summon;
I hail the superhuman;
I call it death-in-life and life-in-death.

Miracle, bird or golden handiwork,
More miracle than bird or handiwork,
Planted on the star-lit golden bough,
Can like the cocks of Hades crow,
Or, by the moon embittered, scorn aloud
In glory of changeless metal
Common bird or petal
And all complexities of mire or blood.

At midnight on the Emperor's pavement flit
Flames that no faggot feeds, nor steel has lit,
Nor storm disturbs, flames begotten of flame,
Where blood-begotten spirits come
And all complexities of fury leave,
Dying into a dance,
An agony of trance,
An agony of flame that cannot singe a sleeve.

Astraddle on the dolphin's mire and blood,
Spirit after spirit! The smithies break the flood,
The golden smithies of the Emperor!
Marbles of the dancing floor
Break bitter furies of complexity,
Those images that yet
Fresh images beget,
That dolphin-torn, that gong-tormented sea.

An Acre of Grass

Picture and book remain,
An acre of green grass
For air and exercise,
Now strength of body goes;
Midnight, an old house
Where nothing stirs but a mouse.

My temptation is quiet.
Here at life's end
Neither loose imagination,
Nor the mill of the mind
Consuming its rag and bone,
Can make the truth known.

Grant me an old man's frenzy,
Myself must I remake
Till I am Timon and Lear
Or that William Blake
Who beat upon the wall
Till Truth obeyed his call;

A mind Michael Angelo knew
That can pierce the clouds,
Or inspired by frenzy
Shake the dead in their shrouds;
Forgotten else by mankind,
An old man's eagle mind.

The Circus Animals' Desertion

I

I sought a theme and sought for it in vain,
I sought it daily for six weeks or so.
Maybe at last, being but a broken man,
I must be satisfied with my heart, although
Winter and summer till old age began
My circus animals were all on show,
Those stilted boys, that burnished chariot,
Lion and woman and the Lord knows what.

2

What can I but enumerate old themes?
First that sea-rider Oisin led by the nose
Through three enchanted islands, allegorical dreams,
Vain gaiety, vain battle, vain repose,
Themes of the embittered heart, or so it seems,
That might adorn old songs or courtly shows;
But what cared I that set him on to ride,
I, starved for the bosom of his faery bride?

And then a counter-truth filled out its play,
The Countess Cathleen was the name I gave it;
She, pity-crazed, had given her soul away,
But masterful Heaven had intervened to save it.
I thought my dear must her own soul destroy,
So did fanaticism and hate enslave it,
And this brought forth a dream and soon enough
This dream itself had all my thought and love.

And when the Fool and Blind Man stole the bread
Cuchulain fought the ungovernable sea;
Heart-mysteries there, and yet when all is said
It was the dream itself enchanted me:
Character isolated by a deed
To engross the present and dominate memory.
Players and painted stage took all my love,
And not those things that they were emblems of.

3

Those masterful images because complete
Grew in pure mind, but out of what began?
A mound of refuse or the sweepings of a street,
Old kettles, old bottles, and a broken can,

Old iron, old bones, old rags, that raving slut
Who keeps the till. Now that my ladder's gone,
I must lie down where all the ladders start,
In the foul rag-and-bone shop of the heart.

CHARLOTTE MEW

Fame

Sometimes in the over-heated house, but not for long,
    Smirking and speaking rather loud,
    I see myself among the crowd,
Where no one fits the singer to his song,
Or sifts the unpainted from the painted faces
Of the people who are always on my stair;
They were not with me when I walked in heavenly places;
        But could I spare
In the blind Earth's great silences and spaces,
    The din, the scuffle, the long stare
    If I went back and it was not there?
Back to the old known things that are the new,
The folded glory of the gorse, the sweet-briar air,
To the larks that cannot praise us, knowing nothing of what
        we do
    And the divine, wise trees that do not care
Yet, to leave Fame, still with such eyes and that bright hair!
God! If I might! And before I go hence
        Take in her stead
        To our tossed bed,
One little dream, no matter how small, how wild.
Just now, I think I found it in a field, under a fence –
A frail, dead, new-born lamb, ghostly and pitiful and white,
        A blot upon the night,
        The moon's dropped child!

The Quiet House

When we were children old Nurse used to say
    The house was like an auction or a fair
    Until the lot of us were safe in bed.
    It has been quiet as the country-side

Since Ted and Janey and then Mother died
And Tom crossed Father and was sent away.
After the lawsuit he could not hold up his head,
    Poor Father, and he does not care
    For people here, or to go anywhere.

To get away to Aunt's for that week-end
    Was hard enough; (since then, a year ago,
    He scarcely lets me slip out of his sight –)
At first I did not like my cousin's friend,
    I did not think I should remember him:
    His voice has gone, his face is growing dim
And if I like him now I do not know.
    He frightened me before he smiled –
    He did not ask me if he might –
    He said that he would come one Sunday night,
    He spoke to me as if I were a child.

No year has been like this that has just gone by;
    It may be that what Father says is true,
If things are so it does not matter why:
    But everything has burned, and not quite through.
    The colours of the world have turned
    To flame, the blue, the gold has burned
In what used to be such a leaden sky.
When you are burned quite through you die.

    Red is the strangest pain to bear;
In Spring the leaves on the budding trees;
In Summer the roses are worse than these,
    More terrible than they are sweet:
    A rose can stab you across the street
        Deeper than any knife:
    And the crimson haunts you everywhere –
Thin shafts of sunlight, like the ghosts of reddened swords
        have struck our stair
As if, coming down, you had spilt your life.

    I think that my soul is red
Like the soul of a sword or a scarlet flower:
    But when these are dead
    They have had their hour.

    I shall have had mine, too,
        For from head to feet,
    I am burned and stabbed half through,
        And the pain is deadly sweet.

The things that kill us seem
  Blind to the death they give:
It is only in our dream
  The things that kill us live.

The room is shut where Mother died,
  The other rooms are as they were,
The world goes on the same outside,
  The sparrows fly across the Square,
  The children play as we four did there,
  The trees grow green and brown and bare,
The sun shines on the dead Church spire,
  And nothing lives here but the fire,
While Father watches from his chair
          Day follows day
The same, or now and then, a different grey,
          Till, like his hair,
Which Mother said was wavy once and bright,
          They will all turn white.

To-night I heard a bell again —
Outside it was the same mist of fine rain,
  The lamps just lighted down the long, dim street,
          No one for me —
  I think it is myself I go to meet:
I do not care; some day I *shall* not think; I shall not *be*!

Not For That City

Not for that city of the level sun,
    Its golden streets and glittering gates ablaze —
    The shadeless, sleepless city of white days,
White nights, or nights and days that are as one —
We weary, when all is said, all thought, all done.
    We strain our eyes beyond this dusk to see
    What, from the threshold of eternity
We shall step into. No, I think we shun
The splendour of that everlasting glare,
    The clamour of that never-ending song.
    And if for anything we greatly long,
It is for some remote and quiet stair
    Which winds to silence and a space of sleep
    Too sound for waking and for dreams too deep.

Rooms

I remember rooms that have had their part
In the steady slowing down of the heart.
The room in Paris, the room at Geneva,
The little damp room with the seaweed smell,
And that ceaseless maddening sound of the tide –
   Rooms where for good or for ill – things died.
But there is the room where we (two) lie dead,
Though every morning we seem to wake and might just as
     well seem to sleep again
  As we shall somewhere in the other quieter, dustier bed
  Out there in the sun – in the rain.

ROBERT FROST

Mowing

There was never a sound beside the wood but one
And that was my long scythe whispering to the ground.
What was it it whispered? I knew not well myself;
Perhaps it was something about the heat of the sun,
Something, perhaps, about the lack of sound –
And that was why it whispered and did not speak.
It was no dream of the gift of idle hours,
Or easy gold at the hand of fay or elf:
Anything more than the truth would have seemed too weak
To the earnest love that laid the swale in rows,
Not without feeble-pointed spikes of flowers
(Pale orchises), and scared a bright green snake.
The fact is the sweetest dream that labour knows.
My long scythe whispered and left the hay to make.

Mending Wall

Something there is that doesn't love a wall,
That sends the frozen-ground-swell under it,
And spills the upper boulders in the sun;
And makes gaps even two can pass abreast.
The work of hunters is another thing:

So low for long, they never right themselves:
You may see their trunks arching in the woods
Years afterwards, trailing their leaves on the ground
Like girls on hands and knees that throw their hair
Before them over their heads to dry in the sun.
But I was going to say when Truth broke in
With all her matter-of-fact about the ice-storm
I should prefer to have some boy bend them
As he went out and in to fetch the cows –
Some boy too far from town to learn baseball,
Whose only play was what he found himself,
Summer or winter, and could play alone.
One by one he subdued his father's trees
By riding them down over and over again
Until he took the stiffness out of them,
And not one but hung limp, not one was left
For him to conquer. He learned all there was
To learn about not launching out too soon
And so not carrying the tree away
Clear to the ground. He always kept his poise
To the top branches, climbing carefully
With the same pains you use to fill a cup
Up to the brim, and even above the brim.
Then he flung outward, feet first, with a swish,
Kicking his way down through the air to the ground.
So was I once myself a swinger of birches.
And so I dream of going back to be.
It's when I'm weary of considerations,
And life is too much like a pathless wood
Where your face burns and tickles with the cobwebs
Broken across it, and one eye is weeping
From a twig's having lashed across it open.
I'd like to get away from earth awhile
And then come back to it and begin over.
May no fate wilfully misunderstand me
And half grant what I wish and snatch me away
Not to return. Earth's the right place for love:
I don't know where it's likely to go better.
I'd like to go by climbing a birch tree,
And climb black branches up a snow-white trunk
Toward heaven, till the tree could bear no more,
But dipped its top and set me down again.
That would be good both going and coming back.
One could do worse than be a swinger of birches.

"Out, Out — "

The buzz saw snarled and rattled in the yard
And made dust and dropped stove-length sticks of wood,
Sweet-scented stuff when the breeze drew across it.
And from there those that lifted eyes could count
Five mountain ranges one behind the other
Under the sunset far into Vermont.
And the saw snarled and rattled, snarled and rattled,
As it ran light, or had to bear a load.
And nothing happened: day was all but done.
Call it a day, I wish they might have said
To please the boy by giving him the half hour
That a boy counts so much when saved from work.
His sister stood beside them in her apron
To tell them "Supper". At the word, the saw,
As if to prove saws knew what supper meant,
Leaped out at the boy's hand, or seemed to leap —
He must have given the hand. However it was,
Neither refused the meeting. But the hand!
The boy's first outcry was a rueful laugh,
As he swung toward them holding up the hand
Half in appeal, but half as if to keep
The life from spilling. Then the boy saw all —
Since he was old enough to know, big boy
Doing a man's work, though a child at heart —
He saw all spoiled. "Don't let him cut my hand off —
The doctor, when he comes. Don't let him, sister!"
So. But the hand was gone already.
The doctor put him in the dark of ether.
He lay and puffed his lips out with his breath.
And then — the watcher at his pulse took fright.
No one believed. They listened at his heart.
Little — less — nothing! — and that ended it.
No more to build on there. And they, since they
Were not the one dead, turned to their affairs.

Stopping by Woods on a Snowy Evening

Whose woods these are I think I know.
His house is in the village though;
He will not see me stopping here
To watch his woods fill up with snow.

My little horse must think it queer
To stop without a farmhouse near
Between the woods and frozen lake
The darkest evening of the year.

He gives his harness bells a shake
To ask if there is some mistake.
The only other sound's the sweep
Of easy wind and downy flake.

The woods are lovely, dark and deep,
But I have promises to keep,
And miles to go before I sleep,
And miles to go before I sleep.

Acquainted with the Night

I have been one acquainted with the night.
I have walked out in rain – and back in rain.
I have outwalked the furthest city light.

I have looked down the saddest city lane.
I have passed by the watchman on his beat
And dropped my eyes, unwilling to explain.

I have stood still and stopped the sound of feet
When far away an interrupted cry
Came over houses from another street,

But not to call me back or say goodbye;
And further still at an unearthly height,
One luminary clock against the sky
Proclaimed the time was neither wrong nor right.
I have been one acquainted with the night.

Desert Places

Snow falling and night falling fast, oh, fast
In a field I looked into going past,
And the ground almost covered smooth in snow,
But a few weeds and stubble showing last.

The woods around it have it – it is theirs.
All animals are smothered in their lairs.
I am too absent-spirited to count;
The loneliness includes me unawares.

And lonely as it is that loneliness
Will be more lonely ere it will be less –
A blanker whiteness of benighted snow
With no expression, nothing to express.

They cannot scare me with their empty spaces
Between stars – on stars where no human race is.
I have it in me so much nearer home,
To scare myself with my own desert places.

Provide, Provide

The witch that came (the withered hag)
To wash the steps with pail and rag,
Was once the beauty Abishag,

The picture pride of Hollywood.
Too many fall from great and good
For you to doubt the likelihood.

Die early and avoid the fate.
Or if predestined to die late,
Make up your mind to die in state.

Make the whole stock exchange your own!
If need be occupy a throne,
Where nobody can call *you* crone.

Some have relied on what they knew;
Others on being simply true.
What worked for them might work for you.

No memory of having starred
Atones for later disregard,
Or keeps the end from being hard.

Better to go down dignified
With boughten friendship at your side
Than none at all. Provide, provide!

The Gift Outright

The land was ours before we were the land's.
She was our land more than a hundred years
Before we were her people. She was ours
In Massachusetts, in Virginia,
But we were England's, still colonials,
Possessing what we still were unpossessed by,
Possessed by what we now no more possessed.
Something we were withholding made us weak
Until we found out that it was ourselves
We were withholding from our land of living,
And forthwith found salvation in surrender.
Such as we were we gave ourselves outright
(The deed of gift was many deeds of war)
To the land vaguely realizing westward,
But still unstoried, artless, unenhanced,
Such as she was, such as she would become.

EDWARD THOMAS

Swedes

They have taken the gable from the roof of clay
On the long swede pile. They have let in the sun
To the white and gold and purple of curled fronds
Unsunned. It is a sight more tender-gorgeous
At the wood-corner where Winter moans and drips
Than when, in the Valley of the Tombs of Kings,
A boy crawls down into a Pharaoh's tomb
And, first of Christian men, beholds the mummy,
God and monkey, chariot and throne and vase,
Blue pottery, alabaster, and gold.

But dreamless long-dead Amen-hotep lies.
This is a dream of Winter, sweet as Spring.

As the Team's Head-Brass

As the team's head-brass flashed out on the turn
The lovers disappeared into the wood.
I sat among the boughs of the fallen elm
That strewed an angle of the fallow, and
Watched the plough narrowing a yellow square
Of charlock. Every time the horses turned
Instead of treading me down, the ploughman leaned
Upon the handles to say or ask a word,
About the weather, next about the war.
Scraping the share he faced towards the wood,
And screwed along the furrow till the brass flashed
Once more.
            The blizzard felled the elm whose crest
I sat in, by a woodpecker's round hole,
The ploughman said. "When will they take it away?"
"When the war's over." So the talk began –
One minute and an interval of ten,
A minute more and the same interval.
"Have you been out?" "No." "And don't want to, perhaps?"
"If I could only come back again, I should.
I could spare an arm. I shouldn't want to lose
A leg. If I should lose my head, why, so,
I should want nothing more . . . Have many gone
From here?" "Yes." "Many lost?" "Yes, a good few.
Only two teams work on the farm this year.
One of my mates is dead. The second day
In France they killed him. It was back in March,
The very night of the blizzard, too. Now if
He had stayed here we should have moved the tree."
"And I should not have sat here. Everything
Would have been different. For it would have been
Another world." "Ay, and a better, though
If we could see all all might seem good." Then
The lovers came out of the wood again:
The horses started and for the last time
I watched the clods crumble and topple over
After the ploughshare and the stumbling team.

The Glory

The glory of the beauty of the morning, –
The cuckoo crying over the untouched dew;
The blackbird that has found it, and the dove
That tempts me on to something sweeter than love;
White clouds ranged even and fair as new-mown hay;
The heat, the stir, the sublime vacancy
Of sky and meadow and forest and my own heart: –
The glory invites me, yet it leaves me scorning
All I can ever do, all I can be,
Beside the lovely of motion, shape, and hue,
The happiness I fancy fit to dwell
In beauty's presence. Shall I now this day
Begin to seek as far as heaven, as hell,
Wisdom or strength to match this beauty, start
And tread the pale dust pitted with small dark drops,
In hope to find whatever it is I seek,
Hearkening to short-lived happy-seeming things
That we know naught of, in the hazel copse?
Or must I be content with discontent
As larks and swallows are perhaps with wings?
And shall I ask at the day's end once more
What beauty is, and what I can have meant
By happiness? And shall I let all go,
Glad, weary, or both? Or shall I perhaps know
That I was happy oft and oft before,
Awhile forgetting how I am fast pent,
How dreary-swift, with naught to travel to,
Is Time? I cannot bite the day to the core.

Adlestrop

Yes. I remember Adlestrop –
The name, because one afternoon
Of heat the express-train drew up there
Unwontedly. It was late June.

The steam hissed. Someone cleared his throat.
No one left and no one came
On the bare platform. What I saw
Was Adlestrop – only the name

And willows, willow-herb, and grass,
And meadowsweet, and haycocks dry,
No whit less still and lonely fair
Than the high cloudlets in the sky.

And for that minute a blackbird sang
Close by, and round him, mistier,
Farther and farther, all the birds
Of Oxfordshire and Gloucestershire.

October

The green elm with the one great bough of gold
Lets leaves into the grass slip, one by one, –
The short hill grass, the mushrooms small, milk-white,
Harebell and scabious and tormentil,
That blackberry and gorse, in dew and sun,
Bow down to; and the wind travels too light
To shake the fallen birch leaves from the fern;
The gossamers wander at their own will.
At heavier steps than birds' the squirrels scold.
The rich scene has grown fresh again and new
As Spring, and to the touch is not more cool
Than it is warm to the gaze; and now I might
As happy be as earth is beautiful,
Were I some other or with earth could turn
In alternation of violet and rose,
Harebell and snowdrop, at their season due,
And gorse that has no time not to be gay.
But if this be not happiness, – who knows?
Some day I shall think this a happy day,
And this mood by the name of melancholy
Shall no more blackened and obscured be.

Rain

Rain, midnight rain, nothing but the wild rain
On this bleak hut, and solitude, and me
Remembering again that I shall die
And neither hear the rain nor give it thanks
For washing me cleaner than I have been

Since I was born into this solitude.
Blessed are the dead that the rain rains upon:
But here I pray that none whom once I loved
Is dying tonight or lying still awake
Solitary, listening to the rain,
Either in pain or thus in sympathy
Helpless among the living and the dead,
Like a cold water among broken reeds,
Myriads of broken reeds all still and stiff,
Like me who have no love which this wild rain
Has not dissolved except the love of death,
If love it be for what is perfect and
Cannot, the tempest tells me, disappoint.

Lights Out

I have come to the borders of sleep,
The unfathomable deep
Forest, where all must lose
Their way, however straight,
Or winding, soon or late;
They cannot choose.

Many a road and track
That, since the dawn's first crack,
Up to the forest brink,
Deceived the travellers,
Suddenly now blurs,
And in they sink.

Here love ends,
Despair, ambition ends;
All pleasure and all trouble,
Although most sweet or bitter,
Here ends, in sleep that is sweeter
Than tasks most noble.

There is not any book
Or face of dearest look
That I would not turn from now
To go into the unknown
I must enter, and leave, alone,
I know not how.

The tall forest towers;
Its cloudy foliage lowers
Ahead, shelf above shelf;
Its silence I hear and obey
That I may lose my way
And myself.

"I never saw that land before"

I never saw that land before,
And now can never see it again;
Yet, as if by acquaintance hoar
Endeared, by gladness and by pain,
Great was the affection that I bore

To the valley and the river small,
The cattle, the grass, the bare ash trees,
The chickens from the farmsteads, all
Elm-hidden, and the tributaries
Descending at equal interval;

The blackthorns down along the brook
With wounds yellow as crocuses
Where yesterday the labourer's hook
Had sliced them cleanly; and the breeze
That hinted all and nothing spoke.

I neither expected anything
Nor yet remembered: but some goal
I touched then; and if I could sing
What would not even whisper my soul
As I went on my journeying,

I should use, as the trees and birds did,
A language not to be betrayed;
And what was hid should still be hid
Excepting from those like me made
Who answer when such whispers bid.

Old Man

Old Man, or Lad's-love, – in the name there's nothing
To one that knows not Lad's-love, or Old Man,
The hoar-green feathery herb, almost a tree,
Growing with rosemary and lavender.
Even to one that knows it well, the names
Half decorate, half perplex, the thing it is:
At least, what that is clings not to the names
In spite of time. And yet I like the names.

The herb itself I like not, but for certain
I love it, as some day the child will love it
Who plucks a feather from the door-side bush
Whenever she goes in or out of the house.
Often she waits there, snipping the tips and shrivelling
The shreds at last on to the path, perhaps
Thinking, perhaps of nothing, till she sniffs
Her fingers and runs off. The bush is still
But half as tall as she, though it is as old;
So well she clips it. Not a word she says;
And I can only wonder how much hereafter
She will remember, with that bitter scent,
Of garden rows, and ancient damson trees
Topping a hedge, a bent path to a door,
A low thick bush beside the door, and me
Forbidding her to pick.
                                As for myself,
Where first I met the bitter scent is lost.
I, too, often shrivel the grey shreds,
Sniff them and think and sniff again and try
Once more to think what it is I am remembering,
Always in vain. I cannot like the scent,
Yet I would rather give up others more sweet,
With no meaning, than this bitter one.

I have mislaid the key. I sniff the spray
And think of nothing; I see and I hear nothing;
Yet seem, too, to be listening, lying in wait
For what I should, yet never can, remember:
No garden appears, no path, no hoar-green bush
Of Lad's-love, or Old Man, no child beside,
Neither father nor mother, nor any playmate;
Only an avenue, dark, nameless, without end.

Roads

I love roads:
The goddesses that dwell
Far along invisible
Are my favourite gods.

Roads go on
While we forget, and are
Forgotten like a star
That shoots and is gone.

On this earth 'tis sure
We men have not made
Anything that doth fade
So soon, so long endure:

The hill road wet with rain
In the sun would not gleam
Like a winding stream
If we trod it not again.

They are lonely
While we sleep, lonelier
For lack of the traveller
Who is now a dream only.

From dawn's twilight
And all the clouds like sheep
On the mountains of sleep
They wind into the night.

The next turn may reveal
Heaven: upon the crest
The close pine clump, at rest
And black, may Hell conceal.

Often footsore, never
Yet of the road I weary,
Though long and steep and dreary,
As it winds on for ever.

Helen of the roads,
The mountain ways of Wales
And the Mabinogion tales
Is one of the true gods,

Abiding in the trees,
The threes and fours so wise,
The larger companies,
That by the roadside be,

And beneath the rafter
Else uninhabited
Excepting by the dead;
And it is her laughter

At morn and night I hear
When the thrush cock sings
Bright irrelevant things,
And when the chanticleer

Calls back to their own night
Troops that make loneliness
With their light footsteps' press
As Helen's own are light.

Now all roads lead to France
And heavy is the tread
Of the living; but the dead
Returning lightly dance:

Whatever the roads bring
To me or take from me,
They keep me company
With their pattering,

Crowding the solitude
Of the loops over the downs,
Hushing the roar of towns
And their brief multitude.

WALLACE STEVENS

The Snow Man

One must have a mind of winter
To regard the frost and the boughs
Of the pine-trees crusted with snow;

And have been cold a long time
To behold the junipers shagged with ice,
The spruces rough in the distant glitter

Of the January sun; and not to think
Of any misery in the sound of the wind,
In the sound of a few leaves,

Which is the sound of the land
Full of the same wind
That is blowing in the same bare place

For the listener, who listens in the snow,
And, nothing himself, beholds
Nothing that is not there and the nothing that is.

Sunday Morning

I

Complacencies of the peignoir, and late
Coffee and oranges in a sunny chair,
And the green freedom of a cockatoo
Upon a rug mingle to dissipate
The holy hush of ancient sacrifice.
She dreams a little, and she feels the dark
Encroachment of that old catastrophe,
As a calm darkens among water-lights.
The pungent oranges and bright, green wings
Seem things in some procession of the dead,
Winding across wide water, without sound.
The day is like wide water, without sound,
Stilled for the passing of her dreaming feet
Over the seas, to silent Palestine,
Dominion of the blood and sepulchre.

2

Why should she give her bounty to the dead?
What is divinity if it can come
Only in silent shadows and in dreams?
Shall she not find in comforts of the sun,
In pungent fruit and bright, green wings, or else
In any balm or beauty of the earth,
Things to be cherished like the thought of heaven?
Divinity must live within herself:
Passions of rain, or moods in falling snow;
Grievings in loneliness, or unsubdued
Elations when the forest blooms; gusty
Emotions on wet roads on autumn nights;
All pleasures and all pains, remembering
The bough of summer and the winter branch.
These are the measures destined for her soul.

3

Jove in the clouds had his inhuman birth.
No mother suckled him, no sweet land gave
Large-mannered motions to his mythy mind
He moved among us, as a muttering king,
Magnificent, would move among his hinds,
Until our blood, commingling, virginal,
With heaven, brought such requital to desire
The very hinds discerned it, in a star.
Shall our blood fail? Or shall it come to be
The blood of paradise? And shall the earth
Seem all of paradise that we shall know?
The sky will be much friendlier then than now,
A part of labor and a part of pain,
And next in glory to enduring love,
Not this dividing and indifferent blue.

4

She says, "I am content when wakened birds,
Before they fly, test the reality
Of misty fields, by their sweet questionings;
But when the birds are gone, and their warm fields
Return no more, where, then, is paradise?"
There is not any haunt of prophecy,
Nor any old chimera of the grave,
Neither the golden underground, nor isle
Melodious, where spirits gat them home,
Nor visionary south, nor cloudy palm

Remote on heaven's hill, that has endured
As April's green endures; or will endure
Like her remembrance of awakened birds,
Or her desire for June and evening, tipped
By the consummation of the swallow's wings.

5

She says, "But in contentment I still feel
The need of some imperishable bliss."
Death is the mother of beauty; hence from her,
Alone, shall come fulfilment to our dreams
And our desires. Although she strews the leaves
Of sure obliteration on our paths,
The path sick sorrow took, the many paths
Where triumph rang its brassy phrase, or love
Whispered a little out of tenderness,
She makes the willow shiver in the sun
For maidens who were wont to sit and gaze
Upon the grass, relinquished to their feet.
She causes boys to pile new plums and pears
On disregarded plate. The maidens taste
And stray impassioned in the littering leaves.

6

Is there no change of death in paradise?
Does ripe fruit never fall? Or do the boughs
Hang always heavy in that perfect sky,
Unchanging, yet so like our perishing earth,
With rivers like our own that seek for seas
They never find, the same receding shores
That never touch with inarticulate pang?
Why set the pear upon those river-banks
Or spice the shores with odors of the plum?
Alas, that they should wear our colors there,
The silken weavings of our afternoons,
And pick the strings of our insipid lutes!
Death is the mother of beauty, mystical,
Within whose burning bosom we devise
Our earthly mothers waiting, sleeplessly.

7

Supple and turbulent, a ring of men
Shall chant in orgy on a summer morn
Their boisterous devotion to the sun,
Not as a god, but as a god might be,

Naked among them, like a savage source.
Their chant shall be a chant of paradise,
Out of their blood, returning to the sky;
And in their chant shall enter, voice by voice,
The windy lake wherein their lord delights,
The trees, like serafin, and echoing hills,
That choir among themselves long afterward.
They shall know well the heavenly fellowship
Of men that perish and of summer morn.
And whence they came and whither they shall go
The dew upon their feet shall manifest.

8

She hears, upon that water without sound,
A voice that cries, "The tomb in Palestine
Is not the porch of spirits lingering.
It is the grave of Jesus, where he lay."
We live in an old chaos of the sun,
Or old dependency of day and night,
Or island solitude, unsponsored, free,
Of that wide water, inescapable.
Deer walk upon our mountains, and the quail
Whistle about us their spontaneous cries;
Sweet berries ripen in the wilderness;
And, in the isolation of the sky,
At evening, casual flocks of pigeons make
Ambiguous undulations as they sink,
Downward to darkness, on extended wings.

Thirteen Ways of Looking at a Blackbird

I

Among twenty snowy mountains,
The only moving thing
Was the eye of the blackbird.

2

I was of three minds,
Like a tree
In which there are three blackbirds.

3

The blackbird whirled in the autumn winds.
It was a small part of the pantomime.

4

A man and a woman
Are one.
A man and a woman and a blackbird
Are one.

5

I do not know which to prefer,
The beauty of inflections
Or the beauty of innuendoes,
The blackbird whistling
Or just after.

6

Icicles filled the long window
With barbaric glass.
The shadow of the blackbird
Crossed it, to and fro.
The mood
Traced in the shadow
An indecipherable cause.

7

O thin men of Haddam,
Why do you imagine golden birds?
Do you not see how the blackbird
Walks around the feet
Of the women about you?

8

I know noble accents
And lucid, inescapable rhythms;
But I know, too,
That the blackbird is involved
In what I know.

9

When the blackbird flew out of sight,
It marked the edge
Of one of many circles.

10

At the sight of blackbirds
Flying in a green light,
Even the bawds of euphony
Would cry out sharply.

11

He rode over Connecticut
In a glass coach.
Once, a fear pierced him,
In that he mistook
The shadow of his equipage
For blackbirds.

12

The river is moving.
The blackbird must be flying.

13

It was evening all afternoon.
It was snowing
And it was going to snow.
The blackbird sat
In the cedar-limbs.

The Idea of Order at Key West

She sang beyond the genius of the sea.
The water never formed to mind or voice,
Like a body wholly body, fluttering
Its empty sleeves; and yet its mimic motion
Made constant cry, caused constantly a cry,
That was not ours although we understood,
Inhuman, of the veritable ocean.

The sea was not a mask. No more was she.
The song and water were not medleyed sound
Even if what she sang was what she heard,
Since what she sang was uttered word by word.
It may be that in all her phrases stirred
The grinding water and the gasping wind;
But it was she and not the sea we heard.

For she was the maker of the song she sang.
The ever-hooded, tragic-gestured sea
Was merely a place by which she walked to sing.
Whose spirit is this? we said, because we knew
It was the spirit that we sought and knew
That we should ask this often as she sang.

If it was only the dark voice of the sea
That rose, or even colored by many waves;
If it was only the outer voice of sky
And cloud, of the sunken coral water-walled,
However clear, it would have been deep air,
The heaving speech of air, a summer sound
Repeated in a summer without end
And sound alone. But it was more than that,
More even than her voice, and ours, among
The meaningless plungings of water and the wind,
Theatrical distances, bronze shadows heaped
On high horizons, mountainous atmospheres
Of sky and sea.
                    It was her voice that made
The sky acutest at its vanishing.
She measured to the hour its solitude.
She was the single artificer of the world
In which she sang. And when she sang, the sea,
Whatever self it had, became the self
That was her song, for she was the maker. Then we,
As we beheld her striding there alone,
Knew that there never was a world for her
Except the one she sang and, singing, made.

Ramon Fernandez, tell me, if you know,
Why, when the singing ended and we turned
Toward the town, tell why the glassy lights,
The lights in the fishing boats at anchor there,
As the night descended, tilting in the air,
Mastered the night and portioned out the sea,
Fixing emblazoned zones and fiery poles,
Arranging, deepening, enchanting night.

Oh! Blessed rage for order, pale Ramon,
The maker's rage to order words of the sea,
Words of the fragrant portals, dimly-starred,
And of ourselves and of our origins,
In ghostlier demarcations, keener sounds.

The Sun This March

The exceeding brightness of this early sun
Makes me conceive how dark I have become,

And re-illumines things that used to turn
To gold in broadest blue, and be a part

Of a turning spirit in an earlier self.
That, too, returns from out the winter's air,

Like an hallucination come to daze
The corner of the eye. Our element,

Cold is our element and winter's air
Brings voices as of lions coming down.

Oh! Rabbi, rabbi, fend my soul for me
And true savant of this dark nature be.

Final Soliloquy of the Interior Paramour

Light the first light of evening, as in a room
In which we rest and, for small reason, think
The world imagined is the ultimate good.

This is, therefore, the intensest rendezvous.
It is in that thought that we collect ourselves,
Out of all the indifferences, into one thing:

Within a single thing, a single shawl
Wrapped tightly round us, since we are poor, a warmth,
A light, a power, the miraculous influence.

Here, now, we forget each other and ourselves.
We feel the obscurity of an order, a whole,
A knowledge, that which arranged the rendezvous.

Within its vital boundary, in the mind.
We say God and the imagination are one . . .
How high that highest candle lights the dark.

Out of this same light, out of the central mind,
We make a dwelling in the evening air,
In which being there together is enough.

MINA LOY

Der Blinde Junge

The dam Bellona
littered
her eyeless offspring
Kreigsopfer
upon the pavements of Vienna

Sparkling precipitate
the spectral day
involves
the visionless obstacle

this slow blind face
pushing
its virginal nonentity
against the light

Pure purposeless eremite
of centripetal sentience

Upon the carnose horologe of the ego
the vibrant tendon index moves not

since the black lightning desecrated
the retinal altar

Void and extinct
this planet of the soul
strains from the craving throat
in static flight upslanting

A downy youth's snout
nozzling the sun
drowned in dumbfounded instinct

Listen!
illuminati of the coloured earth
How this expressionless "thing"
blows out damnation and concussive dark

Upon a mouth-organ

Brancusi's Golden Bird

The toy
become the aesthetic archetype

As if
   some patient peasant God
   had rubbed and rubbed
   the Alpha and Omega
   of Form
   into a lump of metal

   A naked orientation
   unwinged   unplumed
      – the ultimate rhythm
   has lopped the extremities
   of crest and claw
   from
   the nucleus of flight

   The absolute act
   of art
   conformed
   to continent sculpture
   – bare as the brow of Osiris –
   this breast of revelation

   an incandescent curve
   licked by chromatic flames
   in labyrinths of reflections

   This gong
   of polished hyperaesthesia
   shrills with brass
   as the aggressive light
   strikes
   its significance

   The immaculate
   conception
   of the inaudible bird
   occurs
   in gorgeous reticence . . .

On Third Avenue

1

"You should have disappeared years ago" –

so disappear
on Third Avenue
to share the heedless incognito

of shuffling shadow-bodies
animate with frustration

whose silence'   only potence is
respiration
preceding the eroded bronze contours
of their other aromas

through the monstrous air
of this red-lit thoroughfare.

Here and there
saturnine
neon-signs
set afire
a feature
on their hueless overcast
of down-cast countenances.

For their ornateness
Time, the contortive tailor,
on and off,
clowned with sweat-sculptured cloth
to press
upon these irreparable dummies
an eerie undress
of mummies
half unwound.

2

Such are the compensations of poverty,
to see ——

Like an electric fungus
sprung from its own effulgence
of intercircled jewellery
reflected on the pavement,

like a reliquary sedan-chair,
out of a legend, dumped there,

before a ten-cent Cinema,

a sugar-coated box-office
enjail a Goddess
aglitter, in her runt of a tower,
with ritual claustrophobia.

Such are compensations of poverty,
to see ———

Transient in the dust,
the brilliancy
of a trolley
loaded with luminous busts;

lovely in anonymity
they vanish
with the mirage
of their passage.

Jules Pascin

So this is death
to rise to the occasion
a shadow
to a shadowy persuasion

Pascin has passed
with his affectionate swagger
his air
of the Crown in the role of jester.

The side-long derby-slanted Bulgar
cocked his jet eye
in its immaculate leer,
and as a coin,
tossed his destiny

Once a shy ivory boy,
the colour of life
had deepened on his cheek
in a wry irony

Pascin has ceased
to flush with ineffaceable bruises
his innubile Circes

Ceased to dangle
demi-rep angels
in tinsel bordels

Silence bleeds
from his slashed wrists
the dim homunculus
within
cries for the unbirth

The seeds
of his sly spirit
are cast to posterity
in satyric squander

a pigeon-toed populace
whose changeling women
jostle the prodigal son
as swine
Cinderellas awander.

WILLIAM CARLOS WILLIAMS

Portrait of a Lady

Your thighs are appletrees
whose blossoms touch the sky.
Which sky? The sky
where Watteau hung a lady's
slipper. Your knees
are a southern breeze — or
a gust of snow. Agh! what
sort of man was Fragonard?
— as if that answered
anything. Ah, yes — below
the knees, since the tune
drops that way, it is

one of those white summer days,
the tall grass of your ankles
flickers upon the shore –
Which shore? –
the sand clings to my lips –
Which shore?
Agh, petals maybe. How
should I know?
Which shore? Which shore?
I said petals from an appletree.

To the Shade of Po Chü-I

The work is heavy. I see
bare branches laden with snow.
I try to comfort myself
with thought of your old age.
A girl passes, in a red tam,
the coat above her quick ankles
snow smeared from running and falling –
Of what shall I think now
save of death the bright dancer?

"so much depends"

so much depends
upon

a red wheel
barrow

glazed with rain
water

beside the white
chickens

Brilliant Sad Sun

L EE'S
  UNCH

Spaghetti   Oysters
a Specialty   Clams

and raw Winter's done
to a turn – Restaurant: Spring!
Ah, Madam, what good are your thoughts

romantic but true
beside this gaiety of the sun
and that huge appetite?

Look!
from a glass pitcher she serves
clear water to the white chickens.

What are your memories
beside that purity?
The empty pitcher dangling

from her grip
her coarse voice croaks
Bon Jor'

And Patti, on her first concert tour
sang at your house in Mayaguez
and your brother was there

What beauty
beside your sadness – and
what sorrow

Question and Answer

What's wrong with American literature?
You ask me? How much do I get?

Poem

As the cat
climbed over
the top of

the jamcloset
first the right
forefoot

carefully
then the hind
stepped down

into the pit of
the empty
flowerpot

Nantucket

Flowers through the window
lavender and yellow

changed by white curtains –
Smell of cleanliness –

Sunshine of late afternoon –
On the glass tray

a glass pitcher, the tumbler
turned down, by which

a key is lying – And the
immaculate white bed

This Is Just to Say

I have eaten
the plums
that were in
the icebox

and which
you were probably
saving
for breakfast

Forgive me
they were delicious
so sweet
and so cold

The New Clouds

The morning that I first loved you
had a quality of fine division about it
a lightness and a light full of
small round clouds all rose upon the
ground which bore them, a light of
words upon a paper sky, each a meaning
and all a meaning jointly. It was a
quiet speech, at ease but reminiscent
and of praise – with a disturbance
of waiting. Yes! a page that glowed
by all that it was not, a meaning more
of meaning than the text whose
separate edges were the edges of the sky.

The Dance

In Brueghel's great picture, The Kermess,
the dancers go round, they go round and
around, the squeal and the blare and the
tweedle of bagpipes, a bugle and fiddles
tipping their bellies (round as the thick-
sided glasses whose wash they impound)
their hips and their bellies off balance
to turn them. Kicking and rolling about
the Fair Grounds, swinging their butts, those
shanks must be sound to bear up under such
rollicking measures, prance as they dance
in Brueghel's great picture, The Kermess.

Paterson, *Book V: The River of Heaven*

Of asphodel, that greeny flower, the least,
        that is a simple flower
                like a buttercup upon its
branching stem, save
        that it's green and wooden
                We've had a long life
and many things have happened in it.
        There are flowers also
                in hell. So today I've come
to talk to you about them, among
        other things, of flowers
                that we both love, even
of this poor, colorless
        thing which no one living
                prizes but the dead see
and ask among themselves,
        What do we remember that was shaped
                as this thing
is shaped? while their eyes
        fill
                with tears. By which
and by the weak wash of crimson
        colors it, the rose
                is predicated

The Yellow Flower

What shall I say, because talk I must?
        That I have found a cure
                for the sick?
I have found no cure
        for the sick
                but this crooked flower
which only to look upon
        all men
                are cured. This
is that flower
        for which all men
                sing secretly their hymns
of praise. This
        is that sacred
                flower!

Can this be so?
        A flower so crooked
              and obscure? It is
a mustard flower
        and not a mustard flower,
              a single spray
topping the deformed stem
        of fleshy leaves
              in this freezing weather
under glass.

An ungainly flower and
        an unnatural one,
              in this climate; what
can be the reason
        that it has picked me out
              to hold me, openmouthed,
rooted before this window
        in the cold,
              my will
drained from me
        so that I have only eyes
              for these yellow,
twisted petals   .   ?

That the sight,
        though strange to me,
              must be a common one,
is clear: there are such flowers
        with such leaves
              native to some climate
which they can call
        their own.

But why the torture
        and the escape through
              the flower? It is
as if Michelangelo
        had conceived the subject
              of his *Slaves* from this
— or might have done so.
        And did he not make
              the marble bloom? I
am sad
        as he was sad
              in his heroic mood.

But also
                    I have eyes
                              that are made to see and if
they see ruin for myself
                    and all that I hold
                              dear, they see
also
                    through the eyes
                              and through the lips
and tongue the power
                    to free myself
                              and speak of it, as
Michelangelo through his hands
                    had the same, if greater,
                              power.

Which leaves, to account for,
                    the tortured bodies
                              of
the slaves themselves
                    and
                              the tortured body of my flower
which is not a mustard flower at all
                    but some unrecognized
                              and unearthly flower
for me to naturalize
                    and acclimate
                              and choose it for my own.

D. H. LAWRENCE

Discord in Childhood

Outside the house an ash-tree hung its terrible whips,
And at night when the wind rose, the lash of the tree
Shrieked and slashed the wind, as a ship's
Weird rigging in a storm shrieks hideously.

Within the house two voices arose, a slender lash
Whistling she-delirious rage, and the dreadful sound
Of a male thong booming and bruising, until it had drowned
The other voice in a silence of blood, 'neath the noise of
        the ash.

Piano

Softly, in the dusk, a woman is singing to me;
Taking me back down the vista of years, till I see
A child sitting under the piano, in the boom of the tingling
     strings
And pressing the small, poised feet of a mother who smiles as
     she sings.

In spite of myself, the insidious mastery of song
Betrays me back, till the heart of me weeps to belong
To the old Sunday evenings at home, with winter outside
And hymns in the cosy parlour, the tinkling piano our guide.

So now it is vain for the singer to burst into clamour
With the great black piano appassionato. The glamour
Of childish days is upon me, my manhood is cast
Down in the flood of remembrance, I weep like a child for
     the past.

Green

The dawn was apple-green,
     The sky was green wine held up in the sun,
The moon was a golden petal between.

She opened her eyes, and green
     They shone, clear like flowers undone
For the first time, now for the first time seen.

Song of a Man Who Has Come Through

Not I, not I, but the wind that blows through me!
A fine wind is blowing the new direction of Time.
If only I let it bear me, carry me, if only it carry me!
If only I am sensitive, subtle, oh, delicate, a winged gift!
If only, most lovely of all, I yield myself and am borrowed
By the fine, fine wind that takes its course through the chaos
     of the world

Like a fine, an exquisite chisel, a wedge-blade inserted;
If only I am keen and hard like the sheer tip of a wedge
Driven by invisible blows,
The rock will split, we shall come at the wonder, we shall
      find the Hesperides.

Oh, for the wonder that bubbles into my soul,
I would be a good fountain, a good well-head,
Would blur no whisper, spoil no expression.

What is the knocking?
What is the knocking at the door in the night?
It is somebody wants to do us harm.

No, no, it is the three strange angels.
Admit them, admit them.

Snake

A snake came to my water-trough
On a hot, hot day, and I in pyjamas for the heat,
To drink there.

In the deep, strange-scented shade of the great dark carob-tree
I came down the steps with my pitcher
And must wait, must stand and wait, for there he was at the trough
      before me.

He reached down from a fissure in the earth-wall in the gloom
And trailed his yellow-brown slackness soft-bellied down, over the
      edge of the stone trough
And rested his throat upon the stone bottom,
And where the water had dripped from the tap, in a small clearness,
He sipped with his straight mouth,
Softly drank through his straight gums, into his slack long body,
Silently.

Someone was before me at my water-trough,
And I, like a second comer, waiting.

He lifted his head from his drinking, as cattle do,
And looked at me vaguely, as drinking cattle do,

And flickered his two-forked tongue from his lips, and mused a
          moment,
And stooped and drank a little more,
Being earth-brown, earth-golden from the burning bowels
          of the earth
On the day of Sicilian July, with Etna smoking.

The voice of my education said to me
He must be killed,
For in Sicily the black, black snakes are innocent, the gold are
          venomous.

And voices in me said, If you were a man
You would take a stick and break him now, and finish him off.

But must I confess how I liked him,
How glad I was he had come like a guest in quiet, to drink at my
          water-trough
And depart peaceful, pacified, and thankless,
Into the burning bowels of this earth?

Was it cowardice, that I dared not kill him?
Was it perversity, that I longed to talk to him?
Was it humility, to feel so honoured?
I felt so honoured.

And yet those voices:
If you were not afraid, you would kill him!

And truly I was afraid, I was most afraid,
But even so, honoured still more
That he should seek my hospitality
From out the dark door of the secret earth.

He drank enough
And lifted his head, dreamily, as one who has drunken,
And flickered his tongue like a forked night on the air, so black;
Seeming to lick his lips,
And looked around like a god, unseeing, into the air,
And slowly turned his head,
And slowly, very slowly, as if thrice adream,
Proceeded to draw his slow length curving round
And climb again the broken bank of my wall-face.

And as he put his head into that dreadful hole,
And as he slowly drew up, snake-easing his shoulders, and entered
    farther,
A sort of horror, a sort of protest against his withdrawing into that
    horrid black hole,
Deliberately going into the blackness, and slowly drawing himself
    after,
Overcame me now his back was turned.

I looked round, I put down my pitcher,
I picked up a clumsy log
And threw it at the water-trough with a clatter.

I think it did not hit him,
But suddenly that part of him that was left behind convulsed in
    undignified haste,
Writhed like lightning, and was gone
Into the black hole, the earth-lipped fissure in the wallfront,
At which, in the intense still noon, I stared with fascination.

And immediately I regretted it.
I thought how paltry, how vulgar, what a mean act!
I despised myself and the voices of my accursed human education.
And I thought of the albatross,
And I wished he would come back, my snake.

For he seemed to me again like a king,
Like a king in exile, uncrowned in the underworld,
Now due to be crowned again.

And so, I missed my chance with one of the lords
Of life.
And I have something to expiate;
A pettiness.

Bavarian Gentians

Not every man has gentians in his house
in Soft September, at slow, Sad Michaelmas.

Bavarian gentians, big and dark, only dark
darkening the day-time torch-like with the smoking blueness of
    Pluto's gloom,

ribbed and torch-like, with their blaze of darkness spread blue
down flattening into points, flattened under the sweep of white day
torch-flower of the blue-smoking darkness, Pluto's dark-blue daze,
black lamps from the halls of Dio, burning dark blue,
giving off darkness, blue darkness, as Demeter's pale lamps give off
     light,
lead me then, lead me the way.

Reach me a gentian, give me a torch
let me guide myself with the blue, forked torch of this flower
down the darker and darker stairs, where blue is darkened on
     blueness.
even where Persephone goes, just now, from the frosted September
to the sightless realm where darkness is awake upon the dark
and Persephone herself is but a voice
or a darkness invisible enfolded in the deeper dark
of the arms Plutonic, and pierced with the passion of dense gloom,
among the splendour of torches of darkness, shedding darkness on
     the lost bride and her groom.

EZRA POUND

The Tree

I stood still and was a tree amid the wood,
Knowing the truth of things unseen before;
Of Daphne and the laurel bow
And that god-feasting couple old
That grew elm-oak amid the wold.
'Twas not until the gods had been
Kindly entreated, and been brought within
Unto the hearth of their heart's home
That they might do this wonder thing;
Nathless I have been a tree amid the wood
And many a new thing understood
That was rank folly to my head before.

Speech for Psyche in the Golden Book of Apuleius

All night, and as the wind lieth among
The cypress trees, he lay,
Nor held me save as air that brusheth by one
Close, and as the petals of flowers in falling
Waver and seem not drawn to earth, so he
Seemed over me to hover light as leaves
And closer me than air,
And music flowing through me seemed to open
Mine eyes upon new colours.
O winds, what wind can match the weight of him!

The River-Merchant's Wife: A Letter

While my hair was still cut straight across my forehead
I played about the front gate, pulling flowers.
You came by on bamboo stilts, playing horse,
You walked about my seat, playing with blue plums.
And we went on living in the village of Chōkan:
Two small people, without dislike or suspicion.

At fourteen I married My Lord you.
I never laughed, being bashful.
Lowering my head, I looked at the wall.
Called to, a thousand times, I never looked back.

At fifteen I stopped scowling,
I desired my dust to be mingled with yours
Forever and forever and forever.
Why should I climb the look out?

At sixteen you departed,
You went into far Ku-tō-en, by the river of swirling eddies,
And you have been gone five months.
The monkeys make sorrowful noise overhead.

You dragged your feet when you went out.
By the gate now, the moss is grown, the different mosses,
Too deep to clear them away!
The leaves fall early this autumn, in wind.
The paired butterflies are already yellow with August

Over the grass in the West garden;
They hurt me. I grow older.
If you are coming down through the narrows of the river
    Kiang,
Please let me know beforehand,
And I will come out to meet you
As far as Chō-fū-Sa.

By Rihaku (Li T'ai Po)

from *Hugh Selwyn Mauberley*

E. P. Ode Pour L'Élection de Son Sépulcre

2

The age demanded an image
Of its accelerated grimace,
Something for the modern stage,
Not, at any rate, an Attic grace;

Not, not certainly, the obscure reveries
Of the inward gaze;
Better mendacities
Than the classics in paraphrase!

The "age demanded" chiefly a mould in plaster,
Made with no loss of time,
A prose kinema, not, not assuredly, alabaster
Or the "sculpture" of rhyme.

3

The tea-rose tea-gown, etc.
Supplants the mousseline of Cos,
The pianola "replaces"
Sappho's barbitos.

Christ follows Dionysus,
Phallic and ambrosial
Made way for macerations;
Caliban casts out Ariel.

All things are a flowing,
Sage Heracleitus says;
But a tawdry cheapness
Shall outlast our days.

Even the Christian beauty
Defects – after Samothrace;
We see το καλον
Decreed in the market place.

Faun's flesh is not to us,
Nor the saint's vision.
We have the press for wafer;
Franchise for circumcision.

All men, in law, are equals.
Free of Pisistratus,
We choose a knave or an eunuch
To rule over us.

O bright Apollo,
τιν ανδρα, τιν ηρωα, τινα θεον
What god, man, or hero
Shall I place a tin wreath upon!

4

These fought in any case,
and some believing,
                    pro domo, in any case . . .

Some quick to arm,
some for adventure,
some from fear of weakness,
some from fear of censure,
some for love of slaughter, in imagination,
learning later . . .
some in fear, learning love of slaughter;

Died some, pro patria,
                    non "dulce" non "et decor" . . .
walked eye-deep in hell
believing in old men's lies, then unbelieving
came home, home to a lie,
home to many deceits,
home to old lies and new infamy;
usury age-old and age-thick
and liars in public places.

Daring as never before, wastage as never before.
Young blood and high blood,
fair cheeks, and fine bodies;

fortitude as never before

frankness as never before,
disillusions as never told in the old days,
hysterias, trench confessions,
laughter out of dead bellies.

5

There died a myriad,
And of the best, among them,
For an old bitch gone in the teeth,
For a botched civilisation,

Charm, smiling at the good mouth,
Quick eyes gone under earth's lid,

For two gross of broken statues,
For a few thousand battered books.

Canto XXX

Compleynt, compleynt I hearde upon a day,
Artemis singing, Artemis, Artemis
Agaynst Pity lifted her wail:
Pity causeth the forests to fail,
Pity slayeth my nymphs,
Pity spareth so many an evil thing.
Pity befouleth April,
Pity is the root and the spring.
Now if no fayre creature followeth me
It is on account of Pity,
It is on account that Pity forbideth them slaye.
All things are made foul in this season,
This is the reason, none may seek purity
Having for foulnesse pity
And things growne awry;
No more do my shaftes fly
To slay. Nothing is now clean slayne
But rotteth away.

In Paphos, on a day
      I also heard:
. . . goeth not with young Mars to playe
But she hath pity on a doddering fool,
She tendeth his fyre,
She keepeth his embers warm.
Time is the evil. Evil.
      A day, and a day
Walked the young Pedro baffled,
     a day and a day
After Ignez was murdered.

Came the Lords in Lisboa
     a day, and a day
In homage. Seated there
      dead eyes,
Dead hair under the crown,
The King still young there beside her.

Came Madame ΥΛΗ
Clothed with the light of the altar
And with the price of the candles.
"Honour? Balls for yr. honour!
Take two million and swallow it."
      Is come Messire Alfonso
And is departed by boat for Ferrara
And has passed here without saying "O."

Whence have we carved it in metal
Here working in Caesar's fane:
    To the Prince Caesare Borgia
    Duke of Valent and Aemelia
. . . and here have I brought cutters of letters
and printers not vile and vulgar
    (in Fano Caesaris)
notable and sufficient compositors
and a die-cutter for greek fonts and hebrew
named Messire Francesco da Bologna
not only of the usual types but he hath excogitated
a new form called cursive or chancellry letters
nor was it Aldous nor any other but it was
this Messire Francesco who hath cut all Aldous his
     letters

with such grace and charm as is known
    Hieronymous Soncinus 7th July 1503.
and as for text we have taken it
from that of Messire Laurentius
and from a codex once of the Lords Malatesta . . .

And in August that year died Pope Alessandro Borgia,
    Il Papa mori.

Canto XLV

With *Usura*

With usura hath no man a house of good stone
each block cut smooth and well fitting
that design might cover their face,
with usura
hath no man a painted paradise on his church wall
harpes et luthes
or where virgin receiveth message
and halo projects from incision,
with usura
seeth no man Gonzaga his heirs and his concubines
no picture is made to endure nor to live with
but it is made to sell and sell quickly
with usura, sin against nature,
is thy bread ever more of stale rags
is thy bread dry as paper,
with no mountain wheat, no strong flour
with usura the line grows thick
with usura is no clear demarcation
and no man can find site for his dwelling.
Stone cutter is kept from his stone
weaver is kept from his loom
WITH USURA
wool comes not to market
sheep bringeth no gain with usura
Usura is a murrain, usura
blunteth the needle in the maid's hand
and stoppeth the spinner's cunning. Pietro Lombardo
came not by usura
Duccio came not by usura
nor Pier della Francesca; Zuan Bellin' not by usura
nor was "La Calunnia" painted.

Came not by usura Angelico; came not Ambrogio Praedis,
Came no church of cut stone signed: *Adamo me fecit.*
Not by usura St Trophime
Not by usura Saint Hilaire,
Usura rusteth the chisel
It rusteth the craft and the craftsman
It gnaweth the thread in the loom
None learneth to weave gold in her pattern;
Azure hath a canker by usura; cramoisi is unbroidered
Emerald findeth no Memling
Usura slayeth the child in the womb
It stayeth the young man's courting
It hath brought palsey to bed, lyeth
between the young bride and her bridegroom
        CONTRA NATURAM
They have brought whores for Eleusis
Corpses are set to banquet
at behest of usura.

Canto LXXXI

Zeus lies in Ceres' bosom
Taishan is attended of loves
        under Cythera, before sunrise
and he said: Hay aquí mucho catolicismo – (sounded catoli*th*ismo)
        y muy poco reliHion"
and he said: Yo creo que los reyes desparecen"
That was Padre José Elizondo
        in 1906 and in 1917
or about 1917
        and Dolores said: Come pan, niño," eat bread, me lad
Sargent had painted her
        before he descended
(i.e. if he descended
        but in those days he did thumb sketches,
impressions of the Velasquez in the Museo del Prado
and books cost a peseta,
        brass candlesticks in proportion,
hot wind came from the marshes
  and death-chill from the mountains.
And later Bowers wrote: "but such hatred,
  I had never conceived such"
and the London reds wouldn't show up his friends
        (i.e. friends of Franco

working in London) and in Alcazar
forty years gone, they said: "go back to the station to eat
you can sleep here for a peseta"
        goat bells tinkled all night
        and the hostess grinned: Eso es luto, *haw!*
mi marido es muerto
        (it is mourning, my husband is dead)
when she gave me paper to write on
with a black border half an inch or more deep,
        say 5/8ths, of the locanda
"We call *all* foreigners frenchies"
and the egg broke in Cabranez' pocket,
        thus making history. Basil says
they beat drums for three days
till all the drumheads were busted
        (simple village fiesta)
and as for his life in the Canaries . . .
Possum observed that the local   folk dance
was danced by the same dancers in divers localities
        in political welcome . . .
the technique of demonstration
        Cole studied that (not G.D.H., Horace)
"You will find" said old André Spire,
that every man on that board (Crédit Agricole)
has a brother-in-law
        "You the one, I the few"
        said John Adams
speaking of fears in the abstract
    to his volatile friend Mr Jefferson
(to break the pentameter, that was the first heave)
or as Jo Bard says: they never speak to each other,
if it is baker and concierge visibly
        it is La Rouchefoucauld and de Maintenon audibly.
"Te cavero le budelle"
            " La corata a te"
In less than a geological epoch
                said Henry Mencken
"Some cook, some do not cook
    some things cannot be altered"
Ιυγξ . . . εμον ποτι δωμα τον ανδρα
What counts is the cultural level,
    thank Benin for this table ex packing box
    "doan yu tell no one I made it"
        from a mask fine as any in Frankfurt
"It'll get you offn th' groun"
        Light as the branch of Kuanon

And at first disappointed with shoddy
the bare ram-shackle quais, but then saw the
high buggy wheels
        and was reconciled.
George Santayana arriving in the port of Boston
and kept to the end of his life that faint *thethear*
of the Spaniard
        as a grace quasi imperceptible
as did Muss the *v* for *u* of Romagna
and said the grief was a full act
        repeated for each new condoleress
working up to a climax.
and George Horace said he wd/ "get Beveridge" (Senator)
Beveridge wouldn't talk and he wouldn't write for the papers
but George got him by campin' in his hotel
and assailin' him at lunch breakfast an' dinner
        three articles
and my ole man went on hoein' corn
    while George was a-tellin' him,
come across a vacant lot
        where you'd occasionally see a wild rabbit
or mebbe only a loose one
        AOI!
    a leaf in the current
                        at my grates no Althea

libretto Yet
Ere the season died a-cold
Borne upon a zephyr's shoulder
I rose through the aureate sky
                Lawes and Jenkyns guard thy rest
                Dolmetsch ever be thy guest
Has he tempered the viol's wood
To enforce   both the grave   and the acute?
Has he curved us the bowl of the lute?
                Lawes and Jenkyns guard thy rest
                Dolmetsch ever be thy guest
Hast 'ou fashioned so airy a mood
    To draw up leaf from the root?
Hast 'ou found   a cloud   so light
    As seemed neither mist nor shade?

                Then resolve me, tell me aright
                If Waller sang or Dowland played.

            Your eyen two wol sleye me sodenly
            I may the beauté of hem nat susteyne

And for 180 years almost nothing.

Ed ascoltando al leggier mormorio
    there came new subtlety of eyes into my tent,
whether of spirit or hypostasis,
    but what the blindfold hides
or at carneval
            nor any pair showed anger
      Saw but the eyes and stance between the eyes,
colour, diastasis,
    careless or unaware it had not the
  whole tent's room
nor was place for the full Εἰδώς
interpass, penetrate
    casting but shade beyond the other lights
      sky's clear
      night's sea
      green of the mountain pool
      shone from the unmasked eyes in half-mask's space.
What thou lovest well remains,
      the rest is dross
What thou lov'st well shall not be reft from thee
What thou lov'st well is thy true heritage
Whose world, or mine or theirs
      or is it of none?
First came the seen, then thus the palpable
  Elysium, though it were in the halls of hell,
What thou lovest well is thy true heritage

The ant's a centaur in his dragon world.
Pull down thy vanity, it is not man
Made courage, or made order, or made grace,
  Pull down thy vanity, I say pull down.
Learn of the green world what can be thy place
In scaled invention or true artistry,
Pull down thy vanity,
      Paquin pull down!
The green casque has outdone your elegance.

"Master thyself, then others shall thee beare"
  Pull down thy vanity
Thou art a beaten dog beneath the hail,
A swollen magpie in a fitful sun,
Half black half white
Nor knowst'ou wing from tail

Pull down thy vanity
      How mean thy hates
Fostered in falsity,
      Pull down thy vanity,
Rathe to destroy, niggard in charity,
Pull down thy vanity,
      I say pull down.

But to have done instead of not doing
      this is not vanity
To have, with decency, knocked
That a Blunt should open
      To have gathered from the air a live tradition
or from a fine old eye the unconquered flame
This is not vanity.
  Here error is all in the not done,
all in the diffidence that faltered,

HILDA DOOLITTLE (H. D.)

Evening

The light passes
from ridge to ridge,
from flower to flower –
the hepaticas, wide-spread
under the light
grow faint –
the petals reach inward,
the blue tips bend
toward the bluer heart
and the flowers are lost.

The cornel-buds are still white,
but shadows dart
from the cornel-roots –
black creeps from root to root,
each leaf
cuts another leaf on the grass,
shadow seeks shadow,
then both leaf
and leaf-shadow are lost.

The Pool

Are you alive?
I touch you.
You quiver like a sea-fish.
I cover you with my net.
What are you — banded one?

Hippolytus Temporizes

I worship the greatest first —
(it were sweet, the couch,
the brighter ripple of cloth
over the dipped fleece;
the thought: her bones
under the flesh are white
as sand which along a beach
covers but keeps the print
of the crescent shapes beneath:
I thought:
between cloth and fleece,
so her body lies.)

I worship first, the great —
(ah, sweet, your eyes —
what God, invoked in Crete,
gave them the gift to part
as the Sidonian myrtle-flower
suddenly, wide and swart,
then swiftly,
the eye-lids having provoked our hearts —
as suddenly beat and close.)

I worship the feet, flawless,
that haunt the hills —
(ah, sweet, dare I think,
beneath fetter of golden clasp,
of the rhythm, the fall and rise
of yours, carven, slight
beneath straps of gold that keep
their slender beauty caught,
like wings and bodies
of trapped birds.)

I worship the greatest first —
(suddenly into my brain —
the flash of sun on the snow,
the fringe of light and the drift,
the crest and the hill-shadow —
ah, surely now I forget,
ah splendour, my goddess turns:
or was it the sudden heat,
beneath quivering of molten flesh,
of veins, purple as violets?)

from *The Walls Do Not Fall*

I

An incident here and there,
and rails gone (for guns)
from your (and my) old town square:

mist and mist-grey, no colour,
still the Luxor bee, chick and hare
pursue unalterable purpose

in green, rose-red, lapis;
they continue to prophesy
from the stone papyrus:

there, as here, ruin opens
the tomb, the temple; enter,
there as here, there are no doors:

the shrine lies open to the sky,
the rain falls, here, there
sand drifts; eternity endures:

ruin everywhere, yet as the fallen roof
leaves the sealed room
open to the air,

so, through our desolation,
thoughts stir, inspiration stalks us
through gloom:

unaware, Spirit announces the Presence;
shivering overtakes us,
as of old, Samuel:

trembling at a known street-corner,
we know not nor are known;
the Pythian pronounces – we pass on

to another cellar, to another sliced wall
where poor utensils show
like rare objects in a museum;

Pompeii has nothing to teach us,
we know crack of volcanic fissure,
slow flow of terrible lava,

pressure on heart, lungs, the brain
about to burst its brittle case
(what the skull can endure!):

over us, Apocryphal fire,
under us, the earth sway, dip of a floor,
slope of a pavement

where men roll, drunk
with a new bewilderment,
sorcery, bedevilment:

the bone-frame was made for
no such shock knit within terror,
yet the skeleton stood up to it:

the flesh? it was melted away,
the heart burnt out, dead ember,
tendons, muscles shattered, outer husk dismembered,

yet the frame held:
we passed the flame: we wonder
what saved us? what for?

2

Evil was active in the land,
Good was impoverished and sad;

Ill promised adventure,
Good was smug and fat;

Dev-ill was after us,
tricked up like Jehovah;

Good was the tasteless pod,
stripped from the manna-beans, pulse, lentils:

they were angry when we were so hungry
for the nourishment, God;

they snatched off our amulets,
charms are not, they said, grace;

but gods always face two-ways,
so let us search the old highways

for the true-rune, the right-spell,
recover old values;

nor listen if they shout out,
your beauty, Isis, Aset or Astarte,

is a harlot; you are retrogressive,
zealot, hankering after old flesh-pots;

your heart, moreover,
is a dead canker,

they continue, and your
rhythm is the devil's hymn,

your stylus is dipped in corrosive sublimate,
how can you scratch out

indelible ink of the palimpsest
of past misadventure?

3

Let us, however, recover the Sceptre,
the rod of power:

it is crowned with the lily-head
or the lily-bud:

it is Caduceus; among the dying
it bears healing:

or evoking the dead,
it brings life to the living.

from *The Flowering of the Rod*

To Norman Holmes Pearson

. . . pause to give
thanks that we rise again from death and live.

I

O the beautiful garment,
the beautiful raiment —

do not think of His face
or even His hands,

do not think how we will stand
before Him;

remember the snow
on Hermon;

do not look below
where the blue gentian

reflects geometric pattern
in the ice-floe;

do not be beguiled
by the geometry of perfection

for even now,
the terrible banner

darkens the bridge-head;
we have shown

that we could stand;
we have withstood

the anger, frustration,
bitter fire of destruction;

leave the smouldering cities below
(we have done all we could),

we have given until we have no more to give;
alas, it was pity, rather than love, we gave;

now having given all, let us leave all;
above all, let us leave pity

and mount higher
to love – resurrection.

2

I go where I love and where I am loved,
into the snow;

I go to the things I love
with no thought of duty or pity;

I go where I belong, inexorably,
as the rain that has lain long

in the furrow; I have given
or would have given

life to the grain;
but if it will not grow or ripen

with the rain of beauty,
the rain will return to the cloud;

the harvester sharpens his steel on the stone;
but this is not our field,

we have not sown this;
pitiless, pitiless, let us leave

The-place-of-a-skull
to those who have fashioned it.

ROBINSON JEFFERS

Shine, Perishing Republic

While this America settles in the mould of its vulgarity, heavily
    thickening to empire,
And protest, only a bubble in the molten mass, pops and sighs out, and
    the mass hardens,

I sadly smiling remember that the flower fades to make fruit, the fruit
    rots to make earth.
Out of the mother; and through the spring exultances, ripeness and
    decadence; and home to the mother.

You making haste haste on decay: not blameworthy; life is good, be it
    stubbornly long or suddenly
A mortal splendor: meteors are not needed less than mountains: shine,
    perishing republic.

But for my children, I would have them keep their distance from the
    thickening center; corruption
Never has been compulsory, when the cities lie at the monster's feet
    there are left the mountains.

And boys, be in nothing so moderate as in love of man, a clever
    servant, insufferable master.
There is the trap that catches noblest spirits, that caught – they say –
    God, when he walked on earth.

An Artist

That sculptor we knew, the passionate-eyed son of a quarryman,
Who astonished Rome and Paris in his meteor youth, and then was
    gone, at his high tide of triumphs,
Without reason or good-bye; I have seen him again lately, after
    twenty years, but not in Europe.

In desert hills I rode a horse slack-kneed with thirst. Down a steep
    slope a dancing swarm
Of yellow butterflies over a shining rock made me hope water. We
    slid down to the place,
The spring was bitter but the horse drank. I imagined wearings of an
    old path from that wet rock
Ran down the canyon; I followed, soon they were lost, I came to a
    stone valley in which it seemed
No man nor his mount had ever ventured, you wondered whether
    even a vulture'd ever spread sail there.
There were stones of strange form under a cleft in the far hill; I teth-
    ered the horse to a rock
And scrambled over. A heap like a stone current, a moraine,
But monstrously formed limbs of broken carving appeared in the rock-
    fall, enormous breasts, defaced heads
Of giants, the eyes calm through the brute veils of fracture. It was
    natural then to climb higher and go in
Up the cleft gate. The canyon was a sheer-walled crack winding at the
    entrance, but around its bend
The walls grew dreadful with stone giants, presences growing out of
    the rigid precipice, that strove

In dream between stone and life, intense to cast their chaos . . . or to
    enter and return . . . stone-fleshed, nerve-stretched
Great bodies ever more beautiful and more heavy with pain, they
    seemed leading to some unbearable
Consummation of the ecstasy . . . but there, troll among Titans, the
    bearded master of the place accosted me
In a cold anger, a mallet in his hand, filthy and ragged. There was no
    kindness in that man's mind,
But after he had driven me down to the entrance he spoke a little.
    The merciless sun had found the slot now
To hide in, and lit for the wick of that stone lamp-bowl a sky almost, I
    thought, abominably beautiful;
While our lost artist we used to admire: for now I knew him: spoke of
    his passion.

He said, "Marble?
White marble is fit to model a snow-mountain: let man be modest.
    Nor bronze: I am bound to have my tool
In my material, no irrelevances. I found this pit of dark-gray freestone,
    fine-grained, and tough enough
To make sketches that under any weathering will last my lifetime . . . .

The town is eight miles off, I can fetch food and no one follows me
    home. I have water and a cave
Here; and no possible lack of material. I need, therefore, nothing. As
    to companions, I make them.
And models? They are seldom wanted; I know a Basque shepherd I
    sometimes use; and a woman of the town.
What more? Sympathy? Praise? I have never desired them and also I
    have never deserved them. I will not show you
More than the spalls you saw by accident.

                What I see
    is the enormous beauty of things, but what I attempt
Is nothing to that. I am helpless toward that.
It is only to form in stone the mould of some ideal humanity that
    might be worthy to *be*
Under that lightning. Animalcules that God (if he were given to
    laughter) might omit to laugh at.

Those children of my hands are tortured, because they feel," he said,
    "the storm of the outer magnificence.
They are giants in agony. They have seen from my eyes
The man-destroying beauty of the dawns over their notch yonder,
and all the obliterating stars.

But in their eyes they have peace. I have lived a little and I think
Peace marrying pain alone can breed that excellence in the luckless race,
        might make it decent
To exist at all on the star-lit stone breast.

                                        I hope," he said,
        "that when I grow old and the chisel drops,
I may crawl out on a ledge of the rock and die like a wolf."

                                                These
        fragments are all I can remember,
These in the flare of the desert evening. Having been driven so brutally
        forth I never returned;
Yet I respect him enough to keep his name and the place secret. I hope
        that some other traveller
May stumble on that ravine of Titans after their maker has died.
        While he lives, let him alone.

Hurt Hawks

I

The broken pillar of the wing jags from the clotted shoulder,
The wing trails like a banner in defeat,
No more to use the sky forever but live with famine
And pain a few days: cat nor coyote
Will shorten the week of waiting for death, there is game without talons.
He stands under the oak-bush and waits
The lame feet of salvation; at night he remembers freedom
And flies in a dream, the dawns ruin it.
He is strong and pain is worse to the strong, incapacity is worse.
The curs of the day come and torment him
At distance, no one but death the redeemer will humble that head,
The intrepid readiness, the terrible eyes.
The wild God of the world is sometimes merciful to those
That ask mercy, not often to the arrogant.
You do not know him, you communal people, or you have forgotten
        him;
Intemperate and savage, the hawk remembers him;
Beautiful and wild, the hawks, and men that are dying, remember him.

2

I'd sooner, except the penalties, kill a man than a hawk; but the great
        redtail
Had nothing left but unable misery
From the bone too shattered for mending, the wing that trailed under
        his talons when he moved.

We had fed him six weeks, I gave him freedom,
He wandered over the foreland hill and returned in the evening,
    asking for death,
Not like a beggar, still eyed with the old
Implacable arrogance. I gave him the lead gift in the twilight. What
    fell was relaxed,
Owl-downy, soft feminine feathers; but what
Soared: the fierce rush: the night-herons by the flooded river cried fear
    at its rising
Before it was quite unsheathed from reality.

Return

A little too abstract, a little too wise,
It is time for us to kiss the earth again,
It is time to let the leaves rain from the skies,
Let the rich life run to the roots again.
I will go down to the lovely Sur Rivers
And dip my arms in them up to the shoulders.
I will find my accounting where the alder leaf quivers
In the ocean wind over the river boulders.
I will touch things and things and no more thoughts,
That breed like mouthless May-flies darkening the sky,
The insect clouds that blind our passionate hawks
So that they cannot strike, hardly can fly.
Things are the hawk's food and noble is the mountain, Oh noble
Pico Blanco, steep sea-wave of marble.

The Stars Go Over the Lonely Ocean

Unhappy about some far off things
That are not my affair, wandering
Along the coast and up the lean ridges,
I saw in the evening
The stars go over the lonely ocean,
And a black-maned wild boar
Plowing with his snout on Mal Paso Mountain.

The old monster snuffled, "Here are sweet roots,
Fat grubs, slick beetles and sprouted acorns.
The best nation in Europe has fallen,
And that is Finland,

But the stars go over the lonely ocean,"
The old black-bristled boar,
Tearing the sod on Mal Paso Mountain.

"The world's in a bad way, my man,
And bound to be worse before it mends;
Better lie up in the mountain here
Four or five centuries,
While the stars go over the lonely ocean,"
Said the old father of wild pigs,
Plowing the fallow on Mal Paso Mountain.

"Keep clear of the dupes that talk democracy
And the dogs that talk revolution,
Drunk with talk, liars and believers.
I believe in my tusks.
Long live freedom and damn the ideologies,"
Said the gamey black-maned wild boar
Tusking the turf on Mal Paso Mountain.

MARIANNE MOORE

The Steeple-Jack

Dürer would have seen a reason for living
     in a town like this, with eight stranded whales
to look at; with the sweet sea air coming into your house
on a fine day, from water etched
     with waves as formal as the scales
on a fish.

One by one in two's and three's, the seagulls keep
     flying back and forth over the town clock,
or sailing around the lighthouse without moving their wings —
rising steadily with a slight
     quiver of the body — or flock
mewing where

a sea the purple of the peacock's neck is
     paled to greenish azure as Dürer changed
the pine green of the Tyrol to peacock blue and guinea
gray. You can see a twenty-five-
     pound lobster; and fish nets arranged
to dry. The

whirlwind fife-and-drum of the storm bends the salt
    marsh grass, disturbs stars in the sky and the
star on the steeple; it is a privilege to see so
much confusion. Disguised by what
    might seem the opposite, the sea-
side flowers and

trees are favored by the fog so that you have
    the tropics at first hand: the trumpet vine,
foxglove, giant snapdragon, a salpiglossis that has
spots and stripes; morning-glories, gourds,
    or moon-vines trained on fishing twine
at the back door:

cattails, flags, blueberries and spiderwort,
    striped grass, lichens, sunflowers, asters, daisies –
yellow and crab-claw ragged sailors with green bracts –
        toad-plant,
petunias, ferns; pink lilies, blue
    ones, tigers; poppies; black sweet-peas.
The climate

is not right for the banyan, frangipani, or
    jack-fruit trees; or for exotic serpent
life. Ring lizard and snakeskin for the foot, if you see fit;
but here they've cats, not cobras, to
    keep down the rats. The diffident
little newt

with white pin-dots on black horizontal spaced-
    out bands lives here; yet there is nothing that
ambition can buy or take away. The college student
named Ambrose sits on the hillside
    with his not-native books and hat
and sees boats

at sea progress white and rigid as if in
    a groove. Liking an elegance of which
the source is not bravado, he knows by heart the antique
sugar-bowl shaped summerhouse of
    interlacing slats, and the pitch
of the church

spire, not true, from which a man in scarlet lets
    down a rope as a spider spins a thread;
he might be part of a novel, but on the sidewalk a

sign says C. J. Poole, Steeple Jack,
   in black and white; and one in red
and white says

Danger. The church portico has four fluted
   columns, each a single piece of stone, made
modester by whitewash. This would be a fit haven for
waifs, children, animals, prisoners,
   and presidents who have repaid
sin-driven

senators by not thinking about them. The
   place has a schoolhouse, a post-office in a
store, fish-houses, hen-houses, a three-masted
   schooner on
the stocks. The hero, the student,
   the steeple jack, each in his way,
is at home.

It could not be dangerous to be living
   in a town like this, of simple people,
who have a steeple-jack placing danger signs by the church
while he is gilding the solid-
   pointed star, which on a steeple
stands for hope.

Poetry

I, too, dislike it.
   Reading it, however, with a perfect contempt for it, one
      discovers in
   it after all, a place for the genuine.

Silence

My father used to say,
"Superior people never make long visits,
have to be shown Longfellow's grave
or the glass flowers at Harvard.
Self-reliant like the cat —
that takes its prey to privacy,
the mouse's limp tail hanging like a shoelace from its
      mouth —

they sometimes enjoy solitude,
and can be robbed of speech
by speech which has delighted them.
The deepest feeling always shows itself in silence;
not in silence, but restraint."
Nor was he insincere in saying, "Make my house your inn."
Inns are not residences.

What Are Years?

What is our innocence,
what is our guilt? All are
     naked, none is safe. And whence
is courage: the unanswered question,
the resolute doubt –
dumbly calling, deafly listening – that
is misfortune, even death,
     encourages others
     and in its defeat, stirs

the soul to be strong? He
sees deep and is glad, who
     accedes to mortality
and in his imprisonment rises
upon himself as
the sea in a chasm, struggling to be
free and unable to be,
     in its surrendering
     finds its continuing.

So he who strongly feels,
behaves. The very bird,
     grown taller as he sings, steels
his form straight up. Though he is captive,
his mighty singing
says, satisfaction is a lowly
thing, how pure a thing is joy.
     This is mortality,
     this is eternity.

The Paper Nautilus

For authorities whose hopes
are shaped by mercenaries?
    Writers entrapped by
    teatime fame and by
commuters' comforts? Not for these
    the paper nautilus
    constructs her thin glass shell.

    Giving her perishable
souvenir of hope, a dull
    white outside and smooth-
    edged inner surface
glossy as the sea, the watchful
    maker of it guards it
    day and night; she scarcely

    eats until the eggs are hatched.
Buried eightfold in her eight
    arms, for she is in
    a sense a devil-
fish, her glass ram's-horn-cradled freight
    is hid but is not crushed;
    as Hercules, bitten

    by a crab loyal to the hydra,
was hindered to succeed,
    the intensively
    watched eggs coming from
the shell free it when they are freed –
    leaving its wasp-nest flaws
    of white on white, and close-

    laid Ionic chiton-folds
like the lines in the mane of
    a Parthenon horse,
    round which the arms had
wound themselves as if they knew love
    is the only fortress
    strong enough to trust to.

Nevertheless

you've seen a strawberry
   that's had a struggle; yet
   was, where the fragments met,

a hedgehog or a star-
   fish for the multitude
   of seeds. What better food

than apple seeds – the fruit
   within the fruit – locked in
   like counter-curved twin

hazelnuts? Frost that kills
   the little rubber-plant-
   leaves of *kok-saghyz*-stalks, can't

harm the roots; they still grow
   in frozen ground. Once where
   there was a prickly-pear-

leaf clinging to barbed wire,
   a root shot down to grow
   in earth two feet below;

as carrots, form mandrakes
   or a ram's-horn root some-
   times. Victory won't come

to me unless I go
   to it; a grape tendril
   ties a knot in knots till

knotted thirty times – so
   the bound twig that's under-
   gone and over-gone, can't stir.

The weak overcomes its
   menace, the strong over-
   comes itself. What is there

like fortitude! What sap
   went through that little thread
   to make the cherry red!

EDWIN MUIR

Ballad of Hector in Hades

Yes, this is where I stood that day,
  Beside this sunny mound.
The walls of Troy are far away,
  And outward comes no sound.

I wait. On all the empty plain
  A burnished stillness lies,
Save for the chariot's tinkling hum,
  And a few distant cries.

His helmet glitters near. The world
  Slowly turns around,
With some new sleight compels my feet
  From the fighting ground.

I run. If I turned back again
  The earth must turn with me,
The mountains planted on the plain,
  The sky clamped to the sea.

The grasses puff a little dust
  Where my footsteps fall.
I cast a shadow as I pass
  The little wayside wall.

The strip of grass on either hand
  Sparkles in the light;
I only see that little space
  To the left and to the right,

And in that space our shadows run,
  His shadow there and mine,
The little flowers, the tiny mounds,
  The grasses frail and fine.

But narrower still and narrower!
  My course is shrunk and small,
Yet vast as in a deadly dream,
  And faint the Trojan wall.
The sun up in the towering sky
  Turns like a spinning ball.

The sky with all its clustered eyes
   Grows still with watching me,
The flowers, the mounds, the flaunting weeds
   Wheel slowly round to see.

Two shadows racing on the grass,
   Silent and so near,
Until his shadow falls on mine.
   And I am rid of fear.

The race is ended. Far away
   I hang and do not care,
While round bright Troy Achilles whirls
   A corpse with streaming hair.

Troy

He all that time among the sewers of Troy
Scouring for scraps. A man so venerable
He might have been Priam's self, but Priam was dead,
Troy taken. His arms grew meagre as a boy's,
And all that flourished in that hollow famine
Was his long, white, round beard. Oh, sturdily
He swung his staff and sent the bold rats skipping
Across the scurfy hills and worm-wet valleys,
Crying: "Achilles, Ajax, turn and fight!
Stop cowards!" Till his cries, dazed and confounded,
Flew back at him with: "Coward, turn and fight!"
And the wild Greeks yelled round him.
Yet he withstood them, a brave, mad old man,
And fought the rats for Troy. The light was rat-grey,
The hills and dells, the common drain, his Simois,
Rat-grey. Mysterious shadows fell
Affrighting him whenever a cloud offended
The sun up in the other world. The rat-hordes,
Moving, were grey dust shifting in grey dust.
Proud history has such sackends. He was taken
At last by some chance robber seeking treasure
Under Troy's riven roots. Dragged to the surface.
And there he saw Troy like a burial ground
With tumbled walls for tombs, the smooth sward wrinkled
As Time's last wave had long since passed that way,
The sky, the sea, Mount Ida and the islands,

No sail from edge to edge, the Greeks clean gone.
They stretched him on a rock and wrenched his limbs,
Asking: "Where is the treasure?" till he died.

The Myth

My childhood all a myth
Enacted in a distant isle;
Time with his hourglass and his scythe
Stood dreaming on the dial,
And did not move the whole day long
That immobility might save
Continually the dying song,
The flower, the falling wave.
And at each corner of the wood
In which I played the ancient play,
Guarding the traditional day
The faithful watchers stood.

My youth a tragi-comedy,
Ridiculous war of dreams and shames
Waged for a Pyrrhic victory
Of reveries and names,
Which in slow-motion rout were hurled
Before sure-footed flesh and blood
That of its hunger built a world,
Advancing rood by rood.
And there in practical clay compressed
The reverie played its useful part,
Fashioning a diurnal mart
Of radiant east and west.

So manhood went. Now past the prime
I see this life contrived to stay
With all its works of labouring time
By time beguiled away.
Consolidated flesh and bone
And its designs grow halt and lame;
Unshakeable arise alone
The reverie and the name.
And at each border of the land,
Like monuments a deluge leaves,
Guarding the invisible sheaves
The risen watchers stand.

The Late Wasp

You that through all the dying summer
Came every morning to our breakfast table,
A lonely bachelor mummer,
And fed on the marmalade
So deeply, all your strength was scarcely able
To prise you from the sweet pit you had made, –
You and the earth have now grown older,
And your blue thoroughfares have felt a change;
They have grown colder;
And it is strange
How the familiar avenues of the air
Crumble now, crumble; the good air will not hold,
All cracked and perished with the cold;
And down you dive through nothing and through despair.

JOHN CROWE RANSOM

Bells for John Whiteside's Daughter

There was such speed in her little body,
And such lightness in her footfall,
It is no wonder her brown study
Astonishes us all.

Her wars were bruited in our high window.
We looked among orchard trees and beyond
Where she took arms against her shadow,
Or harried unto the pond

The lazy geese, like a snow cloud
Dripping their snow on the green grass,
Tricking and stopping, sleepy and proud,
Who cried in goose, Alas,

For the tireless heart within the little
Lady with rod that made them rise
From their noon apple-dreams and scuttle
Goose-fashion under the skies!

But now go the bells, and we are ready,
In one house we are sternly stopped
To say we are vexed at her brown study,
Lying so primly propped.

Piazza Piece

– I am a gentleman in a dustcoat trying
To make you hear. Your ears are soft and small
And listen to an old man not at all,
They want the young men's whispering and sighing.
But see the roses on your trellis dying
And hear the spectral singing of the moon;
For I must have my lovely lady soon,
I am a gentleman in a dustcoat trying.

– I am a lady young in beauty waiting
Until my truelove comes, and then we kiss.
But what grey man among the vines is this
Whose words are dry and faint as in a dream?
Back from my trellis, Sir, before I scream!
I am a lady young in beauty waiting.

Vision by Sweetwater

Go and ask Robin to bring the girls over
To Sweetwater, said my Aunt; and that was why
It was like a dream of ladies sweeping by
The willows, clouds, deep meadowgrass, and river.

Robin's sisters and my Aunt's lily daughter
Laughed and talked, and tinkled light as wrens
If there were a little colony all hens
To go walking by the steep turn of Sweetwater.

Let them alone, dear Aunt, just for one minute
Till I go fishing in the dark of my mind:
Where have I seen before, against the wind,
These bright virgins, robed and bare of bonnet,

Flowing with music of their strange quick tongue
And adventuring with delicate paces by the stream, –
Myself a child, old suddenly at the scream
From one of the white throats which it hid among?

Dead Boy

The little cousin is dead, by foul subtraction,
A green bough from Virginia's aged tree,
And none of the county kin like the transaction,
Nor some of the world of outer dark, like me.

A boy not beautiful, nor good, nor clever,
A black cloud full of storms too hot for keeping,
A sword beneath his mother's heart – yet never
Woman bewept her babe as this is weeping.

A pig with a pasty face, so I had said,
Squealing for cookies, kinned by poor pretense
With a noble house. But the little man quite dead,
I see the forbears' antique lineaments.

The elder men have strode by the box of death
To the wide flag porch, and muttering low send round
The bruit of the day. O friendly waste of breath!
Their hearts are hurt with a deep dynastic wound.

He was pale and little, the foolish neighbors say;
The first-fruits, saith the Preacher, the Lord hath taken;
But this was the old tree's late branch wrenched away,
Grieving the sapless limbs, the shorn and shaken.

T. S. ELIOT

The Love Song of J. Alfred Prufrock

*S'io credesse che mia risposta fosse
A persona che mai tornasse al mondo,
Questa fiamma staria senza piu scosse.
Ma perciocche giammai di questo fondo
Non torno vivo alcun, s'i'odo il vero,
Senza tema d'infamia ti rispondo.*

Let us go then, you and I,
When the evening is spread out against the sky
Like a patient etherised upon a table;
Let us go, through certain half-deserted streets,
The muttering retreats

Of restless nights in one-night cheap hotels
And sawdust restaurants with oyster-shells:
Streets that follow like a tedious argument
Of insidious intent
To lead you to an overwhelming question . . .
Oh, do not ask, "What is it?"
Let us go and make our visit.

In the room the women come and go
Talking of Michelangelo.

The yellow fog that rubs its back upon the window-panes,
The yellow smoke that rubs its muzzle on the window-panes
Licked its tongue into the corners of the evening,
Lingered upon the pools that stand in drains,
Let fall upon its back the soot that falls from chimneys,
Slipped by the terrace, made a sudden leap,
And seeing that it was a soft October night,
Curled once about the house, and fell asleep.

And indeed there will be time
For the yellow smoke that slides along the street,
Rubbing its back upon the window-panes;
There will be time, there will be time
To prepare a face to meet the faces that you meet;
There will be time to murder and create,
And time for all the works and days of hands
That lift and drop a question on your plate;
Time for you and time for me,
And time yet for a hundred indecisions,
And for a hundred visions and revisions,
Before the taking of a toast and tea.

In the room the women come and go
Talking of Michelangelo.

And indeed there will be time
To wonder, "Do I dare?" and, "Do I dare?"
Time to turn back and descend the stair,
With a bald spot in the middle of my hair –
(They will say: "How his hair is growing thin!")
My morning coat, my collar mounting firmly to the chin,
My necktie rich and modest, but asserted by a simple pin –
(They will say: "But how his arms and legs are thin!")
Do I dare

Disturb the universe?
In a minute there is time
For decisions and revisions which a minute will reverse.

For I have known them all already, known them all: –
Have known the evenings, mornings, afternoons,
I have measured out my life with coffee spoons;
I know the voices dying with a dying fall
Beneath the music from a farther room.
So how should I presume?

And I have known the eyes already, known them all –
The eyes that fix you in a formulated phrase,
And when I am formulated, sprawling on a pin,
When I am pinned and wriggling on the wall,
Then how should I begin
To spit out all the butt-ends of my days and ways?
And how should I presume?

And I have known the arms already, known them all –
Arms that are braceleted and white and bare
(But in the lamplight, downed with light brown hair!)
Is it perfume from a dress
That makes me so digress?
Arms that lie along a table, or wrap about a shawl.
And should I then presume?
And how should I begin?

                    *   *   *

Shall I say, I have gone at dusk through narrow streets
And watched the smoke that rises from the pipes
Of lonely men in shirt-sleeves, leaning out of windows? . . .

I should have been a pair of ragged claws
Scuttling across the floors of silent seas.

                    *   *   *

And the afternoon, the evening, sleeps so peacefully!
Smoothed by long fingers,
Asleep . . . tired . . . or it malingers,
Stretched on the floor, here beside you and me.
Should I, after tea and cakes and ices,
Have the strength to force the moment to its crisis?

But though I have wept and fasted, wept and prayed,
Though I have seen my head (grown slightly bald) brought
    in upon a platter,
I am no prophet — and here's no great matter;
I have seen the moment of my greatness flicker,
And I have seen the eternal Footman hold my coat, and
    snicker,
And in short, I was afraid.

And would it have been worth it, after all,
After the cups, the marmalade, the tea,
Among the porcelain, among some talk of you and me,
Would it have been worth while,
To have bitten off the matter with a smile,
To have squeezed the universe into a ball
To roll it toward some overwhelming question,
To say: "I am Lazarus, come from the dead,
Come back to tell you all, I shall tell you all" —
If one, settling a pillow by her head,
    Should say: "That is not what I meant at all.
    That is not it, at all."

And would it have been worth it, after all,
Would it have been worth while,
After the sunsets and the dooryards and the sprinkled streets,
After the novels, after the teacups, after the skirts that trail
    along the floor —
And this, and so much more? —
It is impossible to say just what I mean!
But as if a magic lantern threw the nerves in patterns on a
    screen:
Would it have been worth while
If one, settling a pillow or throwing off a shawl,
And turning toward the window, should say:
    "That is not it at all,
    That is not what I meant, at all."

*   *   *

No! I am not Prince Hamlet, nor was meant to be;
Am an attendant lord, one that will do
To swell a progress, start a scene or two,
Advise the prince; no doubt, an easy tool,
Deferential, glad to be of use,
Politic, cautious, and meticulous;
Full of high sentence, but a bit obtuse;

At times, indeed, almost ridiculous —
Almost, at times, the Fool.

   I grow old . . . I grow old . . .
I shall wear the bottoms of my trousers rolled.

   Shall I part my hair behind? Do I dare to eat a peach?
I shall wear white flannel trousers, and walk upon the beach.
I have heard the mermaids singing, each to each.

   I do not think that they will sing to me.

   I have seen them riding seaward on the waves
Combing the white hair of the waves blown back
When the wind blows the water white and black.

   We have lingered in the chambers of the sea
By sea-girls wreathed with seaweed red and brown
Till human voices wake us, and we drown.

La Figlia che Piange

O quam te memorem virgo . . .

Stand on the highest pavement of the stair —
Lean on a garden urn —
Weave, weave the sunlight in your hair —
Clasp your flowers to you with a pained surprise —
Fling them to the ground and turn
With a fugitive resentment in your eyes:
But weave, weave the sunlight in your hair.

   So I would have had him leave,
So I would have had her stand and grieve,
So he would have left
As the soul leaves the body torn and bruised,
As the mind deserts the body it has used.
I should find
Some way incomparably light and deft,
Some way we both should understand,
Simple and faithless as a smile and shake of the hand.

   She turned away, but with the autumn weather
Compelled my imagination many days,

Many days and many hours:
Her hair over her arms and her arms full of flowers.
And I wonder how they should have been together!
I should have lost a gesture and a pose.
Sometimes these cogitations still amaze
The troubled midnight and the noon's repose.

Sweeney Among the Nightingales

ωμοι πεπληγμαι καιριαν πληγην εσω

Apeneck Sweeney spreads his knees
Letting his arms hang down to laugh,
The zebra stripes along his jaw
Swelling to maculate giraffe.

The circles of the stormy moon
Slide westward toward the River Plate,
Death and the Raven drift above
And Sweeney guards the hornèd gate.

Gloomy Orion and the Dog
Are veiled; and hushed the shrunken seas;
The person in the Spanish cape
Tries to sit on Sweeney's knees

Slips and pulls the table cloth
Overturns a coffee-cup,
Reorganized upon the floor
She yawns and draws a stocking up;

The silent man in mocha brown
Sprawls at the window-sill and gapes;
The waiter brings in oranges
Bananas figs and hothouse grapes;

The silent vertebrate in brown
Contracts and concentrates, withdraws;
Rachel *née* Rabinovitch
Tears at the grapes with murderous paws;

She and the lady in the cape
Are suspect, thought to be in league;
Therefore the man with heavy eyes
Declines the gambit, shows fatigue,

Leaves the room and reappears
Outside the window, leaning in,
Branches of wistaria
Circumscribe a golden grin;

The host with someone indistinct
Converses at the door apart,
The nightingales are singing near
The Convent of the Sacred Heart,

And sang within the bloody wood
When Agamemnon cried aloud,
And let their liquid siftings fall
To stain the stiff dishonoured shroud.

from *The Waste Land*

II. *A Game of Chess*

The Chair she sat in, like a burnished throne,
Glowed on the marble, where the glass
Held up by standards wrought with fruited vines
From which a golden Cupidon peeped out
(Another hid his eyes behind his wing)
Doubled the flames of sevenbranched candelabra
Reflecting light upon the table as
The glitter of her jewels rose to meet it,
From satin cases poured in rich profusion;
In vials of ivory and coloured glass
Unstoppered, lurked her strange synthetic perfumes,
Unguent, powdered, or liquid – troubled, confused
And drowned the sense in odours; stirred by the air
That freshened from the window, these ascended
In fattening the prolonged candle-flames,
Flung their smoke into the laquearia,
Stirring the pattern on the coffered ceiling.
Huge sea-wood fed with copper
Burned green and orange, framed by the coloured stone,
In which sad light a carvèd dolphin swam.
Above the antique mantel was displayed
As though a window gave upon the sylvan scene
The change of Philomel, by the barbarous king
So rudely forced; yet there the nightingale
Filled all the desert with inviolable voice
And still she cried, and still the world pursues,

"Jug Jug" to dirty ears.
And other withered stumps of time
Were told upon the walls; staring forms
Leaned out, leaning, hushing the room enclosed.
Footsteps shuffled on the stair.
Under the firelight, under the brush, her hair
Spread out in fiery points
Glowed into words, then would be savagely still.

　　"My nerves are bad tonight. Yes, bad. Stay with me.
"Speak to me. Why do you never speak. Speak.
　　"What are you thinking of? What thinking? What?
"I never know what you are thinking. Think."

　　I think we are in rats' alley
Where the dead men lost their bones.

　　"What is that noise?"
　　　　　　　　　　　　　The wind under the door.
"What is that noise now? What is the wind doing?"
　　　　　　　　　　　　　Nothing again nothing.

　　　　　　　　　　　　　　　　　　　　　"Do
"You know nothing? Do you see nothing? Do you remember
"Nothing?"

　　I remember
Those are pearls that were his eyes.
"Are you alive, or not? Is there nothing in your head?"
　　　　　　　　　　　　　　　　　　　　　　　　But

O O O O that Shakespeherian Rag –
It's so elegant
So intelligent
"What shall I do now? What shall I do?"
"I shall rush out as I am, and walk the street
"With my hair down, so. What shall we do tomorrow?
"What shall we ever do?"
　　　　　　　　　　　　　The hot water at ten.
And if it rains, a closed car at four.
And we shall play a game of chess,
Pressing lidless eyes and waiting for a knock upon the door.

　　When Lil's husband got demobbed, I said –
I didn't mince my words, I said to her myself,
HURRY UP PLEASE ITS TIME
Now Albert's coming back, make yourself a bit smart.

He'll want to know what you done with that money he
    gave you
To get yourself some teeth. He did, I was there.
You have them all out, Lil, and get a nice set,
He said, I swear, I can't bear to look at you.
And no more can't I, I said, and think of poor Albert,
He's been in the army four years, he wants a good time,
And if you don't give it him, there's others will, I said.
Oh is there, she said. Something o' that, I said.
Then I'll know who to thank, she said, and give me a
    straight look.
HURRY UP PLEASE ITS TIME
If you don't like it you can get on with it, I said.
Others can pick and choose if you can't.
But if Albert makes off, it won't be for lack of telling.
You ought to be ashamed, I said, to look so antique.
(And her only thirty-one.)
I can't help it, she said, pulling a long face,
It's them pills I took, to bring it off, she said.
(She's had five already, and nearly died of young George.)
The chemist said it would be all right, but I've never been
    the same.
You are a proper fool, I said.
Well, if Albert won't leave you alone, there it is, I said,
What you get married for if you don't want children?
HURRY UP PLEASE ITS TIME
Well, that Sunday Albert was home, they had a hot gammon,
And they asked me in to dinner, to get the beauty of it hot —
HURRY UP PLEASE ITS TIME
HURRY UP PLEASE ITS TIME
Goonight Bill. Goonight Lou. Goonight May. Goonight.
Ta ta. Goonight. Goonight.
Good night, ladies, good night, sweet ladies, good night,
    good night.

III. *The Fire Sermon*

The river's tent is broken: the last fingers of leaf
Clutch and sink into the wet bank. The wind
Crosses the brown land, unheard. The nymphs are departed.
Sweet Thames, run softly, till I end my song.
The river bears no empty bottles, sandwich papers,
Silk handkerchiefs, cardboard boxes, cigarette ends
Or other testimony of summer nights. The nymphs are
    departed.

And their friends, the loitering heirs of city directors;
Departed, have left no addresses.
By the waters of Leman I sat down and wept . . .
Sweet Thames, run softly till I end my song,
Sweet Thames, run softly, for I speak not loud or long.
But at my back in a cold blast I hear
The rattle of the bones, and chuckle spread from ear to ear.
A rat crept softly through the vegetation
Dragging its slimy belly on the bank
While I was fishing in the dull canal
On a winter evening round behind the gashouse
Musing upon the king my brother's wreck
And on the king my father's death before him.
White bodies naked on the low damp ground
And bones cast in a little low dry garret,
Rattled by the rat's foot only, year to year.
But at my back from time to time I hear
The sound of horns and motors, which shall bring
Sweeney to Mrs Porter in the spring.
O the moon shone bright on Mrs Porter
And on her daughter
They wash their feet in soda water
Et O ces voix d'enfants, chantant dans la coupole!

    Twit twit twit
Jug jug jug jug jug jug
So rudely forc'd.
Tereu

    Unreal City
Under the brown fog of a winter noon
Mr Eugenides, the Smyrna merchant
Unshaven, with a pocket full of currants
C.i.f. London: documents at sight,
Asked me in demotic French
To luncheon at the Cannon Street Hotel
Followed by a weekend at the Metropole.

    At the violet hour, when the eyes and back
Turn upward from the desk, when the human engine waits
Like a taxi throbbing waiting,
I Tiresias, though blind, throbbing between two lives,
Old man with wrinkled female breasts, can see
At the violet hour, the evening hour that strives
Homeward, and brings the sailor home from sea,
The typist home at teatime, clears her breakfast, lights

Her stove, and lays out food in tins.
Out of the window perilously spread
Her drying combinations touched by the sun's last rays,
On the divan are piled (at night her bed)
Stockings, slippers, camisoles, and stays.
I Tiresias, old man with wrinkled dugs
Perceived the scene, and foretold the rest –
I too awaited the expected guest.
He, the young man carbuncular, arrives,
A small house agent's clerk, with one bold stare,
One of the low on whom assurance sits
As a silk hat on a Bradford millionaire.
The time is now propitious, as he guesses,
The meal is ended, she is bored and tired,
Endeavours to engage her in caresses
Which still are unreproved, if undesired.
Flushed and decided, he assaults at once;
Exploring hands encounter no defence;
His vanity requires no response,
And makes a welcome of indifference.
(And I Tiresias have foresuffered all
Enacted on this same divan or bed;
I who have sat by Thebes below the wall
And walked among the lowest of the dead.)
Bestows one final patronising kiss,
And gropes his way, finding the stairs unlit . . .

  She turns and looks a moment in the glass,
Hardly aware of her departed lover;
Her brain allows one half-formed thought to pass:
"Well now that's done: and I'm glad it's over."
When lovely woman stoops to folly and
Paces about her room again, alone,
She smoothes her hair with automatic hand,
And puts a record on the gramophone.

  "This music crept by me upon the waters"
And along the Strand, up Queen Victoria Street.
O City city, I can sometimes hear
Beside a public bar in Lower Thames Street,
The pleasant whining of a mandoline
And a clatter and a chatter from within
Where fishmen lounge at noon: where the walls
Of Magnus Martyr hold   .
Inexplicable splendour of Ionian white and gold.

The river sweats
Oil and tar
The barges drift
With the turning tide
Red sails
Wide
To leeward, swing on the heavy spar.
The barges wash
Drifting logs
Down Greenwich reach
Past the Isle of Dogs.
                   Weialala leia
                   Wallala leialala

    Elizabeth and Leicester
Beating oars
The stern was formed
A gilded shell
Red and gold
The brisk swell
Rippled both shores
Southwest wind
Carried down stream
The peal of bells
White towers
                   Weialala leia
                   Wallala leialala

"Trams and dusty trees.
Highbury bore me. Richmond and Kew
Undid me. By Richmond I raised my knees
Supine on the floor of a narrow canoe."

    "My feet are at Moorgate, and my heart
Under my feet. After the event
He wept. He promised 'a new start'.
I made no comment. What should I resent?"

    "On Margate Sands.
I can connect
Nothing with nothing.
The broken fingernails of dirty hands.
My people humble people who expect
Nothing."
                   la la

To Carthage then I came

Burning burning burning burning
O Lord Thou pluckest me out
O Lord Thou pluckest

burning

from *Four Quartets*

Burnt Norton

του λογου δεντος ξυνου ζωουσιν οι πολλοι
ως ιδιαν εχοντες φρονησιν
I. p. 77. Fr. 2.

οδος ανω κατω μια και ωυτη
I. p. 89. Fr. 60.

Diels: *Die Fragmente der Vorsokratiker* (Herakleitos).

I

Time present and time past
Are both perhaps present in time future,
And time future contained in time past.
If all time is eternally present
All time is unredeemable.
What might have been is an abstraction
Remaining a perpetual possibility
Only in a world of speculation.
What might have been and what has been
Point to one end, which is always present.
Footfalls echo in the memory
Down the passage which we did not take
Towards the door we never opened
Into the rose-garden. My words echo
Thus, in your mind.
                    But to what purpose
Disturbing the dust on a bowl of rose-leaves
I do not know.
                    Other echoes
Inhabit the garden. Shall we follow?
Quick, said the bird, find them, find them,
Round the corner. Through the first gate,

Into our first world, shall we follow
The deception of the thrush? Into our first world.
There they were, dignified, invisible,
Moving without pressure, over the dead leaves.
In the autumn heat, through the vibrant air,
And the bird called, in response to
The unheard music hidden in the shrubbery,
And the unseen eyebeam crossed, for the roses
Had the look of flowers that are looked at.
There they were as our guests, accepted and accepting.
So we moved, and they, in a formal pattern,
Along the empty alley, into the box circle,
To look down into the drained pool.
Dry the pool, dry concrete, brown edged,
And the pool was filled with water out of sunlight,
And the lotos rose, quietly, quietly,
The surface glittered out of heart of light,
And they were behind us, reflected in the pool.
Then a cloud passed, and the pool was empty.
Go, said the bird, for the leaves were full of children,
Hidden excitedly, containing laughter.
Go, go, go, said the bird: human kind
Cannot bear very much reality.
Time past and time future
What might have been and what has been
Point to one end, which is always present.

                                  2

Garlic and sapphires in the mud
Clot the bedded axle-tree.
The trilling wire in the blood
Sings below inveterate scars
And reconciles forgotten wars.
The dance along the artery
The circulation of the lymph
Are figured in the drift of stars
Ascend to summer in the tree
We move above the moving tree
In light upon the figured leaf
And hear upon the sodden floor
Below, the boarhound and the boar
Pursue their pattern as before
But reconciled among the stars.

At the still point of the turning world. Neither flesh nor fleshless;
Neither from nor towards; at the still point, there the dance is,
But neither arrest nor movement. And do not call it fixity,
Where past and future are gathered. Neither movement from nor
    towards,
Neither ascent nor decline. Except for the point, the still point,
There would be no dance, and there is only the dance.
I can only say, *there* we have been: but I cannot say where.
And I cannot say, how long, for that is to place it in time.

The inner freedom from the practical desire,
The release from action and suffering, release from the inner
And the outer compulsion, yet surrounded
By a grace of sense, a white light still and moving,
Erhebung without motion, concentration
Without elimination, both a new world
And the old made explicit, understood
In the completion of its partial ecstasy,
The resolution of its partial horror.
Yet the enchainment of past and future
Woven in the weakness of the changing body,
Protects mankind from heaven and damnation
Which flesh cannot endure.
                  Time past and time future
Allow but a little consciousness.
To be conscious is not to be in time
But only in time can the moment in the rose-garden,
The moment in the arbour where the rain beat,
The moment in the draughty church at smokefall
Be remembered; involved with past and future.
Only through time time is conquered.

3

Here is a place of disaffection
Time before and time after
In a dim light: neither daylight
Investing form with lucid stillness
Turning shadow into transient beauty
With slow rotation suggesting permanence
Nor darkness to purify the soul
Emptying the sensual with deprivation
Cleansing affection from the temporal.
Neither plenitude nor vacancy. Only a flicker
Over the strained time-ridden faces
Distracted from distraction by distraction
Filled with fancies and empty of meaning

Tumid apathy with no concentration
Men and bits of paper, whirled by the cold wind
That blows before and after time,
Wind in and out of unwholesome lungs
Time before and time after.
Eructation of unhealthy souls
Into the faded air, the torpid
Driven on the wind that sweeps the gloomy hills of London,
Hampstead and Clerkenwell, Campden and Putney,
Highgate, Primrose and Ludgate. Not here
Not here the darkness, in this twittering world.

    Descend lower, descend only
Into the world of perpetual solitude,
World not world, but that which is not world,
Internal darkness, deprivation
And destitution of all property,
Desiccation of the world of sense,
Evacuation of the world of fancy,
Inoperancy of the world of spirit;
This is the one way, and the other
Is the same, not in movement
But abstention from movement; while the world moves
In appetency, on its metalled ways
Of time past and time future.

4

Time and the bell have buried the day,
The black cloud carries the sun away.
Will the sunflower turn to us, will the clematis
Stray down, bend to us; tendril and spray
Clutch and cling?
Chill
Fingers of yew be curled
Down on us? After the kingfisher's wing
Has answered light to light, and is silent, the light is still
At the still point of the turning world.

5

Words move, music moves
Only in time; but that which is only living
Can only die. Words, after speech, reach
Into the silence. Only by the form, the pattern,
Can words or music reach
The stillness, as a Chinese jar still
Moves perpetually in its stillness.

Not the stillness of the violin, while the note lasts,
Not that only, but the co-existence,
Or say that the end precedes the beginning,
And the end and the beginning were always there
Before the beginning and after the end.
And all is always now. Words strain,
Crack and sometimes break, under the burden,
Under the tension, slip, slide, perish,
Decay with imprecision, will not stay in place,
Will not stay still. Shrieking voices
Scolding, mocking, or merely chattering,
Always assail them. The Word in the desert
Is most attacked by voices of temptation,
The crying shadow in the funeral dance,
The loud lament of the disconsolate chimera.

   The detail of the pattern is movement,
As in the figure of the ten stairs.
Desire itself is movement
Not in itself desirable;
Love is itself unmoving,
Only the cause and end of movement,
Timeless, and undesiring
Except in the aspect of time
Caught in the form of limitation
Between un-being and being.
Sudden in a shaft of sunlight
Even while the dust moves
There rises the hidden laughter
Of children in the foliage
Quick now, here, now, always –
Ridiculous the waste sad time
Stretching before and after.

IVOR GURNEY

Bach and the Sentry

Watching the dark my spirit rose in flood
   On that most dearest Prelude of my delight.
The low-lying mist lifted its hood,
   The October stars showed nobly in clear night.

When I return, and to real music-making,
   And play that Prelude, how will it happen then?
Shall I feel as I felt, a sentry hardly waking,
   With a dull sense of No Man's Land again?

Song

Only the wanderer
   Knows England's graces,
Or can anew see clear
   Familiar faces.

And who loves joy as he
   That dwells in shadows?
Do not forget me quite,
   O Severn meadows.

After War

One got peace of heart at last, the dark march over,
And the straps slipped, the warmth felt under roof's low cover,
Lying slack the body, let sink in straw giving;
And some sweetness, a great sweetness felt in mere living.
And to come to this haven after sorefooted weeks,
The dark barn roof, and the glows and the wedges and streaks;
Letters from home, dry warmth and still sure rest taken
Sweet to the chilled frame, nerves soothed were so sore shaken.

The Silent One

Who died on the wires, and hung there, one of two –
Who for his hours of life had chattered through
Infinite lovely chatter of Bucks accent;
Yet faced unbroken wires; stepped over, and went,
A noble fool, faithful to his stripes – and ended.
But I weak, hungry, and willing only for the chance
Of line – to fight in the line, lay down under unbroken
Wires, and saw the flashes, and kept unshaken.
Till the politest voice – a finicking accent, said:
"Do you think you might crawl through, there; there's a
      hole:" In the afraid
Darkness, shot at; I smiled, as politely replied –
"I'm afraid not, Sir." There was no hole, no way to be seen.

Nothing but chance of death, after tearing of clothes.
Kept flat, and watched the darkness, hearing bullets whizzing –
And thought of music – and swore deep heart's deep oaths
(Polite to God –) and retreated and came on again.
Again retreated – and a second time faced the screen.

Behind the Line

I suppose France this morning is as white as here
High white clouds veiling the sun, and the mere
Cabbage fields and potato plants lovely to see,
Back behind at Robecq there with the day free.

In the estaminets I suppose the air as cool, and the floor
Grateful dark red; the beer and the different store
Of citron, grenadine, red wine as surely delectable
As in Nineteen Sixteen; with the round stains on the dark table.

Journals Français tell the same news and the queer
Black printed columns give news, but no longer the fear
Of shrapnel or any evil metal torments.
High white morning as here one is sure is on France.

Old Dreams

Once I had dreamed of return to a sunlit land,
Of summer and firelight winter with inns to visit,
But here are tangles of fate one does not understand,
And as for rest or true ease, where is it or what is it?

With criss-cross purposes and spoilt threads of life,
Perverse pathways, the savour of life is gone.
What have I then with crumbling wood or glowing coals,
Or a four-hours' walking, to work, through a setting sun?

The Not-Returning

Never comes now the through-and-through clear
Tiredness of body on crisp straw down laid,
Nor the tired thing said
Content before the clean sleep close the eyes,
Or ever resistless rise
Pictures of far country westward, westward out of sight of the eyes.

Never more delight comes of the roof dark lit
With under-candle-flicker nor rich gloom on it,
The limned faces and moving hands shuffling the cards,
The clear conscience, the free mind moving towards
Poetry, friends, the old earthly rewards.
No more they come. No more.
Only the restless searching, the bitter labour,
The going out to watch stars, stumbling blind through the
      difficult door.

The Mangel-Bury

It was after war; Edward Thomas had fallen at Arras –
I was walking by Gloucester musing on such things
As fill his verse with goodness; it was February; the long house
Straw-thatched of the mangels stretched two wide wings;
And looked as part of the earth heaped up by dead soldiers
In the most fitting place – along the hedge's yet-bare lines.
West spring breathed there early, that none foreign divines.
Across the flat country the rattling of the cart sounded;
Heavy of wood, jingling of iron; as he neared me I waited
For the chance perhaps of heaving at those great rounded
Ruddy or orange things – and right to be rolled and hefted
By a body like mine, soldier still, and clean from water.
Silent he assented; till the cart was drifted
High with those creatures, so right in size and matter.
We threw with our bodies swinging, blood in my ears singing;
His was the thick-set sort of farmer, but well-built –
Perhaps, long before, his blood's name ruled all,
Watched all things for his own. If my luck had so willed
Many questions of lordship I had heard him tell – old
Names, rumours. But my pain to more moving called
And him to some barn business far in the fifteen acre field.

ISAAC ROSENBERG

Chagrin

    Caught still as Absalom,
    Surely the air hangs
    From the swayless cloud-boughs,
    Like hair of Absalom
    Caught and hanging still.

From the imagined weight
Of spaces in a sky
Of mute chagrin, my thoughts
Hang like branch-clung hair
To trunks of silence swung,
With the choked soul weighing down
Into thick emptiness.
Christ! end this hanging death,
For endlessness hangs therefrom.

Invisibly – branches break
From invisible trees –
The cloud-woods where we rush,
Our eyes holding so much,
Which we must ride dim ages round
Ere the hands (we dream) can touch,
We ride, we ride, before the morning
The secret roots of the sun to tread,
And suddenly
We are lifted of all we know
And hang from implacable boughs.

On Receiving News of the War

Snow is a strange white word.
No ice or frost
Has asked of bud or bird
For Winter's cost.

Yet ice and frost and snow
From earth to sky
This Summer land doth know.
No man knows why.

In all men's hearts it is.
Some spirit old
Hath turned with malign kiss
Our lives to mould.

Red fangs have torn His face.
God's blood is shed.
He mourns from His lone place
His children dead.

O! ancient crimson curse!
Corrode, consume.
Give back this universe
Its pristine bloom.

August 1914

What in our lives is burnt
In the fire of this?
The heart's dear granary?
The much we shall miss?

Three lives hath one life –
Iron, honey, gold.
The gold, the honey gone –
Left is the hard and cold.

Iron are our lives
Molten right through our youth.
A burnt space through ripe fields
A fair mouth's broken tooth.

Break of Day in the Trenches

The darkness crumbles away –
It is the same old druid Time as ever.
Only a live thing leaps my hand –
A queer sardonic rat –
As I pull the parapet's poppy
To stick behind my ear.
Droll rat, they would shoot you if they knew
Your cosmopolitan sympathies.
Now you have touched this English hand
You will do the same to a German –
Soon, no doubt, if it be your pleasure
To cross the sleeping green between.
It seems you inwardly grin as you pass
Strong eyes, fine limbs, haughty athletes
Less chanced than you for life,
Bonds to the whims of murder,
Sprawled in the bowels of the earth,
The torn fields of France.

What do you see in our eyes
At the shrieking iron and flame
Hurled through still heavens?
What quaver — what heart aghast?
Poppies whose roots are in man's veins
Drop, and are ever dropping;
But mine in my ear is safe,
Just a little white with the dust.

Returning, We Hear the Larks

Sombre the night is.
And though we have our lives, we know
What sinister threat lurks there.

Dragging these anguished limbs, we only know
This poison-blasted track opens on our camp —
On a little safe sleep.

But hark! joy — joy — strange joy.
Lo! heights of night ringing with unseen larks.
Music showering on our upturned list'ning faces.

Death could drop from the dark
As easily as song —
But song only dropped,
Like a blind man's dreams on the sand
By dangerous tides,
Like a girl's dark hair for she dreams no ruin lies there,
Or her kisses where a serpent hides.

Dead Man's Dump

The plunging limbers over the shattered track
Racketed with their rusty freight,
Stuck out like many crowns of thorns,
And the rusty stakes like sceptres old
To stay the flood of brutish men
Upon our brothers dear.

The wheels lurched over sprawled dead
But pained them not, though their bones crunched,
Their shut mouths made no moan.
They lie there huddled, friend and foeman,
Man born of man, and born of woman,
And shells go crying over them
From night till night and now.

Earth has waited for them,
All the time of their growth
Fretting for their decay:
Now she has them at last!
In the strength of their strength
Suspended – stopped and held.

What fierce imaginings their dark souls lit?
Earth! have they gone into you!
Somewhere they must have gone,
And flung on your hard back
Is their soul's sack
Emptied of God-ancestralled essences.
Who hurled them out? Who hurled?

None saw their spirits' shadow shake the grass,
Or stood aside for the half used life to pass
Out of those doomed nostrils and the doomed mouth,
When the swift iron burning bee
Drained the wild honey of their youth.

What of us who, flung on the shrieking pyre,
Walk, our usual thoughts untouched,
Our lucky limbs as on ichor fed,
Immortal seeming ever?
Perhaps when the flames beat loud on us,
A fear may choke in our veins
And the startled blood may stop.

The air is loud with death,
The dark air spurts with fire,
The explosions ceaseless are.
Timelessly now, some minutes past,
These dead strode time with vigorous life,
Till the shrapnel called "An end!"
But not to all. In bleeding pangs
Some borne on stretchers dreamed of home,
Dear things, war-blotted from their hearts.

Maniac Earth! howling and flying, your bowel
Seared by the jagged fire, the iron love,
The impetuous storm of savage love.
Dark Earth! dark Heavens! swinging in chemic smoke,
What dead are born when you kiss each soundless soul
With lightning and thunder from your mined heart,
Which man's self dug, and his blind fingers loosed?

A man's brains splattered on
A stretcher-bearer's face;
His shook shoulders slipped their load,
But when they bent to look again
The drowning soul was sunk too deep
For human tenderness.

They left this dead with the older dead,
Stretched at the cross roads.

Burnt black by strange decay
Their sinister faces lie,
The lid over each eye,
The grass and coloured clay
More motion have than they,
Joined to the great sunk silences.

Here is one not long dead;
His dark hearing caught our far wheels,
And the choked soul stretched weak hands
To reach the living word the far wheels said,
The blood-dazed intelligence beating for light,
Crying through the suspense of the far torturing wheels
Swift for the end to break
Or the wheels to break.
Cried as the tide of the world broke over his sight.

Will they come? Will they ever come?
Even as the mixed hoofs of the mules,
The quivering-bellied mules,
And the rushing wheels all mixed
With his tortured upturned sight.
So we crashed round the bend,
We heard his weak scream,
We heard his very last sound,
And our wheels grazed his dead face.

HUGH MacDIARMID

The Bonnie Broukit Bairn

(For Peggy)

Mars is braw in crammasy,
Venus in a green silk goun,
The auld mune shak's her gowden feathers,
Their starry talk's a wheen o' blethers,
Nane for thee a thochtie sparin',
Earth, thou bonnie broukit bairn!
— But greet, an' in your tears ye'll droun
The haill clanjamfrie!

The Watergaw

Ae weet forenicht i' the yow-trummle
I saw yon antrin thing,
A watergaw wi' its chitterin' licht
Ayont the on-ding;
An' I thocht o' the last wild look ye gied
Afore ye deed!

There was nae reek i' the laverock's hoose
That nicht — an' nane i' mine;
But I hae thocht o' that foolish licht
Ever sin' syne;
An' I think that mebbe at last I ken
What your look meant then.

broukit neglected   bairn child   braw handsome   crammasy crimson
wheen o' blethers pack of nonsense   greet weep   clanjamfrie collection

watergaw indistinct rainbow   ae weet one wet   forenicht early evening
yow-trummle cold weather in July after sheep-shearing   antrin rare
chitterin' shivering   on-ding downpour   reek smoke   laverock lark
sin' syne since then

The Innumerable Christ

Other stars may have their Bethlehem, and their Calvary too.
                              Professor J. Y. Simpson

Wha kens on whatna Bethlehems
Earth twinkles like a star the nicht,
An' whatna shepherds lift their heids
In its unearthly licht?

'Yont a' the stars oor een can see
An' farther than their lichts can fly,
I' mony an unco warl' the nicht
The fatefu' bairnies cry.

I' mony an unco warl' the nicht
The lift gaes black as pitch at noon,
An' sideways on their chests the heids
O' endless Christs roll doon.

An' when the earth's as cauld's the mune
An' a' its folk are lang syne deid,
On coontless stars the Babe maun cry
An' the Crucified maun bleed.

At My Father's Grave

The sunlicht still on me, you row'd in clood,
We look upon each ither noo like hills
Across a valley. I'm nae mair your son.
It is my mind, nae son o' yours, that looks,
And the great darkness o' your death comes up
And equals it across the way.
A livin' man upon a deid man thinks
And ony sma'er thocht's impossible.

kens knows   *whatna* whichever   *'yont* beyond   *een* eyes
unco strange   *lang syne* long since

row'd wrapped

Of John Davidson

I remember one death in my boyhood
That next to my father's, and darker, endures;
Not Queen Victoria's, but Davidson, yours,
And something in me has always stood
Since then looking down the sandslope
On your small black shape by the edge of the sea,
– A bullet-hole through a great scene's beauty,
God through the wrong end of a telescope.

Light and Shadow

Like memories of what cannot be
Within the reign of memory . . .
That shake our mortal frames to dust.
                    Shelley

On every thought I have the countless shadows fall
Of other thoughts as valid that I cannot have;
Cross-lights of errors, too, impossible to me,
Yet somehow truer than all these thoughts, being with more
        power aglow.

May I never lose these shadowy glimpses of unknown thoughts
That modify and minify my own, and never fail
To keep some shining sense of the way all thoughts at last
Before life's dawning meaning like the stars at sunrise pale.

Poetry and Science

Science is the Differential Calculus of the mind,
Art is the Integral Calculus; they may be
Beautiful apart, but are great only when combined.
                    Sir Ronald Ross

The rarity and value of scientific knowledge
Is little understood – even as people
Who are not botanists find it hard to believe
Special knowledge of the subject can add
Enormously to the aesthetic appreciation of flowers!

Partly because in order to identify a plant
You must study it very much more closely
Than you would otherwise have done, and in the process
Exquisite colours, proportions, and minute shapes spring to
    light
Too small to be ordinarily noted.
And more than this – it seems the botanist's knowledge
Of the complete structure of the plant
(Like a sculptor's of bone and muscle)
– Of the configuration of its roots stretching under the earth,
The branching of stems,
Enfolding of buds by bracts,
Spreading of veins on a leaf –
Enriches and makes three-dimensional
His awareness of its complex beauty.

Wherefore I seek a poetry of facts. Even as
The profound kinship of all living substance
Is made clear by the chemical route.
Without some chemistry one is bound to remain
Forever a dumbfounded savage
In the face of vital reactions.
The beautiful relations
Shown only by biochemistry
Replace a stupefied sense of wonder
With something more wonderful
Because natural and understandable.
Nature is more wonderful
When it is at least partly understood.
Such an understanding dawns
On the lay reader when he becomes
Acquainted with the biochemistry of the glands
In their relation to diseases such as goitre
And their effects on growth, sex, and reproduction.
He will begin to comprehend a little
The subtlety and beauty of the action
Of enzymes, viruses, and bacteriophages,
These substances which are on the borderland
Between the living and the non-living.

He will understand why the biochemist
Can speculate on the possibility
Of the synthesis of life without feeling
That thereby he is shallow or blasphemous.
He will understand that, on the contrary,
He finds all the more

Because he seeks for the endless
– "Even our deepest emotions
May be conditioned by traces
Of a derivative of phenanthrene!"

Crystals Like Blood

I remember how, long ago, I found
Crystals like blood in a broken stone.

I picked up a broken chunk of bed-rock
And turned it this way and that,
It was heavier than one would have expected
From its size. One face was caked
With brown limestone. But the rest
Was a hard greenish-grey quartz-like stone
Faintly dappled with darker shadows,
And in this quartz ran veins and beads
Of bright magenta.

And I remember how later on I saw
How mercury is extracted from cinnabar
– The double ring of iron piledrivers
Like the multiple legs of a fantastically symmetrical spider
Rising and falling with monotonous precision,
Marching round in an endless circle
And pounding up and down with a tireless, thunderous
    force,
While, beyond, another conveyor drew the crumbled ore
From the bottom and raised it to an opening high
In the side of a gigantic grey-white kiln.

So I remember how mercury is got
When I contrast my living memory of you
And your dear body rotting here in the clay
– And feel once again released in me
The bright torrents of felicity, naturalness, and faith
My treadmill memory draws from you yet.

EDNA ST VINCENT MILLAY

"Time does not bring relief; you all have lied"

Time does not bring relief; you all have lied
Who told me time would ease me of my pain!
I miss him in the weeping of the rain;
I want him at the shrinking of the tide;
The old snows melt from every mountain-side,
And last year's leaves are smoke in every lane;
But last year's bitter loving must remain
Heaped on my heart, and my old thoughts abide.
There are a hundred places where I fear
To go, – so with his memory they brim.
And entering with relief some quiet place
Where never fell his foot or shone his face
I say, "There is no memory of him here!"
And so stand stricken, so remembering him.

Passer Mortuus Est

Death devours all lovely things:
    Lesbia with her sparrow
Shares the darkness, – presently
    Every bed is narrow.

Unremembered as old rain
    Dries the sheer libation;
And the little petulant hand
    Is an annotation.

After all, my erstwhile dear,
    My no longer cherished,
Need we say it was not love,
    Just because it perished?

Inland

People that build their houses inland,
  People that buy a plot of ground
Shaped like a house, and build a house there,
  Far from the sea-board, far from the sound

Of water sucking the hollow ledges,
  Tons of water striking the shore, –
What do they long for, as I long for
  One salt smell of the sea once more?

People the waves have not awakened,
  Spanking the boats at the harbour's head,
What do they long for, as I long for, –
  Starting up in my inland bed,

Beating the narrow walls, and finding
  Neither a window nor a door,
Screaming to God for death by drowning, –
  One salt taste of the sea once more?

Wild Swans

I looked in my heart while the wild swans went over.
And what did I see I had not seen before?
Only a question less or a question more;
Nothing to match the flight of wild birds flying.
Tiresome heart, forever living and dying,
House without air, I leave you and lock your door.
Wild swans, come over the town, come over
The town again, trailing your legs and crying!

"I, being born a woman and distressed"

I, being born a woman and distressed
By all the needs and notions of my kind,
Am urged by your propinquity to find
Your person fair, and feel a certain zest
To bear your body's weight upon my breast:
So subtly is the fume of life designed,
To clarify the pulse and cloud the mind,

And leave me once again undone, possessed.
Think not for this, however, the poor treason
Of my stout blood against my staggering brain,
I shall remember you with love, or season
My scorn with pity, – let me make it plain:
I find this frenzy insufficient reason
For conversation when we meet again.

On the Wide Heath

On the wide heath at evening overtaken,
    When the fast-reddening sun
Drops, and against the sky the looming bracken
    Waves, and the day is done,

Though no unfriendly nostril snuffs his bone,
    Though English wolves be dead,
The fox abroad on errands of his own,
    The adder gone to bed,

The weary traveler from his aching hip
    Lengthens his long stride;
Though home be but a humming on his lip,
    No happiness, no pride,

He does not drop him under the yellow whin
    To sleep the darkness through;
Home to the yellow light that shines within
    The kitchen of a loud shrew,

Home over stones and sand, through stagnant water
    He goes, mile after mile
Home to a wordless poaching son and a daughter
    With a disdainful smile,

Home to the worn reproach, the disagreeing,
    The shelter, the stale air; content to be
Pecked at, confined, encroached upon, – it being
    Too lonely, to be free.

WILFRED OWEN

The Parable of the Old Men and the Young

So Abram rose, and clave the wood, and went,
And took the fire with him, and a knife.
And as they sojourned both of them together,
Isaac the first-born spake and said, My Father,
Behold the preparations, fire and iron,
But where the lamb for this burnt-offering?
Then Abram bound the youth with belts and straps,
And builded parapets and trenches there,
And stretchèd forth the knife to slay his son.
When lo! an angel called him out of heaven,
Saying, Lay not thy hand upon the lad,
Neither do anything to him. Behold,
A ram, caught in a thicket by its horns;
Offer the Ram of Pride instead of him.
But the old man would not so, but slew his son, –
And half the seed of Europe, one by one.

The Send-Off

Down the close, darkening lanes they sang their way
To the siding-shed,
And lined the train with faces grimly gay.

Their breasts were stuck all white with wreath and spray
As men's are, dead.

Dull porters watched them, and a casual tramp
Stood staring hard,
Sorry to miss them from the upland camp.
Then, unmoved, signals nodded, and a lamp
Winked to the guard.

So secretly, like wrongs hushed-up, they went.
They were not ours:
We never heard to which front these were sent.

Nor there if they yet mock what women meant
Who gave them flowers.

Shall they return to beatings of great bells
In wild train-loads?
A few, a few, too few for drums and yells,
May creep back, silent, to still village wells
Up half-known roads.

Dulce et Decorum Est

Bent double, like old beggars under sacks,
Knock-kneed, coughing like hags, we cursed through sludge,
Till on the haunting flares we turned our backs,
And towards our distant rest began to trudge.
Men marched asleep. Many had lost their boots,
But limped on, blood-shod. All went lame; all blind;
Drunk with fatigue; deaf even to the hoots
Of gas-shells dropping softly behind.

Gas! GAS! Quick, boys! – An ecstasy of fumbling,
Fitting the clumsy helmets just in time
But someone still was yelling out and stumbling
And floundering like a man in fire or lime. –
Dim, through the misty panes and thick green light,
As under a green sea, I saw him drowning.

In all my dreams before my helpless sight
He plunges at me, guttering, choking, drowning.

If in some smothering dreams, you too could pace
Behind the wagon that we flung him in,
And watch the white eyes writhing in his face,
His hanging face, like a devil's sick of sin;
If you could hear, at every jolt, the blood
Come gargling from the froth-corrupted lungs,
Obscene as cancer, bitter as the cud
Of vile, incurable sores on innocent tongues, –
My friend, you would not tell with such high zest
To children ardent for some desperate glory,
The old lie: *Dulce et decorum est*
Pro patria mori.

Futility

Move him into the sun –
Gently its touch awoke him once,
At home, whispering of fields unsown.
Always it woke him, even in France,
Until this morning and this snow.
If anything might rouse him now
The kind old sun will know.

Think how it wakes the seeds, –
Woke, once, the clays of a cold star.
Are limbs, so dear-achieved, are sides,
Full-nerved – still warm – too hard to stir?
Was it for this the clay grew tall?
– O what made fatuous sunbeams toil
To break earth's sleep at all?

Anthem for Doomed Youth

What passing-bells for these who die as cattle?
Only the monstrous anger of the guns.
Only the stuttering rifles' rapid rattle
Can patter out their hasty orisons.
No mockeries for them from prayers or bells,
Nor any voice of mourning save the choirs, –
The shrill, demented choirs of wailing shells;
And bugles calling for them from sad shires.

What candles may be held to speed them all?
Not in the hands of boys, but in their eyes
Shall shine the holy glimmers of good-byes.
The pallor of girls' brows shall be their pall;
Their flowers the tenderness of silent minds,
And each slow dusk a drawing-down of blinds.

Hospital Barge at Cérisy

Budging the sluggard ripples of the Somme,
A barge round old Cérisy slowly slewed.
Softly her engines down the current screwed
And chuckled in her, with contented hum.

Till fairy tinklings struck their croonings dumb.
The waters rumpling at the stern subdued.
The lock-gate took her bulging amplitude.
Gently from out the gurgling lock she swum.

One reading by that sunset raised his eyes
To watch her lessening westward quietly;
Till, as she neared the bend, her funnel screamed.
And that long lamentation made him wise
How unto Avalon in agony
Kings passed in the dark barge which Merlin dreamed.

Strange Meeting

It seemed that out of battle I escaped
Down some profound dull tunnel, long since scooped
Through granites which titanic wars had groined.
Yet also there encumbered sleepers groaned,
Too fast in thought or death to be bestirred.
Then, as I probed them, one sprang up, and stared
With piteous recognition in fixed eyes,
Lifting distressful hands as if to bless.
And by his smile, I knew that sullen hall,
By his dead smile I knew we stood in Hell.
With a thousand pains that vision's face was grained;
Yet no blood reached there from the upper ground,
And no guns thumped, or down the flues made moan.
"Strange friend," I said, "here is no cause to mourn."
"None," said the other, "save the undone years,
The hopelessness. Whatever hope is yours,
Was my life also; I went hunting wild
After the wildest beauty in the world,
Which lies not calm in eyes, or braided hair,
But mocks the steady running of the hour,
And if it grieves, grieves richlier than here.
For by my glee might many men have laughed,
And of my weeping something had been left,
Which must die now. I mean the truth untold,
The pity of war, the pity war distilled.
Now men will go content with what we spoiled.
Or, discontent, boil bloody, and be spilled.
They will be swift with swiftness of the tigress,
None will break ranks, though nations trek from progress.

Courage was mine, and I had mystery,
Wisdom was mine, and I had mastery;
To miss the march of this retreating world
Into vain citadels that are not walled.
Then, when much blood had clogged their chariot-wheels
I would go up and wash them from sweet wells,
Even with truths that lie too deep for taint.
I would have poured my spirit without stint
But not through wounds; not on the cess of war.
Foreheads of men have bled where no wounds were.
I am the enemy you killed, my friend.
I knew you in this dark: for so you frowned
Yesterday through me as you jabbed and killed.
I parried; but my hands were loath and cold.
Let us sleep now . . . "

E. E. CUMMINGS

"in Just-"

in Just-
spring   when the world is mud-
luscious the little
lame balloonman

whistles   far   and wee

and eddieandbill come
running from marbles and
piracies and it's
spring

when the world is puddle-wonderful

the queer
old balloonman whistles
far   and   wee
and bettyandisbel come dancing

from hop-scotch and jump-rope and

it's
spring
and
   the

     goat-footed

balloonMan   whistles
far
and
wee

"what if a much of a which of a wind"

what if a much of a which of a wind
gives the truth to summer's lie;
bloodies with dizzying leaves the sun
and yanks immortal stars awry?
Blow king to beggar and queen to seem
(blow friend to fiend:blow space to time)
—when skies are hanged and oceans drowned,
the single secret will still be man

what if a keen of a lean wind flays
screaming hills with sleet and snow:
strangles valleys by ropes of thing
and stifles forests in white ago?
Blow hope to terror;blow seeing to blind
(blow pity to envy and soul to mind)
—whose hearts are mountains, roots are trees,
it's they shall cry hello to the spring

what if a dawn of a doom of a dream
bites this universe in two,
peels forever out of his grave
and sprinkles nowhere with me and you?
Blow soon to never and never to twice
(blow life to isn't:blow death to was)
—all nothing's only our hugest home;
the most who die, the more we live

"a wind has blown the rain away and blown"

a wind has blown the rain away and blown
the sky away and all the leaves away,
and the trees stand.   I think i too have known
autumn too long

                 (and what have you to say,
wind wind wind–did you love somebody
and have you the petal of somewhere in your heart
pinched from dumb summer?
                       O crazy daddy
of death dance cruelly for us and start

the last leaf whirling in the final brain
of air!)Let us as we have seen see
doom's integration . . . . a wind has blown the rain

away and the leaves and the sky and the
trees stand:
             the trees stand.   The trees,
suddenly wait against the moon's face.

Poem, or Beauty Hurts Mr Vinal

take it from me kiddo
believe me
my country,'tis of

you,land of the Cluett
Shirt Boston Garter and Spearmint
Girl With The Wrigley Eyes(of you
land of the Arrow Ide
and Earl &
Wilson
Collars)of you i
sing:land of Abraham Lincoln and Lydia E. Pinkham,
land above all of Just Add Hot Water And Serve—
from every B.V.D.

let freedom ring

amen.   i do however protest,anent the un
-spontaneous and otherwise scented merde which
greets one(Everywhere Why)as divine poesy per
that and this radically defunct periodical.   i would

suggest that certain ideas gestures
rhymes,like Gillette Razor Blades
having been used and reused
to the mystical moment of dullness emphatically are
Not To Be Resharpened.   (Case in point

if we are to believe these gently O sweetly
melancholy trillers amid the thrillers
these crepuscular violinists among my and your
skyscrapers–Helen & Cleopatra were Just Too Lovely,
The Snail's On The Thorn enter Morn and God's
In His andsoforth

do you get me?)according
to such supposedly indigenous
throstles Art is O World O Life
a formula:example,Turn Your Shirttails Into
Drawers and If It Isn't An Eastman It Isn't A
Kodak therefore my friends let
us now sing each and all fortissimo A-
mer
i

ca,I
love,
You.   And there're a
hun-dred-mil-lion-oth-ers,like
all of you successfully if
delicately gelded(or spaded)
gentlemen(and ladies)–pretty

littleliverpill-
hearted-Nujolneeding-There's-A-Reason
americans(who tensetendoned and with
upward vacant eyes,painfully
perpetually crouched,quivering,upon the
sternly allotted sandpile
–how silently
emit a tiny violetflavoured nuisance:Odor?

ono.
comes out like a ribbon lies flat on the brush

"pity this busy monster,manunkind"

pity this busy monster,manunkind,

not.   Progress is a comfortable disease:
your victim(death and life safely beyond)

plays with the bigness of his littleness
—electrons deify one razorblade
into a mountainrange;lenses extend

unwish through curving wherewhen till unwish
returns on its unself.
                              A world of made
is not a world of born—pity poor flesh

and trees,poor stars and stones,but never this
fine specimen of hypermagical

ultraomnipotence.   We doctors know

a hopeless case if—listen:there's a hell
of a good universe next door;let's go

ROBERT GRAVES

The Cool Web

Children are dumb to say how hot the day is,
How hot the scent is of the summer rose,
How dreadful the black wastes of evening sky,
How dreadful the tall soldiers drumming by.

But we have speech, that cools the hottest sun,
And speech that dulls the hottest rose's scent.
We spell away the overhanging night,
We spell away the soldiers and the fright.

There's a cool web of language winds us in,
Retreat from too much gladness, too much fear:
We grow sea-green at last and coldly die
In brininess and volubility.

But if we let our tongues lose self-possession,
Throwing off language and its wateriness
Before our death, instead of when death comes,
Facing the brightness of the children's day,
Facing the rose, the dark sky and the drums,
We shall go mad no doubt and die that way.

Sick Love

O love, be fed with apples while you may
And feel the sun and go in royal array,
A smiling innocent on the heavenly causeway.

Though in what listening horror for the cry
That soars in outer blackness dismally,
The dumb blind beast, the paranoiac fury,

Be warm, enjoy the season, lift your head,
Exquisite in the pulse of tainted blood,
That shivering glory not to be despised.

Take your delight in momentariness,
Walk between dark and dark, a shining space
With the grave's narrowness, though not its peace.

In Broken Images

He is quick, thinking in clear images;
I am slow, thinking in broken images.

He becomes dull, trusting to his clear images;
I become sharp, mistrusting my broken images.

Trusting his images, he assumes their relevance;
Mistrusting my images, I question their relevance.

Assuming their relevance, he assumes the fact,
Questioning their relevance, I question the fact.

When the fact fails him, he questions his senses;
When the fact fails me, I approve my senses.

He continues quick and dull in his clear images;
I continue slow and sharp in my broken images.

He in a new confusion of his understanding;
I in a new understanding of my confusion.

Warning to Children

Children, if you dare to think
All the many largeness, smallness,
Fewness of this single only
Endless world in which you say
You live, you think of things like this: –
Lumps of slate enclosing dappled
Red and green, enclosing tawny
Yellow nets, enclosing white
And black acres of dominoes.
In the acres a brown paper
Parcel, then untie the string.
In the parcel a small island,
On the island a large tree,
On the tree a husky fruit,
Strip the husk and cut the rind off.
In the centre you will see
Lumps of slate enclosed by dappled
Red and green, enclosed by tawny
Yellow nets, enclosed by white
And black acres of dominoes.
In the acres a brown paper
Parcel, leave the string untied.
If you dare undo the parcel
You will find yourself inside it,
On the island, in the fruit,
With the parcel still untied,
Just like any lump of slate,
Find yourself enclosed by dappled
Green and red, enclosed by yellow
Tawny nets, enclosed by black
And white acres of dominoes.
And, children, if you dare to think
All the many largeness, smallness,
Fewness of this single only
Endless world in which you say
You live, you then untie the string.

On Portents

If strange things happen where she is,
So that men say that graves open
And the dead walk, or that futurity
Becomes a womb and the unborn are shed,
Such portents are not to be wondered at
Being tourbillions in Time made
By the strong pulling of her bladed mind
Through that ever-reluctant element.

Down, Wanton, Down!

Down, wanton, down! Have you no shame
That at the whisper of Love's name
Or Beauty's, presto! up you raise
Your angry head and stand at gaze?

Poor bombard-captain, sworn to reach
The ravelin and effect a breach,
Indifferent what you storm or why
So be that in the breach you die!

Love may be blind, but Love at least
Knows what is man and what mere beast:
Or beauty, wayward, but requires
More delicacy from her squires.

Tell me, my witless, whose one boast
Could be your staunchness at the post,
When were you made a man of parts
To think fine and profess the arts?

Will many-gifted Beauty come
Bowing to your bald rule of thumb,
Or Love swear loyalty to your crown?
Be gone, have done! Down, wanton, down!

Nobody

Nobody, ancient mischief, nobody
Harasses always with an absent body.

Nobody coming up the road, nobody,
Like a tall man in a dark cloak, nobody.

Nobody about in the house, nobody,
Like children creeping up the stairs, nobody.

Nobody anywhere in the garden, nobody,
Like a young girl quiet with needlework, nobody.

Nobody coming, nobody, not yet here,
Incessantly welcomed by the wakeful ear.

Until this nobody shall consent to die
Under his curse must every man lie –

The curse of his jealousy, of his grief and fright,
Of sudden rape and murder screamed in the night.

The Cloak

Into exile with only a few shirts,
Some gold coin and the necessary papers.
But winds are contrary: the Channel packet
Time after time returns the sea-sick peer
To Sandwich, Deal or Rye. He does not land,
But keeps his cabin; so at last we find him
In humble lodging at perhaps Dieppe,
His shirts unpacked, his night-cap on a peg,
Passing the day with cards and swordsmanship
Or merry passages with chambermaids,
By night at his old work. And all is well –
The country wine wholesome although so sharp,
And French his second tongue; a faithful valet
Brushes his hat and brings him newspapers.
This nobleman is at home anywhere,
His castle being, the valet says, his title.
The cares of an estate would incommode
Such tasks as now his Lordship has in hand.
His Lordship, says the valet, contemplates

A profitable absence of some years.
Has he no friend at Court to intercede?
He wants none: exile's but another name
For an old habit of non-residence
In all but the recesses of his cloak.
It was this angered a great personage.

Recalling War

Entrance and exit wounds are silvered clean,
The track aches only when the rain reminds.
The one-legged man forgets his leg of wood,
The one-armed man his jointed wooden arm.
The blinded man sees with his ears and hands
As much or more than once with both his eyes.
Their war was fought these twenty years ago
And now assumes the nature-look of time,
As when the morning traveller turns and views
His wild night-stumbling carved into a hill.

What, then, was war? No mere discord of flags
But an infection of the common sky
That sagged ominously upon the earth
Even when the season was the airiest May.
Down pressed the sky and we, oppressed, thrust out
Boastful tongue, clenched fist and valiant yard.
Natural infirmities were out of mode,
For Death was young again: patron alone
Of healthy dying, premature fate-spasm.

Fear made fine bed-fellows. Sick with delight
At life's discovered transitoriness,
Our youth became all-flesh and waived the mind.
Never was such antiqueness of romance,
Such tasteless honey oozing from the heart.
And old importances came swimming back –
Wine, meat, log-fires, a roof over the head,
A weapon at the thigh, surgeons at call.
Even there was a use again for God –
A word of rage in lack of meat, wine, fire,
In ache of wounds beyond all surgeoning.

War was return of earth to ugly earth,
War was foundering of sublimities,

Extinction of each happy art and faith
By which the world had still kept head in air,
Protesting logic or protesting love,
Until the unendurable moment struck –
The inward scream, the duty to run mad.

And we recall the merry ways of guns –
Nibbling the walls of factory and church
Like a child, piecrust; felling groves of trees
Like a child, dandelions with a switch!
Machine-guns rattle toy-like from a hill,
Down in a row the brave tin-soldiers fall:
A sight to be recalled in elder days
When learnedly the future we devote
To yet more boastful visions of despair.

To Evoke Posterity

To evoke posterity
Is to weep on your own grave,
Ventriloquizing for the unborn:
"Would you were present in flesh, hero,
What wreaths and junketings!"

And the punishment is known:
To be found fully ancestral,
To be cast in bronze for a city square,
To dribble green in times of rain
And stain the pedestal.

Spiders in the spread beard;
A life proverbial
On clergy lips a-cackle;
Eponymous institutes,
Their luckless architecture.

Two more dates of life and birth
For the hour of special study
From which all boys and girls of mettle
Twice a week play truant
And worn excuses try.

Alive, you have abhorred
The crowds on holiday
Jostling and whistling – yet you would air
Your death-mask, smoothly lidded,
Along the promenade?

To Juan at the Winter Solstice

There is one story and one story only
That will prove worth your telling,
Whether as learned bard or gifted child;
To it all lines or lesser gauds belong
That startle with their shining
Such common stories as they stray into.

Is it of trees you tell, their months and virtues,
Of strange beasts that beset you,
Of birds that croak at you the Triple will?
Or of the Zodiac and how slow it turns
Below the Boreal Crown,
Prison of all true kings that ever reigned?

Water to water, ark again to ark,
From woman back to woman:
So each new victim treads unfalteringly
The never altered circuit of his fate,
Bringing twelve peers as witness
Both to his starry rise and starry fall.

Or is it of the Virgin's silver beauty,
All fish below the thighs?
She in her left hand bears a leafy quince;
When with her right she crooks a finger, smiling,
How may the King hold back?
Royally then he barters life for love.

Or of the undying snake from chaos hatched,
Whose coils contain the ocean,
Into whose chops with naked sword he springs,
Then in black water, tangled by the reeds,
Battles three days and nights,
To be spewed up beside her scalloped shore?

Much snow is falling, winds roar hollowly,
The owl hoots from the elder,
Fear in your heart cries to the loving-cup:
Sorrow to sorrow as the sparks fly upward.
The log groans and confesses
There is one story and one story only.

Dwell on her graciousness, dwell on her smiling,
Do not forget what flowers
The great boar trampled down in ivy time.
Her brow was creamy as the long ninth wave,
Her sea-blue eyes were wild
But nothing promised that is not performed.

The White Goddess

All saints revile her, and all sober men
Ruled by the God Apollo's golden mean –
In scorn of which we sailed to find her
In distant regions likeliest to hold her
Whom we desired above all things to know,
Sister of the mirage and echo.
It was a virtue not to stay,
To go our headstrong and heroic way
Seeking her out at the volcano's head,
Among pack ice, or where the track had faded
Beyond the cavern of the seven sleepers:
Whose broad high brow was white as any leper's,
Whose eyes were blue, with rowan-berry lips,
With hair curled honey-coloured to white hips.

The sap of Spring in the young wood a-stir
Will celebrate with green the Mother,
Anti every song-bird shout awhile for her;
But we are gifted, even in November
Rawest of seasons, with so huge a sense
Of her nakedly worn magnificence
We forget cruelty and past betrayal,
Heedless of where the next bright bolt may fall.

Counting the Beats

You, love, and I,
(He whispers) you and I,
And if no more than only you and I
What care you or I?

Counting the beats,
Counting the slow heart beats,
The bleeding to death of time in slow heart beats,
Wakeful they lie.

Cloudless day,
Night, and a cloudless day;
Yet the huge storm will burst upon their heads
      one day
From a bitter sky.

Where shall we be,
(She whispers) where shall we be,
When death strikes home, O where then shall we be
Who were you and I?

Not there but here,
(He whispers) only here,
As we are, here, together, now and here,
Always you and I.

Counting the beats,
Counting the slow heart beats,
The bleeding to death of time in slow heart beats,
Wakeful they lie.

DAVID JONES

A, a, a, Domine Deus

I said, Ah! what shall I write?
I enquired up and down.
                    (He's tricked me before
with his manifold lurking-places.)
I looked for His symbol at the door.

I have looked for a long while
                         at the textures and contours.
I have run a hand over the trivial intersections.
I have journeyed among the dead forms
causation projects from pillar to pylon.
I have tired the eyes of the mind
                         regarding the colours and lights.
I have felt for His Wounds
                         in nozzles and containers.
I have wondered for the automatic devices.
I have tested the inane patterns
                         without prejudice.
I have been on my guard
                         not to condemn the unfamiliar.
For it is easy to miss Him
                         at the turn of a civilisation.

I have watched the wheels go round in case I might see the living creatures like the appearance of lamps, in case I might see the Living God projected from the Machine. I have said to the perfected steel, be my sister and for the glassy towers I thought I felt some beginnings of His creature, but *A, a, a, Domine Deus*, my hands found the glazed work unrefined and the terrible crystal a stage-paste . . . *Eia, Domine Deus.*

from *The Anathemata*

Angle-Land

Did he strike soundings off Vecta Insula?
           or was it already the gavelkind *ígland*?[1]

Did he lie by
           in the East Road?
was it a kindly *numen* of the Sleeve that headed him clear of
South Sand Head?
Did he shelter in the Small Downs?
Keeping close in, did he feel his way
between the Flats and the Brake?
But, what was her draught, and, what was the ocean doing?

---

1. When I wrote this I was associating the system of gavelkind with the Isle of Wight solely on account of its being occupied by Jutes, who also occupied Kent, which county is particularly associated with that system and there is evidence of a sort of succession by gavelkind in the Jutish area in Hampshire opposite Wight.

Did he stand on toward the Gull?
did his second mate sound
                with more than care?
was it perforce or Fortuna's rudder, circumstance or superb
pilotage or clean oblation
                that sheered him from smother
(the unseen necropolis[1] banking to starboard of her).
Or was it she
                Sea-born and Sea-star
whose own, easy and free
                the pious matlos are[2]
or, was it a whim of Poseidon's
(master o' the cinque masters o' lodemanage)[3]
whose own the Island's approaches are
                that kept her?
Was the Foreland?
                was the Elbow?
under fog.
        He might have been deeped in the Oaze![4]
Or
        by the brumous numen drawn on
or
        in preclear visibility
by the invisible wind laboured
it might have been Dogger or Well
        to bank her a mound
without a sheet to wrap her
without a shroud to her broken back.
                Past where they placed their *ingas*-names
where they speed the coulter deep
                in the open Engel fields
to this day.
                How many poles
of their broad Angle hidage

1. It so happens that it was at Deal, *c.*1903, that "I first beheld the ocean" and I particularly remember that sometimes, in certain conditions of weather and tide, a number of hulks were visible on the Goodwins which then seemed like a graveyard of ships.
2. Cf. Archbishop David Mathew, *British Seamen*, p. 48, "Easy and gallant they defend the freedom of the seas and the shores of England". And cf. song, *All the Nice Girls Love a Sailor*, line 5, "Bright and breezy, free and easy".
3. "Cinque" and "lodemanage" to be said as in English, indeed as in Cockney English. (Each of the Cinque Ports had a pilot called the Master of Lodemanage.)
4. Cf. Oaze Deep, an area of water so named in the mouth of the Thames.

to the small scattered plots, to the lightly furrowed *erwau*,[1]
that once did guilt Boudícca's róyal *gwely*?[2]

Past where they urn'd their calcined dead from Schleswig
over the foam.

(Close the south-west wall of the chester, without the orbit,
if but a stone's throw: you don't want to raise an Icenian
Venta's Brettisc[3] ghost.
He'll latin-runes tellan in his horror-coat standing:
IAM REDIT ROMA
        his lifted palm his VERBVM is.)

Past where the ancra-man, deeping his holy rule
in the fiendish marsh
      at the *Geisterstunde*
        on *Calangaeaf* night[4]
heard the bogee-*baragouinage*.
        Crowland-*diawliaidd*[5]
Waelisc-man lingo speaking?
      or Britto-Romani gone *diaboli*?
or Romanity gone *Waelisc*?[6]
Is Marianus wild Meirion?[7]
is Sylvánus
      Urbigéna's son?
has toga'd Rhufon[8]
      (gone Actaéon)
come away to the Wake
      in the bittern's low aery?
along with his towny
      Patricius gone the *wilde Jäger*?

1. *Erwau*, plural of *erw*, acre; érr-wye (err as in the Latin *errare*), accent on first syllable. Not in fact an acre or any fixed unit, but land equally divided among the members of a plough-team under the Celtic system of co-aration.
2. *gwely*, gwel-ly, bed, but also used of the collective lands of a group. Typical Celtic ploughing was less deep than that of subsequent invaders.
3. Pronounce bret-tish.
4. *Calangaeaf*, Winter Calands, November 1, cal-lan-gei-av, accent on ei pronounced as in height.
5. *diawliaidd*, devils, deeowl-yithe, accent on first syllable. The Mercian saint, Guthlac, when an anchorite on Crowland island in the Fens, hearing the speech of surviving Britons thought it the language of devils.
6. Pronounce wye-lish.
7. The Roman name Marianus gave Meirion in Welsh; hence 'Merioneth'.
8. Rhufon, rhiv-von, Romanus. Urbigena; cf. Urbgen in Nennius, Urien in the Romances. The late Gilbert Sheldon wrote: "The Latin name *Urbigena*, city-born, is disguised as Urien". Pronounce as urr-bee-gain-ah, accent on gain.

From the *fora*
        to the forests.
Out from *gens Romulum*
      into the *Weal*-kin[1]
dinas-man gone *aethwlad*[2]
cives gone wold-men
            . . . from Lindum to London
bridges broken down.

What was his *Hausname*?
       he whose North Holstein urn
they sealed against the seep of the Yare?
If there are *Wealas*[3] yet
       in the Waltons
what's the cephalic index of the *môrforynion*,[4] who knell the
bell, who thread the pearls that were Ned Mizzen's eyes, at
the five fathom line off the Naze?
       On past the low low lands of the Holland that
Welland winds to the Deepings north of the Soke
past where Woden's gang *is gens Julia* for Wuffingas new to
old Nene and up with the Lark[5]
past the south hams and the north tons
past the weathered thorps and
       the Thorpe
that bore, that bred
       him whom Nike did bear
her tears at flood
and over the scatter of the forebrace bitts
       down to the orlop
at twenty five minutes after one of the clock
in the afternoon, on a Monday
twelve days before the Calends of November
outside the Pillars
       where they closed like a forest
       . . . in 13 fathoms' water

---

1. Cf. *Wealcyn* used by the Teutonic invaders of any group of kindred within those
lands which had been part of Roman Britain. Pronounce, wa-ahl.
2. *dinas*, city, din-ass, accent on first syllable.
   aethwlad, outlaw, aeth-oolahd, ae as ah+eh, accent on first syllable.
3. *Wealas*, wa-ahl-ass, plural of *Wealh*, a Welshman.
4. *môrforynion*, water-maidens, morr-vorr-un-yon, accent on third syllable.
5. The Wuffingas, that during the fifth-century invasions made settlements in the Fen
Country, through which flow the Nene and the Lark, seem later on to have claimed
descent from both Odin and Caesar.

unanchored in the worsening weather.[1]

Far drawn on away
from the island's field-floor, upwards of a hundred fathoms
over where, beyond where, in the fifties, toward the sixties,
north latitude

all our easting waters
are confluent with the fathering river and tributary to him:
where Tamesis, Great Ouse, Tyne from the Wall's end, de-
marking Tweed, Forth that winds the middle march, Tummel
and wide looping Tay (that laps the wading files when Birnam
boughs deploy toward Dunsinane – out toward the Goat Flats).

Spey of the Symbol stones and Ness from the serpentine mere
all mingle Rhenus-flow
and are oned with him
in Cronos-*meer*.
I speak of before the whale-roads or the keel-paths were from
Orcades to the fiord-havens, or the greyed green wastes that
they strictly grid
quadrate and number on the sea-green *Quadratkarte*
one eight six one G
for the fratricides
of the latter-day, from east-shore of Iceland
bis Norwegen[2]
(O Balin O Balan![3]
how blood you both
the *Brudersee*
toward the last pháse
of our dear West.)

1. See Collingwood's dispatch to the Admiralty Lords as reported in a contemporary edition of *The Times*, giving particulars of the action on Monday, October 21, 1805, and also James, *Naval History*, Vol. IV, 1837 edtn.
"Seeing by the direction of her course that the Victory was about to follow the example of the Royal-Sovereign, the French and Spanish ships ahead of the British weather column closed like a forest." p. 38.
"To add to the perilous condition of the British fleet and prizes, the ships were then in 13 fathoms' water, with the shoals of Trafalgar but a few miles to leeward." p. 87.
2. I had in mind a squared chart issued for special service requirements by the German Naval Command, described as *Europäisches Nordmeer. Ostküste von Island bis Norwegen, 1861* G., on which the grid, numerals and other markings are imposed in green on a large-scale map of that area. Date *c.*1940.
3. Cf. Malory Bk. II, Cp. 18. How Balin met with his brother Balan and how each slew other unknown.

HART CRANE

Forgetfulness

Forgetfulness is like a song
That, freed from beat and measure, wanders.
Forgetfulness is like a bird whose wings are reconciled,
Outspread and motionless, –
A bird that coasts the wind unwearyingly.

Forgetfulness is rain at night,
Or an old house in a forest, – or a child.
Forgetfulness is white, – white as a blasted tree,
And it may stun the sybil into prophecy,
Or bury the Gods.

I can remember much forgetfulness.

Sunday Morning Apples

To William Sommer

The leaves will fall again sometime and fill
The fleece of nature with those purposes
That are your rich and faithful strength of line.

But now there are challenges to spring
In that ripe nude with head
                reared
Into a realm of swords, her purple shadow
Bursting on the winter of the world
From whiteness that cries defiance to the snow.

A boy runs with a dog before the sun, straddling
Spontaneities that form their independent orbits,
Their own perennials of light
In the valley where you live
              (called Brandywine).

I have seen the apples there that toss you secrets, –
Beloved apples of seasonable madness
That feed your inquiries with aerial wine.

Put them again beside a pitcher with a knife,
And poise them full and ready for explosion –
The apples, Bill, the apples!

Repose of Rivers

The willows carried a slow sound,
A sarabande the wind mowed on the mead.
I could never remember
That seething, steady leveling of the marshes
Till age had brought me to the sea.

Flags, weeds. And remembrance of steep alcoves
Where cypresses shared the noon's
Tyranny; they drew me into hades almost.
And mammoth turtles climbing sulphur dreams
Yielded, while sun-silt rippled them
Asunder . . .

How much I would have bartered! the black gorge
And all the singular nestings in the hills
Where beavers learn stitch and tooth.
The pond I entered once and quickly fled –
I remember now its singing willow rim.

And finally, in that memory all things nurse;
After the city that I finally passed
With scalding unguents spread and smoking darts
The monsoon cut across the delta
At gulf gates . . . There, beyond the dykes

I heard wind flaking sapphire, like this summer,
And willows could not hold more steady sound.

At Melville's Tomb

Often beneath the wave, wide from this ledge
The dice of drowned men's bones he saw bequeath
An embassy. Their numbers as he watched,
Beat on the dusty shore and were obscured.

And wrecks passed without sound of bells,
The calyx of death's bounty giving back
A scattered chapter, livid hieroglyph,
The portent wound in corridors of shells.

Then in the circuit calm of one vast coil,
Its lashings charmed and malice reconciled,
Frosted eyes there were that lifted altars;
And silent answers crept across the stars.

Compass, quadrant and sextant contrive
No farther tides . . . High in the azure steeps
Monody shall not wake the mariner.
This fabulous shadow only the sea keeps.

To Brooklyn Bridge

How many dawns, chill from his rippling rest
The seagull's wings shall dip and pivot him,
Shedding white rings of tumult, building high
Over the chained bay waters Liberty –

Then, with inviolate curve, forsake our eyes
As apparitional as sails that cross
Some page of figures to be filed away;
– Till elevators drop us from our day . . .

I think of cinemas, panoramic sleights
With multitudes bent toward some flashing scene
Never disclosed, but hastened to again,
Foretold to other eyes on the same screen;

And Thee, across the harbor, silver-paced
As though the sun took step of thee, yet left
Some motion ever unspent in thy stride,
Implicitly thy freedom staying thee!

Out of some subway scuttle, cell or loft
A bedlamite speeds to thy parapets,
Tilting there momently, shrill shirt ballooning,
A jest falls from the speechless caravan.

Down Wall, from girder into street noon leaks,
A rip-tooth of the sky's acetylene;
All afternoon the cloud-flown derricks turn . . .
Thy cables breathe the North Atlantic still.

And obscure as that heaven of the Jews,
Thy guerdon . . . Accolade thou dost bestow
Of anonymity time cannot raise:
Vibrant reprieve and pardon thou dost show.

O harp and altar, of the fury fused,
(How could mere toil align thy choiring strings!)
Terrific threshold of the prophet's pledge,
Prayer of pariah, and the lover's cry, –

Again the traffic lights that skim thy swift
Unfractioned idiom, immaculate sigh of stars,
Beading thy path – condense eternity:
And we have seen night lifted in thine arms.

Under thy shadow by the piers I waited;
Only in darkness is thy shadow clear.
The City's fiery parcels all undone,
Already snow submerges an iron year . . .

O Sleepless as the river under thee,
Vaulting the sea, the prairies' dreaming sod,
Unto us lowliest sometime sweep, descend
And of the curveship lend a myth to God.

To the Cloud Juggler

In Memoriam: Harry Crosby

What you may cluster 'round the knees of space
We hold in vision only, asking trace
Of districts where cliff, sea and palm advance
The falling wonder of a rainbow's trance.

Your light lifts whiteness into virgin azure . . .
Disclose your lips, O Sun, nor long demure
With snore of thunder, crowding us to bleed
The green preëmption of the deep seaweed.

You, the rum-giver to that slide-by-night, –
The moon's best lover, – guide us by a sleight
Of quarts to faithfuls – surely smuggled home –
As you raise temples fresh from basking foam.

Expose vaunted validities that yawn
Past pleasantries . . . Assert the ripened dawn
As you have yielded balcony and room
Or tempests – in a silver, floating plume.

Wrap us and lift us; drop us then, returned
Like water, undestroyed, – like mist, unburned . . .
But do not claim a friend like him again,
Whose arrow must have pierced you beyond pain.

BASIL BUNTING

from *Briggflatts*

Brag, sweet tenor bull,
descant on Rawthey's madrigal,
each pebble its part
for the fells' late spring.
Dance tiptoe, bull,
black against may.
Ridiculous and lovely
chase hurdling shadows
morning into noon.
May on the bull's hide
and through the dale
furrows fill with may,
paving the slowworm's way.

A mason times his mallet
to a lark's twitter,
listening while the marble rests,
lays his rule
at a letter's edge,
fingertips checking,
till the stone spells a name
naming none,
a man abolished.

Painful lark, labouring to rise!
The solemn mallet says:
In the grave's slot
he lies. We rot.

Decay thrusts the blade,
wheat stands in excrement
trembling. Rawthey trembles.
Tongue stumbles, ears err
for fear of spring.
Rub the stone with sand,
wet sandstone rending
roughness away. Fingers
ache on the rubbing stone.
The mason says: Rocks
happen by chance.
No one here bolts the door,
love is so sore.

Stone smooth as skin,
cold as the dead they load
on a low lorry by night.
The moon sits on the fell
but it will rain.
Under sacks on the stone
two children lie,
hear the horse stale,
the mason whistle,
harness mutter to shaft,
felloe to axle squeak,
rut thud the rim,
crushed grit.

Stocking to stocking, jersey to jersey,
head to a hard arm,
they kiss under the rain,
bruised by their marble bed.
In Garsdale, dawn;
at Hawes, tea from the can.
Rain stops, sacks
steam in the sun, they sit up.
Copper-wire moustache,
sea-reflecting eyes
and Baltic plainsong speech
declare: By such rocks
men killed Bloodaxe.

Fierce blood throbs in his tongue,
lean words.
Skulls cropped for steel caps
huddle round Stainmore.
Their becks ring on limestone,
whisper to peat.
The clogged cart pushes the horse downhill.
In such soft air
they trudge and sing,
laying the tune frankly on the air.
All sounds fall still,
fellside bleat,
hide-and-seek peewit.

Her pulse their pace,
palm countering palm,
till a trench is filled,
stone white as cheese
jeers at the dale.
Knotty wood, hard to rive,
smoulders to ash;
smell of October apples.
The road again,
at a trot.
Wetter, warmed, they watch
the mason meditate
on name and date.

Rain rinses the road,
the bull streams and laments.
Sour rye porridge from the hob
with cream and black tea,
meat, crust and crumb.
Her parents in bed
the children dry their clothes.
He has untied the tape
of her striped flannel drawers
before the range. Naked
on the pricked rag mat
his fingers comb
thatch of his manhood's home.

Gentle generous voices weave
over bare night
words to confirm and delight
till bird dawn.

Rainwater from the butt
she fetches and flannel
to wash him inch by inch,
kissing the pebbles.
Shining slowworm part of the marvel.
The mason stirs:
Words!
Pens are too light.
Take a chisel to write.

Every birth a crime,
every sentence life.
Wiped of mould and mites
would the ball run true?
No hope of going back.
Hounds falter and stray,
shame deflects the pen.
Love murdered neither bleeds nor stifles
but jogs the draftsman's elbow.
What can he, changed, tell
her, changed, perhaps dead?
Delight dwindles. Blame
stays the same.

Brief words are hard to find,
shapes to carve and discard:
Bloodaxe, king of York,
king of Dublin, king of Orkney.
Take no notice of tears;
letter the stone to stand
over love laid aside lest
insufferable happiness impede
flight to Stainmore,
to trace
lark, mallet,
becks, flocks
and axe knocks.

Dung will not soil the slowworm's
mosaic. Breathless lark
drops to nest in sodden trash;
Rawthey truculent, dingy.
Drudge at the mallet, the may is down,
fog on fells. Guilty of spring
and spring's ending

amputated years ache after
the bull is beef, love a convenience.
It is easier to die than to remember.
Name and date
split in soft slate
a few months obliterate.

Ode 17

To Mina Loy

Now that sea's over that island
so that barely on a calm day sun sleeks
a patchwork hatching of combed weed
over stubble and fallow alike
I resent drowned blackthorn hedge, choked ditch,
gates breaking from rusty hinges,
the submerged copse,
Trespassers will be prosecuted.

Sea's over that island,
weed over furrow and dungheap:
but how I should recognise the place
under the weeds and sand
who was never in it on land I don't know:
some trick of refraction,
a film of light in the water crumpled and spread
like a luminous frock on a woman walking
alone in her garden.

Oval face, thin eyebrows wide of the eyes,
a premonition in the gait
of this subaqueous persistence
of a particular year —
for you had prepared it for preservation
not vindictively, urged
by the economy of passions.

Nobody said: She is organising
these knicknacks her dislike collects
into a pattern nature will adopt and perpetuate.

Weed over meadowgrass, sea over weed,
no step on the gravel.
Very likely I shall never meet her again
or if I do, fear the latch as before.

Ode 37: *On the Fly-Leaf of Pound's* Cantos

There are the Alps. What is there to say about them?
They don't make sense. Fatal glaciers, crags cranks climb,
jumbled boulder and weed, pasture and boulder, scree,
et l'on entend, maybe, *le refrain joyeux et leger.*
Who knows what the ice will have scraped on the rock it is
    smoothing?

There they are, you will have to go a long way round
if you want to avoid them.
It takes some getting used to. There are the Alps,
fools! Sit down and wait for them to crumble!

"A thrush in the syringa sings"

A thrush in the syringa sings.

"Hunger ruffles my wings, fear,
lust, familiar things.

Death thrusts hard. My sons
by hawk's beak, by stones,
trusting weak wings
by cat and weasel, die.

Thunder smothers the sky.
From a shaken bush I
list familiar things,
fear, hunger, lust."

O gay thrush!

YVOR WINTERS

The Realization

Death. Nothing is simpler. One is dead.
The set face now will fade out; the bare fact,
Related movement, regular, intact,
Is reabsorbed, the clay is on the bed.
The soul is mortal, nothing: the dim head
On the dim pillow, less. But thought clings flat
To this, since it can never follow that
Where no precision of the mind is bred.

Nothing to think of between you and All!
Screaming processionals of infinite
Logic are grinding down receding cold!
O fool! Madness again! Turn not, for it
Lurks in each paintless cranny, and you sprawl
Blurring a definition. Quick! you are old.

The Slow Pacific Swell

Far out of sight forever stands the sea,
Bounding the land with pale tranquillity.
When a small child, I watched it from a hill
At thirty miles or more. The vision still
Lies in the eye, soft blue and far away:
The rain has washed the dust from April day;
Paint-brush and lupine lie against the ground;
The wind above the hill-top has the sound
Of distant water in unbroken sky;
Dark and precise the little steamers ply –
Firm in direction they seem not to stir.
That is illusion. The artificer
Of quiet, distance holds me in a vise
And holds the ocean steady to my eyes.

Once when I rounded Flattery, the sea
Hove its loose weight like sand to tangle me
Upon the washing deck, to crush the hull;
Subsiding, dragged flesh at the bone. The skull
Felt the retreating wash of dreaming hair.
Half drenched in dissolution, I lay bare.

I scarcely pulled myself erect; I came
Back slowly, slowly knew myself the same.
That was the ocean. From the ship we saw
Gray whales for miles: the long sweep of the jaw,
The blunt head plunging clean above the wave.
And one rose in a tent of sea and gave
A darkening shudder; water fell away;
The whale stood shining, and then sank in spray.

A landsman, I. The sea is but a sound.
I would be near it on a sandy mound,
And hear the steady rushing of the deep
While I lay stinging in the sand with sleep.
I have lived inland long. The land is numb.
It stands beneath the feet, and one may come
Walking securely, till the sea extends
Its limber margin, and precision ends.
By night a chaos of commingling power,
The whole Pacific hovers hour by hour.
The slow Pacific swell stirs on the sand,
Sleeping to sink away, withdrawing land,
Heaving and wrinkled in the moon, and blind;
Or gathers seaward, ebbing out of mind.

On a View of Pasadena from the Hills

From the high terrace porch I watch the dawn.
No light appears, though dark has mostly gone,
Sunk from the cold and monstrous stone. The hills
Lie naked but not light. The darkness spills
Down the remoter gulleys; pooled, will stay
Too low to melt, not yet alive with day.
Below the windows, the lawn, matted deep
Under its close-cropped tips with dewy sleep,
Gives off a faint hush, all its plushy swarm
Alive with coolness reaching to be warm.
Gray windows at my back, the massy frame
Dull with the blackness that has not a name;
But down below, the garden is still young,
Of five years' growth, perhaps, and terrace-hung,
Drop by slow drop of seeping concrete walls.
Such are the bastions of our pastorals!

Here are no palms! They once lined country ways,
Where old white houses glared down dusty days,
With small round towers, blunt-headed through small trees.
Those towers are now the hiving place of bees.
The palms were coarse; their leaves hung thick with dust;
The roads were muffled deep. But now deep rust
Has fastened on the wheels that labored then.
Peace to all such, and to all sleeping men!
I lived my childhood there, a passive dream
In the expanse of that recessive scheme.

Slow air, slow fire! O deep delay of Time!
That summer crater smoked like slaking lime,
The hills so dry, so dense the underbrush,
That where I pushed my way the giant hush
Was changed to soft explosion as the sage
Broke down to powdered ash, the sift of age,
And fell along my path, a shadowy rift.

On these rocks now no burning ashes drift;
Mowed lawn has crept along the granite bench;
The yellow blossoms of acacia drench
The dawn with pollen; and, with waxen green,
The long leaves of the eucalypti screen
The closer hills from view – lithe, tall, and fine,
And nobly clad with youth, they bend and shine.
The small dark pool, jutting with living rock,
Trembles at every atmospheric shock,
Blurred to its depth with the cold living ooze.
From cloudy caves, heavy with summer dews,
The shyest and most tremulous beings stir,
The pulsing of their fins a lucent blur,
That, like illusion, glances off the view.
The pulsing mouths, like metronomes, are true.

This is my father's house, no homestead here
That I shall live in, but a shining sphere
Of glass and glassy moments, frail surprise,
My father's phantasy of Paradise;
Which melts upon his death, which he attained
With loss of heart for every step he gained.
Too firmly gentle to displace the great,
He crystallised this vision somewhat late;
Forbidden now to climb the garden stair,
He views the terrace from a window chair.

His friends, hard shaken by some twenty years,
Tremble with palsy and with senile fears,
In their late middle age gone cold and gray.
Fine men, now broken. That the vision stay,
They spend astutely their depleted breath,
With tired ironic faces wait for death.

Below the garden the hills fold away.
Deep in the valley, a mist fine as spray,
Ready to shatter into spinning light,
Conceals the city at the edge of night.
The city, on the tremendous valley floor,
Draws its dream deeper for an instant more,
Superb on solid loam, and breathing deep,
Poised for a moment at the edge of sleep.

Cement roads mark the hills, wide, bending free
Of cliff and headland. Dropping toward the sea,
Through suburb after suburb, vast ravines
Swell to the summer drone of fine machines.
The driver, melting down the distance here,
May cast in flight the faint hoof of a deer
Or pass the faint head set perplexedly.
And man-made stone outgrows the living tree,
And at its rising, air is shaken, men
Are shattered, and the tremor swells again,
Extending to the naked salty shore,
Rank with the sea, which crumbles evermore.

Time and the Garden

The spring has darkened with activity.
The future gathers in vine, bush, and tree:
Persimmon, walnut, loquat, fig, and grape,
Degrees and kinds of color, taste, and shape.
These will advance in their due series, space
The season like a tranquil dwelling-place.
And yet excitement swells me, vein by vein:
I long to crowd the little garden, gain
Its sweetness in my hand and crush it small
And taste it in a moment, time and all!
These trees, whose slow growth measures off my years,
I would expand to greatness. No one hears,

And I am still retarded in duress!
And this is like that other restlessness
To seize the greatness not yet fairly earned,
One which the tougher poets have discerned –
Gascoigne, Ben Jonson, Greville, Raleigh, Donne,
Poets who wrote great poems, one by one,
And spaced by many years, each line an act
Through which few labor, which no men retract.
This passion is the scholar's heritage,
The imposition of a busy age,
The passion to condense from book to book
Unbroken wisdom in a single look,
Though we know well that when this fix the head,
The mind's immortal, but the man is dead.

LAURA RIDING

A City Seems

A city seems between us. It is only love,
Love like a sorrow still
After a labor, after light.
The crowds are one.
Sleep is a single heart
Filling the old avenues we used to know
With miracles of dark and dread
We dare not go to meet
Save as our own dead stalking
Or as two dreams walking
One tread and terrible,
One cloak of longing in the cold,
Though we stand separate and wakeful
Measuring death in miles between us
Where a city seems and memories
Sleep like a populace.

The Mask

Cover up,
Oh, quickly cover up
All the new spotted places,
All the unbeautifuls,
The insufficiently beloved.

With what? with what?
With the uncovering of the lovelies,
With the patches that transformed
The more previous corruptions.

Is there no pure then?
The eternal taint wears beauty like a mask.
But a mask eternal.

One Self

Under apparel, apparel lies
The recurring body:
O multiple innocence, O fleshfold dress.

One self, one manyness,
Is first confusion, then simplicity.
Smile, death, O simultaneous mouth.
Cease, inner and outer,
Continuous flight and overtaking.

The Troubles of a Book

The trouble of a book is first to be
No thoughts to nobody,
Then to lie as long unwritten
As it will lie unread,
Then to build word for word an author
And occupy his head
Until the head declares vacancy
To make full publication
Of running empty.

The trouble of a book is secondly
To keep awake and ready
And listening like an innkeeper,
Wishing, not wishing for a guest,
Torn between hope of no rest
And hope of rest.
Uncertainly the pages doze
And blink open to passing fingers
With landlord smile, then close.

The trouble of a book is thirdly
To speak its sermon, then look the other way,
Arouse commotion in the margin,
Where tongue meets the eye,
But claim no experience of panic,
No complicity in the outcry.
The ordeal of a book is to give no hint
Of ordeal, to be flat and witless
Of the upright sense of print.

The trouble of a book is chiefly
To be nothing but book outwardly;
To wear binding like binding,
Bury itself in book-death,
Yet to feel all but book;
To breathe live words, yet with the breath
Of letters; to address liveliness
In reading eyes, be answered with
Letters and bookishness.

The World and I

This is not exactly what I mean
Any more than the sun is the sun.
But how to mean more closely
If the sun shines but approximately?
What a world of awkwardness!
What hostile implements of sense!
Perhaps this is as close a meaning
As perhaps becomes such knowing.
Else I think the world and I
Must live together as strangers and die —

A sour love, each doubtful whether
Was ever a thing to love the other.
No, better for both to be nearly sure
Each of each – exactly where
Exactly I and exactly the world
Fail to meet by a moment, and a word.

Poet: A Lying Word

You have now come with me, I have now come with you, to the season that should be winter, and is not: we have not come back.

We have not come back: we have not come round: we have not moved. I have taken you, you have taken me, to the next and next span, and the last – and it is the last. Stand against me then and stare well through me then. It is a wall not to be scaled and left behind like the old seasons, like the poets who were the seasons.

Stand against me then and stare well through me then. I am no poet as you have span by span leapt the high words to the next depth and season, the next season always, the last always, and the next. I am a true wall: you may but stare me through.

It is a false wall, a poet: it is a lying word. It is a wall that closes and does not.

This is no wall that closes and does not. It is a wall to see into, it is no other season's height. Beyond it lies no depth and height of further travel, no partial courses. Stand against me then and stare well through me then. Like wall of poet here I rise, but am no poet as walls have risen between next and next and made false end to leap. A last, true wall am I: you may but stare me through.

And the tale is no more of the going: no more a poet's tale of a going false-like to a seeing. The tale is of a seeing true-like to a knowing: there's but to stare the wall through now, well through.

It is not a wall, it is not a poet. It is not a lying wall, it is not a lying word. It is a written edge of time. Step not across, for then into my mouth, my eyes, you fall. Come close, stare me well through, speak as you see. But, oh, infatuated drove of lives, step not across now. Into my mouth, my eyes, shall you thus fall, and be yourselves no more.

Into my mouth, my eyes, I say, I say. I am no poet like transitory wall to lead you on into such slow terrain of time as measured out your single span to broken turns of season once and once again. I lead you not. You have now come with me, I have now come with you, to your last turn and season: thus could I come with you, thus only.

I say, I say, I am, it is, such wall, such poet, such not lying, such not leading into. Await the sight, and look well through, know by such standing still that next comes none of you.

Comes what? Comes this even I, even this not-I, this not lying season when death holds the year at steady count – this every-year.

Would you not see, not know, not mark the count? What would you then? Why have you come here then? To leap a wall that is no wall, and a true wall? To step across into my eyes and mouth not yours? To cry me down like wall or poet as often your way led past down-falling height that seemed?

I say, I say, I am, it is: such wall, such end of graded travel. And if you will not hark, come tumbling then upon me, into my eyes, my mouth, and be the backward utterance of yourselves expiring angrily through instant seasons that played you time-false.

My eyes, my mouth, my hovering hands, my intransmutable head: wherein my eyes, my mouth, my hands, my head, my body-self, are not such mortal simulacrum as everlong you builded against very-death, to keep you everlong in boasted death-course, neverlong? I say, I say, I am not builded of you so.

This body-self, this wall, this poet-like address, is that last barrier long shied of in your elliptic changes: out of your leaping, shying, season-quibbling, have I made it, is it made. And if now poet-like it rings with one-more-time as if, this is the mounted stupor of your everlong outbiding worn prompt and lyric, poet-like – the forbidden one-more-time worn time-like.

Does it seem I ring, I sing, I rhyme, I poet-wit? Shame on me then! Grin me your foulest humour then of poet-piety, your eyes rolled up in white hypocrisy – should I be one sprite more of your versed fame – or turned from me into your historied brain, where the lines read more actual. Shame on me then!

And haste unto us both, my shame is yours. How long I seem to beckon like a wall beyond which stretches longer length of fleshsome traverse: it is your lie of flesh and my flesh-seeming stand of words. Haste then unto us both. I say, I say. This wall reads "Stop!" This poet verses "Poet: a lying word!"

Shall the wall then not crumble, as to walls is given? Have I not said: "Stare me well through"? It is indeed a wall, crumble it shall. It is a wall of walls, stare it well through: the reading gentles near, the name of death passes with the season that it was not.

Death is a very wall. The going over walls, against walls, is a dying and a learning. Death is a knowing-death. Known death is truth sighted at the halt. The name of death passes. The mouth that moves with death forgets the word.

And the first page is the last of death. And haste unto us both, lest the wall seem to crumble not, to lead mock-onward. And the first page reads: "Haste unto us both!" And the first page reads: "Slowly, it is the first page only."

Slowly, it is the page before the first page only, there is no haste. The page before the first page tells of death, haste, slowness: how truth falls true now at the turn of page, at time of telling. Truth one by one falls true. And the first page reads, the page which is the page before the first page only: "This once-upon-a-time when seasons failed, and time stared through the wall nor made to leap across, is the hour, the season, seasons, year and years, no wall and wall, where when and when the classic lie dissolves and nakedly time salted is with truth's sweet flood nor yet to mix with, but be salted tidal-sweet – O sacramental ultimate by which shall time be old-renewed nor yet another season move." I say, I say.

Divestment of Beauty

She, she and she and she –
Which of these is not lovely?
In her long robe of glamour now
And her beauty like a ribbon tied
The wisdom of her head round?

To call these "women"
Is homage of the eye:
Such sights to greet as natural,
Such beings to proclaim
Companion to expectance.

But were they now who take
This gaudy franchise from
The accolade of stilted vision

Their lady-swaddlings to unwrap
And shed the timorous scales of nakedness –

It were a loathsome spectacle, you think?
Eventual entrails of deity
Worshipful eye offending?
It were the sign, man.
To pluck the loathsome eye,

Forswear the imbecile
Theology of loveliness,
Be no more doctor in antiquities –
Chimeras of the future
In archaic daze embalmed –

And grow to later youth,
Felling the patriarchal leer
That it lie reft of all obscenities
While she and she, she, she, disclose
The recondite familiar to your candour.

The Reasons of Each

The reason of the saint that he is saintly,
And of the hero that to him
Glory the mirror and the beauty;
And of the brigand that to prowl abhorred
Makes him renowned unto himself
And dear the evil name;

Of girls like evening angels
From the mass of heaven fluttering
To earth in wanton whispers –
That they invite their flesh to loose
All yet unbaptized terrors on them
And will tomorrow change the virgin glance
For the long wandering gaze;

The reason of the dark one that his heart
For love of hell is empty
And that the empty maze consoles
In that the bare heart is
Of heaven the augury
As of hell;

The reasons of each are lone,
And lone the fate of each.
To private death-ear will they tell
Why they have done so.
Such were the reasons of the lives they lived.
Then they are dead,
And the cause was themselves.

Each to himself is the cause of himself.
These are the agencies of freedom
Which necessity compels,
As birds are flown from earth
By that earth utters no command
Of fixity, but waits on motion
To consume itself, and stillness
To be earth of earth, ingenerate
Cohesion without cause.

For they are uncaused, the minds
Which differ not in sense.
They are the mind which saves
Sense to itself
Against interpretation's waste;
They are the sense dispartable
Which senses cannot change.

The reasons, then, of this one, that one,
That they unlike are this one, that one –
This is as the telling of beads.
The chain hangs round the neck of lamentation –
They are lost.
Or as to watch the sun's purposeful clouds
Mingle with moonlight and be nothing.

The brow of unanimity
Perplexes as each goes his unlike way.
But soon the vagrant thought is out of sight.
To go is short,
Though slow the shadow trailing after
Which the backward look a reason names.

LANGSTON HUGHES

The Negro Speaks of Rivers

I've known rivers:
I've known rivers ancient as the world and older than the
    flow of human blood in human veins.

My soul has grown deep like the rivers.

I bathed in the Euphrates when dawns were young.
I built my hut near the Congo and it lulled me to sleep.
I looked upon the Nile and raised the pyramids above it.
I heard the singing of the Mississippi when Abe Lincoln went
    down to New Orleans, and I've seen its muddy bosom
    turn all golden in the sunset.

I've known rivers:
Ancient, dusky rivers.

My soul has grown deep like rivers.

The Weary Blues

Droning a drowsy syncopated tune,
Rocking back and forth to a mellow croon,
    I heard a Negro play.
Down on Lenox Avenue the other night
By the pale dull pallor of an old gas light
    He did a lazy sway . . .
    He did a lazy sway . . .
To the tune o'those Weary Blues.
With his ebony hands on each ivory key
He made that poor piano moan with melody.
    O Blues!
Swaying to and fro on his rickety stool
He played that sad raggy tune like a musical fool.
    Sweet Blues!
Coming from a black man's soul.
    O Blues!
In a deep song voice with a melancholy tone
I heard that Negro sing, that old piano moan —

"Ain't got nobody in all this world,
Ain't got nobody but ma self
I's gwine to quit ma frownin'
And put ma troubles on the shelf."
Thump, thump, thump, went his foot on the floor.
He played a few chords then he sang some more –
"I got the Weary Blues
And I can't be satisfied.
Got the Weary Blues
And can't be satisfied –
I ain't happy no mo'
And I wish that I had died."
And far into the night he crooned that tune.
The stars went out and so did the moon.
The singer stopped playing and went to bed
While the Weary Blues echoed through his head.
He slept like a rock or a man that's dead.

Cross

My old man's a white old man
And my old mother's black.
If ever I cursed my white old man
I take my curses back.

If ever I cursed my black old mother
And wished she were in hell,
I'm sorry for that evil wish
And now I wish her well.

My old man died in a fine big house.
My ma died in a shack.
I wonder where I'm gonna die,
Being neither white nor black?

Old Walt

Old Walt Whitman
Went finding and seeking,
Finding less than sought
Seeking more than found,
Every detail minding
Of the seeking or the finding.

Pleasured equally
In seeking as in finding,
Each detail minding,
Old Walt went seeking
And finding.

I, Too

I, too, sing America.

I am the darker brother.
They send me to eat in the kitchen
When company comes,
But I laugh,
And eat well,
And grow strong.

Tomorrow,
I'll be at the table
When company comes.
Nobody'll dare
Say to me,
"Eat in the kitchen,"
Then.

Besides,
They'll see how beautiful I am
And be ashamed –

I, too, am America.

STEVIE SMITH

Dirge

From a friend's friend I taste friendship,
From a friend's friend love,
My spirit in confusion,
Long years I strove,
But now I know that never
Nearer I shall move,

Than a friend's friend to friendship,
To love than a friend's love.

Into the dark night
Resignedly I go,
I am not so afraid of the dark night
As the friends I do not know,
I do not fear the night above,
As I fear the friends below.

Not Waving but Drowning

Nobody heard him, the dead man,
But still he lay moaning:
I was much further out than you thought
And not waving but drowning.

Poor chap, he always loved larking
And now he's dead
It must have been too cold for him his heart
        gave way,
They said.

Oh, no no no, it was too cold always
(Still the dead one lay moaning)
I was much too far out all my life
And not waving but drowning.

The Jungle Husband

Dearest Evelyn, I often think of you
Out with the guns in the jungle stew
Yesterday I hittapotamus
I put the measurements down for you but they got
        lost in the fuss
It's not a good thing to drink out here
You know, I've practically given it up dear.
Tomorrow I am going alone a long way
Into the jungle. It is all gray
But green on top
Only sometimes when a tree has fallen
The sun comes down plop, it is quite appalling.

You never want to go in a jungle pool
In the hot sun, it would be the act of a fool
Because it's always full of anacondas, Evelyn, not looking
    ill-fed
I'll say. So no more now, from your loving husband,
    Wilfred.

Tenuous and Precarious

Tenuous and Precarious
Were my guardians,
Precarious and Tenuous,
Two Romans.

My father was Hazardous,
Hazardous,
Dear old man,
Three Romans.

There was my brother Spurious,
Spurious Posthumous,
Spurious was spurious
Was four Romans.

My husband was Perfidious,
He was perfidious,
Five Romans.

Surreptitious, our son,
Was surreptitious,
He was six Romans.

Our cat Tedious
Still lives,
Count not Tedious
Yet.

My name is Finis,
Finis, Finis,
I am Finis,
Six, five, four, three, two,
One Roman,
Finis.

A House of Mercy

It was a house of female habitation,
Two ladies fair inhabited the house,
And they were brave. For although Fear knocked loud
Upon the door, and said he must come in,
They did not let him in.

There were also two feeble babes, two girls,
That Mrs S. had by her husband had,
He soon left them and went away to sea,
Nor sent them money, nor came home again
Except to borrow back
Her Naval Officer's Wife's Allowance from Mrs S.
Who gave it him at once, she thought she should.

There was also the ladies' aunt
And babes' great aunt, a Mrs Martha Hearn Clode,
And she was elderly.
These ladies put their money all together
And so we lived.

I was the younger of the feeble babes
And when I was a child my mother died
And later Great Aunt Martha Hearn Clode died
And later still my sister went away.

Now I am old I tend my mother's sister
The noble aunt who so long tended us,
Faithful and True her name is. Tranquil.
Also Sardonic. And I tend the house.

It is a house of female habitation
A house expecting strength as it is strong
A house of aristocratic mould that looks apart
When tears fall; counts despair
Derisory. Yet it has kept us well. For all its faults,
If they are faults, of sternness and reserve,
It is a Being of warmth I think; at heart
A house of mercy.

The Donkey

It was such a pretty little donkey
It had such pretty ears
And it used to gallop round the field so briskly
Though well down in years.

It was a retired donkey,
After a life-time of working
Between the shafts of regular employment
It was now free to go merrymaking.

Oh in its eyes was such a gleam
As is usually associated with youth
But it was not a youthful gleam really,
But full of mature truth.

And of the hilarity that goes with age,
As if to tell us sardonically
No hedged track lay before this donkey longer
But the sweet prairies of anarchy.

But the sweet prairies of anarchy
And the thought that keeps my heart up
That at last, in Death's odder anarchy,
Our pattern will be broken all up.
Though precious we are momentarily, donkey,
I aspire to be broken up.

LORINE NIEDECKER

Poet's work

Grandfather
   advised me:
      Learn a trade

I learned
   to sit at desk
      and condense

No layoff
   from this
      condensery

Thomas Jefferson

I

My wife is ill!
And I sit
　　　　waiting
for a quorum

2

Fast ride
his horse collapsed
Now *he* saddled walked

Borrowed a farmer's
unbroken colt
To Richmond

Richmond How stop –
Arnold's redcoats
there

3

Elk Hill destroyed –
Cornwallis
carried off 30 slaves

Jefferson:
Were it to give them freedom
he'd have done right

4

Latin and Greek
my tools
to understand
humanity

I rode horse
away from a monarch
to an enchanting
philosophy

5
The South of France

Roman temple
"simple and sublime"

Maria Cosway
        harpist
on his mind

white column
and arch

6

To daughter Patsy: Read –
read Livy

No person full of work
was ever hysterical

Know music, history
dancing

(I calculate 14 to 1
in marriage
she will draw
a blockhead)

Science also
Patsy

7

Agreed with Adams:
send spermaceti oil to Portugal
for their church candles

(light enough to banish mysteries?:
three are one and one is three
and yet the one not three
and the three not one)

and send salt fish
U.S. salt fish preferred
above all other

8

Jefferson of Patrick Henry
backwoods fiddler statesman:

"He spoke as Homer wrote"
Henry eyed our minister at Paris —

the Bill of Rights hassle —
"he remembers . . .

in splendor and dissipation
he thinks yet of bills of rights"

9

True, French frills and lace
for Jefferson, sword and belt

but follow the Court to Fontainebleau
he could not —

house rent would have left him
nothing to eat

* * *

He bowed to everyone he met
and talked with arms folded

He could be trimmed
by a two-month migraine

and yet
            stand up

10

Dear Polly:
I said No — no frost

in Virginia — the strawberries
were safe

I'd have heard — I'm in that kind
of correspondence

with a young daughter –
if they were not

Now I must retract
I shrink from it

11

Political honors
      "splendid torments"
"If one could establish
      an absolute power
of silence over oneself"

When I set out for Monticello
    (my grandchildren
      will they know me?)
How are my young
          chestnut trees –

12

Hamilton and the bankers
would make my country Carthage

I am abandoning the rich –
their dinner parties –

I shall eat my simlins
with the class of science

or not at all
Next year the last of labors

among conflicting parties
Then my family

we shall sow our cabbages
together

13

Delicious flower
of the acacia

or rather

Mimosa Nilotica
from Mr Lomax

14

Polly Jefferson, 8, had crossed
to father and sister in Paris

by way of London – Abigail
embraced her – Adams said

"in all my life I never saw
more charming child"

Death of Polly, 25,
Monticello

15

My harpsichord
my alabaster vase
and bridle bit
bound for Alexandria
Virginia

The good sea weather
of retirement
The drift and suck
and die-down of life
but there is land

16

These were my passions:
Monticello and the villa-temples
I passed on to carpenters
bricklayers what I knew

and to an Italian sculptor
how to turn a volute
on a pillar

You may approach the campus rotunda
from lower to upper terrace
Cicero had levels

17

John Adams' eyes
            dimming
Tom Jefferson's rheumatism
                    cantering

18

Ah soon must Monticello be lost
            to debts
and Jefferson himself
                    to death

19

Mind leaving, let body leave
Let dome live, spherical dome
and colonnade

Martha (Patsy) stay
"The Committee of Safety
must be warned"

Stay youth – Anne and Ellen
all my books, the bantams
and the seeds of the senega root

PATRICK KAVANAGH

Shancoduff

My black hills have never seen the sun rising,
Eternally they look north towards Armagh.
Lot's wife would not be salt if she had been
Incurious as my black hills that are happy
When dawn whitens Glassdrummond chapel.

My hills hoard the bright shillings of March
While the sun searches in every pocket.
They are my Alps and I have climbed the Matterhorn
With a sheaf of hay for three perishing calves
In the field under the Big Forth of Rocksavage.

The sleety winds fondle the rushy beards of Shancoduff
While the cattle-drovers sheltering in the Featherna Bush
Look up and say: "Who owns them hungry hills
That the water-hen and snipe must have forsaken?
A poet? Then by heavens he must be poor."
I hear and is my heart not badly shaken?

Stony Grey Soil

O stony grey soil of Monaghan
The laugh from my love you thieved;
You took the gay child of my passion
And gave me your clod-conceived.

You clogged the feet of my boyhood
And I believed that my stumble
Had the poise and stride of Apollo
And his voice my thick-tongued mumble.

You told me the plough was immortal!
O green-life-conquering plough!
Your mandril strained, your coulter blunted
In the smooth lea-field of my brow.

You sang on steaming dunghills
A song of cowards' brood,
You perfumed my clothes with weasel itch,
You fed me on swinish food.

You flung a ditch on my vision
Of beauty, love and truth.
O stony grey soil of Monaghan
You burgled my bank of youth!

Lost the long hours of pleasure
All the women that love young men.
O can I still stroke the monster's back
Or write with unpoisoned pen

His name in these lonely verses
Or mention the dark fields where
The first gay flight of my lyric
Got caught in a peasant's prayer.

Mullahinsha, Drummeril, Black Shanco –
Wherever I turn I see
In the stony grey soil of Monaghan
Dead loves that were born for me.

The Long Garden

It was the garden of the golden apples,
A long garden between a railway and a road,
In the sow's rooting where the hen scratches
We dipped our fingers in the pockets of God.

In the thistly hedge old boots were flying sandals
By which we travelled through the childhood skies,
Old buckets rusty-holed with half-hung handles
Were drums to play when old men married wives.

The pole that lifted the clothes-line in the middle
Was the flag-pole on a prince's palace when
We looked at it through fingers crossed to riddle
In evening sunlight miracles for men.

It was the garden of the golden apples,
And when the Carrick train went by we knew
That we could never die till something happened
Like wishing for a fruit that never grew,

Or wanting to be up on Candle-Fort
Above the village with its shops and mill.
The racing cyclists' gasp-gapped reports
Hinted of pubs where life can drink his fill.

And when the sun went down into Drumcatton
And the New Moon by its little finger swung
From the telegraph wires, we knew how God had
        happened
And what the blackbird in the whitethorn sang.

It was the garden of the golden apples,
The half-way house where we had stopped a day
Before we took the west road to Drumcatton
Where the sun was always setting on the play.

Memory of Brother Michael

It would never be morning, always evening,
Golden sunset, golden age –
When Shakespeare, Marlowe and Jonson were writing
The future of England page by page
A nettle-wild grave was Ireland's stage.

It would never be spring, always autumn
After a harvest always lost,
When Drake was winning seas for England
We sailed in puddles of the past
Chasing the ghost of Brendan's mast.

The seeds among the dust were less than dust,
Dust we sought, decay,
The young sprout rising smothered in it,
Cursed for being in the way –
And the same is true today.

Culture is always something that was,
Something pedants can measure,
Skull of bard, thigh of chief,
Depth of dried-up river.
Shall we be thus for ever?
Shall we be thus for ever?

Epic

I have lived in important places, times
When great events were decided: who owned
That half a rood of rock, a no-man's land
Surrounded by our pitchfork-armed claims.
I heard the Duffys shouting "Damn your soul"
And old McCabe stripped to the waist, seen
Step the plot defying blue cast-steel –
"Here is the march along these iron stones"
That was the year of the Munich bother. Which
Was most important? I inclined
To lose my faith in Ballyrush and Gortin
Till Homer's ghost came whispering to my mind
He said: I made the *Iliad* from such
A local row. Gods make their own importance.

Come Dance with Kitty Stobling

No, no, no, I know I was not important as I moved
Through the colourful country, I was but a single
Item in the picture, the namer not the beloved.
O tedious man with whom no gods commingle.

Beauty, who has described beauty? Once upon a time
I had a myth that was a lie but it served:
Trees walking across the crests of hills and my rhyme
Cavorting on mile-high stilts and the unnerved
Crowds looking up with terror in their rational faces.
O dance with Kitty Stobling I outrageously
Cried out-of-sense to them, while their timorous paces
Stumbled behind Jove's page boy paging me.
I had a very pleasant journey, thank you sincerely
For giving me my madness back, or nearly.

JOHN BETJEMAN

Slough

Come, friendly bombs, and fall on Slough
It isn't fit for humans now,
There isn't grass to graze a cow
   Swarm over, Death!

Come, bombs, and blow to smithereens
Those air-conditioned, bright canteens,
Tinned fruit, tinned meat, tinned milk, tinned beans
   Tinned minds, tinned breath.

Mess up the mess they call a town –
A house for ninety-seven down
And once a week a half-a-crown
   For twenty years,

And get that man with double chin
Who'll always cheat and always win,
Who washes his repulsive skin
   In women's tears,

And smash his desk of polished oak
And smash his hands so used to stroke
And stop his boring dirty joke
   And make him yell.

But spare the bald young clerks who add
The profits of the stinking cad;
It's not their fault that they are mad,
   They've tasted Hell.

It's not their fault they do not know
The birdsong from the radio,
It's not their fault they often go
    To Maidenhead

And talk of sports and makes of cars
In various bogus Tudor bars
And daren't look up and see the stars
    But belch instead.

In labour-saving homes, with care
Their wives frizz out peroxide hair
And dry it in synthetic air
    And paint their nails.

Come, friendly bombs, and fall on Slough
To get it ready for the plough.
The cabbages are coming now;
    The earth exhales.

City

When the great bell
BOOMS over the Portland stone urn, and
From the carved cedar wood
Rises the odour of incense,
I SIT DOWN
In St Botolph Bishopsgate Churchyard
And wait for the spirit of my grandfather
Toddling along from the Barbican.

A Shropshire Lad

N.B. – This should be recited with a Midland accent.
Captain Webb, the swimmer and a relation of
Mary Webb by marriage, was born at Dawley in
an industrial district in Salop.

The gas was on in the Institute,
    The flare was up in the gym,
A man was running a mineral line,
    A lass was singing a hymn,
When Captain Webb the Dawley man,
    Captain Webb from Dawley,

Came swimming along the old canal
    That carried the bricks to Lawley.
        Swimming along –
        Swimming along –
        Swimming along from Severn,
And paying a call at Dawley Bank while swimming
    along to Heaven.

The sun shone low on the railway line
    And over the bricks and stacks,
And in at the upstairs windows
    Of the Dawley houses' backs,
When we saw the ghost of Captain Webb,
    Webb in a water sheeting,
Come dripping along in a bathing dress
    To the Saturday evening meeting.
        Dripping along –
        Dripping along –
        To the Congregational Hall;
Dripping and still he rose over the sill and faded away
    in a wall.

There wasn't a man in Oakengates
    That hadn't got hold of the tale,
And over the valley in Ironbridge,
    And round by Coalbrookdale,
How Captain Webb the Dawley man,
    Captain Webb from Dawley,
Rose rigid and dead from the old canal
    That carries the bricks to Lawley.
        Rigid and dead –
        Rigid and dead –
        To the Saturday congregation,
Paying a call at Dawley Bank on his way to his
    destination.

In Westminster Abbey

Let me take this other glove off
    As the vox humana swells,
And the beauteous fields of Eden
    Bask beneath the Abbey bells.
Here, where England's statesmen lie,
Listen to a lady's cry.

Gracious Lord, oh bomb the Germans.
  Spare their women for Thy Sake,
And if that is not too easy
  We will pardon Thy Mistake.
But, gracious Lord, whate'er shall be,
Don't let anyone bomb me.

Keep our Empire undismembered
  Guide Our Forces by Thy Hand,
Gallant blacks from far Jamaica,
  Honduras and Togoland;
Protect them Lord in all their fights,
And, even more, protect the whites.

Think of what our Nation stands for,
  Books from Boots' and country lanes,
Free speech, free passes, class distinction,
  Democracy and proper drains.
Lord, put beneath Thy special care
One-eighty-nine Cadogan Square.

Although dear Lord I am a sinner,
  I have done no major crime;
Now I'll come to Evening Service
  Whensoever I have the time.
So, Lord, reserve for me a crown,
And do not let my shares go down.

I will labour for Thy Kingdom,
  Help our lads to win the war,
Send white feathers to the cowards
  Join the Women's Army Corps,
Then wash the Steps around Thy Throne
In the Eternal Safety Zone.

Now I feel a little better,
  What a treat to hear Thy Word,
Where the bones of leading statesmen
  Have so often been interr'd.
And now, dear Lord, I cannot wait
Because I have a luncheon date.

Before the Anaesthetic,
or *A Real Fright*

Intolerably sad, profound
St Giles's bells are ringing round,
They bring the slanting summer rain
To tap the chestnut boughs again
Whose shadowy cave of rainy leaves
The gusty belfry-song receives.
Intolerably sad and true,
Victorian red and jewel blue,
The mellow bells are ringing round
And charge the evening light with sound,
And I look motionless from bed
On heavy trees and purple red
And hear the midland bricks and tiles
Throw back the bells of stone St Giles,
Bells, ancient now as castle walls,
Now hard and new as pitchpine stalls,
Now full with help from ages past,
Now dull with death and hell at last.
Swing up! and give me hope of life,
Swing down! and plunge the surgeon's knife.
I, breathing for a moment, see
Death wing himself away from me
And think, as on this bed I lie,
Is it extinction when I die?
I move my limbs and use my sight;
Not yet, thank God, not yet the Night.
Oh better far those echoing hells
Half-threaten'd in the pealing bells
Than that this "I" should cease to be —
Come quickly, Lord, come quick to me.
St Giles's bells are asking now
"And hast thou known the Lord, hast thou?"
St Giles's bells, they richly ring
"And was that Lord our Christ the King?"
St Giles's bells they hear me call
I never knew the Lord at all.
Oh not in me your Saviour dwells
You ancient, rich St Giles's bells.
Illuminated missals — spires —
Wide screens and decorated quires —

All these I loved, and on my knees
I thanked myself for knowing these
And watched the morning sunlight pass
Through richly stained Victorian glass
And in the colour-shafted air
I, kneeling, thought the Lord was there.
Now, lying in the gathering mist
I know that Lord did not exist;
Now, lest this "I" should cease to be,
Come, real Lord, come quick to me.
With every gust the chestnut sighs,
With every breath, a mortal dies;
The man who smiled alone, alone,
And went his journey on his own
With "Will you give my wife this letter,
In case, of course, I don't get better?"
Waits for his coffin lid to close
On waxen head and yellow toes.
Almighty Saviour, had I Faith
There'd be no fight with kindly Death.
Intolerably long and deep
St Giles's bells swing on in sleep:
"But still you go from here alone"
Say all the bells about the Throne.

WILLIAM EMPSON

Rolling the Lawn

You can't beat English lawns. Our final hope
Is flat despair. Each morning therefore ere
I greet the office, through the weekday air,
Holding the Holy Roller at the slope
(The English fetish, not the Texas Pope)
Hither and thither on my toes with care
I roll ours flatter and flatter. Long, in prayer,
I grub for daisies at whose roots I grope.

Roll not the abdominal wall; the walls of Troy
Lead, since a plumb-line ordered, could destroy.
Roll rather, where no mole dare sap, the lawn,
And ne'er his tumuli shall tomb your brawn.
World, roll yourself, and bear your roller, soul,
As martyrs gridirons, when God calls the roll.

Villanelle

It is the pain, it is the pain, endures.
Your chemic beauty burned my muscles through.
Poise of my hands reminded me of yours.

What later purge from this deep toxin cures?
What kindness now could the old salve renew?
It is the pain, it is the pain, endures.

The infection slept (custom or change inures)
And when pain's secondary phase was due
Poise of my hands reminded me of yours.

How safe I felt, whom memory assures,
Rich that your grace safely by heart I knew.
It is the pain, it is the pain, endures.

My stare drank deep beauty that still allures.
My heart pumps yet the poison draught of you.
Poise of my hands reminded me of yours.

You are still kind whom the same shape immures.
Kind and beyond adieu. We miss our cue.
It is the pain, it is the pain, endures.
Poise of my hands reminded me of yours.

Legal Fiction

Law makes long spokes of the short stakes of men.
Your well fenced out real estate of mind
No high flat of the nomad citizen
Looks over, or train leaves behind.

Your rights extend under and above your claim
Without bound; you own land in Heaven and Hell;
Your part of earth's surface and mass the same,
Of all cosmos' volume, and all stars as well.

Your rights reach down where all owners meet, in Hell's
Pointed exclusive conclave, at earth's centre
(Your spun farm's root still on that axis dwells);
And up, through galaxies, a growing sector.

You are nomad yet; the lighthouse beam you own
Flashes, like Lucifer, through the firmament.
Earth's axis varies; your dark central cone
Wavers, a candle's shadow, at the end.

This Last Pain

This last pain for the damned the Fathers found:
"They knew the bliss with which they were not
    crowned."
　　Such, but on earth, let me foretell,
　　Is all, of heaven or of hell.

Man, as the prying housemaid of the soul,
May know her happiness by eye to hole:
　　He's safe; the key is lost; he knows
　　Door will not open, nor hole close.

"What is conceivable can happen too,"
Said Wittgenstein, who had not dreamt of you;
　　But wisely; if we worked it long
　　We should forget where it was wrong.

Those thorns are crowns which, woven into knots,
Crackle under and soon boil fool's pots;
　　And no man's watching, wise and long,
　　Would ever stare them into song.

Thorns burn to a consistent ash, like man;
A splendid cleanser for the frying-pan:
　　And those who leap from pan to fire
　　Should this brave opposite admire.

All those large dreams by which men long live well
Are magic-lanterned on the smoke of hell;
　　This then is real, I have implied,
　　A painted, small, transparent slide.

These the inventive can hand-paint at leisure,
Or most emporia would stock our measure;
　　And feasting in their dappled shade
　　We should forget how they were made.

Feign then what's by a decent tact believed
And act that state is only so conceived,
    And build an edifice of form
    For house where phantoms may keep warm.

Imagine, then, by miracle, with me,
(Ambiguous gifts, as what gods give must be)
    What could not possibly be there,
    And learn a style from a despair.

Missing Dates

Slowly the poison the whole blood stream fills.
It is not the effort nor the failure tires.
The waste remains, the waste remains and kills.

It is not your system or clear sight that mills
Down small to the consequence a life requires;
Slowly the poison the whole blood stream fills.

They bled an old dog dry yet the exchange rills
Of young dog blood gave but a month's desires
The waste remains, the waste remains and kills.

It is the Chinese tombs and the slag hills
Usurp the soil, and not the soil retires.
Slowly the poison the whole blood stream fills.

Not to have fire is to be a skin that shrills.
The complete fire is death. From partial fires
The waste remains, the waste remains and kills.

It is the poems you have lost, the ills
From missing dates, at which the heart expires.
Slowly the poison the whole blood stream fills.
The waste remains, the waste remains and kills.

The Teasers

Not but they die, the teasers and the dreams,
Not but they die,
                    and tell the careful flood
To give them what they clamour for and why.

You could not fancy where they rip to blood,
You could not fancy
     nor that mud
I have heard speak that will not cake or dry.

Our claims to act appear so small to these,
Our claims to act
    colder lunacies
That cheat the love, the moment, the small fact.

Make no escape because they flash and die,
Make no escape
     build up your love,
Leave what you die for and be safe to die.

Let It Go

It is this deep blankness is the real thing strange.
 The more things happen to you the more you can't
  Tell or remember even what they were.

The contradictions cover such a range.
 The talk would talk and go so far aslant.
  You don't want madhouse and the whole thing there.

W. H. AUDEN

The Wanderer

Doom is dark and deeper than any sea-dingle.
Upon what man it fall
In spring, day-wishing flowers appearing,
Avalanche sliding, white snow from rock-face,
That he should leave his house,
No cloud-soft hand can hold him, restraint by women;
But ever that man goes
Through place-keepers, through forest trees,
A stranger to strangers over undried sea,
Houses for fishes, suffocating water,
Or lonely on fell as chat,
By pot-holed becks
A bird stone-haunting, an unquiet bird.

There head falls forward, fatigued at evening,
And dreams of home,
Waving from window, spread of welcome,
Kissing of wife under single sheet;
But waking sees
Bird-flocks nameless to him, through doorway voices
Of new men making another love.

Save him from hostile capture,
From sudden tiger's leap at corner;
Protect his house,
His anxious house where days are counted
From thunderbolt protect,
From gradual ruin spreading like a stain;
Converting number from vague to certain,
Bring joy, bring day of his returning,
Lucky with day approaching, with leaning dawn.

Paysage Moralisé

Hearing of harvests rotting in the valleys,
Seeing at end of street the barren mountains,
Round corners coming suddenly on water,
Knowing them shipwrecked who were launched for islands,
We honour founders of these starving cities
Whose honour is the image of our sorrow,

Which cannot see its likeness in their sorrow
That brought them desperate to the brink of valleys;
Dreaming of evening walks through learned cities
They reined their violent horses on the mountains,
Those fields like ships to castaways on islands,
Visions of green to them who craved for water.

They built by rivers and at night the water
Running past windows comforted their sorrow;
Each in his little bed conceived of islands
Where every day was dancing in the valleys
And all the green trees blossomed on the mountains,
Where love was innocent, being far from cities.

But dawn came back and they were still in cities;
No marvellous creature rose up from the water;
There was still gold and silver in the mountains

But hunger was a more immediate sorrow,
Although to moping villagers in valleys
Some waving pilgrims were describing islands . . .

"The gods," they promised, "visit us from islands,
Are stalking, head-up, lovely, through our cities;
Now is the time to leave your wretched valleys
And sail with them across the lime-green water,
Sitting at their white sides, forget your sorrow,
The shadow cast across your lives by mountains."

So many, doubtful, perished in the mountains,
Climbing up crags to get a view of islands,
So many, fearful, took with them their sorrow
Which stayed them when they reached unhappy cities,
So many, careless, dived and drowned in water,
So many, wretched, would not leave their valleys.

It is our sorrow. Shall it melt? Then water
Would gush, flush, green these mountains and these valleys,
And we rebuild our cities, not dream of islands.

Our Hunting Fathers

Our hunting fathers told the story
Of the sadness of the creatures,
Pitied the limits and the lack
Set in their finished features;
Saw in the lion's intolerant look,
Behind the quarry's dying glare,
Love raging for the personal glory
That reason's gift would add,
The liberal appetite and power,
The rightness of a god.

Who, nurtured in that fine tradition,
Predicted the result,
Guessed Love by nature suited to
The intricate ways of guilt,
That human ligaments could so
His southern gestures modify
And make it his mature ambition
To think no thought but ours,
To hunger, work illegally,
And be anonymous?

On This Island

Look, stranger, on this island now
The leaping light for your delight discovers,
Stand stable here
And silent be,
That through the channels of the ear
May wander like a river
The swaying sound of the sea.

Here at a small field's ending pause
Where the chalk wall falls to the foam and its tall
    ledges
Oppose the pluck
And knock of the tide,
And the shingle scrambles after the suck-
ing surf, and a gull lodges
A moment on its sheer side.

Far off like floating seeds the ships
Diverge on urgent voluntary errands,
And this full view
Indeed may enter
And move in memory as now these clouds do,
That pass the harbour mirror
And all the summer through the water saunter.

Lullaby

Lay your sleeping head, my love,
Human on my faithless arm;
Time and fevers burn away
Individual beauty from
Thoughtful children, and the grave
Proves the child ephemeral:
But in my arms till break of day
Let the living creature lie,
Mortal, guilty, but to me
The entirely beautiful.

Soul and body have no bounds:
To lovers as they lie upon
Her tolerant enchanted slope
In their ordinary swoon,

Grave the vision Venus sends
Of supernatural sympathy,
Universal love and hope;
While an abstract insight wakes
Among the glaciers and the rocks
The hermit's carnal ecstasy.

Certainty, fidelity
On the stroke of midnight pass
Like vibrations of a bell
And fashionable madmen raise
Their pedantic boring cry:
Every farthing of the cost,
All the dreaded cards foretell,
Shall be paid, but from this night
Not a whisper, not a thought,
Not a kiss nor look be lost.

Beauty, midnight, vision dies:
Let the winds of dawn that blow
Softly round your dreaming head
Such a day of welcome show
Eye and knocking heart may bless,
Find our mortal world enough;
Noons of dryness find you fed
By the involuntary powers,
Nights of insult let you pass
Watched by every human love.

September 1, 1939

I sit in one of the dives
On Fifty-Second Street
Uncertain and afraid
As the clever hopes expire
Of a low dishonest decade:
Waves of anger and fear
Circulate over the bright
And darkened lands of the earth,
Obsessing our private lives;
The unmentionable odour of death
Offends the September night.

Accurate scholarship can
Unearth the whole offence
From Luther until now
That has driven a culture mad,
Find what occurred at Linz,
What huge imago made
A psychopathic god:
I and the public know
What all schoolchildren learn,
Those to whom evil is done
Do evil in return.

Exiled Thucydides knew
All that a speech can say
About Democracy,
And what dictators do,
The elderly rubbish they talk
To an apathetic grave;
Analysed all in his book,
The enlightenment driven away,
The habit-forming pain,
Mismanagement and grief:
We must suffer them all again.

Into this neutral air
Where blind skyscrapers use
Their full height to proclaim
The strength of Collective Man,
Each language pours its vain
Competitive excuse:
But who can live for long
In an euphoric dream;
Out of the mirror they stare,
Imperialism's face
And the international wrong.

Faces along the bar
Cling to their average day:
The lights must never go out,
The music must always play,
All the conventions conspire
To make this fort assume
The furniture of home;
Lest we should see where we are,
Lost in a haunted wood,
Children afraid of the night
Who have never been happy or good.

The windiest militant trash
Important Persons shout
Is not so crude as our wish:
What mad Nijinsky wrote
About Diaghilev
Is true of the normal heart;
For the error bred in the bone
Of each woman and each man
Craves what it cannot have,
Not universal love
But to be loved alone.

From the conservative dark
Into the ethical life
The dense commuters come,
Repeating their morning vow,
"I *will* be true to the wife,
I'll concentrate more on my work,"
And helpless governors wake
To resume their compulsory game:
Who can release them now,
Who can reach the deaf,
Who can speak for the dumb?

All I have is a voice
To undo the folded lie,
The romantic lie in the brain
Of the sensual man-in-the-street
And the lie of Authority
Whose buildings grope the sky:
There is no such thing as the State
And no one exists alone;
Hunger allows no choice
To the citizen or the police;
We must love one another or die.

Defenceless under the night
Our world in stupor lies;
Yet, dotted everywhere,
Ironic points of light
Flash out wherever the Just
Exchange their messages:
May I, composed like them
Of Eros and of dust,
Beleaguered by the same
Negation and despair,
Show an affirming flame.

If I Could Tell You

Time will say nothing but I told you so,
Time only knows the price we have to pay;
If I could tell you I would let you know.

If we should weep when clowns put on their show,
If we should stumble when musicians play,
Time will say nothing but I told you so.

There are no fortunes to be told, although,
Because I love you more than I can say,
If I could tell you I would let you know.

The winds must come from somewhere when they blow,
There must be reasons why the leaves decay;
Time will say nothing but I told you so.

Perhaps the roses really want to grow,
The vision seriously intends to stay;
If I could tell you I would let you know.

Suppose the lions all get up and go,
And all the brooks and soldiers run away;
Will Time say nothing but I told you so?
If I could tell you I would let you know.

In Praise of Limestone

If it form the one landscape that we, the inconstant ones,
    Are consistently homesick for, this is chiefly
Because it dissolves in water. Mark these rounded slopes
    With their surface fragrance of thyme and, beneath,
A secret system of caves and conduits; hear the springs
    That spurt out everywhere with a chuckle,
Each filling a private pool for its fish and carving
    Its own little ravine whose cliffs entertain
The butterfly and the lizard; examine this region
    Of short distances and definite places:
What could be more like Mother or a fitter background
    For her son, the flirtatious male who lounges
Against a rock in the sunlight, never doubting
    That for all his faults he is loved; whose works are but

Extensions of his power to charm? From weathered outcrop
    To hill-top temple, from appearing waters to
Conspicuous fountains, from a wild to a formal vineyard,
    Are ingenious but short steps that a child's wish
To receive more attention than his brothers, whether
    By pleasing or teasing, can easily take.
Watch, then, the band of rivals as they climb up and down
    Their steep stone gennels in twos and threes, at times
Arm in arm, but never, thank God, in step; or engaged
    On the shady side of a square at midday in
Voluble discourse, knowing each other too well to think
    There are any important secrets, unable
To conceive a god whose temper-tantrums are moral
    And not to be pacified by a clever line
Or a good lay: for, accustomed to a stone that responds,
    They have never had to veil their faces in awe
Of a crater whose blazing fury could not be fixed;
    Adjusted to the local needs of valleys
Where everything can be touched or reached by walking,
    Their eyes have never looked into infinite space
Through the lattice-work of a nomad's comb; born lucky,
    Their legs have never encountered the fungi
And insects of the jungle, the monstrous forms and lives
    With which we have nothing, we like to hope, in common.
So, when one of them goes to the bad, the way his mind
       works
    Remains comprehensible: to become a pimp
Or deal in fake jewellery or ruin a fine tenor voice
    For effects that bring down the house, could happen to all
But the best and the worst of us . . .
                            That is why, I suppose,
    The best and worst never stayed here long but sought
Immoderate soils where the beauty was not so external,
    The light less public and the meaning of life
Something more than a mad camp. "Come!" cried the
       granite wastes,
    "How evasive is your humor, how accidental
Your kindest kiss, how permanent is death." (Saints-to-be
    Slipped away sighing.) "Come!" purred the clays and
       gravels,
"On our plains there is room for armies to drill; rivers
    Wait to be tamed and slaves to construct you a tomb
In the grand manner: soft as the earth is mankind and both
    Need to be altered." (Intendant Caesars rose and
Left, slamming the door.) But the really reckless were fetched
    By an older colder voice, the oceanic whisper:

"I am the solitude that asks and promises nothing;
    That is how I shall set you free. There is no love;
There are only the various envies, all of them sad."

    They were right, my dear, all those voices were right
And still are; this land is not the sweet home that it looks,
    Nor its peace the historical calm of a site
Where something was settled once and for all: A backward
    And dilapidated province, connected
To the big busy world by a tunnel, with a certain
    Seedy appeal, is that all it is now? Not quite:
It has a worldly duty which in spite of itself
    It does not neglect, but calls into question
All the Great Powers assume; it disturbs our rights. The poet,
    Admired for his earnest habit of calling
The sun the sun, his mind Puzzle, is made uneasy
    By these marble statues which so obviously doubt
His antimythological myth; and these gamins,
    Pursuing the scientist down the tiled colonnade
With such lively offers, rebuke his concern for Nature's
    Remotest aspects: I, too, am reproached, for what
And how much you know. Not to lose time, not to get
        caught,
    Not to be left behind, not, please! to resemble
The beasts who repeat themselves, or a thing like water
    Or stone whose conduct can be predicted, these
Are our Common Prayer, whose greatest comfort is music
    Which can be made anywhere, is invisible,
And does not smell. In so far as we have to look forward
    To death as a fact, no doubt we are right: But if
Sins can be forgiven, if bodies rise from the dead,
    These modifications of matter into
Innocent athletes and gesticulating fountains,
    Made solely for pleasure, make a further point:
The blessed will not care what angle they are regarded from,
    Having nothing to hide. Dear, I know nothing of
Either, but when I try to imagine a faultless love
    Or the life to come, what I hear is the murmur
Of underground streams, what I see is a limestone landscape.

A New Year Greeting

After an article by Mary J. Marples in
Scientific American, *January, 1969*

(*for Vassily Yanowsky*)

On this day tradition allots
   to taking stock of our lives,
my greetings to all of you, Yeasts,
   Bacteria, Viruses,
Aerobics and Anaerobics:
   A Very Happy New Year
to all for whom my ectoderm
   is as Middle-Earth to me.

For creatures your size I offer
   a free choice of habitat,
so settle yourselves in the zone
   that suits you best, in the pools
of my pores or the tropical
   forests of arm-pit and crotch,
in the deserts of my fore-arms,
   or the cool woods of my scalp.

Build colonies: I will supply
   adequate warmth and moisture,
the sebum and lipids you need,
   on condition you never
do me annoy with your presence,
   but behave as good guests should,
not rioting into acne
   or athlete's-foot or a boil.

Does my inner weather affect
   the surfaces where you live?
Do unpredictable changes
   record my rocketing plunge
from fairs when the mind is in tift
   and relevant thoughts occur
to fouls when nothing will happen
   and no one calls and it rains.

I should like to think that I make
   a not impossible world,

but an Eden it cannot be:
    my games, my purposive acts,
may turn to catastrophes there.
    If you were religious folk,
how would your dramas justify
    unmerited suffering?

By what myths would your priests account
    for the hurricanes that come
twice every twenty-four hours,
    each time I dress or undress,
when, clinging to keratin rafts,
    whole cities are swept away
to perish in space, or the Flood
    that scalds to death when I bathe?

Then, sooner or later, will dawn
    a Day of Apocalypse,
when my mantle suddenly turns
    too cold, too rancid, for you,
appetising to predators
    of a fiercer sort, and I
am stripped of excuse and nimbus,
    a Past, subject to Judgement.

A. D. HOPE

The Wandering Islands

You cannot build bridges between the wandering islands;
The Mind has no neighbours, and the unteachable heart
Announces its armistice time after time, but spends
Its love to draw them closer and closer apart.

They are not on the chart; they turn indifferent shoulders
On the island-hunters; they are not afraid
Of Cook or De Quiros, nor of the empire-builders;
By missionary bishops and the tourist trade

They are not annexed; they claim no fixed position;
They take no pride in a favoured latitude;
The committee of atolls inspires in them no devotion
And the earthquake belt no special attitude.

A refuge only for the shipwrecked sailor;
He sits on the shore and sullenly masturbates,
Dreaming of rescue, the pubs in the ports of call or
The big-hipped harlots at the dockyard gates.

But the wandering islands drift on their own business,
Incurious whether the whales swim round or under,
Investing no fear in ultimate forgiveness.
If they clap together, it is only casual thunder

And yet they are hurt – for the social polyps never
Girdle their bare shores with a moral reef;
When the icebergs grind them they know both beauty
      and terror;
They are not exempt from ordinary grief;

And the sudden ravages of love surprise
Them like acts of God – its irresistible function
They have never treated with convenient lies
As a part of geography or an institution.

An instant of fury, a bursting mountain of spray,
They rush together, their promontories lock,
An instant the castaway hails the castaway,
But the sounds perish in that earthquake shock.

And then, in the crash of ruined cliffs, the smother
And swirl of foam, the wandering islands part.
But all that one mind ever knows of another,
Or breaks the long isolation of the heart,

Was in that instant. The shipwrecked sailor senses
His own despair in a retreating face.
Around him he hears in the huge monotonous voices
Of wave and wind: "The Rescue will not take place."

Imperial Adam

Imperial Adam, naked in the dew,
Felt his brown flanks and found the rib was gone.
Puzzled he turned and saw where, two and two,
The mighty spoor of Jahweh marked the lawn.

Then he remembered through mysterious sleep
The surgeon fingers probing at the bone,
The voice so far away, so rich and deep:
"It is not good for him to live alone."

Turning once more he found Man's counterpart
In tender parody breathing at his side.
He knew her at first sight, he knew by heart
Her allegory of sense unsatisfied.

The pawpaw drooped its golden breasts above
Less generous than the honey of her flesh;
The innocent sunlight showed the place of love;
The dew on its dark hairs winked crisp and fresh.

This plump gourd severed from his virile root,
She promised on the turf of Paradise
Delicious pulp of the forbidden fruit;
Sly as the snake she loosed her sinuous thighs,

And waking, smiled up at him from the grass;
Her breasts rose softly and he heard her sigh –
From all the beasts whose pleasant task it was
In Eden to increase and multiply

Adam had learned the jolly deed of kind:
He took her in his arms and there and then,
Like the clean beasts, embracing from behind,
Began in joy to found the breed of men.

Then from the spurt of seed within her broke
Her terrible and triumphant female cry,
Split upward by the sexual lightning stroke.
It was the beasts now who stood watching by:

The gravid elephant, the calving hind,
The breeding bitch, the she-ape big with young
Were the first gentle midwives of mankind;
The teeming lioness rasped her with her tongue;

The proud vicuña nuzzled her as she slept
Lax on the grass; and Adam watching too
Saw how her dumb breasts at their ripening wept,
The great pod of her belly swelled and grew,

And saw its water break, and saw, in fear,
Its quaking muscles in the act of birth,
Between her legs a pigmy face appear,
And the first murderer lay upon the earth.

On an Engraving by Casserius

For Dr John Z. Bowers

Set on this bubble of dead stone and sand,
Lapped by its frail balloon of lifeless air,
Alone in the inanimate void, they stand,
These clots of thinking molecules who stare
Into the night of nescience and death,
And, whirled about with their terrestrial ball,
Ask of all being its motion and its frame:
This of all human images takes my breath;
Of all the joys in being a man at all,
This folds my spirit in its quickening flame.

Turning the leaves of this majestic book
My thoughts are with those great cosmographers,
Surgeon adventurers who undertook
To probe and chart time's other universe.
This one engraving holds me with its theme:
More than all maps made in that century
Which set true bearings for each cape and star,
De Quiros' vision or Newton's cosmic dream,
This reaches towards the central mystery
Of whence our being draws and what we are.

It came from that great school in Padua:
Casserio and Spiegel made this page.
Vesalius, who designed the *Fabrica*,
There strove, but burned his book at last in rage;
Fallopius by its discipline laid bare
The elements of this Humanity
Without which none knows that which treats the soul;
Fabricius talked with Galileo there:
Did those rare spirits in their colloquy
Divine in their two skills the single goal?

"One force that moves the atom and the star,"
Says Galileo, "one basic law beneath
All change!" "Would light from Achernar
Reveal how embryon forms within its sheath?"
Fabricius asks, and smiles. Talk such as this,
Ranging the bounds of our whole universe,
Could William Harvey once have heard? And once
Hearing, strike out that strange hypothesis,
Which in *De Motu Cordis* twice recurs,
Coupling the heart's impulsion with the sun's?

Did Thomas Browne at Padua, too, in youth
Hear of their talk of universal law
And form that notion of particular truth
Framed to correct a science they foresaw,
That darker science of which he used to speak
In later years and called the Crooked Way
Of Providence? Did *he* foresee perhaps
An age in which all sense of the unique,
And singular dissolves, like ours today,
In diagrams, statistics, tables, maps?

Not here! The graver's tool in this design
Aims still to give not general truth alone,
Blue-print of science or data's formal line:
Here in its singularity he has shown
The image of an individual soul;
Bodied in this one woman, he makes us see
The shadow of his anatomical laws.
An artist's vision animates the whole,
Shines through the scientist's detailed scrutiny
And links the person and the abstract cause.

Such were the charts of those who pressed beyond
Vesalius their master, year by year
Tracing each bone, each muscle, every frond
Of nerve until the whole design lay bare.
Thinking of this dissection, I descry
The tiers of faces, their teacher in his place,
The talk at the cadaver carried in:
"A woman – with child!"; I hear the master's dry
Voice as he lifts a scalpel from its case:
"With each new step in science, we begin."

Who was she? Though they never knew her name,
Dragged from the river, found in some alley at dawn,
This corpse none cared, or dared perhaps, to claim,
The dead child in her belly still unborn,
Might have passed, momentary as a shooting star,
Quenched like the misery of her personal life,
Had not the foremost surgeon of Italy,
Giulio Casserio of Padua,
Bought her for science, questioned her with his knife,
And drawn her for his great *Anatomy*;

Where still in the abundance of her grace,
She stands among the monuments of time
And, with a feminine delicacy displays
His elegant dissection: the sublime
Shaft of her body opens like a flower
Whose petals, folded back expose the womb,
Cord and placenta and the sleeping child,
Like instruments of music in a room
Left when her grieving Orpheus left his tower
Forever, for the desert and the wild.

Naked she waits against a tideless shore,
A sibylline stance, a noble human frame
Such as those old anatomists loved to draw.
She turns her head as though in trouble or shame,
Yet with a dancer's gesture holds the fruit
Plucked, though not tasted, of the Fatal Tree.
Something of the first Eve is in this pose
And something of the second in the mute
Offering of her child in death to be
Love's victim and her flesh its mystic rose.

No figure with wings of fire and back-swept hair
Swoops with his: Blessed among Women!; no sword
Of the spirit cleaves or quickens her; yet there
She too was overshadowed by the Word,
Was chosen, and by her humble gift of death
The lowly and the poor in heart give tongue,
Wisdom puts down the mighty from their seat;
The vile rejoice and rising, hear beneath
Scalpel and forceps, tortured into song,
Her body utter their magnificat.

Four hundred years since first that cry rang out:
Four hundred years, the patient, probing knife

Cut towards its answer – yet we stand in doubt:
Living, we cannot tell the source of life.
Old science, old certainties that lit our way
Shrink to poor guesses, dwindle to a myth.
Today's truths teach us how we were beguiled;
Tomorrow's how blind our vision of today.
The universals we thought to conjure with
Pass: there remain the mother and the child.

Loadstone, loadstar, alike to each new age,
There at the crux of time they stand and scan,
Past every scrutiny of prophet or sage,
Still unguessed prospects in this venture of Man.
To generations which we leave behind,
They taught a difficult, selfless skill: to show
The mask beyond the mask beyond the mask;
To ours another vista, where the mind
No longer asks for answers, but to know:
What questions are there which we fail to ask?

Who knows, but to the age to come they speak
Words that our own is still unapt to hear:
"These are the limits of all you sought and seek;
More our yet unborn nature cannot bear.
Learn now that all man's intellectual quest
Was but the stirrings of a foetal sleep;
The birth you cannot haste and cannot stay
Nears its appointed time; turn now and rest
Till that new nature ripens, till the deep
Dawns with that unimaginable day."

LOUIS MacNEICE

Snow

The room was suddenly rich and the great bay-window was
Spawning snow and pink roses against it
Soundlessly collateral and incompatible:
World is suddener than we fancy it.

World is crazier and more of it than we think,
Incorrigibly plural. I peel and portion
A tangerine and spit the pips and feel
The drunkenness of things being various.

And the fire flames with a bubbling sound for world
Is more spiteful and gay than one supposes –
On the tongue on the eyes on the ears in the palms of one's
    hands –
There is more than glass between the snow and the huge
    roses.

The Sunlight on the Garden

The sunlight on the garden
Hardens and grows cold,
We cannot cage the minute
Within its nets of gold,
When all is told
We cannot beg for pardon.

Our freedom as free lances
Advances towards its end;
The earth compels, upon it
Sonnets and birds descend;
And soon, my friend,
We shall have no time for dances.

The sky was good for flying
Defying the church bells
And every evil iron
Siren and what it tells:
The earth compels,
We are dying, Egypt, dying

And not expecting pardon,
Hardened in heart anew,
But glad to have sat under
Thunder and rain with you,
And grateful too
For sunlight on the garden.

Bagpipe Music

It's no go the merrygoround, it's no go the rickshaw,
All we want is a limousine and a ticket for the peepshow.
Their knickers are made of crêpe-de-chine, their shoes are made of
    python,
Their halls are lined with tiger rugs and their walls with heads of
    bison.

John MacDonald found a corpse, put it under the sofa,
Waited till it came to life and hit it with a poker,
Sold its eyes for souvenirs, sold its blood for whiskey,
Kept its bones for dumb-bells to use when he was fifty.

It's no go the Yogi-Man, it's no go Blavatsky,
All we want is a bank balance and a bit of skirt in a taxi.

Annie MacDougall went to milk, caught her foot in the heather,
Woke to hear a dance record playing of Old Vienna.
It's no go your maidenheads, it's no go your culture,
All we want is a Dunlop tyre and the devil mend the puncture.

The Laird o' Phelps spent Hogmanay declaring he was sober,
Counted his feet to prove the fact and found he had one foot over.
Mrs Carmichael had her fifth, looked at the job with repulsion,
Said to the midwife "Take it away; I'm through with
    overproduction."

It's no go the gossip column, it's no go the Ceilidh,
All we want is a mother's help and a sugar-stick for the baby.

Willie Murray cut his thumb, couldn't count the damage,
Took the hide of an Ayrshire cow and used it for a bandage.
His brother caught three hundred cran when the seas were lavish,
Threw the bleeders back in the sea and went upon the parish.

It's no go the Herring Board, it's no go the Bible,
All we want is a packet of fags when our hands are idle.

It's no go the picture palace, it's no go the stadium,
It's no go the country cot with a pot of pink geraniums,
It's no go the Government grants, it's no go the elections,
Sit on your arse for fifty years and hang your hat on a pension.

It's no go my honey love, it's no go my poppet;
Work your hands from day to day, the winds will blow the profit.
The glass is falling hour by hour, the glass will fall for ever,
But if you break the bloody glass you won't hold up the weather.

Evening in Connecticut

Equipoise: becalmed
Trees, a dome of kindness;
Only the scissory noise of the grasshoppers;
Only the shadows longer and longer.

The lawn a raft
In a sea of singing insects,
Sea without waves or mines or premonitions:
Life on a china cup.

But turning. The trees turn
Soon to brocaded autumn.
Fall. The fall of dynasties; the emergence
Of sleeping kings from caves –

Beard over the breastplate,
Eyes not yet in focus, red
Hair on the back of the hands, unreal
Heraldic axe in the hands.

Unreal but still can strike.
And in defence we cannot call on the evening
Or the seeming-friendly woods –
Nature is not to be trusted,

Nature whose falls of snow,
Falling softer than catkins,
Bury the lost and over their grave a distant
Smile spreads in the sun.

Not to be trusted, no,
Deaf at the best; she is only
And always herself, Nature is only herself,
Only the shadows longer and longer.

Prayer before Birth

I am not yet born; O hear me.
Let not the bloodsucking bat or the rat or the stoat or the
    club-footed ghoul come near me.

I am not yet born, console me.
I fear that the human race may with tall walls wall me,
    with strong drugs dope me, with wise lies lure me,
        on black racks rack me, in blood-baths roll me.

I am not yet born; provide me
With water to dandle me, grass to grow for me, trees to talk
    to me, sky to sing to me, birds and a white light
        in the back of my mind to guide me.

I am not yet born; forgive me
For the sins that in me the world shall commit, my words
    when they speak me, my thoughts when they think me,
        my treason engendered by traitors beyond me,
            my life when they murder by means of my
                hands, my death when they live me.

I am not yet born; rehearse me
In the parts I must play and the cues I must take when
    old men lecture me, bureaucrats hector me, mountains
        frown at me, lovers laugh at me, the white
            waves call me to folly and the desert calls
                me to doom and the beggar refuses
                    my gift and my children curse me.

I am not yet born; O hear me,
Let not the man who is beast or who thinks he is God
    come near me.

I am not yet born; O fill me
With strength against those who would freeze my
    humanity, would dragoon me into a lethal automaton,
        would make me a cog in a machine, a thing with
            one face, a thing, and against all those
                who would dissipate my entirety, would
                    blow me like thistledown hither and
                        thither or hither and thither
                          like water held in the
                            hands would spill me.

Let them not make me a stone and let them not spill me.
Otherwise kill me.

House on a Cliff

Indoors the tang of a tiny oil lamp. Outdoors
The winking signal on the waste of sea.
Indoors the sound of the wind. Outdoors the wind.
Indoors the locked heart and the lost key.

Outdoors the chill, the void, the siren. Indoors
The strong man pained to find his red blood cools,
While the blind clock grows louder, faster. Outdoors
The silent moon, the garrulous tides she rules.

Indoors ancestral curse-cum-blessing. Outdoors
The empty bowl of heaven, the empty deep.
Indoors a purposeful man who talks at cross
Purposes, to himself, in a broken sleep.

Selva Oscura

A house can be haunted by those who were never there
If there was where they were missed. Returning to such
Is it worse if you miss the same or another or none?
The haunting anyway is too much.
You have to leave the house to clear the air.

A life can be haunted by what it never was
If that were merely glimpsed. Lost in the maze
That means yourself and never out of the wood
These days, though lost, will be all your days;
Life, if you leave it, must be left for good.

And yet for good can be also where I am,
Stumbling among dark treetrunks, should I meet
One sudden shaft of light from the hidden sky
Or, finding bluebells bathe my feet,
Know that the world, though more, is also I.

Perhaps suddenly too I strike a clearing and see
Some unknown house – or was it mine? – but now
It welcomes whom I miss in welcoming me;
The door swings open and a hand
Beckons to all the life my days allow.

E. J. SCOVELL

Past Time

You'll never understand *No Road This Way*,
But like a lost bird, on the window pane
Beating for skies, you'll throw yourself again
On the glass daylight of departed day.
For there seems open country: "There," you'll say,
"The high streams flow between the sky and plain,
Between the hills so bright with hanging rain
The sky's thin atoms are less clear than they."
But light of yesterday is cold like glass.
Time that is past harder than diamond
Turns the fine air, and freezes to the bone.
The sap stirs once and slumbers when we pass.
The breath we breathe just thaws the air beyond,
Till stone we waked returns to harder stone.

The Ghosts

The days of our ghosthood were these:
When we were children, when we had no keys
We entered through closed doors, unseen went out again.
Our souls were the dissolved, ungathered, filtering rain.
Our bodies sat upon our parents' knees.

In the second days of our ghosthood
We went on foot among a multitude,
In time of drought, in our hard youth, we winter-born.
And those were visible to men as flowers in corn
Whose souls were eyes unseen that gaze from dark.

We entered flesh and took our veil, our state.
The third days of our ghosthood wait.
When we are stripped by pain, by coming death far-seen,
Of earthly loves, earth's fruit, that came so late to hand,
With that waking or falling into dream
We shall not cross into an unfamiliar land.

Shadows of Chrysanthemums

Where the flowers lean to their shadows on the wall
The shadow flowers outshine them all,
Answering their wild lightness with a deeper tone
And clearer pattern than their own
(For they are like flames in sun, or saints in trance,
Almost invisible, dissolved in radiance).

But space in that shadow world lengthens, its creatures
Fall back and distance takes their features;
The shadows of the flowers that lean away
Are blurred like milky nebulae;
And faint as though a ghost had risen between
The lamplight and the wall, they seem divined, not seen.

The dying wild chrysanthemums, the white,
Yellow and pink are levelled in light;
But here in their shadows, tones remain, where deep
Is set on deep, and pallors keep
Their far-off stations, and the florets more
Subtly crisp their bright profiles, or are lost in the flower.

The River Steamer

Waiting for a spirit to trouble the water.

Waiting for a spirit from beneath or over
To trouble the surface of the river
From which the hours like clouds reflected gaze
White, and the daylight shines of all earth's days,

Waiting for a spirit to dissolve the glass,
I see, in the unbreaking wave that fans from us,
Incline and circle the reeds and sedges;
And see the ripples on the under sides of bridges

And under the dark green leaves of deepest summer
And the green awning of the river steamer,
The secondary ripple, the shadow's shadow,
Abstract and pure appearance, follow and follow;

And see the roan banks flecked with rose and seed
Of willow-herb, and fields beside the river-bed
Freshened by total light in day's decline,
And the elms standing in the heart of the sun;

And hear the passengers telling the day's praises,
And the tired wildness of their children's voices
Too young for the journey's hours; and all of these
Clear in the river's glass, I also praise,

Waiting for a spirit to transpierce the glaze.

The Sandy Yard

One day at noon I crossed
A sandy yard planted with citrus trees
Behind a small hotel. I walked slowly in the sun
With feet in the hot sand which the leaf-cutting ants
Crossed too, under their little sails of green, filing
Intent; and I thought, this
I will keep, I will register with time: I am here;
And always, shall have been here – that is the wonder –
Never, now, not have been here; for now I am here,
Crossing the sandy yard
Between the citrus trees, behind the small hotel.

Listening to Collared Doves

I am homesick now for middle age, as then
For youth. For youth is our home-land: we were born
And lived there long, though afterwards moved on
From state to state, too slowly acclimatising
Perhaps and never fluent, through the surprising
Countries, in any languages but one.

This mourning now for middle age, no more
For youth, confirms me old as not before.
Age rounds the world, they say, to childhood's far
Archaic shores; it may be so at last.
But what now (strength apart) I miss the most
Is time unseen like air, since everywhere.

And yet, when in the months and in the skies
That were the cuckoos', and in the nearer trees
That were the deep-voiced wood-pigeons', it is
Instead now the collared doves that call and call
(Their three flat notes growing traditional),
I think we live long enough, listening to these.

I draw my line out from their simple curve
And say, our natural span may be enough;
And think of one I knew and her long life;
And how the climate changed and how the sign-
Posts changed, defaced, from her Victorian
Childhood and youth, through our century of grief;

And how she adapted as she could, not one
By nature adaptable, bred puritan
(Though quick to be pleased and having still her own
Lightness of heart). She died twenty years ago,
Aged, of life – it seems, all she could do
Having done, all the change that she could know having
     known.

Water Images

The Tidal River

The trees descend, image of love,
To drink the brackish water of
Estuary or tidal river,
To lean their inland fulness over
That bright and far-brought mineral other.

The Stream

So turbid though I am,
Rooted in me the young
Floated like water lilies –
That now alight like swans.

The Well

The stone you let fall in me will not resile
Nor echo nor give any sign awhile.
Wait for my word. A lifetime you may wait,
I am so deep, my depth so obdurate,
Not with my will but through my fate.

THEODORE ROETHKE

The Premonition

Walking this field I remember
Days of another summer.
Oh that was long ago! I kept
Close to the heels of my father,
Matching his stride with half-steps
Until we came to a river.
He dipped his hand in the shallow:
Water ran over and under
Hair on a narrow wrist bone;
His image kept following after, –
Flashed with the sun in the ripple.
But when he stood up, that face
Was lost in a maze of water.

Mid-Country Blow

All night and all day the wind roared in the trees,
Until I could think there were waves rolling high as my bedroom
    floor;
When I stood at the window, an elm bough swept to my knees;
The blue spruce lashed like a surf at the door.

The second dawn I would not have believed:
The oak stood with each leaf stiff as a bell.
When I looked at the altered scene, my eye was undeceived,
But my ear still kept the sound of the sea like a shell.

Root Cellar

Nothing would sleep in that cellar, dank as a ditch,
Bulbs broke out of boxes hunting for chinks in the dark,
Shoots dangled and drooped,
Lolling obscenely from mildewed crates,
Hung down long yellow evil necks, like tropical snakes.
And what a congress of stinks! –
Roots ripe as old bait,

Pulpy stems, rank, silo–rich,
Leaf–mold, manure, lime, piled against slippery planks.
Nothing would give up life:
Even the dirt kept breathing a small breath.

Orchids

They lean over the path,
Adder–mouthed,
Swaying close to the face,
Coming out, soft and deceptive,
Limp and damp, delicate as a young bird's tongue;
Their fluttery fledgling lips
Move slowly,
Drawing in the warm air.

And at night,
The faint moon falling through whitewashed glass,
The heat going down
So their musky smell comes even stronger,
Drifting down from their mossy cradles:
So many devouring infants!
Soft luminescent fingers,
Lips neither dead nor alive,
Loose ghostly mouths
Breathing.

Big Wind

Where were the greenhouses going,
Lunging into the lashing
Wind driving water
So far down the river
All the faucets stopped?—
So we drained the manure-machine
For the steam plant,
Pumping the stale mixture
Into the rusty boilers,
Watching the pressure gauge
Waver over to red,
As the seams hissed
And the live steam

Drove to the far
End of the rose-house,
Where the worst wind was,
Creaking the cypress window-frames,
Cracking so much thin glass
We stayed all night,
Stuffing the holes with burlap;
But she rode it out,
That old rose-house,
She hove into the teeth of it,
The core and the pith of that ugly storm,
Ploughing with her stiff prow,
Bucking into the wind-waves
That broke over the whole of her,
Flailing her sides with spray,
Flinging long string of wet across the roof-top,
Finally veering, wearing themselves out, merely
Whistling thinly under the wind-vents;
She sailed until the calm morning,
Carrying her full cargo of roses.

All the Earth, All the Air

1

I stand with standing stones.
The stones stay where they are.
The twiny winders wind;
The little fishes move.
A ripple wakes the pond.

2

This joy's my fall. I am! —
A man rich as a cat,
A cat in the fork of a tree,
When she shakes out her hair.
I think of that, and laugh.

3

All innocence and wit,
She keeps my wishes warm;
When, easy as a beast,
She steps along the street,
I start to leave myself.

4

The truly beautiful,
Their bodies cannot lie:
The blossom stings the bee.
The ground needs the abyss,
Say the stones, say the fish.

5

A field recedes in sleep.
Where are the dead? Before me
Floats a single star.
A tree glides with the moon.
The field is mine! Is mine!

6

In a lurking-place I lurk,
One with the sullen dark.
What's hell but a cold heart?
But who, faced with her face,
Would not rejoice?

Otto

1

He was the youngest son of a strange brood,
A Prussian who learned early to be rude
To fools and frauds: He does not put on airs
Who lived above a potting shed for years.
I think of him, and I think of his men,
As close to him as any kith or kin.
Max Laurisch had the greenest thumb of all.
A florist does not woo the beautiful:
He potted plants as if he hated them.
What root of his ever denied its stem?
When flowers grew, their bloom extended him.

2

His hand could fit into a woman's glove,
And in a wood he knew whatever moved;
Once when he saw two poachers on his land,
He threw his rifle over with one hand;
Dry bark flew in their faces from his shot, –
He always knew what he was aiming at.

They stood there with their guns; he walked toward,
Without his rifle, and slapped each one hard;
It was no random act, for those two men
Had slaughtered game, and cut young fir trees down.
I was no more than seven at the time.

3

A house with flowers! House upon house they built,
Whether for love or out of obscure guilt
For ancestors who loved a warlike show,
Or Frenchmen killed a hundred years ago,
And yet still violent men, whose stacked-up guns
Killed every cat that neared their pheasant runs;
When Hattie Wright's angora died as well,
My father took it to her, by the tail.
Who loves the small can be both saint and boor,
(And some grow out of shape, their seed impure;)
The Indians loved him, and the Polish poor.

4

In my mind's eye I see those fields of glass,
As I looked out at them from the high house,
Riding beneath the moon, hid from the moon,
Then slowly breaking whiter in the dawn;
When George the watchman's lantern dropped from sight
The long pipes knocked: it was the end of night.
I'd stand upon my bed, a sleepless child
Watching the waking of my father's world. –
O world so far away! O my lost world!

GEORGE OPPEN

"No interval of manner"

No interval of manner
Your body in the sun.
You? A solid, this that the dress
    insisted,
Your face unaccented, your mouth a mouth?
    Practical knees:
It is you who truly
Excel the vegetable,
The fitting of grasses – more bare than
    that.

Pointedly bent, your elbow on a car-edge
Incognito as summer
Among mechanics.

Product

There is no beauty in New England like the boats.
Each itself, even the paint white
Dipping to each wave each time
At anchor, mast
And rigging tightly part of it
Fresh from the dry tools
And the dry New England hands.
The bow soars, finds the waves
The hull accepts. Once someone
Put a bowl afloat
And there for all to see, for all the children,
Even the New Englander
Was boatness. What I've seen
Is all I've found: myself.

Psalm

Veritas sequitur . . .

In the small beauty of the forest
The wild deer bedding down –
That they are there!

            Their eyes
Effortless, the soft lips
Nuzzle and the alien small teeth
Tear at the grass

            The roots of it
Dangle from their mouths
Scattering earth in the strange woods.
They who are there.

            Their paths
Nibbled thru the fields, the leaves that shade them
Hang in the distances
Of sun

                        The small nouns
Crying faith
In this in which the wild deer
Startle, and stare out.

Penobscot

Children of the early
Countryside

Talk on the back stoops
Of that locked room
Of their birth

Which they cannot remember

In these small stony worlds
In the ocean

Like a core
Of an antiquity

Non classic, anti-classic, not the ocean
But the flat
Water of the harbor
Touching the stone

They stood on –

I think we will not breach the world
These small worlds least
Of all with secret names

Or unexpected phrases –

Penobscot
Half deserted, has an air
Of northern age, the rocks and pines

And the inlets of the sea
Shining among the islands

And these innocent
People
In their carpentered

Homes, nailed
Against the weather – It is more primitive

Than I know
To live like this, to tinker
And to sleep

Near the birches
That shine in the moonlight

Distant
From the classic world – the north

Looks out from its rock
Bulging into the fields, wild flowers
Growing at its edges! It is a place its women

Love, which is the country's
Distinction –

The canoes in the forest
And the small prows of the fish boats
Off the coast in the dead of winter

That burns like a Tyger
In the night sky. One sees their homes and lawns,
The pale wood houses

And the pale green
Terraced lawns.
"It brightens up into the branches

And against the buildings"
Early. That was earlier.

Confession

"neither childhood
nor future

are growing less" guilts   guilts
pour in

to memory things leak I am an old ship
and leaky   oceans

in the bilges ordinary

oceans in the bilges I come to know it is so guilts
    guilts

failures in the creaking
timbers but to have touched

foundations keels on the cellars
as all this becomes strange

enough
I come to know it is home a groping

down a going
down middle-voice the burgeoning

desolate   magic   the dark
grain

of sand and eternity

STEPHEN SPENDER

"My parents kept me from children who were rough"

My parents kept me from children who were rough
Who threw words like stones and who wore torn clothes.
Their thighs showed through rags. They ran in the street
And climbed cliffs and stripped by the country streams.

I feared more than tigers their muscles like iron
Their jerking hands and their knees tight on my arms.
I feared the salt coarse pointing of those boys
Who copied my lisp behind me on the road.

They were lithe, they sprang out behind hedges
Like dogs to bark at my world. They threw mud
While I looked the other way, pretending to smile.
I longed to forgive them, but they never smiled.

"What I expected, was"

What I expected, was
Thunder, fighting,
Long struggles with men
And climbing.
After continual straining
I should grow strong;
Then the rocks would shake,
And I rest long.

What I had not foreseen
Was the gradual day
Weakening the will
Leaking the brightness away,
The lack of good to touch,
The fading of body and soul
– Smoke before wind,
Corrupt, unsubstantial.

The wearing of Time,
And the watching of cripples pass
With limbs shaped like questions
In their odd twist,
The pulverous grief
Melting the bones with pity,
The sick falling from earth –
These, I could not foresee.

Expecting always
Some brightness to hold in trust,
Some final innocence
Except from dust,
That, hanging solid,
Would dangle through all,
Like the created poem,
Or faceted crystal.

"I think continually of those who were truly great"

I think continually of those who were truly great.
Who, from the womb, remembered the soul's history
Through corridors of light where the hours are suns,
Endless and singing. Whose lovely ambition

Was that their lips, still touched with fire,
Should tell of the Spirit, clothed from head to foot in song.
And who hoarded from the Spring branches
The desires falling across their bodies like blossoms.

What is precious, is never to forget
The essential delight of the blood drawn from ageless springs
Breaking through rocks in worlds before our earth.
Never to deny its pleasure in the morning simple light
Nor its grave evening demand for love.
Never to allow gradually the traffic to smother
With noise and fog, the flowering of the Spirit.

Near the snow, near the sun, in the highest fields,
See how these names are fêted by the waving grass
And by the streamers of white cloud
And whispers of wind in the listening sky.
The names of those who in their lives fought for life,
Who wore at their hearts the fire's centre.
Born of the sun, they travelled a short while toward the sun
And left the vivid air signed with their honour.

NORMAN MacCAIG

Climbing Suilven

I nod and nod to my own shadow and thrust
A mountain down and down.
Between my feet a loch shines in the brown,
Its silver paper crinkled and edged with rust.
My lungs say No;
But down and down this treadmill hill must go.

Parishes dwindle. But my parish is
This stone, that tuft, this stone
And the cramped quarters of my flesh and bone.
I claw that tall horizon down to this;
And suddenly
My shadow jumps huge miles away from me.

Feeding Ducks

One duck stood on my toes.
The others made watery rushes after bread
Thrown by my momentary hand; instead,
She stood duck-still and got far more than those.

An invisible drone boomed by
With a beetle in it; the neighbour's yearning bull
Bugled across five fields. And an evening full
Of other evenings quietly began to die.

And my everlasting hand
Dropped on my hypocrite duck her grace of bread.
And I thought, "The first to be fattened, the first
    to be dead,"
Till my gestures enlarged, wide over the darkening land.

No Consolation

I consoled myself for not being able to describe
water trickling down a wall or
a wall being trickled down by water
by reflecting that I can see
these two things are not the same thing:
which is more than a wall can do,
or water.
    – But how hard it is
to live at a remove
from a common wall, that keeps out and
keeps in, and from water, that
saves you and drowns you.

But when I went on to notice
that I could see the pair of them
as a trickling wall or as a wall
of water,
it became clear that I can describe only
my own inventions.
    – And how odd to suppose
you prove you love your wife
by continually committing adultery
with her.

Crossing the Border

I sit with my back to the engine, watching
the landscape pouring away out of my eyes.
I think I know where I'm going and have
some choice in the matter.

I think, too, that this was a country
of bog-trotters, moss-troopers,
fired ricks and roof-trees in the black night – glinting
on tossed horns and red blades.
I think of lives
bubbling into the harsh grass.

What difference now?
I sit with my back to the future, watching
time pouring away into the past. I sit, being helplessly
lugged backwards
through the Debatable Lands of history, listening
to the execrations, the scattered cries, the
falling of roof-trees
in the lamentable dark.

So Many Summers

Beside one loch, a hind's neat skeleton,
Beside another, a boat pulled high and dry:
Two neat geometries drawn in the weather:
Two things already dead and still to die.

I passed them every summer, rod in hand,
Skirting the bright blue or the spitting gray,
And, every summer, saw how the bleached timbers
Gaped wider and the neat ribs fell away.

Time adds one malice to another one –
Now you'd look very close before you knew
If it's the boat that ran, the hind went sailing.
So many summers, and I have lived them too.

Toad

Stop looking like a purse. How could a purse
squeeze under the rickety door and sit,
full of satisfaction, in a man's house?

You clamber towards me on your four corners –
right hand, left foot, left hand, right foot.

I love you for being a toad,
for crawling like a Japanese wrestler,
and for not being frightened.

I put you in my purse hand, not shutting it,
and set you down outside directly under
every star.

A jewel in your head? Toad,
you've put one in mine,
a tiny radiance in a dark place.

CHARLES OLSON

The Kingfishers

I

I

What does not change / is the will to change

He woke, fully clothed, in his bed. He
remembered only one thing, the birds, how
when he came in, he had gone around the rooms
and got them back in their cage, the green one first,
she with the bad leg, and then the blue,
the one they had hoped was a male

Otherwise? Yes, Fernand, who had talked lispingly of Albers &
    Angkor Vat.
He had left the party without a word. How he got up, got into his
    coat,
I do not know. When I saw him, he was at the door, but it did not
    matter,

he was already sliding along the wall of the night, losing himself
in some crack of the ruins. That it should have been he who said,
    "The kingfishers!
who cares
for their feathers
now?"

His last words had been, "The pool is slime." Suddenly everyone,
ceasing their talk, sat in a row around him, watched
they did not so much hear, or pay attention, they
wondered, looked at each other, smirked, but listened,
he repeated and repeated, could not go beyond his thought
"The pool   the kingfishers' feathers were wealth   why
did the export stop?"

It was then he left

2

I thought of the E on the stone, and of what Mao said
la lumiere"
        but the kingfisher
de l'aurore"
        but the kingfisher flew west
est devant nous!
        he got the color of his breast
        from the heat of the setting sun!

The features are, the feebleness of the feet (syndactylism of the 3rd
    & 4th digit)
the bill, serrated, sometimes a pronounced beak, the wings
where the color is, short and round, the tail
inconspicuous.

But not these things were the factors. Not the birds.
The legends are
legends. Dead, hung up indoors, the kingfisher
will not indicate a favoring wind,
or avert the thunderbolt. Nor, by its nesting,
still the waters, with the new year, for seven days.
It is true, it does nest with the opening year, but not on the waters.
It nests at the end of a tunnel bored by itself in a bank. There,
six or eight white and translucent eggs are laid, on fishbones
not on bare clay, on bones thrown up in pellets by the birds.

On these rejectamenta
(as they accumulate they form a cup-shaped structure) the young
    are born.
And, as they are fed and grow, this nest of excrement and decayed
    fish becomes

                    a dripping, fetid mass

Mao concluded:
              nous devons
                    nous lever
                        et agir!

                  3
When the attentions change/the jungle
leaps in
        even the stones are split
                they rive

Or,
enter
that other conqueror we more naturally recognize
he so resembles ourselves

But the E
cut so rudely on that oldest stone
sounded otherwise,
was differently heard

as, in another time, were treasures used:

(and, later, much later, a fine ear thought
a scarlet coat)

              "of green feathers   feet, beaks and eyes
              of gold

              "animals likewise,
              resembling snails

              "a large wheel, gold, with figures of unknown
                  four-foots,
               and worked with tufts of leaves, weight
              3800 ounces

              "last, two birds, of thread and featherwork, the quills
              gold, the feet

gold, the two birds perched on two reeds
 gold, the reeds arising from two embroidered
      mounds,
one yellow, the other
white.

     "And from each reed hung
     seven feathered tassels."

In this instance, the priests
(in dark cotton robes, and dirty,
their dishevelled hair matted with blood, and flowing wildly
over their shoulders)
rush in among the people, calling on them
to protect their gods

And all now is war
where so lately there was peace,
and the sweet brotherhood, the use
of tilled fields.

                    4

Not one death but many,
not accumulation but change, the feed-back proves, the feed-back is
the law

               Into the same river no man steps twice
               When fire dies air dies
               No one remains, nor is, one

Around an appearance, one common model, we grow up
many. Else how is it,
if we remain the same,
we take pleasure now
in what we did not take pleasure before? love
contrary objects? admire and/or find fault? use
other words, feel other passions, have
nor figure, appearance, disposition, tissue
the same?
     To be in different states without a change
     is not a possibility

We can be precise. The factors are
in the animal and/or the machine the factors are
communication and/or control, both involve

the message. And what is the message? The message is
a discrete or continuous sequence of measurable events distributed
     in time

is the birth of air, is
the birth of water, is
a state between
the origin and
the end, between
birth and the beginning of
another fetid nest

is change, presents
no more than itself
And the too strong grasping of it,
when it is pressed together and condensed,
loses it

This very thing you are

II

    They buried their dead in a sitting posture
    serpent   cane   razor   ray of the sun

    And she sprinkled water on the head of the child, crying
    "Cioa-coatl! Cioa-coatl!"
    with her face to the west

    Where the bones are found, in each personal heap
    with what each enjoyed, there is always
    the Mongolian louse

The light is in the east. Yes. And we must rise, act. Yet
in the west, despite the apparent darkness (the whiteness
which covers all), if you look, if you can bear, if you can, long
    enough

                as long as it was necessary for him, my guide
                to look into the yellow of that longest-lasting rose

so you must, and, in that whiteness, into that face, with what
    candor, look

and, considering the dryness of the place
        the long absence of an adequate race

(of the two who first came, each a conquistador, one
            healed, the other
tore the eastern idols down, toppled
the temple walls, which, says the excuser
were black from human gore)

hear
hear, where the dry blood talks
        where the old appetite walks

                        la piu saporita et migliore
                        che si possa truovar al mondo

where it hides, look
in the eye how it runs
in the flesh / chalk

                but under these petals
                in the emptiness
                regard the light, contemplate
                the flower

whence it arose

        with what violence benevolence is bought
        what cost in gesture justice brings
        what wrongs domestic rights involve
        what stalks
        this silence

        what pudor pejorocracy affronts
        how awe, night-rest and neighborhood can rot
        what breeds where dirtiness is law
        what crawls
        below

                        III
        I am no Greek, hath not th'advantage.
        And of course, no Roman:
        he can take no risk that matters,
        the risk of beauty least of all.

        But I have my kin, if for no other reason than
        (as he said, next of kin) I commit myself, and,
        given my freedom, I'd be a cad
        if I didn't. Which is most true.

It works out this way, despite the disadvantage.
I offer, in explanation, a quote:
si j'ai du goût, ce n'est guères
que pour la terre et les pierres.

Despite the discrepancy (an ocean   courage   age)
this is also true: if I have any taste
it is only because I have interested myself
in what was slain in the sun

  I pose you your question:

shall you uncover honey / where maggots are?

  I hunt among stones

At Yorktown

I

At Yorktown the church

at Yorktown the dead

at Yorktown the grass

are live

                at York-town the earth

piles itself in shallows,

declares itself, like water,

by pools and mounds

2

At Yorktown the dead

are soil

at Yorktown the church

is marl

at Yorktown the swallows

dive where it is greenest,

                              the hollows

are eyes are flowers, the heather,

equally accurate, is hands

          at York-town only the flies

dawdle, like history,

in the sun

          3

at Yorktown the earthworks

braw

at Yorktown the mortars

of brass, weathered green, of mermaids

for handles, of Latin

for texts, scream

without noise

like a gull

          4

At Yorktown the long dead

loosen the earth, heels

sink in, over an abatis

a bird wheels

and time is a shine caught blue

from a martin's

back

The Moon Is the Number 18

is a monstrance,
the blue dogs bay,
and the son sits,
grieving

is a grinning god, is
the mouth of, is
the dripping moon

while in the tower the cat
preens
and all motion
is a crab

and there is nothing he can do but what they do, watch
the face of waters, and fire

The blue dogs paw,
lick the droppings, dew
or blood, whatever
results are. And night,
the crab, rays round
attentive as the cat to catch
human sound

The blue dogs rue,
as he does, as he would howl, confronting
the wind which rocks what was her, while prayers
striate the snow, words blow
as questions cross fast, fast
as flames, as flames form, melt
along any darkness

Birth is an instance as is a host, namely, death

The moon has no air

In the red tower
in that tower where she also sat
in that particular tower where watching & moving
    are,
there,
there where what triumph there is, is: there
is all substance, all creature
all there is against the dirty moon, against
number, image, sortilege –

alone with cat & crab,
and sound is, is, his
conjecture

ELIZABETH BISHOP

The Fish

I caught a tremendous fish
and held him beside the boat
half out of water, with my hook
fast in a corner of his mouth.
He didn't fight.
He hadn't fought at all.
He hung a grunting weight,
battered and venerable
and homely. Here and there
his brown skin hung in strips
like ancient wallpaper,
and its pattern of darker brown
was like wallpaper:
shapes like full-blown roses
stained and lost through age.
He was speckled with barnacles,
fine rosettes of lime,
and infested
with tiny white sea-lice,
and underneath two or three
rags of green weed hung down.
While his gills were breathing in
the terrible oxygen
– the frightening gills,
fresh and crisp with blood,

that can cut so badly —
I thought of the coarse white flesh
packed in like feathers,
the big bones and the little bones,
the dramatic reds and blacks
of his shiny entrails,
and the pink swim-bladder
like a big peony.
I looked into his eyes
which were far larger than mine
but shallower, and yellowed,
the irises backed and packed
with tarnished tinfoil
seen through the lenses
of old scratched isinglass.
They shifted a little, but not
to return my stare.
— It was more like the tipping
of an object toward the light.
I admired his sullen face,
the mechanism of his jaw,
and then I saw
that from his lower lip
— if you could call it a lip —
grim, wet, and weaponlike,
hung five old pieces of fish-line,
or four and a wire leader
with the swivel still attached,
with all their five big hooks
grown firmly in his mouth.
A green line, frayed at the end
where he broke it, two heavier lines,
and a fine black thread
still crimped from the strain and snap
when it broke and he got away.
Like medals with their ribbons
frayed and wavering,
a five-haired beard of wisdom
trailing from his aching jaw.
I stared and stared
and victory filled up
the little rented boat,
from the pool of bilge
where oil had spread a rainbow
around the rusted engine

to the bailer rusted orange,
the sun-cracked thwarts,
the oarlocks on their strings,
the gunnels – until everything
was rainbow, rainbow, rainbow!
And I let the fish go.

Over 2,000 Illustrations and a Complete Concordance

Thus should have been our travels:
serious, engravable.
The Seven Wonders of the World are tired
and a touch familiar, but the other scenes,
innumerable, though equally sad and still,
are foreign. Often the squatting Arab,
or group of Arabs, plotting, probably,
against our Christian Empire,
while one apart, with outstretched arm and hand
points to the Tomb, the Pit, the Sepulcher.
The branches of the date-palms look like files.
The cobbled courtyard, where the Well is dry,
is like a diagram, the brickwork conduits
are vast and obvious, the human figure
far gone in history or theology,
gone with its camel or its faithful horse.
Always the silence, the gesture, the specks of birds
suspended on invisible threads above the Site,
or the smoke rising solemnly, pulled by threads.
Granted a page alone or a page made up
of several scenes arranged in cattycornered rectangles
or circles set on stippled gray,
granted a grim lunette,
caught in the toils of an initial letter,
when dwelt upon, they all resolve themselves.
The eye drops, weighted, through the lines
the burin made, the lines that move apart
like ripples above sand,
dispersing storms, God's spreading fingerprint,
and painfully, finally, that ignite
in watery prismatic white-and-blue.

Entering the Narrows at St Johns
the touching bleat of goats reached to the ship.

We glimpsed them, reddish, leaping up the cliffs
among the fog-soaked weeds and butter-and-eggs.
And at St Peter's the wind blew and the sun shone madly.
Rapidly, purposefully, the Collegians marched in lines,
crisscrossing the great square with black, like ants.
In Mexico the dead man lay
in a blue arcade; the dead volcanoes
glistened like Easter lilies.
The jukebox went on playing "Ay, Jalisco!"
And at Volubilis there were beautiful poppies
splitting the mosaics; the fat old guide made eyes.
In Dingle harbor a golden length of evening
the rotting hulks held up their dripping plush.
The Englishwoman poured tea, informing us
that the Duchess was going to have a baby.
And in the brothels of Marrakesh
the little pockmarked prostitutes
balanced their tea-trays on their heads
and did their belly-dances; flung themselves
naked and giggling against our knees,
asking for cigarettes. It was somewhere near there
I saw what frightened me most of all:
A holy grave, not looking particularly holy,
one of a group under a keyhole-arched stone baldaquin
open to every wind from the pink desert.
An open, gritty, marble trough, carved solid
with exhortation, yellowed
as scattered cattle-teeth;
half-filled with dust, not even the dust
of the poor prophet paynim who once lay there.
In a smart burnoose Khadour looked on amused.

Everything only connected by "and" and "and".
Open the book. (The gilt rubs off the edges
of the pages and pollinates the fingertips.)
Open the heavy book. Why couldn't we have seen
this old Nativity while we were at it?
– the dark ajar, the rocks breaking with light,
an undisturbed, unbreathing flame,
colorless, sparkless, freely fed on straw,
and, lulled within, a family with pets,
– and looked and looked our infant sight away.

The Shampoo

The still explosions on the rocks,
the lichens, grow
by spreading, gray, concentric shocks.
They have arranged
to meet the rings around the moon, although
within our memories they have not changed.

And since the heavens will attend
as long on us,
you've been, dear friend,
precipitate and pragmatical;
and look what happens. For Time is
nothing if not amenable.

The shooting stars in your black hair
in bright formation
are flocking where,
so straight, so soon?
– Come, let me wash it in this big tin basin,
battered and shiny like the moon.

Questions of Travel

There are too many waterfalls here; the crowded streams
hurry too rapidly down to the sea,
and the pressure of so many clouds on the mountaintops
makes them spill over the sides in soft slow-motion,
turning to waterfalls under our very eyes.
– For if those streaks, those mile-long, shiny, tearstains,
aren't waterfalls yet,
in a quick age or so, as ages go here,
they probably will be.
But if the streams and clouds keep travelling, travelling,
the mountains look like the hulls of capsized ships,
slime-hung and barnacled.

Think of the long trip home.
Should we have stayed at home and thought of here?
Where should we be today?
Is it right to be watching strangers in a play
in this strangest of theatres?
What childishness is it that while there's a breath of life

in our bodies, we are determined to rush
to see the sun the other way around?
The tiniest green hummingbird in the world?
To stare at some inexplicable old stonework,
inexplicable and impenetrable,
at any view,
instantly seen and always, always delightful?
Oh, must we dream our dreams
and have them, too?
And have we room
for one more folded sunset, still quite warm?

But surely it would have been a pity
not to have seen the trees along this road,
really exaggerated in their beauty,
not to have seen them gesturing
like noble pantomimists, robed in pink.
– Not to have had to stop for gas and heard
the sad, two-noted, wooden tune
of disparate wooden clogs
carelessly clacking over
a grease-stained filling-station floor.
(In another country the clogs would all be tested.
Each pair there would have identical pitch.)
– A pity not to have heard
the other, less primitive music of the fat brown bird
who sings above the broken gasoline pump
in a bamboo church of Jesuit baroque:
three towers, five silver crosses.
– Yes, a pity not to have pondered,
blurr'dly and inconclusively,
on what connection can exist for centuries
between the crudest wooden footwear
and, careful and finicky,
the whittled fantasies of wooden cages.
– Never to have studied history in
the weak calligraphy of songbirds' cages.
– And never to have had to listen to rain
so much like politicians' speeches:
two hours of unrelenting oratory
and then a sudden golden silence
in which the traveller takes a notebook, writes:

*"Is it lack of imagination that makes us come
to imagined places, not just stay at home?
Or could Pascal have been not entirely right
about just sitting quietly in one's room?*

*Continent, city, country, society:
the choice is never wide and never free.
And here, or there . . . No. Should we have stayed at home,
wherever that may be?"*

First Death in Nova Scotia

In the cold, cold parlor
my mother laid out Arthur
beneath the chromographs:
Edward, Prince of Wales,
with Princess Alexandra,
and King George with Queen Mary.
Below them on the table
stood a stuffed loon
shot and stuffed by Uncle
Arthur, Arthur's father.

Since Uncle Arthur fired
a bullet into him,
he hadn't said a word.
He kept his own counsel
on his white, frozen lake,
the marble-topped table.
His breast was deep and white,
cold and caressable;
his eyes were red glass,
much to be desired.

"Come," said my mother,
"Come and say good-bye
to your little cousin Arthur."
I was lifted up and given
one lily of the valley
to put in Arthur's hand.
Arthur's coffin was
a little frosted cake,
and the red-eyed loon eyed it
from his white, frozen lake.

Arthur was very small.
He was all white, like a doll
that hadn't been painted yet.
Jack Frost had started to paint him
the way he always painted
the Maple Leaf (Forever).
He had just begun on his hair,
a few red strokes, and then
Jack Frost had dropped the brush
and left him white, forever.

The gracious royal couples
were warm in red and ermine;
their feet were well wrapped up
in the ladies' ermine trains.
They invited Arthur to be
the smallest page at court.
But how could Arthur go,
clutching his tiny lily,
with his eyes shut up so tight
and the roads deep in snow?

One Art

The art of losing isn't hard to master;
so many things seem filled with the intent
to be lost that their loss is no disaster.

Lose something every day. Accept the fluster
of lost door keys, the hour badly spent.
The art of losing isn't hard to master.

Then practice losing farther, losing faster:
places, and names, and where it was you meant
to travel. None of these will bring disaster.

I lost my mother's watch. And look! my last, or
next-to-last, of three loved houses went.
The art of losing isn't hard to master.

I lost two cities, lovely ones. And, vaster,
some realms I owned, two rivers, a continent.
I miss them, but it wasn't a disaster.

– Even losing you (the joking voice, a gesture
I love) I shan't have lied. It's evident
the art of losing's not too hard to master
though it may look like (*Write* it!) like disaster.

ALLEN CURNOW

Country School

You know the school; you call it old –
Scrub-worn floors and paint all peeled
On barge-board, weatherboard and gibbet belfry.

Pinus betrays, with rank tufts topping
The roof-ridge, scattering bravely
Nor'west gale as a reef its waves
While the small girls squeal at skipping
And magpies hoot from the eaves.

For scantling *Pinus* stands mature
In less than the life of a man;
The rusty saplings, the school, and you
Together your lives began.

O sweet antiquity! Look, the stone
That skinned your knees. How small
Are the terrible doors; how sad the dunny
And the things you drew on the wall.

This Beach Can Be Dangerous

*The fatalities of his nature cannot be disentangled from the
fatality of all that which has been and will be.*
Nietzsche

WARNING
They came back, a well known face
familiarly transfigured, lifelikeness only
cancer, coronary, burning, mutilation
could have bestowed, they came by millions
and a friend or two calling me by my name
and my father, by a name no other could know.

BATHE BETWEEN THE FLAGS
Each with the same expression, his own,
mirrored in the sand or the mind, came back
the way they went calling like winter waves
pick-a-back on the humped horizon they rode
the strong disturbed westerly airstream
which covered the North Island.

    DO NOT BATHE ALONE
It was their company that made it possible
for me to walk there, cracking the odd shell
with the butt of a manuka stick,
happy to the point of hopelessness.

You Get What You Pay For

One more of those perfections
of still water with houses
growing like trees with trees dipped
in first light
           that pearl of a
cloud excited by sunrise
may or may not be priceless
fine weather is not what it
was and you pay more every
day yesterday's blue was of
a depth and a brilliance you
don't find now
             rich eccentric
having wisely ingested
his cake has it too dying
among treasures the weather
troubles him very little
you too Ananias keep
back part of the price
              it all
hangs by a breath from the south
you too pushing seventy
wishing the weather were here
to stay the morning's moment
free
    knowing that it is not.

On the Road to Erewhon

The Author wishes it to be understood that Erewhon is pronounced
as a word of three syllables, all short — thus, E-re-whon.
— Samuel Butler, Preface to *Erewhon*, 1872.

Once past the icefalls and the teeth of
noon, already descending the pass,
out of a cloud blackened by lightning,
if mirrors can spell and maps don't lie,
that's the Erewhon road, the ambush

can't be far. Gigantic statues shock
you down to size. Before the Hyksos
their senate debated what's to be
done with you. They have mouths the mountain
blast vociferates in, a people

had need of these or these of themselves
were the need *causa sui*. Inhuman
syllables, harmony that howls and
hails, halting you. Patches of old snow
squeak underfoot. Goat-tracks, lost writings.

Six or seven times larger than life,
of great antiquity, worn and lichen
grown. They were ten in number . . . I saw
that their heads had been hollowed. Fear,
pain, hate, cruelty once chopped into stone

stare out again, each head *a sort of*
organ-pipe, so that their mouths should catch
the wind. Earthly, unaccompanied
voices empty wind into wind, mist
into mist, rock into rock, these ten

commandments. Eight of them still seated,
two had fallen. The God who thinks aloud's
the worst, your own shadow's a friendlier
fright. Physical, *superhumanly*
malevolent faces look back, too

hard for your nature to bear, only
the legs and how fast they can carry
you the hell out of here *as though one*
of them would rush after me and grip
me . . . If it were just one of those dreams

where running gets you nowhere! This is
the mirrored map, the Erewhon road,
where you came from is where you're going,
the hammers in the brain keep time with
feet pounding downhill, the rivers are

swollen in the mind's eye. Back there, in
the cloud the trumpeting heads perform
their own *Te Deum*. Panicky antiphons
die down in the blood. You can shiver
suddenly, for no reason at all.

Continuum

The moon rolls over the roof and falls behind
my house, and the moon does neither of these things,
I am talking about myself.

It's not possible to get off to sleep or
the subject or the planet, nor to think thoughts.
Better barefoot it out the front

door and lean from the porch across the privets
and the palms into the washed-out creation,
a dark place with two particular

bright clouds dusted (query) by the moon, one's mine
the other's an adversary, which may depend
on the wind, or something.

A long moment stretches, the next one is not
on time. Not unaccountably the chill of
the planking underfoot rises

in the throat, for its part the night sky empties
the whole of its contents down. Turn on a bare
heel, close the door behind

on the author, cringing demiurge, who picks up
his litter and his tools and paces me back
to bed, stealthily in step.

Pacific 1945–1995

A Pantoum

> . . . if th'assassination
> could trammel up the consequence, and catch,
> with his surcease, success; that but this blow
> might be the be-all and the end-all . . . here,
> but here, upon this bank and shoal of time
> we'ld jump the life to come . . .
>
> — Macbeth

Quantifiable griefs. The daily kill.
  One bullet, with his name on, his surcease.
"The casualties were few, the damage nil" –
  The scale was blown up, early in the piece.

One bullet, with his name on, his surcease.
  Laconic fire, short work the long war mocks.
The scale was blown up, early in the piece –
  How many is few? After the aftershocks,

laconic fire – short work! The long war mocks,
  dragging out our dead. What calibration says
how many is few, after the aftershocks
  of just such magnitude? We heard the news,

dragging out our dead. What calibration says,
  right! You can stop crying now, was it really
of just such magnitude? We heard the news
  again, the statistical obscene, the cheery

right! You can stop crying now, was it really
  the sky that fell, that boiling blue lagoon?
Again, the statistical obscene, the cheery
  salutation and bright signature tune.

The sky that fell! That boiling blue lagoon!
  Jacques Chirac's rutting tribe – with gallic
salutation and bright signature tune –
  thermonuclear hard-on. Ithyphallic

Jacques! Chirac's rutting tribe, with gallic
  eye for the penetrable, palm-fringed hole –
thermonuclear hard-on, ithyphallic
  BANG! full kiloton five below the atoll.

Eye for the penetrable, palm-fringed hole,
   whose trigger-finger, where he sat or knelt down –
BANG! full kiloton five, below the atoll
   had it off, bedrock deep orgasmic meltdown –

whose trigger-finger, where he sat or knelt down,
   fifty years back, fired one as huge as then
had it off bedrock deep, orgasmic meltdown –
   whose but Ferebee's? – Hiroshima come again! –

fifty years back, fired one as huge as then
   fireballed whole cities while "People . . . copulate, pray . . ."
Whose but Ferebee's – Hiroshima come again! –
   bombardier, U.S. Army? *Enola Gay*

fireballed whole cities while "People . . . copulate, pray . . ."
   Not God fingering Gomorrah but the man,
bombardier, U.S. Army. *Enola Gay*
   shuddering at 30,000 feet began –

not God fingering Gomorrah, but the man,
   the colonel her pilot who named her for his Mom –
shuddering at 30,000 feet began –
   'Little Boy' delivered – her run for home:

the colonel her pilot, who named her for his Mom,
   flew her to roost (at last) in the Smithsonian.
"Little Boy" delivered, her run for home
   lighter by the Beast's birth, her son's companion:

flew her to roost (at last) in the Smithsonian:
   are tourists' hearts and hopes, viewing her there,
lighter by the Beast's birth, her son's companion?
   Jacques' Marianne's delivery, is that near?

Are tourists' hearts and hopes, viewing her there,
   pronounced infection-free and safely tested –
Jacques' Marianne's delivery, is that near? –
   What effluent, what fall-out's to be trusted?

pronounced infection-free and safely tested
   for carcinogenic isotope unseen fall-out –
what effluent, what fall-out's to be trusted?
   The Beast once born, who's answering the call-out?

For carcinogenic isotope, unseen fall-out,
   for the screaming city under the crossed hairs,
the Beast once born. Who's answering the call-out?
   no time even to know it's one of THEIRS –

for the screaming city under the crossed hairs,
   "The casualties were few, the damage nil" – ?
No time even to know! It's one of theirs –
   quantifiable griefs. The daily kill.

October–November, 1995

SORLEY MacLEAN

Am Buaireadh

Cha do chuir de bhuaireadh riamh
no thrioblaid dhian 'nam chré
allaban Chrìosda air an talamh
no muillionan nan speur.

'S cha d' ghabh mi suim de aisling bhaoith –
coille uaine tìr an sgeòil –
mar leum mo chridhe rag ri tuar
a gàire 's cuailein òir.

Agus chuir a h-àiléachd sgleò
air bochdainn 's air creuchd sheirbh
agus air saoghal tuigse Leninn,
air fhoighidinn 's air fheirg.

The Turmoil

Never has such turmoil
nor vehement trouble been put in my flesh
by Christ's suffering on the earth
or by the millions of the skies.

And I took no such heed of a vapid dream –
green wood of the land of story –
as when my stubborn heart leaped to the glint
of her smile and golden head.

And her beauty cast a cloud
over poverty and a bitter wound
and over the world of Lenin's intellect,
over his patience and his anger.

Ban-Ghàidheal

Am faca Tu i, Iùdhaich mhóir,
ri 'n abrar Aon Mhac Dhé?
Am fac' thu 'coltas air Do thriall
ri strì an fhìon-lios chéin?

An cuallach mhiosan air a druim,
fallus searbh air mala is gruaidh;
's a' mhios chreadha trom air cùl
a cinn chrùibte bhochd thruaigh.

Chan fhaca Tu i, Mhic an t-saoir,
ri 'n abrar Rìgh na Glòir,
a miosg nan cladach carrach siar,
fo fhallus cliabh a lòin.

An t-earrach so agus so chaidh
's gach fichead earrach bho 'n an tùs
tharruing ise 'n fheamainn fhuar
chum biadh a cloinne 's duais an tùir.

'S gach fichead foghar tha air triall
chaill i samhradh buidh nam blàth;
is threabh an dubh-chosnadh an clais
tarsuinn mìnead ghil a clàir.

Agus labhair T' eaglais chaomh
mu staid chaillte a h-anama thruaigh;
agus leag an cosnadh dian
a corp gu sàmhchair dhuibh an uaigh.

Is thriall a tìm mar shnighe dubh
a' drùdhadh tughaidh fàrdaich bochd;
mheal ise an dubh-chosnadh cruaidh;
is glas a cadal suain an nochd.

A Highland Woman

Hast Thou seen her, great Jew,
who art called the One Son of God?
Hast Thou seen on Thy way the like of her
labouring in the distant vineyard?

The load of fruits on her back,
a bitter sweat on brow and cheek,
and the clay basin heavy on the back
of her bent poor wretched head.

Thou hast not seen her, Son of the carpenter,
who art called the King of Glory,
among the rugged western shores
in the sweat of her food's creel.

This Spring and last Spring
and every twenty Springs from the beginning,
she has carried the cold seaweed
for her children's food and the castle's reward.

And every twenty Autumns gone
she has lost the golden summer of her bloom,
and the Black Labour has ploughed the furrow
across the white smoothness of her forehead.

And Thy gentle church has spoken
about the lost state of her miserable soul,
and the unremitting toil has lowered
her body to a black peace in a grave.

And her time has gone like a black sludge
seeping through the thatch of a poor dwelling:
the hard Black Labour was her inheritance;
grey is her sleep tonight.

Ceann Loch Aoineart

Còmhlan bheanntan, stòiteachd bheanntan,
còrr-lios bheanntan fàsmhor,
cruinneachadh mhullaichean, thulaichean, shléibhtean,
tighinn 'sa' bheucaich ghàbhaidh.

Eirigh ghleanntan, choireachan ùdlaidh,
laighe 's a' bhùirich chràcaich;
sìneadh chluaineagan, shuaineagan srùlach,
brìodal 's an dùbhlachd àrsaidh.

Eachraidh bheanntan, marcachd mhullaichean,
deann-ruith shruthanach càthair,
sleamhnachd leacannan, seangachd chreachainnean,
strannraich leacanach àrd-bheann.

Onfhadh-chrios mhullaichean,
confhadh-shlios thulaichean,
monmhar luim thurraidean màrsail,
gorm-shliosan Mhosgaraidh,
stoirm-shliosan mosganach,
borb-bhiodan mhonaidhean àrda.

Kinloch Ainort

A company of mountains, an upthrust of mountains,
a great garth of growing mountains,
a concourse of summits, of knolls, of hills
coming on with a fearsome roaring.

A rising of glens, of gloomy corries,
a lying down in the antlered bellowing;
a stretching of green nooks, of brook mazes,
prattling in the age-old mid-winter.

A cavalry of mountains, horse-riding summits,
a streaming headlong haste of foam,
a slipperiness of smooth flat rocks, small-bellied bare
　　　　summits,
flat-rock snoring of high mountains.

A surge-belt of hill-tops,
impetuous thigh of peaks,
the murmuring bareness of marching turrets,
green flanks of Mosgary,
crumbling storm-flanks,
barbarous pinnacles of high moorlands.

Hallaig

"Tha tìm, am fiadh, an coille Hallaig"

Tha bùird is tàirnean air an uinneig
troimh 'm faca mi an Aird an Iar
's tha mo ghaol aig Allt Hallaig
'na craoibh bheithe,'s bha i riamh

eadar an t-Inbhir 's Poll a' Bhainne,
thall 's a bhos mu Bhaile-Chùirn:
tha i 'na beithe, 'na calltuinn,
'na caorunn dhìreach sheang ùir.

Ann an Screapadal mo chinnidh,
far robh Tarmad 's Eachunn Mór,
tha 'n nigheanan 's am mic 'nan coille
ag gabhail suas ri taobh an lóin.

Uaibhreach a nochd na coilich ghiuthais
ag gairm air mullach Cnoc an Rà,
dìreach an druim ris a' ghealaich –
chan iadsan coille mo ghràidh.

Fuirichidh mi ris a' bheithe
gus an tig i mach an Càrn,
gus am bi am bearradh uile
o Bheinn na Lice f' a sgàil.

Mura tig 's ann theàrnas mi a Hallaig
a dh' ionnsaigh sàbaid nam marbh,
far a bheil an sluagh a' tathaich,
gach aon ghinealach a dh' fhalbh.

Tha iad fhathast ann a Hallaig,
Clann Ghill-Eain 's Clann MhicLeòid,
na bh'ann ri linn Mhic Ghille-Chaluim:
Chunnacas na mairbh beò.

Na fir 'nan laighe air an lianaig
aig ceann gach taighe a bh' ann,
na h-ighenan 'nan coille bheithe,
dìreach an druim, crom an ceann.

Eadar an Leac is na Feàrnaibh
tha 'n rathad mór fo chóinnich chiùin,
's na h-igheanan 'nam badan sàmhach
a' dol a Chlachan mar o thùs.

Agus a' tilleadh as a' Chlachan,
á Suidhisnis 's á tir nam beò;
a chuile té òg uallach
gun bhristeadh cridhe an sgeòil.

O Allt na Feàrnaibh gus an fhaoilinn
tha soilleir an dìomhaireachd narn beann
chan eil ach coimhthional nan nighean
ag cumail na coiseachd gun cheann.

A' tilleadh a Hallaig anns an fheasgar,
anns a' chamhanaich bhalbh bheò,
a' lìonadh nan leathadan casa,
an gàireachdaich 'nam chluais 'na ceò,

's am bòidhche 'na sgleò air mo chridhe
mun tig an ciaradh air na caoil,
's nuair theàrnas grian air cùl Dhùn Cana
thig peileir dian à gunna Ghaoil;

's buailear am fiadh a tha 'na thuaineal
a' snòtach nan làraichean feòir;
thig reothadh air a shùil 'sa' choille:
chan fhaighear lorg air fhuil ri m' bheò.

Hallaig

"Time, the deer, is in the wood of Hallaig"

The window is nailed and boarded
through which I saw the West
and my love is at the Burn of Hallaig,
a birch tree, and she has always been

between Inver and Milk Hollow,
here and there about Baile-chuirn:
she is a birch, a hazel,
a straight, slender young rowan.

In Screapadal of my people
where Norman and Big Hector were,
their daughters and their sons are a wood
going up beside the stream.

Proud tonight the pine cocks
crowing on the top of Cnoc an Ra,
straight their backs in the moonlight –
they are not the wood I love.

I will wait for the birch wood
until it comes up by the cairn,
until the whole ridge from Beinn na Lice
will be under its shade.

If it does not, I will go down to Hallaig,
to the Sabbath of the dead,
where the people are frequenting,
every single generation gone.

They are still in Hallaig,
MacLeans and MacLeods,
all who were there in the time of Mac Gille Chaluim
the dead have been seen alive.

The men lying on the green
at the end of every house that was,
the girls a wood of birches,
straight their backs, bent their heads.

Between the Leac and Fearns
the road is under mild moss
and the girls in silent bands
go to Clachan as in the beginning,

and return from Clachan
from Suisnish and the land of the living;
each one young and light-stepping,
without the heartbreak of the tale.

From the Burn of Fearns to the raised beach
that is clear in the mystery of the hills,
there is only the congregation of the girls
keeping up the endless walk,

coming back to Hallaig in the evening,
in the dumb living twilight,
filling the steep slopes,
their laughter a mist in my ears,

and their beauty a film on my heart
before the dimness comes on the kyles,
and when the sun goes down behind Dun Cana
a vehement bullet will come from the gun of Love;

and will strike the deer that goes dizzily,
sniffing at the grass-grown ruined homes;
his eye will freeze in the wood,
his blood will not be traced while I live.

F. T. PRINCE

An Epistle to a Patron

My lord, hearing lately of your opulence in promises and your house
Busy with parasites, of your hands full of favours, your statutes
Admirable as music, and no fear of your arms not prospering, I have
Considered how to serve you and breed from my talents
These few secrets which I shall make plain
To your intelligent glory. You should understand that I have plotted,
Being in command of all the ordinary engines
Of defence and offence, a hundred and fifteen buildings
Less others less complete: complete, some are courts of serene stone,
Some the civil structures of a war-like elegance as bridges,
Sewers, aqueducts and citadels of brick, with which I declare the fact
That your nature is to vanquish. For these I have acquired a
     knowledge
Of the habits of numbers and of various tempers, and skill in setting
Firm sets of pure bare members which will rise, hanging together
Like an argument, with beams, ties and sistering pilasters:
The lintels and windows with mouldings as round as a girl's chin;
     thresholds
To libraries; halls that cannot be entered without a sensation as of
     myrrh
By your vermilion officers, your sages and dancers. There will be
     chambers
Like the recovery of a sick man, your closet waiting not
Less suitably shadowed than the heart, and the coffers of a ceiling

To reflect your diplomatic taciturnities. You may commission
Hospitals, huge granaries that will smile to bear your filial plunders,
And stables washed with a silver lime in whose middle tower seated
In the slight acridity you may watch
The copper thunder kept in the sulky flanks of your horse, a rolling
    field
Of necks glad to be groomed, the strong crupper, the edged hoof
And the long back, seductive and rebellious to saddles.
And barracks, fortresses, in need of no vest save light, light
That to me is breath, food and drink, I live by effects of light, I live
To catch it, to break it, as an orator plays off
Against each other and his theme his casual gems, and so with light,
Twisted in strings, plucked, crossed or knotted or crumbled
As it may be allowed to be by leaves,
Or clanged back by lakes and rocks or otherwise beaten,
Or else spilt and spread like a feast of honey, dripping
Through delightful voids and creeping along long fractures, brimming
Carved canals, bowls and lachrymatories with pearls: all this the work
Of now advancing, now withdrawing faces, whose use I know.
I know what slabs thus will be soaked to a thumb's depth by the sun,
And where to rob them, what colour stifles in your intact quarries,
    what
Sand silted in your river-gorges will well mix with the dust of flint; I
    know
What wood to cut by what moon in what weather
Of your sea-winds, your hill-wind: therefore tyrant, let me learn
Your high-ways, ways of sandstone, roads of the oakleaf, and your
    sea-ways.
Send me to dig dry graves, exposing what you want: I must
Attend your orgies and debates (let others apply for austerities), admit
    me
To your witty table, stuff me with urban levities, feed me, bind me
To a prudish luxury, free me thus, and with a workshop
From my household consisting
Of a pregnant wife, one female and one boy child and an elder bastard
With other properties; these let me regard, let me neglect, and let
What I begin be finished. Save me, noble sir, from the agony
Of starved and privy explorations such as those I stumble
From a hot bed to make, to follow lines to which the night-sky
Holds only faint contingencies. These flights with no end but failure,
And failure not to end them, these palliate or prevent.
I wish for liberty, let me then be tied: and seeing too much
I aspire to be constrained by your emblems of birth and triumph,
And between the obligations of your future and the checks of actual
    state
To flourish, adapt the stubs of an interminable descent, and place

The crested key to confident vaults; with a placid flurry of petals,
And bosom and lips, will stony functionaries support
The persuasion, so beyond proof, of your power. I will record
In peculiar scrolls your alien alliances,
Fit an apartment for your eastern hostage, extol in basalt
Your father, praise with white festoons the goddess your lady;
And for your death which will be mine prepare
An encasement as if of solid blood. And so let me
Forget, let me remember, that this is stone, stick, metal, trash
Which I will pile and hack, my hands will stain and bend
(None better knowing how to gain from the slow pains of a marble
Bruised, breathing strange climates). Being pressed as I am, being
       broken
By wealth and poverty, torn between strength and weakness, take me,
       choose
To relieve me, to receive of me, and must you not agree
As you have been to some – a great giver of banquets, of respite from
       swords,
Who shook out figured cloths, who rained coin,
A donor of laurel and of grapes, a font of profuse intoxicants – and so,
To be so too for me? And none too soon, since the panting mind
Rather than barren will be prostitute, and once
I served a herd of merchants; but since I will be faithful
And my virtue is such, though far from home let what is yours be
       mine, and this be a match
As many have been proved, enduring exiles and blazed
Not without issue in returning shows: your miserly freaks
Your envies, racks and poisons not out of mind
Although not told, since often borne – indeed how should it be
That you employed them less than we? but now be flattered a little
To indulge the extravagant gist of this communication,
For my pride puts all in doubt and at present I have no patience,
I have simply hope, and I submit me
To your judgement which will be just.

False Bay

She I love leaves me, and I leave my friends
In the dusky capital where I spent two years
In the cultivation of divinity.
Sitting beside my window above the sea
In this unvisited land I feel once more
How little ingenious I am. The winter ends,
The seaward slopes are covered to the shore

With a press of lilies that have silver ears.
And although I am perplexed and sad, I say
"Now indulge in no dateless lamentations;
Watch only across the water the lapsed nations
And the fisherman twitch a boat across the bay."

For Fugitives

For you who loved me too
As the mistress of transparent towns that showed
Like sea-beasts the embodied ruins
As their bones, it is I who loved you
And crossed the sea, the flawed air
Allayed, now feel beneath my fingers
The seal melt from the fountain,
And recall the lost palatinate.

And for you whose it was
Who can forgive me? what may I offer? as
On this the other shore, unless
A dream rehearses loss,
Air of its charity will flush, the thin moon
From the white kernel of her filmy almond
Leans, and a causeless radiance fills
The palm I dip among these hills.

Cœur de Lion

Forbecause a prisoner lies
With no air or exercise
He has need, to save his health,
Of thoughts that will not give him grief:
I have friends of name and wealth,
But few of them have sent relief.

Ask what they have done for me,
Those who yet go rich and free,
All my barons, tall young men
Of Poitou, England and Touraine;
Once they were my friends, and then
They never knew me false or vain.

Much dishonour they may fear,
Should I lie two winters here.
Men and barons, they all know
Not one could be so poor to me,
I would let him stifle so
For want of money paid in fee.

Some may think my capture sent
As deserved, in punishment;
Others resting from alarms
Live unconcerned in heart or head,
Though the fields are bare of arms
And I do homage to a bed.

Not that I intend excuse
From the chance of war, ill-use,
Close confinement, fear and pain;
But this is over and above.
Of the others none complain,
But worse than all is loss of love.

R. S. THOMAS

Song for Gwydion

When I was a child and the soft flesh was forming
Quietly as snow on the bare boughs of bone,
My father brought me trout from the green river
From whose chill lips the water song had flown.

Dull grew their eyes, the beautiful, blithe garland
Of stipples faded, as light shocked the brain;
They were the first sweet sacrifice I tasted,
A young god, ignorant of the blood's stain.

The Village

Scarcely a street, too few houses
To merit the title; just a way between
The one tavern and the one shop
That leads nowhere and fails at the top

Of the short hill, eaten away
By long erosion of the green tide
Of grass creeping perpetually nearer
This last outpost of time past.

So little happens; the black dog
Cracking his fleas in the hot sun
Is history. Yet the girl who crosses
From door to door moves to a scale
Beyond the bland day's two dimensions.

Stay, then, village, for round you spins
On slow axis a world as vast
And meaningful as any poised
By great Plato's solitary mind.

Taliesin 1952

I have been all men known to history,
Wondering at the world and at time passing;
I have seen evil, and the light blessing
Innocent love under a spring sky.

I have been Merlin wandering in the woods
Of a far country, where the winds waken
Unnatural voices, my mind broken
By sudden acquaintance with man's rage.

I have been Glyn Dŵr set in the vast night,
Scanning the stars for the propitious omen,
A leader of men, yet cursed by the crazed women
Mourning their dead under the same stars.

I have been Goronwy, forced from my own land
To taste the bitterness of the salt ocean;
I have known exile and a wild passion
Of longing changing to a cold ache.

King, beggar and fool, I have been all by turns,
Knowing the body's sweetness, the mind's treason;
Taliesin still, I show you a new world, risen,
Stubborn with beauty, out of the heart's need.

In a Country Church

To one kneeling down no word came,
Only the wind's song, saddening the lips
Of the grave saints, rigid in glass;
Or the dry whisper of unseen wings,
Bats not angels, in the high roof.

Was he balked by silence? He kneeled long,
And saw love in a dark crown
Of thorns blazing, and a winter tree
Golden with fruit of a man's body.

Period

It was a time when wise men
Were not silent, but stifled
By vast noise. They took refuge
In books that were not read.

Two counsellors had the ear
Of the public. One cried "Buy"
Day and night, and the other,
More plausibly, "Sell your repose".

Pavane

Convergences
Of the spirit! What
Century, love? I,
Too; you remember –
Brescia? This sunlight reminds
Of the brocade. I dined
Long. And now the music
Of darkness in your eyes
Sounds. But Brescia,
And the spreading foliage
Of smoke! With Yeats' birds
Grown hoarse.
             Artificer
Of the years, is this

Your answer? The long dream
Unwound; we followed
Through time to the tryst
With ourselves. But wheels roll
Between and the shadow
Of the plane falls. The
Victim remains
Nameless on the tall
Steps. Master, I
Do not wish, I do not wish
To continue.

Navigation

(*for Lee McOwan*)

There go the storeyed liners,
the tankers, the thudding substitutes
for the billowing schooners
that were blown away as though
they were time's clouds. I wave
to them on their way – where?
They are, as I am, outward
bound over multitudinous
fathoms. The crew lean over
the taffrail, I over myself
and suffer the old nausea
of the unknown. Sometimes when there is
fog, I hear the horn calling
to them to be careful. When I
kneel down in the obscurity
that is God, there is no comparable
voice, however melancholy,
to direct me.
                    Never mind,
traveller, there are the heights,
too, where the intellect
meets with God in its own
weather. By day I see the 'planes
reflecting him with the clarity
that is thought. By night
their instruments deputise
for him and are unerring.

God, on this latest stage
of my journey let me profit
from my inventions by christening
them yours. Amid the shoals and hazards
that are about me, let me employ
radar as though it were your gift.

Evening

The archer with time
as his arrow – has he broken
his strings that the rainbow
is so quiet over our village?

Let us stand, then, in the interval
of our wounding, till the silence
turn golden and love is
a moment eternally overflowing.

GEORGE BARKER

Summer Song I

I looked into my heart to write
    And found a desert there.
But when I looked again I heard
Howling and proud in every word
    The hyena despair.

Great summer sun, great summer sun,
    All loss burns in trophies;
And in the cold sheet of the sky
Lifelong the fish-lipped lovers lie
    Kissing catastrophes.

O loving garden where I lay
    When under the breasted tree
My son stood up behind my eyes
And groaned: Remember that the price
    Is vinegar for me.

Great summer sun, great summer sun,
    Turn back to the designer:
I would not be the one to start
The breaking day and the breaking heart
    For all the grief in China.

My one, my one, my only love,
    Hide, hide your face in a leaf,
And let the hot tear falling burn
The stupid heart that will not learn
    The everywhere of grief.

Great summer sun, great summer sun,
    Turn back to the never-never
Cloud-cuckoo, happy, far-off land
Where all the love is true love, and
    True love goes on for ever.

"Turn on your side and bear the day to me"

Turn on your side and bear the day to me
Beloved, sceptre-struck, immured
In the glass wall of sleep. Slowly
Uncloud the borealis of your eye
And show your iceberg secrets, your midnight prizes
To the green-eyed world and to me. Sin
Coils upward into thin air when you awaken
And again morning announces amnesty over
The serpent-kingdomed bed. Your mother
Watched with as dove an eye the unforgivable night
Sigh backward into innocence when you
Set a bright monument in her amorous sea.
Look down, Undine, on the trident that struck
Sons from the rock of vanity. Turn in the world
Sceptre-struck, spellbound, beloved,
Turn in the world and bear the day to me.

Morning in Norfolk

As it has for so long
Come wind and all weather
the house glimmers along
the mists of a little
river that splinters, it
seems, a landscape of
winter dreams. In the far
fields stand a few
bare trees decorating
those mists like the fanned
patterns of Georgian
skylights. The home land
of any heart persists
there, suffused with
memories and mists not
quite concealing the
identities and lost
lives of those loved once
but loved most. They haunt it
still. To the watermeadows
that lie by the heart they
return as do flocks of swallows
to the fields they have known
and flickered and flown so
often and so unforgettably over.
What fish
play in the bright wishing
wells of your painted
stretches, O secret
untainted little Bure,
I could easily tell,
for would they not be
those flashing dashers
and sometimes glittering
presentiments, images
and idealizations
of what had to be?
The dawn has brightened the
shallows and shadows and
the Bure sidles and idles
through weed isles and fallen
willows, and under

Itteringham Mill, and
there is a kind of rain-
drenched flittering in the
air, the night swan still
sleeps in her wings and over it all
the dawn heaps up the hanging
fire of the day.

Fowell's tractor blusters
out of its shed and drags
a day's work, like a piled sled
behind it. The crimson
December morning brims over
Norfolk, turning
to burning Turner
this aqueous water colour
idyll that earlier gleamed
so green that it seemed
drowned. What further
sanction, what blessing
can the man of heart intercede for
than the supreme remission
of dawn? For then the mind
looking backward upon its
too sullied yesterday,
that rotting stack of
resolution and refuse,
reads in the rainbowed sky
a greater covenant,
the tremendous pronouncement:
the day forgives.

Holy the heart in
its proper occupation
praising and appraising this
godsend, the dawn.
Will you lift up your eyes
my blind spirit and see
such evidence of
forgiveness in the heavens
morning after golden
morning that even
the blind can see?

To Whom Else

Had I more carefully cultivated the Horatian pentameter, then
this verse would live longer in your remembrance than
things being what they are, I suppose, it briefly will.
Or do I think these verses may survive you, and, well,
do I really care? I do not give a damn.
For I know that if you read them you will condemn
them simply because they were made by that over
devoted zealot who was once, not briefly, your lover.

JOHN BERRYMAN

Winter Landscape

The three men coming down the winter hill
In brown, with tall poles and a pack of hounds
At heel, through the arrangement of the trees,
Past the five figures at the burning straw,
Returning cold and silent to their town,

Returning to the drifted snow, the rink
Lively with children, to the older men,
The long companions they can never reach,
The blue light, men with ladders, by the church
The sledge and shadow in the twilit street,

Are not aware that in the sandy time
To come, the evil waste of history
Outstretched, they will be seen upon the brow
Of that same hill: when all their company
Will have been irrecoverably lost,

These men, this particular three in brown
Witnessed by birds will keep the scene and say
By their configuration with the trees,
The small bridge, the red houses and the fire,
What place, what time, what morning occasion

Sent them into the wood, a pack of hounds
At heel and the tall poles upon their shoulders,
Thence to return as now we see them and
Ankle-deep in snow down the winter hill
Descend, while three birds watch and the fourth flies.

Scholars at the Orchid Pavilion

I

Sozzled, Mo-tsu, after a silence, vouchsafed
a word alarming: "We must love them all!"
Affronted, the fathers jumped.
"Yes" he went madly on and waved in quest
of his own dreadful subject "O the fathers"
he cried "must not be all!"
Whereat upon consent we broke up for the day.

2

The bamboo's bending power formed our theme
next dawn, under a splendid wind. The water
flapped to our tender gaze.
Girls came & crouched with tea. Great Wu pinched one,
forgetting his later nature. How the wind howled,
tranquil was our pavilion,
watching & reflecting, fingering bamboo.

3

"Wild geese & bamboo" muttered Ch'en Hung-shou
"block out our boundaries of fearful wind.
Neither requires shelter. I shelter
among painters, doing bamboo.
The young shoots unaffected by the wind
mock our love for their elders."
Mo-tsu opened his mouth & closed it to again.

4

"The bamboo of the Ten Halls," went on Ch'en
"of my time, are excellently made.
I cannot find so well
ensorcelled those of later or former time.
Let us apply the highest praise, pure wind,
to those surpassing masters; –
having done things, a thing, along that line myself."

He Resigns

Age, and the deaths, and the ghosts.
Her having gone away
in spirit from me. Hosts
of regrets come & find me empty.

I don't feel this will change.
I don't want any thing
or person, familiar or strange.
I don't think I will sing

any more just now;
ever. I must start
to sit with a blind brow
above an empty heart.

Dream Song 4

Filling her compact & delicious body
with chicken páprika, she glanced at me
twice.
Fainting with interest, I hungered back
and only the fact of her husband & four other people
kept me from springing on her

or falling at her little feet and crying
"You are the hottest one for years of night
Henry's dazed eyes
have enjoyed, Brillance." I advanced upon
(despairing) my spumoni. – Sir Bones: is stuffed,
de world, wif feeding girls.

– Black hair, complexion Latin, jewelled eyes
downcast . . . The slob beside her   feasts . . . What wonders is
she sitting on, over there?
The restaurant buzzes. She might as well be on Mars.
Where did it all go wrong? There ought to be a law against Henry.
—Mr. Bones: there is.

Dream Song 8

The weather was fine. They took away his teeth,
white & helpful; bothered his backhand;
halved his green hair.
They blew out his loves, his interests. "Underneath,"
(they called in iron voices) "understand,
is nothing. So there."

The weather was very fine. They lifted off
his covers till he showed, and cringed & pled
to see himself less.
They installed mirrors till he flowed. "Enough"
(murmured they) "if you will watch Us instead,
yet you may saved be. Yes."

The weather fleured. They weakened all his eyes,
and burning thumbs into his ears, and shook
his hand like a notch.
They flung long silent speeches. (Off the hook!)
They sandpapered his plumpest hope. (So capsize.)
They took away his crotch.

Dream Song 14

Life, friends, is boring. We must not say so.
After all, the sky flashes, the great sea yearns,
we ourselves flash and yearn,
and moreover my mother told me as a boy
(repeatingly) "Ever to confess you're bored
means you have no

Inner Resources." I conclude now I have no
inner resources, because I am heavy bored.
Peoples bore me,
literature bores me, especially great literature,
Henry bores me, with his plights & gripes
as bad as achilles,

who loves people and valiant art, which bores me.
And the tranquil hills, & gin, look like a drag
and somehow a dog
has taken itself & its tail considerably away
into mountains or sea or sky, leaving
behind: me, wag.

Dream Song 26

The glories of the world struck me, made me aria, once.
— What happen then, Mr Bones?
if be you cares to say.
— Henry. Henry became interested in women's bodies,
his loins were & were the   scene of stupendous achievement
Stupor. Knees, dear. Pray.

All the knobs & softnesses of, my God,
the ducking & trouble it swarm on Henry,
at one time.
— What happen then, Mr Bones?
you seems excited-like.
— Fell Henry back into   the original crime: art, rime

besides a sense of others, my God, my God,
and a jealousy for the honour (alive) of his country,
what can get more odd?
and discontent with the thriving gangs & pride.
— What happen then, Mr Bones?
— I had a most marvellous   piece of luck. I died.

Dream Song 29

There sat down, once, a thing on Henry's heart
so heavy, if he had a hundred years
& more, & weeping, sleepless, in all them time
Henry could not make good.
Starts again always in Henry's ears
the little cough somewhere, an odour, a chime.

And there is another thing he has in mind
like a grave Sienese face a thousand years
would fail to blur the still profiled reproach of. Ghastly,
with open eyes, he attends, blind.
All the bells say: too late. This is not for tears;
thinking.

But never did Henry, as he thought he did,
end anyone and hacks her body up
and hide the pieces, where they may be found.
He knows: he went over everyone, & nobody's missing.
Often he reckons, in the dawn, them up.
Nobody is ever missing.

Dream Song 61

Full moon. Our Narragansett gales subside
and the land is celebrating men of war
more or less, less or more.
In valleys, thin on headlands, narrow & wide
our targets rest. In us we trust. Far, near,
the bivouacs of fear

are solemn in the moon somewhere tonight,
in turning time. It's late for gratitude,
an annual, rude
roar of a moment's turkey's "Thanks". Bright & white
their ordered markers undulate away
awaiting no day.

Away from us, from Henry's feel or fail,
campaigners lie with mouldered toes, disarmed,
out of order,
with whom we will one. The war is real,
and a sullen glory pauses over them harmed,
incident to murder.

Dream Song 255

My twin, the nameless one, wild in the woods
whilst I at Pippin's court flourish, am knighted:
we met & fighted
on a red road, made friends, and all my goods
now are half his. I pull this out of the past,
St Valentine's forecast.

Trim, the complex lace, whitest on red:
my baby's kindergarten had a ball
save one got none at all
& tears, like those for the Roman martyr shed
& the bishop of Terni who suffered the same day,
so ancient writers say.

I say, said Henry (all degrees of love
from sky-blue down to spiriting blood, down to
the elder from the new,
loom sanctuaries we are pilgrims of,
the pierced heart over there seems to be mine)
this is my Valentine.

HENRY REED

A Map of Verona

Quelle belle heure, quels bons bras me
rendront ces régions d'où viennent mes
sommeils et mes moindres mouvements?

A map of Verona is open, the small strange city;
With its river running round and through, it is river-
    embraced,
And over this city for a whole long winter season,
Through streets on a map, my thoughts have hovered and
    paced.

Across the river there is a wandering suburb,
An unsolved smile on a now familiar mouth;
Some enchantments of earlier towns are about you:
Once I was drawn to Naples in the south.

Naples I know now, street and hovel and garden,
The look of the islands from the avenue,
Capri and Ischia, like approaching drum-beats –
My youthful Naples, how I remember you!

You were an early chapter, a practice in sorrow,
Your shadows fell, but were only a token of pain,
A sketch in tenderness, lust, and sudden parting,
And I shall not need to trouble with you again.

But I remember, once your map lay open,
As now Verona's, under the still lamp-light.
I thought, are these the streets to walk in in the mornings,
Are these the gardens to linger in at night?

And all was useless that I thought I learned:
Maps are of place, not time, nor can they say
The surprising height and colour of a building,
Nor where the groups of people bar the way.

It is strange to remember those thoughts and to try to catch
The underground whispers of music beneath the years,
The forgotten conjectures, the clouded, forgotten vision,
Which only in vanishing phrases reappears.

Again, it is strange to lead a conversation
Round to a name, to a cautious questioning
Of travellers, who talk of Juliet's tomb and fountains
And a shining smile of snowfall, late in Spring.

Their memories calm this winter of expectation,
Their talk restrains me, for I cannot flow
Like your impetuous river to embrace you;
Yet you are there, and one day I shall go.

The train will bring me perhaps in utter darkness
And drop me where you are blooming, unaware
That a stranger has entered your gates, and a new devotion
Is about to attend and haunt you everywhere.

The flutes are warm: in to-morrow's cave the music
Trembles and forms inside the musician's mind,
The lights begin, and the shifting crowds in the causeways
Are discerned through the dusk, and the rolling river behind.

And in what hour of beauty, in what good arms,
Shall I those regions and that city attain
From whence my dreams and slightest movements rise?
And what good Arms shall take them away again?

The Door and the Window

My love, you are timely come, let me lie by your heart.
For waking in the dark this morning, I woke to that mystery,
Which we can all wake to, at some dark time or another:
Waking to find the room not as I thought it was,
But the window further away, and the door in another direction.

This was not home, and you were far away,
And I woke sick, and held by another passion,
In the icy grip of a dead, tormenting flame,
Consumed by the night, watched by the door and the window,
On a bed of stone, waiting for the day to bring you.

The window is sunlit now, the spring day sparkles beyond it,
The door has opened: and can you, at last beside me,
Drive under the day that frozen and faithless darkness,
With its unseen torments flickering, which neither
The dearest look nor the longest kiss assuages?

Philoctetes

I have changed my mind; or my mind is changed in me.
A shadow lifts, a light comes down, the agony
Of years ceases, the blind eyes open, and the blinded body
Feels the sensation of a god descending,
A shudder of wind through the caves, the shiver of the dawn-wind
    crossing,
The wind which pauses a moment, to bless and caress and kiss
The waters pausing between the last slow wave of night,
And the first slow wave of morning.
It is a god that clasps and releases me thus. Day breaks,
And draws me up from the deepest well of night,
Where I am all and nothing, never and forever,
And sets me brimming on the lip of day, wherein
I am but Philoctetes, at only one point in a story.

On such a day in summer, before a temple,
The wound first broke and bled.
To my companions become unbearable,
I was put on this island. But the story
As you have heard it is with time distorted,
And passion and pity have done their best for it.
They could only report as they saw, who saw the struggle
In the boat that took off from the ship, manned by the strongest,
Taking me to the island. They seized me and forced me ashore,
And wept. They heard, as the boat drew clear again from the rocks,
My final scream of rage, which some have carried
Until the earth has locked their ears against it.
And that for them was the end.
But I, who was left alone in the island's silence,
I lay on the rock in the creek where the sailors placed me,
And slept or drowsed. How should I know how long?
The pain had died and time had lost its meaning.
How should I know how long?
As after death, I lay in peace and triumph,
My only motion, to stretch my left arm outward:
It was satisfactory. The bow was there,
And Troy would not be taken.
Night fell and passed, and day broke clear and cool,
As day breaks now.

This was my home, the winter's gales, the summer,
The cave and the rotting wound,
Where the singing wheel of the seasons became the cycle
Of an endless repeated ritual of sickness and pain.

First the suspicion during the common tasks
Of hewing and killing, or fetching and carrying water;
The hesitation before a memory,
The stumbling thought by which we recognize
That pain is already here, but is still beyond our feeling,
And will soon return to us, returning again
To-morrow or the next day.
And under the noisy disguises we arouse
To drown and confound that onset, quickly as we turn
To press back a wanton branch, or kick a stone from the way,
The noiseless chant has begun in the heart of the wound,
The heavy procession of pain along the nerve,
The torture-music, the circling and approach
Of the fiery dancers, the days of initiation,
The surge through the heat to the babbling, sweating vault
Of muttering, unanswered questions, on,
Through a catechism of ghosts and a toiling litany,
To the ultimate sanctum of delirium, unremembered,
The recapitulation of the bitterly forgotten,
And then forgotten again in the break of day.

Exhausted and wan in the light of those other daybreaks,
I saw myself, watched my sad days, and prayed
That I might be a grotto below the cliff and the sea,
With the hoarse waters in and around me, forever pelting,
Stilly, forever in place; or a rock, or in winter storms,
A wave which the sea throws perpetually forwards, and
Again and again withdraws, forever in its moving place.
But I am not such a thing. And gliding on a gliding sea,
I must seem to make my choice.

That was my choice which now is my rejection:
The caves of alienation, and the chant
Of phantom dancers, the anger and the fury.
And still between rifts of smoke in the acrid darkness,
For a gleaming moment, still the bright daggers besieging
This fiery lump which passes for a heart.
There is one sort of daybreak, a death renewed;
Here is another, a life that glimmers and wakes.
A desert or an ocean perhaps divides them,
Or as rock on rock they lie so close on each other
That our hands can neither persuade them nor tear them apart.
I can only point to one time and speak of it,
And point to another which is different.
One is the buildings of hell, when over a crime
We plaster darkness on darkness, and pray for silence,

While the light grows louder above the disordered days,
The bells with their loud ringing pull down the tower,
And the walled-up entry of death lies exposed and broken.
The other is the beach, unmoving in this other daybreak,
Where Neoptolemus and his companions lie.
The morning mounts and hovers over them.
Time with his patient hand has taken and led them
There where the sailors placed me on that distant morning.
And they lie sleeping, who will bear me back to Troy.
And somewhere between such scenes a god descends
Or a man cries out: "I am here!"
Unfathomable the light and the darkness between them.

I have lived too long on Lemnos, lonely and desperate,
Quarrelling with conjured demons, with the ghosts
Of the men and women with whom I learned to people
The loneliness and despair; and with those others:
The silent circle
Of the men and women I have been and tried to be.
I cannot look at them now in brake or coomb or fountain,
Silent and watchful round the double mouth of the cave,
As in or out I go; nor if they spoke,
Could bear their agonized frustrated voice
(For they would have one voice only), as in or out I go.
I cannot look at them now, when from over the sea, new ghosts
Lean from the future smiling.

Decision is uncertain, made uncertainly
Under ambiguous omens, which here and now cannot question.
Oh, days to come! Give me power to unpick the plots
Which gods and men arrange, to disengage
The gold and silver fragments of their story
And power to let them slip together, accepted,
Their artifice made art.
(I will pick them apart in a year or a generation
After this time. Here they are close together.)

Day breaks: the isle is silent, under the sun,
Which ponders it as though to interpret its silence.
I have changed my mind; or my mind is changed in me.
Unalterable of cliff and water,
The vast ravines are violet, revealing sea.
Here they are close together, the singing fragments
Which gods and men arrange, a chorus of birds and gardens.
The god departs, the men remain, day breaks,
And the bow is ready and burnished.

The arrows are newly fledged with the sun's first feathers.
It is the last still stillness of the morning
Before the first gull screams.
I lie on the rock, the wound is quiet, its death
Is dead within me, and treachery is powerless here.
Under the caves, in the hollows of sheltered beaches
Slowly the sailors wake.
The bushes twitch in the wind on the glowing cliff-sides;
The ghosts dislimn and vanish; the god departs;
My life begins; and a man plants a tree at daybreak.

RANDALL JARRELL

The Island

"While sun and sea – and I, and I –
Were warped through summer on our spar,
I guessed beside the fin, the gull,
And Europe ebbing like a sail
A life indifferent as a star.

"My lids were grating to their close,
My palms were loosening to die,
When – failing through its drift of surf,
Whale-humped, its beaches cracked with salt –
The island gave its absent sigh.

"Years notched my hut, my whiskers soughed
Through summer's witless stare: blue day
Flickered above the nothingness
That rimmed me, the unguessed abyss
Broke on my beaches, and its spray

"Frosted or salted with its curling smile
The printless hachures of the sand . . .
I lay with you, Europe, in a net of snows:
And all my trolls – their noses flattened into Lapps'
Against the thin horn of my windows – wept;

"Vole, kobold, the snowshoe-footed hare
– Crowned with the smoke of steamboats, shagg'd with stars –
Whispered to my white mistress: *He is Mars*;
Till I called, laughing: *Friends! subjects! customers!*
And her face was a woman's, theirs were men's.

"All this I dreamed in my great ragged bed . . .
Or so I dreamed. The dawn's outspeaking smile
Curled through my lashes, felled the Märchen's wood;
The sun stripped my last cumulus of stars,
And the sea graved all the marshes of the swan.

"So, so. The years ticked past like crabs
Or an hour inched out to heaven, like the sea.
One day, by my black hand, my beard
Shone silver; I looked in astonishment
And pinched my lean calves, drawn with many scars,

"With my stiff fingers, till the parrot called
In my grum, quavering voice: *Poor Robinson!*
My herd came bleating, licked my salty cheeks;
I sobbed, and petted with a kind of love
These joys of mine – the old, half-human loves

"That had comforted my absent life . . .
I have dreamed of men, and I am old.
There is no Europe." The man, the goats, the parrot
Wait in their grove for death; and there floods to them
In its last thundering spray, the sea, the sea!

The Märchen

(GRIMM'S TALES)

Listening, listening; it is never still.
This is the forest: long ago the lives
Edged armed into its tides (the axes were its stone
Lashed with the skins of dwellers to its boughs);
We felled our islands there, at last, with iron.
The sunlight fell to them, according to our wish,
And we believed, till nightfall, in that wish;
And we believed, till nightfall, in our lives.

The bird is silent; but its cold breast stirs
Raggedly, and the gloom the moonlight bars
Is blurred with the fluff its long death strewed
In the crumpled fern; and far off something falls.
If the firs forget their breath, if the leaf that perishes
Holds, a bud, to spring; sleeps, fallen, under snow –
It is never still. The darkness quakes with blood;

From its pulse the dark eyes of the hunter glow
Green as their forest, fading images
Of the dream in the firelight: shudder of the coals
In their short Hell, vined skeleton
Of the charcoal-burner dozing in the snow.
Hänsel, to map the hard way, cast his bones
Up clouds to Paradise; His sparrows ate
And he plunged home, past peat and measures, to his kin
Furred in the sooty darkness of the cave
Where the old gods nodded. How the devil's beard
Coiled round the dreaming Hänsel, till his limbs
Grew gnarled as a fakir's on the spindling Cross
The missions rowed from Asia: eternal corpse
Of the Scapegoat, gay with His blood's watered beads,
Red wax in the new snow (strange to His warmed stare);
The wooden mother and the choir of saints, His stars;
And God and His barons, always, iron behind.
Gorged Hänsel felt His blood burn thin as air
In a belly swollen with the airy kine;
How many ages boiled Christ's bark for soup!
Giddy with emptiness, a second wife
Scolding the great-eyed children of a ghost,
He sends them, in his tale, not out to death
(Godfather Death, the reaping messenger),
Nor to the devil cringing in the gloom,
Shifting his barred hooves with a crunch like snow –
But to a king: the blind untroubled Might
Renting a destiny to men on terms –
Come, mend me and wed half of me, my son!
Behind, the headsman fondles his gnawn block.
So men have won a kingdom – there are kings;
Are giants, warlocks, the unburied dead
Invulnerable to any power – the Necessity
Men spring from, die under: the unbroken wood.

Noon, the gold sun of hens and aldermen
Inked black as India, on the green ground,
Our patterns, homely, mercenary, magnified –
Bewitching as the water of Friar Bacon's glass.
(*Our* farmer fooled the devil with a turnip,
Our tailor won a queen with seven flies;
Mouser and mousie and a tub of fat
Kept house together – and a louse, a louse
Brewed small beer in an eggshell with a flea.)
But at evening the poor light, far-off, fantastic –
Sun of misers and of mermen, the last foolish gold

Of soldiers wandering through the country with a crutch –
Scattered its leagues of shadows on the plots
Where life, horned sooty lantern patched with eyes,
Hides more than it illumines, dreams the hordes
Of imps and angels, all of its own hue.
In the great world everything is just the same
Or just the opposite, we found (we never went).
The tinkers, peddlers brought their pinch of salt:
In our mouths the mill of the unresting sea
Ground till their very sores were thirsty.
Quaking below like quicksand, there is fire –
The dowser's twig dips not to water but to Hell;
And the Father, uncomfortable overseer,
Shakes from the rain-clouds Heaven's branding bolt.
Beyond, the Alps ring, avalanche on avalanche,
And the lost palmers freeze to bliss, a smile
Baring their poor teeth, blackened as the skulls
Of sanctuaries – splinters of the Cross, the Ark, the Tree
Jut from a saint's set jawbone, to put out
With one bought vision many a purging fire.
As the circles spread, the stone hopes like a child.
The weak look to the helpless for their aid –
The beasts who, ruled by their god, Death,
Bury the son with their enchanted thanks
For the act outside their possibility:
The victim spared, the labors sweated through, for love
Neither for mate nor litter, but for – anything.
When had it mattered whom we helped? It always paid.
When the dead man's heart broke they found written there
(He could not write): *The wish has made it so.*
Or so he wished. The platter appliquéd
With meals for parents, scraps for children, gristle
For Towser, a poor dog; the walnut jetting wine;
The broom that, fretting for a master, swept a world;
The spear that, weeping for a master, killed a child;
And gold to bury, from the deepest mines –
These neither to wisdom nor to virtue, but to Grace,
The son remembered in the will of God –
These were wishes. The glass in which I saw
Somewhere else, someone else: the field upon which sprawled
Dead, and the ruler of the dead, my twin –
Were wishes? Hänsel, by the eternal sea,
Said to the flounder for his first wish, *Let me wish
And let my wish be granted;* it was granted.
Granted, granted . . . Poor Hänsel, once too powerless
To shelter your own children from the cold

Or quiet their bellies with the thinnest gruel,
It was not power that you lacked, but wishes.
Had you not learned – have we not learned, from tales
Neither of beasts nor kingdoms nor their Lord,
But of our own hearts, the realm of death –
Neither to rule nor die? to change, to change!

90 North

At home, in my flannel gown, like a bear to its floe,
I clambered to bed; up the globe's impossible sides
I sailed all night – till at last, with my black beard,
My furs and my dogs, I stood at the northern pole.

There in the childish night my companions lay frozen,
The stiff furs knocked at my starveling throat,
And I gave my great sigh: the flakes came huddling,
Were they really my end? In the darkness I turned to my rest.

– Here, the flag snaps in the glare and silence
Of the unbroken ice. I stand here,
The dogs bark, my beard is black, and I stare
At the North Pole . . .
                                   And now what? Why, go back.

Turn as I please, my step is to the south.
The world – my world spins on this final point
Of cold and wretchedness: all lines, all winds
End in this whirlpool I at last discover.

And it is meaningless. In the child's bed
After the night's voyage, in that warm world
Where people work and suffer for the end
That crowns the pain – in that Cloud-Cuckoo-Land

I reached my North and it had meaning.
Here at the actual pole of my existence,
Where all that I have done is meaningless,
Where I die or live by accident alone –

Where, living or dying, I am still alone;
Here where North, the night, the berg of death
Crowd me out of the ignorant darkness,
I see at last that all the knowledge

I wrung from the darkness – that the darkness flung me –
Is worthless as ignorance: nothing comes from nothing,
The darkness from the darkness. Pain comes from the
    darkness
And we call it wisdom. It is pain.

The Death of the Ball Turret Gunner

From my mother's sleep I fell into the State,
And I hunched in its belly till my wet fur froze.
Six miles from earth, loosed from its dream of life,
I woke to black flak and the nightmare fighters.
When I died they washed me out of the turret with a hose.

Next Day

Moving from Cheer to joy, from joy to All,
I take a box
And add it to my wild rice, my Cornish game hens.
The slacked or shorted, basketed, identical
Food-gathering flocks
Are selves I overlook. Wisdom, said William James,

Is learning what to overlook. And I am wise
If that is wisdom.
Yet somehow, as I buy All from these shelves
And the boy takes it to my station wagon,
What I've become
Troubles me even if I shut my eyes.

When I was young and miserable and pretty
And poor, I'd wish
What all girls wish: to have a husband,
A house and children. Now that I'm old, my wish
Is womanish:
That the boy putting groceries in my car

See me. It bewilders me he doesn't see me.
For so many years
I was good enough to eat: the world looked at me
And its mouth watered. How often they have undressed me,
The eyes of strangers!
And, holding their flesh within my flesh, their vile

Imaginings within my imagining,
I too have taken
The chance of life. Now the boy pats my dog
And we start home. Now I am good.
The last mistaken,
Ecstatic, accidental bliss, the blind

Happiness that, bursting, leaves upon the palm
Some soap and water –
It was so long ago, back in some Gay
Twenties, Nineties, I don't know . . . Today I miss
My lovely daughter
Away at school, my sons away at school,

My husband away at work – I wish for them.
The dog, the maid,
And I go through the sure unvarying days
At home in them. As I look at my life,
I am afraid
Only that it will change, as I am changing:

I am afraid, this morning, of my face.
It looks at me
From the rear-view mirror, with the eyes I hate,
The smile I hate. Its plain, lined look
Of gray discovery
Repeats to me: "You're old." That's all, I'm old.

And yet I'm afraid, as I was at the funeral
I went to yesterday.
My friend's cold made-up face, granite among its flowers,
Her undressed, operated-on, dressed body
Were my face and body.
As I think of her I hear her telling me

How young I seem; I *am* exceptional;
I think of all I have.
But really no one is exceptional,
No one has anything, I'm anybody,
I stand beside my grave
Confused with my life, that is commonplace and solitary.

C. H. SISSON

The Un-Red Deer

The un-red deer
In the un-green forest

The antlers which do not appear
And are not like branches

The hounds which do not bay
With tails which do not swish

The heather beyond and the insignificant stumble
Of the horse not pulled up

By the rider who does not see all this
Nor hear nor smell it

Or does so but it does not matter
The horn sounds Gone away

Or, if it does not, is there hunter,
Hunted, or the broken tree

Swept by the wind from the channel?

A Letter to John Donne

On 27 July 1617, Donne preached at the parish church at Sevenoaks, of which he was rector, and was entertained at Knole, then the country residence of Richard Sackville, third Earl of Dorset.

I understand you well enough, John Donne
First, that you were a man of ability
Eaten by lust and by the love of God
Then, that you crossed the Sevenoaks High Street
As rector of Saint Nicholas:
I am of that parish.

To be a man of ability is not much
You may see them on the Sevenoaks platform any day
Eager men with despatch cases

Words when I have them, come out, the Devil
Encouraging, grinning from the other side of the street
And my tears
Streaming, a blubbered face, when I am not laughing
Where in all this
Is calm, measure,
Exactness
The Lord's peace?

2

Nothing is in my own voice because I have not
Any. Nothing in my own name
Here inscribed on water, nothing but flow
A ripple, outwards. Standing beside the Usk
You flow like truth, river, I will get in
Over me, through me perhaps, river let me by crystalline
As I shall not be, shivering upon the bank.
A swan passed. So is it, the surface, sometimes
Benign like a mirror, but not I passing, the bird.

3

Under the bridge, meet reward, the water
Falling in cascades or worse, you devil, for truthfulness
Is no part of the illusion, the clear sky
Is not yours, the water
Falling not yours
Only the sheep
Munching at the river brim
Perhaps

4

What I had hoped for, the clear line
Tremulous like water but
Clear also to the stones underneath
Has not come that way, for my truth
Was not public enough, nor perhaps true.
Holy Father, Almighty God
Stop me before I speak

— per Christum.

5

Lies on my tongue. Get up and bolt the door
For I am coming not to be believed
The messenger of anything I say.

So I am come, stand in the cold tonight
The servant of the grain upon my tongue,
Beware, I am the man, and let me in.

6

So speech is treasured, for the things it gives
Which I can not have, for I speak too plain
Yet not so plain as to be understood
It is confusion and a madman's tongue.
Where drops the reason, there is no one by.
Torture my mind: and so swim through the night
As envy cannot touch you, or myself

Sleep comes, and let her, warm at my side, like death.
The Holy Spirit and the Holy One
Of Israel be my guide. So among tombs
Truth may be sought, and found, if we rejoice
With Ham and Shem and Japhet in the dark
The ark rolls onward over a wide sea.
Come sleep, come lightning, comes the dove at last.

The Herb-Garden

When a stream ran across my path
I stopped, dazzled, though the sparkle was at my feet;
The blind head moving forward, Gulliver
Walking toweringly over the little people.

Not that smaller in size meant, in any way, lesser;
It was merely that I could not see them, my eyes
Crunched on them as if they had been pebbles,
And I blundering without understanding.

Large is inept: how my loping arms fall,
The hands not prehensile, perpendicular
Before an inclined trunk. The legs do the damage,
Like the will of God without rhyme or reason.

Epithalamia are dreamed in this atmosphere
Which towers like a blue fastness over my head.
My head is full of rumours, but the perceptions
Dry like lavender within my skull.

Herb-garden, dream, scent of rosemary,
Scent of thyme, the deep error of sage,
Fennel that falls like a fountain, rue that says nothing,
Blue leaves, in a garden of green.

The Red Admiral

The wings tremble, it is the red admiral
Ecstatically against the garden wall;
September is his enjoyment, but he does not know it,
Name it, or refer to it at all.

The old light fades upon the old stones;
The day is old: how is there such light
From grey clouds? It is the autumnal equinox,
And we shall all have shrunk before daylight.

A woman, a horse and a walnut-tree: old voices
Out of recessed time, in the cracks,
It may be, where the plaster has crumbled:
But the butterfly hugs the blue lias.

The mystery is only the close of day,
Remembered love, which is also present:
Layer upon layer, old times, the fish turning
Once more in the pond, and the absent.

All could not be at once without memory
Crowding out what cannot be remembered;
Better to have none, best of all when
The evening sunlight has ended.

Its finger lighter than spiders, the red admiral
Considers, as I do, with little movement;
With little of anything that is meant:
But let the meaning go, movement is all.

In Flood

A word for everybody, myself nobody,
Hardly a ripple over the wide mere:
There is the winter sunshine over the water,
The spirits everywhere, myself here.

Do you know it? It is Arthur's territory
— Agravaine, Mordred, Guinevere and Igraine —
Do you hear them? Or see them in the distant sparkle?
Likely not, but they are there all the same.

And I who am here, actually and statistically,
Have a wide absence as I look at the sea,
— Waters which "wap and wan", Malory said —
And the battle-pile of those he accounted dead.

Yet his word breathes still upon the ripple
Which is innumerable but, more like a leaf
Curled in autumn and blown through the winter,
I on this hillside take my last of life:

Only glad that when I go to join them
I shall be speechless, no one will ask my name,
Yet among the named dead I shall be gathered,
Speaking to no man, not spoken to, but in place.

Tristia

I

It is because of exile I am here,
The utmost tip of the world, for old age
Brings one to the edge of what one lived among.
Before departure I was of that race
Which passed the time but thought of something else,
But now time fills the whole horizon:
Not what yesterday was or what tomorrow
Will bring, for what it brought is dead,
And what it will, will never come to life.
When will it pass? is all I have to ask.
No one is implicated in that question
But I who now no longer live among
Even those who see me now as I do them.
But "as" is not the word I should have used,
For age has given sight in its own blindness,
And no impression is conveyed to me
Which tells me it is here that I belong.
I am the utmost tip of what once was,
Beyond which there is nothing but the sea;
The stationary Pontic cold holds all.

I look towards it, not to those I know,
Though casual bodies hurrying in the street
May hold the eye enough to make a glance,
But where they go is not where I will go:
I turn back to the water and I am lost.

2

No one will speak to you, nor you to any:
This is the end of all communication
Which was the hope which brought you to this end
And served delusively to coax you on.
The road that leads to death goes single file,
And so it always was. Though each in turn
Surrounds himself with dreams of other minds,
The bodies which should hold them have no voice.
The voice of every lonely traveller
Is loud with silence as the company
He sees around him as he passes on.
Why then these verses? Nothing can be heard.
But speak on as you will, you who are young.
Collude with one another on the way:
Proximity may do what words will not.

3

The hollow name of Love sounds through the streets,
The newsboy crying while the city burns.
The lack of any purpose of my own
Cries louder, and the city is consumed.
The state denies the Church, the Church the state;
The promises of neither have come true,
Or so it seems, here at the door of death.

4

The past is only past which never present was:
Nor is there present now but that vain show of past.
Reality has faded into dream
— A dream without cohesion or event.
Oddities now show nothing but oddities,
For meaning has escaped. Where purpose was
Is nothing but consecutive array
Of matters past which do not matter now.

5

The day is over and the night begins,
But what is day which so resembles night?
Forgetfulness and sleep are of a piece.
The tail-end of the world: and here am I
Pledged to a narrowing prospect. I stand here
While the world fails or falters in my eye.

6

Here on this promontory by the sea,
Speech has no meaning, yet we use it still:
The flagged signal, the gesticulation,
Serve better to elicit a reply.
Yet we walk on, dazed and with hollow voice.
The empty shell you see is what you hear:
The tolling bell will tell the truth at last.

7

The crystal world that was, when I was there:
The broken morning and the silver eve,
The flashing woodland and the dew on grass,
The moon lighting up what the sun has left.
Such a world must be somewhere, but not here.
Even the sea breaking upon the rocks.
Crashes no more, but laps this final shore,
Soon to be frozen. There is wind,
But only hissing as it sidles by.
O send the blustering past in new array,
And let me find the quartz within the stone.

8

The naked person is the only one
Who speaks within the chatter of our speech:
There is no truth in reason or abstraction.
They are the garments that the body wears,
The chatter of the magpie, not the bird
Which walks before the eye in black and white.
The body gives direction to our speech,
As to our thoughts: your shape is what you are,
And what you are is what I seek to know.
The brilliant knowledge which escapes me here,
At this far tip of the world, is what the mind
Can take immediately from what it sees,
Plain without any need for explanation.
So strip before my eyes and speak in tune
With what you are, and that will be the truth

– A momentary revelation
To clear the clouds which else envelop me.
But if you think cloud is where I belong,
Pile on your clothes and chatter in the words
The magpie uses and the world applauds.

9

Speech cannot be betrayed, for speech betrays,
And what we say reveals the men we are.
But, once come to a land where no one is,
We long for conversation, and a voice
Which answers what we say when we succeed
In saying for a moment that which is.
O careless world, which covers what is there
With what it hopes, or what best cheats and pays,
But speech with others needs another tongue.
For *a* to speak to *b*, and *b* to *a*,
A stream of commonalty must be found,
Rippling at times, at times in even flow,
And yet it turns to Lethe in the end.

10

I am the place where I belong,
For other self or place is not:
The horror of the world extends
Beyond that bourn and never ends.
No friend, no other haunts that space
Which, empty as infinity,
Means no more to me than myself.
Send me particulars and limits,
The tactile and the visible.
Here only nullity is left:
What was lost has lost its place
– No, place has gone as time has gone,
And I have never been, nor am.

DYLAN THOMAS

The Hand that Signed the Paper

The hand that signed the paper felled a city;
Five sovereign fingers taxed the breath,
Doubled the globe of dead and halved a country;
These five kings did a king to death.

The mighty hand leads to a sloping shoulder,
The finger joints are cramped with chalk;
A goose's quill has put an end to murder
That put an end to talk.

The hand that signed the treaty bred a fever,
And famine grew, and locusts came;
Great is the hand that holds dominion over
Man by a scribbled name.

The five kings count the dead but do not soften
The crusted wound nor stroke the brow;
A hand rules pity as a hand rules heaven;
Hands have no tears to flow.

"The force that through the green fuse drives the flower"

The force that through the green fuse drives the flower
Drives my green age; that blasts the roots of trees
Is my destroyer.
And I am dumb to tell the crooked rose
My youth is bent by the same wintry fever.

The force that drives the water through the rocks
Drives my red blood; that dries the mouthing streams
Turns mine to wax.
And I am dumb to mouth unto my veins
How at the mountain spring the same mouth sucks.

The hand that whirls the water in the pool
Stirs the quicksand; that ropes the blowing wind
Hauls my shroud sail.
And I am dumb to tell the hanging man
How of my clay is made the hangman's lime.

The lips of time leech to the fountain head;
Love drips and gathers, but the fallen blood
Shall calm her sores.
And I am dumb to tell a weather's wind
How time has ticked a heaven round the stars.

And I am dumb to tell the lover's tomb
How at my sheet goes the same crooked worm.

A Refusal to Mourn the Death, by Fire, of a Child in London

Never until the mankind making
Bird beast and flower
Fathering and all humbling darkness
Tells with silence the last light breaking
And the still hour
Is come of the sea tumbling in harness

And I must enter again the round
Zion of the water bead
And the synagogue of the ear of corn
Shall I let pray the shadow of a sound
Or sow my salt seed
In the least valley of sackcloth to mourn

The majesty and burning of the child's death.
I shall not murder
The mankind of her going with a grave truth
Nor blaspheme down the stations of the breath
With any further
Elegy of innocence and youth.

Deep with the first dead lies London's daughter,
Robed in the long friends,
The grains beyond age, the dark veins of her mother,
Secret by the unmourning water
Of the riding Thames.
After the first death, there is no other.

Fern Hill

Now as I was young and easy under the apple boughs
About the lilting house and happy as the grass was green,
   The night above the dingle starry,
      Time let me hail and climb
   Golden in the heydays of his eyes,
And honoured among wagons I was prince of the apple towns
And once below a time I lordly had the trees and leaves
      Trail with daisies and barley
   Down the rivers of the windfall light.

And as I was green and carefree, famous among the barns
About the happy yard and singing as the farm was home,
   In the sun that is young once only,
      Time let me play and be
   Golden in the mercy of his means,
And green and golden I was huntsman and herdsman, the calves
Sang to my horn, the foxes on the hills barked clear and cold,
      And the sabbath rang slowly
   In the pebbles of the holy streams.

All the sun long it was running, it was lovely, the hay
Fields high as the house, the tunes from the chimneys, it was air
   And playing, lovely and watery
      And fire green as grass.
   And nightly under the simple stars
As I rode to sleep the owls were bearing the farm away,
All the moon long I heard, blessed among stables, the nightjars
   Flying with the ricks, and the horses
      Flashing into the dark.

And then to awake, and the farm, like a wanderer white
With the dew, come back, the cock on his shoulder: it was all
   Shining, it was Adam and maiden,
      The sky gathered again
   And the sun grew round that very day.
So it must have been after the birth of the simple light
In the first, spinning place, the spellbound horses walking warm
   Out of the whinnying green stable
      On to the fields of praise.

And honoured among foxes and pheasants by the gay house
Under the new made clouds and happy as the heart was long,
   In the sun born over and over,
      I ran my heedless ways,
   My wishes raced through the house high hay
And nothing I cared, at my sky blue trades, that time allows
In all his tuneful turning so few and such morning songs
   Before the children green and golden
      Follow him out of grace,

Nothing I cared, in the lamb white days, that time would take me
Up to the swallow thronged loft by the shadow of my hand,
   In the moon that is always rising,
      Nor that riding to sleep
   I should hear him fly with the high fields

And wake to the farm forever fled from the childless land.
Oh as I was young and easy in the mercy of his means,
　　Time held me green and dying
　Though I sang in my chains like the sea.

"Do not go gentle into that good night"

Do not go gentle into that good night,
Old age should burn and rave at close of day;
Rage, rage against the dying of the light.

Though wise men at their end know dark is right,
Because their words had forked no lightning they
Do not go gentle into that good night.

Good men, the last wave by, crying how bright
Their frail deeds might have danced in a green bay,
Rage, rage against the dying of the light.

Wild men who caught and sang the sun in flight,
And learn, too late, they grieved it on its way,
Do not go gentle into that good night.

Grave men, near death, who see with blinding sight
Blind eyes could blaze like meteors and be gay,
Rage, rage against the dying of the light.

And you, my father, there on the sad height,
Curse, bless, me now with your fierce tears, I pray.
Do not go gentle into that good night.
Rage, rage against the dying of the light.

JUDITH WRIGHT

At Cooloolah

The blue crane fishing in Cooloolah's twilight
has fished there longer than our centuries.
He is the certain heir of lake and evening,
and he will wear their colour till he dies;

but I'm a stranger, come of a conquering people.
I cannot share his calm, who watch his lake,
being unloved by all my eyes delight in
and made uneasy, for an old murder's sake.

Those dark-skinned people who once named Cooloolah
knew that no land is lost or won by wars,
for earth is spirit; the invader's feet will tangle
in nets there and his blood be thinned by fears.

Riding at noon and ninety years ago,
my grandfather was beckoned by a ghost –
a black accoutred warrior armed for fighting,
who sank into bare plain, as now into time past.

White shores of sand, plumed reed and paperbark,
clear heavenly levels frequented by crane and swan –
I know that we are justified only by love,
but oppressed by arrogant guilt, have room for none.

And walking on clean sand among the prints
of bird and animal, I am challenged by a driftwood spear
thrust from the water; and, like my grandfather,
must quiet a heart accused by its own fear.

Australia 1970

Die, wild country, like the eaglehawk,
dangerous till the last breath's gone,
clawing and striking. Die
cursing your captor through a raging eye.

Die like the tigersnake
that hisses such pure hatred from its pain
as fills the killer's dreams
with fear like suicide's invading stain.

Suffer, wild country, like the ironwood
that gaps the dozer-blade.
I see your living soil ebb with the tree
to naked poverty.

Die like the soldier-ant
mindless and faithful to your million years.
Though we corrupt you with our torturing mind,
stay obstinate; stay blind.

For we are conquerors and self-poisoners
more than scorpion or snake
and dying of the venoms that we make
even while you die of us.

I praise the scoring drought, the flying dust,
the drying creek, the furious animal,
that they oppose us still;
that we are ruined by the thing we kill.

Lament for Passenger Pigeons

(*"Don't ask for the meaning, ask for the use."* – Wittgenstein)

The voice of water as it flows and falls,
the noise air makes against earth-surfaces
have changed; are changing to the tunes we choose.

What wooed and echoed in the pigeon's voice?
We have not heard the bird. How reinvent
that passenger, its million wings and hues,

when we have lost the bird, the thing itself,
the sheen of life on flashing long migrations?
Might human musics hold it, could we hear?

Trapped in the fouling nests of time and space,
we turn the music on; but it is man,
and it is man who lends a deafening ear.

And it is man we eat and man we drink
and man who thickens round us like a stain.
Ice at the polar axis smells of men.

A word, a class, a formula, a use:
that is the rhythm, the cycle we impose.
The sirens sang us to the ends of sea,

and changed to us; their voices were our own,
jug-jug to dirty ears in dirtied brine.
Pigeons and angels sang us to the sky

and turned to metal and a dirty need.
The height of sky, the depth of sea we are,
sick with a yellow stain, a fouling dye.

Whatever Being is, that formula,
it dies as we pursue it past the word.
We have not asked the meaning, but the use.

What is the use of water when it dims?
The use of air that whines an emptiness?
The use of glass-eyed pigeons caged in glass?

We listen to the sea, that old machine,
to air that hoarsens on earth-surfaces
and has no angel, no migrating cry.

What is the being and the end of man?
Blank surfaces reverb a human voice
whose echo tells us that we choose to die:

or else, against the blank of everything,
to reinvent that passenger, that bird-
siren-and-angel image we contain
essential in a constellating word.
To sing of Being, its escaping wing,
to utter absence in a human chord
and recreate the meaning as we sing.

from *Notes at Edge*
Brevity

Old Rhythm, old Metre,
these days I don't draw
very deep breaths. There isn't
much left to say.

Rhyme, my old cymbal,
I don't clash you as often,
or trust your old promises
of music and unison.

I used to love Keats, Blake;
now I try haiku
for its honed brevities,
its inclusive silences.

Issa. Shiki. Buson. Bashō.
Few words and with no rhetoric.
Enclosed by silence
as is the thrush's call.

from *The Shadow of Fire: Ghazals*

Rockpool

My generation is dying, after long lives
swung from war to depression to war to fatness.

I watch the claws in the rockpool, the scuttle, the crouch –
green humps, the biggest barnacled, eaten by seaworms.

In comes the biggest wave, the irresistible
clean wash and backswirl. Where have the dead gone?

At night on the beach the galaxy looks like a grin.
Entropy has unbraided Berenice's hair.

We've brought on our own cancers, one with the world.
I hang on the rockpool's edge, its wild embroideries:

admire it, pore on it, this, the devouring, the mating,
ridges of coloured tracery, occupants, all the living,

the stretching of toothed claws to food, the breeding
on the ocean's edge. "Accept it? Gad, madam, you had better."

Summer

This place's quality is not its former nature
but a struggle to heal itself after many wounds.

Upheaved ironstone, mudstone, quartz and clay
drank dark blood once, heard cries and the running of feet.

Now that the miners' huts are a tumble of chimney-stones,
shafts near the river shelter a city of wombats.

Scabs of growth form slowly over the rocks.
Lichens, algae, wind-bent saplings grow.

I'll never know its inhabitants. Evening torchlight
catches the moonstone eyes of big wolf-spiders.

All day the jenny-lizard dug hard ground
watching for shadows of hawk or kookaburra.

At evening, her pearl-eggs hidden, she raked back earth
over the tunnel, wearing a wide grey smile.

In a burned-out summer, I try to see without words
as they do. But I live through a web of language.

Oppositions

Today I was caught alone in a summer storm
counting heartbeats from flash to crash of thunder.

From a small plane once I looked down a cliff of cloud.
Like God to Moses, it exploded into instructions.

Home, a yellow frog on the shower-pipe
startled my hand and watched me as I watch lightning.

Frog, my towel is wet, my hair dripping,
but you don't for such reasons take me to be a refuge.

Small damp peaceful sage with a loony grin,
("one minute of sitting, one inch of Buddha")[1]

a long time back we clambered up the shore
and learned to play with fire. Now there's no stopping us.

Back to the drainpipe, frog, don't follow me.
I'm off to dry my hair by the radiator.

I can't believe that wine's warm solaces
don't help the searcher: the poet on the wineshop floor

1. Manzan (1635–1714)

was given his revelations. The hermit of Cold Mountain
laughs as loudly perhaps – I choose fire, not snow.

Dust

In my sixty-eighth year drought stopped the song of the rivers,
sent ghosts of wheatfields blowing over the sky.

In the swimming-hole the water's dropped so low
I bruise my knees on rocks which are new acquaintances.

The daybreak moon is blurred in a gauze of dust.
Long ago my mother's face looked through a grey motor-veil.

Fallen leaves on the current scarcely move.
But the azure kingfisher flashes upriver still.

Poems written in age confuse the years.
We all live, said Bashō, in a phantom dwelling.

Winter

Today's white fog won't rise above the tree-tops.
Yesterday's diamond frost has melted to icewater.

Old age and winter are said to have much in common.
Let's pile more wood on the fire and drink red wine.

These hundreds of books on the shelves have all been read,
but I can't force my mind to recall their wisdom.

Let's drink while we can. The sum of it all is Energy,
and that went into the wood, the wine, the poems.

Logs on the fire burn out into smoke and ash.
Let's talk today, though words die out on the air.

Out of the past and the books we must have learned something.
What do we know, what path does the red wine take?

I cleared white hair from my brush on the dressing-table
and dropped it into the fire. Some protein-chains the less.

How long would my hair be now if all the clippings
from the salon-floors returned to join their links?

The paths that energy takes on its way to exhaustion
are not to be forecast. These pathways, you and me,

followed unguessable routes. But all of us end
at the same point, like the wood on the fire,

the wine in the belly. Let's drink to that point – like Hafiz.

Patterns

"Brighter than a thousand suns" – that blinding glare
circled the world and settled in our bones.

Human eyes impose a human pattern,
decipher constellations against featureless dark.

All's fire, said Heraclitus; measures of it
kindle as others fade. All changes yet all's one.

We are born of ethereal fire and we return there.
Understand the Logos; reconcile opposing principles.

Perhaps the dark itself is the source of meaning,
the fires of the galaxy its visible destruction.

Round earth's circumference and atmosphere
bombs and warheads crouch waiting their time.

Strontium in the bones (the mass-number of 90)
is said to be "a good conductor of electricity".

Well, Greek, we have not found the road to virtue.
I shiver by the fire this winter day.

The play of opposites, their interpenetration –
there's the reality, the fission and the fusion.

Impossible to choose between absolutes, ultimates.
Pure light, pure lightlessness cannot be perceived.

"Twisted are the hearts of men – dark powers possess them.
Burn the distant evildoer, the unseen sinner."

That prayer to Agni, fire-god, cannot be prayed.
We are all of us born of fire, possessed by darkness.

ROBERT LOWELL

Mr Edwards and the Spider

I saw the spiders marching through the air,
Swimming from tree to tree that mildewed day
  In latter August when the hay
   Came creaking to the barn. But where
    The wind is westerly,
Where gnarled November makes the spiders fly
Into the apparitions of the sky,
They purpose nothing but their ease and die
Urgently beating east to sunrise and the sea;

What are we in the hands of the great God?
It was in vain you set up thorn and briar
  In battle array against the fire
   And treason crackling in your blood;
    For the wild thorns grow tame
And will do nothing to oppose the flame;
Your lacerations tell the losing game
You play against a sickness past your cure.
How will the hands be strong? How will the heart endure?

A very little thing, a little worm,
Or hourglass-blazoned spider, it is said,
  Can kill a tiger. Will the dead
   Hold up his mirror and affirm
    To the four winds the smell
And flash of his authority? It's well
If God who holds you to the pit of hell,
Much as one holds a spider, will destroy,
Baffle and dissipate your soul. As a small boy

On Windsor Marsh, I saw the spider die
When thrown into the bowels of fierce fire:
  There's no long struggle, no desire
   To get up on its feet and fly –
    It stretches out its feet
And dies. This is the sinner's last retreat;
Yes, and no strength exerted on the heat
Then sinews the abolished will, when sick
And full of burning, it will whistle on a brick.

But who can plumb the sinking of that soul?
Josiah Hawley, picture yourself cast
   Into a brick-kiln where the blast
   Fans your quick vitals to a coal –
     If measured by a glass,
How long would it seem burning! Let there pass
A minute, ten, ten trillion; but the blaze
Is infinite, eternal: this is death,
To die and know it. This is the Black Widow, death.

Skunk Hour

(For Elizabeth Bishop)

Nautilus Island's hermit
heiress still lives through winter in her Spartan
     cottage;
her sheep still graze above the sea.
Her son's a bishop. Her farmer
is first selectman in our village,
she's in her dotage.

Thirsting for
the hierarchic privacy
of Queen Victoria's century,
she buys up all
the eyesores facing her shore,
and lets them fall.

The season's ill –
we've lost our summer millionaire,
who seemed to leap from an L. L. Bean
catalogue. His nine-knot yawl
was auctioned off to lobstermen.
A red fox stain covers Blue Hill.

And now our fairy
decorator brightens his shop for fall,
his fishnet's filled with orange cork,
orange, his cobbler's bench and awl,
there is no money in his work,
he'd rather marry.

One dark night,
my Tudor Ford climbed the hill's skull,
I watched for love-cars. Lights turned down,
they lay together, hull to hull,
where the graveyard shelves on the town . . .
My mind's not right.

A car radio bleats,
"Love, O careless Love . . . " I hear
my ill-spirit sob in each blood cell,
as if my hand were at its throat . . .
I myself am hell,
nobody's here —

only skunks, that search
in the moonlight for a bite to eat.
They march on their soles up Main Street:
white stripes, moonstruck eyes' red fire
under the chalk-dry and spar spire
of the Trinitarian Church.

I stand on top
of our back steps and breathe the rich air —
a mother skunk with her column of kittens swills the
        garbage pail.
She jabs her wedge head in a cup
of sour cream, drops her ostrich tail,
and will not scare.

The Flaw

A seal swims like a poodle through the sheet
of blinding salt. A country graveyard, here
and there a rock, and here and there a pine,
throbs on the essence of the gasoline.
Some mote, some eye-flaw, wobbles in the heat,
hair-thin, hair-dark, the fragment of a hair —

a noose, a question? All is possible;
if there's free will, it's something like this hair,
inside my eye, outside my eye, yet free,
airless as grace, if the good God . . . I see.
Our bodies quiver. In this rustling air,
all's possible, all's unpredictable.

Old wives and husbands! Look, their gravestones wait
in couples with the names and half the date –
one future and one freedom. In a flash,
I see us whiten into skeletons,
our eager, sharpened cries, a pair of stones,
cutting like shark-fins through the boundless wash.

Two walking cobwebs, almost bodiless,
crossed paths here once, kept house, and lay in beds.
Your fingertips once touched my fingertips
and set us tingling through a thousand threads.
Poor pulsing *Fête Champêtre!* The summer slips
between our fingers into nothingness.

We too lean forward, as the heat waves roll
over our bodies, grown insensible,
ready to dwindle off into the soul,
two motes or eye-flaws, the invisible . . .
Hope of the hopeless launched and cast adrift
on the great flaw that gives the final gift.

Dear Figure curving like a questionmark,
how will you hear my answer in the dark?

Night Sweat

Work-table, litter, books and standing lamp,
plain things, my stalled equipment, the old broom –
but I am living in a tidied room,
for ten nights now I've felt the creeping damp
float over my pajamas' wilted white . . .
Sweet salt embalms me and my head is wet,
everything streams and tells me this is right;
my life's fever is soaking in night sweat –
one life, one writing! But the downward glide
and bias of existing wrings us dry –
always inside me is the child who died,
always inside me is his will to die –
one universe, one body . . . in this urn
the animal night sweats of the spirit burn.

Behind me! You! Again I feel the light
lighten my leaded eyelids, while the gray
skulled horses whinny for the soot of night.
I dabble in the dapple of the day,
a heap of wet clothes, seamy, shivering,
I see my flesh and bedding washed with light,
my child exploding into dynamite,
my wife . . . your lightness alters everything,
and tears the black web from the spider's sack,
as your heart hops and flutters like a hare.
Poor turtle, tortoise, if I cannot clear
the surface of these troubled waters here,
absolve me, help me, Deart Heart, as you bear
this world's dead weight and cycle on your back.

For the Union Dead

"Relinquunt Omnia Servare Rem Publicam."

The old South Boston Aquarium stands
in a Sahara of snow now. Its broken windows are boarded.
The bronze weathervane cod has lost half its scales.
The airy tanks are dry.

Once my nose crawled like a snail on the glass;
my hand tingled
to burst the bubbles
drifting from the noses of the cowed, compliant fish.

My hand draws back. I often sigh still
for the dark downward and vegetating kingdom
of the fish and reptile. One morning last March,
I pressed against the new barbed and galvanized

fence on the Boston Common. Behind their cage,
yellow dinosaur steamshovels were grunting
as they cropped up tons of mush and grass
to gouge their underworld garage.

Parking spaces luxuriate like civic
sandpiles in the heart of Boston.
A girdle of orange, Puritan-pumpkin colored girders
braces the tingling Statehouse,

shaking over the excavations, as it faces Colonel Shaw
and his bell-cheeked Negro infantry
on St. Gaudens' shaking Civil War relief,
propped by a plank splint against the garage's earthquake.

Two months after marching through Boston,
half the regiment was dead;
at the dedication,
William James could almost hear the bronze Negroes
        breathe.

Their monument sticks like a fishbone
in the city's throat.
Its Colonel is as lean
as a compass-needle.

He has an angry wrenlike vigilance,
a greyhound's gentle tautness;
he seems to wince at pleasure,
and suffocate for privacy.

He is out of bounds now. He rejoices in man's lovely,
peculiar power to choose life and die –
when he leads his black soldiers to death,
he cannot bend his back.

On a thousand small town New England greens,
the old white churches hold their air
of sparse, sincere rebellion; frayed flags
quilt the graveyards of the Grand Army of the Republic.

The stone statues of the abstract Union Soldier
grow slimmer and younger each year –
wasp-waisted, they doze over muskets
and muse through their sideburns . . .

Shaw's father wanted no monument
except the ditch,
where his son's body was thrown
and lost with his "niggers."

The ditch is nearer.
There are no statues for the last war here;
on Boyleston Street, a commercial photograph
shows Hiroshima boiling

over a Mosler Safe, the "Rock of Ages"
that survived the blast. Space is nearer.
When I crouch to my television set,
the drained faces of Negro school-children rise like balloons.

Colonel Shaw
is riding on his bubble,
he waits
for the bléssed break.

The Aquarium is gone. Everywhere,
giant finned cars nose forward like fish;
a savage servility
slides by on grease.

Waking Early Sunday Morning

O to break loose, like the chinook
salmon jumping and falling back,
nosing up to the impossible
stone and bone-crushing waterfall –
raw-jawed, weak-fleshed there, stopped by ten
steps of the roaring ladder, and then
to clear the top on the last try,
alive enough to spawn and die.

Stop, back off. The salmon breaks
water, and now my body wakes
to feel the unpolluted joy
and criminal leisure of a boy –
no rainbow smashing a dry fly
in the white run is free as I,
here squatting like a dragon on
time's hoard before the day's begun!

Vermin run for their unstopped holes;
in some dark nook a fieldmouse rolls
a marble, hours on end, then stops;
the termite in the woodwork sleeps –
listen, the creatures of the night
obsessive, casual, sure of foot,
go on grinding, while the sun's
daily remorseful blackout dawns.

Fierce, fireless mind, running downhill.
Look up and see the harbour fill:
business as usual in eclipse
goes down to the sea in ships –
wake of refuse, dacron rope,
bound for Bermuda or Good Hope,
all bright before the morning watch
the wine-dark hulls of yawl and ketch.

I watch a glass of water wet
with a fine fuzz of icy sweat,
silvery colours touched with sky,
serene in their neutrality –
yet if I shift, or change my mood,
I see some object made of wood,
background behind it of brown grain,
to darken it, but not to stain.

O that the spirit could remain
tinged but untarnished by its strain!
Better dressed and stacking birch,
or lost with the Faithful at Church –
anywhere, but somewhere else!
And now the new electric bells,
clearly chiming, 'Faith of our fathers',
and now the congregation gathers.

O Bible chopped and crucified
in hymns we hear but do not read,
none of the milder subtleties
of grace or art will sweeten these
stiff quatrains shovelled out four-square –
they sing of peace, and preach despair;
yet they gave darkness some control,
and left a loophole for the soul.

No, put old clothes on, and explore
the corners of the woodshed for
its dregs and dreck: tools with no handle,
ten candle-ends not worth a candle,
old lumber banished from the Temple,
damned by Paul's precept and example,
cast from the kingdom, banned in Israel,
the wordless sign, the tinkling cymbal.

When will we see Him face to face?
Each day, He shines through darker glass –
In this small town where everything
is known, I see His vanishing
emblems, His white spire and flag-
pole sticking out above the fog,
like old white china doorknobs, sad,
slight, useless things to calm the mad.

Hammering military splendour,
top-heavy Goliath in full armour –
little redemption in the mass
liquidations of their brass,
elephant and phalanx moving
with the times and still improving,
when that kingdom hit the crash:
a million foreskins stacked like trash . . .

Sing softer! But what if a new
diminuendo brings no true
tenderness, only restlessness,
excess, the hunger for success,
sanity of self-deception
fixed and kicked by reckless caution,
while we listen to the bells –
anywhere, but somewhere else!

O to break loose. All life's grandeur
is something with a girl in summer . . .
elated as the President
girdled by his establishment
this Sunday morning, free to chaff
his own thoughts with his bear-cuffed staff,
swimming nude, unbuttoned, sick
of his ghost-written rhetoric!

No weekends for the gods now. Wars
flicker, earth licks its open sores,
fresh breakage, fresh promotions, chance
assassinations, no advance.
Only man thinning out his kind
sounds through the Sabbath noon, the blind
swipe of the pruner and his knife
busy about the tree of life . . .

Pity the planet, all joy gone
from this sweet volcanic cone;
peace to our children when they fall
in small war on the heels of small
war – until the end of time
to police the earth, a ghost
orbiting forever lost
in our monotonous sublime.

Epilogue

Those blessèd structures, plot and rhyme –
why are they no help to me now
I want to make
something imagined, not recalled?
I hear the noise of my own voice:
The painter's vision is not a lens,
it trembles to caress the light.
But sometimes everything I write
with the threadbare art of my eye
seems a snapshot,
lurid, rapid, garish, grouped,
heightened from life,
yet paralyzed by fact.
All's misalliance.
Yet why not say what happened?
Pray for the grace of accuracy
Vermeer gave to the sun's illumination
stealing like the tide across a map
to his girl solid with yearning.
We are poor passing facts,
warned by that to give
each figure in the photograph
his living name.

W. S. GRAHAM

The Thermal Stair

For the painter Peter Lanyon
killed in a gliding accident 1964

I called today, Peter, and you were away.
I look out over Botallack and over Ding
Dong and Levant and over the jasper sea.

Find me a thermal to speak and soar to you from
Over Lanyon Quoit and the circling stones standing
High on the moor over Gurnard's Head where some

Time three foxglove summers ago, you came.
The days are shortening over Little Parc Owles.
The poet or painter steers his life to maim

Himself somehow for the job. His job is Love
Imagined into words or paint to make
An object that will stand and will not move.

Peter, I called and you were away, speaking
Only through what you made and at your best.
Look, there above Botallack, the buzzard riding

The salt updraught slides off the broken air
And out of sight to quarter a new place.
The Celtic sea, the Methodist sea is there.

        You said once in the Engine
        House below Morvah
        That words make their world
        In the same way as the painter's
        Mark surprises him
        Into seeing new.
        Sit here on the sparstone
        In this ruin where
        Once the early beam
        Engine pounded and broke
        The air with industry.

        Now the chuck of daws
        And the listening sea.

"Shall we go down" you said
"Before the light goes
And stand under the old
Tinworkings around
Morvah and St Just?"
You said "Here is the sea
Made by alfred wallis
Or any poet or painter's
Eye it encountered.
Or is it better made
By all those vesselled men
Sometime it maintained?
We all make it again."

Give me your hand, Peter,
To steady me on the word.

Seventy-two by sixty,
Italy hangs on the wall.
A woman stands with a drink
In some polite place
And looks at SARACINESCO
And turns to mention space.
That one if she could
Would ride Artistically
The thermals you once rode.

Peter, the phallic boys
Begin to wink their lights.
Godrevy and the Wolf
Are calling Opening Time.
We'll take the quickest way
The tin singers made.
Climb here where the hand
Will not grasp on air.
And that dark-suited man
Has set the dominoes out
On the Queen's table.
Peter, we'll sit and drink
And go in the sea's roar
To Labrador with wallis
Or rise on Lanyon's stair.

Uneasy, lovable man, give me your painting
Hand to steady me taking the word-road home.
Lanyon, why is it you're earlier away?
Remember me wherever you listen from.
Lanyon, dingdong dingdong from carn to carn.
It seems tonight all Closing bells are tolling
Across the Duchy shire wherever I turn.

Imagine a Forest

Imagine a forest
A real forest.

You are walking in it and it sighs
Round you where you go in a deep
Ballad on the border of a time
You have seemed to walk in before.
It is nightfall and you go through
Trying to find between the twittering
Shades the early starlight edge
Of the open moor land you know.
I have set you here and it is not a dream
I put you through. Go on between
The elephant bark of those beeches
Into that lightening, almost glade.

And he has taken
My word and gone

Through his own Ettrick darkening
Upon himself and he's come across
A glinted knight lying dying
On needles under a high tree.
Ease his visor open gently
To reveal whatever white, encased
Face will ask out at you who
It is you are or if you will
Finish him off. His eyes are open.
Imagine he does not speak. Only
His beard moving against the metal
Signs that he would like to speak.

Imagine a room
Where you are home

Taking your boots off from the wood
In that deep ballad very not
A dream and the fire noisily
Kindling up and breaking its sticks.
Do not imagine I put you there
For nothing. I put you through it
There in that holt of words between
The bearded liveoaks and the beeches
For you to meet a man alone
Slipping out of whatever cause
He thought he lay there dying for.

Hang up the ballad
Behind the door.

You are come home but you are about
To not fight hard enough and die
In a no less desolate dark wood
Where a stranger shall never enter.

Imagine a forest
A real forest.

Johann Joachim Quantz's Five Lessons

The First Lesson

So that each person may quickly find that
Which particularly concerns him, certain metaphors
Convenient to us within the compass of this
Lesson are to be allowed. It is best I sit
Here where I am to speak on the other side
Of language. You, of course, in your own time
And incident (I speak in the small hours.)
Will listen from your side. I am very pleased
We have sought us out. No doubt you have read
My Flute Book. Come. The Guild clock's iron men
Are striking out their few deserted hours
And here from my high window Brueghel's winter
Locks the canal below. I blow my fingers.

The Second Lesson

Good morning, Karl. Sit down. I have been thinking
About your progress and my progress as one
Who teaches you, a young man with talent
And the rarer gift of application. I think
You must now be becoming a musician
Of a certain calibre. It is right maybe
That in our lessons now I should expect
Slight and very polite impatiences
To show in you. Karl, I think it is true,
You are now nearly able to play the flute.

Now we must try higher, aware of the terrible
Shapes of silence sitting outside your ear
Anxious to define you and really love you.
Remember silence is curious about its opposite
Element which you shall learn to represent.

Enough of that. Now stand in the correct position
So that the wood of the floor will come up through you.
Stand, but not too stiff. Keep your elbows down.
Now take a simple breath and make me a shape
Of clear unchained started and finished tones.
Karl, as well as you are able, stop
Your fingers into the breathing apertures
And speak and make the cylinder delight us.

The Third Lesson

Karl, you are late. The traverse flute is not
A study to take lightly. I am cold waiting.
Put one piece of coal in the stove. This lesson
Shall not be prolonged. Right. Stand in your place.

Ready? Blow me a little ladder of sound
From a good stance so that you feel the heavy
Press of the floor coming up through you and
Keeping your pitch and tone in character.
Now that is something, Karl. You are getting on.
Unswell your head. One more piece of coal.
Go on now but remember it must be always
Easy and flowing. Light and shadow must
Be varied but be varied in your mind
Before you hear the eventual return sound.

Play me the dance you made for the barge-master.
Stop stop Karl. Play it as you first thought
Of it in the hot boat-kitchen. That is a pleasure
For me. I can see I am making you good.
Keep the stove red. Hand me the matches. Now
We can see better. Give me a shot at the pipe.
Karl, I can still put on a good flute-mouth
And show you in this high cold room something
You will be famous to have said you heard.

The Fourth Lesson

You are early this morning. What we have to do
Today is think of you as a little creator
After the big creator. And it can be argued
You are as necessary, even a composer
Composing in the flesh an attitude
To slay the ears of the gentry. Karl,
I know you find great joy in the great
Composers. But now you can put your lips to
The messages and blow them into sound
And enter and be there as well. You must
Be faithful to who you are speaking from
And yet it is all right. You will be there.

Take your coat off. Sit down. A glass of Bols
Will help us both. I think you are good enough
To not need me anymore. I think you know
You are not only an interpreter.
What you will do is always something else
And they will hear you simultaneously with
The Art you have been given to read. Karl,

I think the Spring is really coming at last.
I see the canal boys working. I realise
I have not asked you to play the flute today.
Come and look. Are the barges not moving?
You must forgive me. I am not myself today.
Be here on Thursday. When you come, bring
Me five herrings. Watch your fingers. Spring
Is apparent but it is still chilblain weather.

The Last Lesson

Dear Karl, this morning is our last lesson.
I have been given the opportunity to
Live in a certain person's house and tutor
Him and his daughters on the traverse flute.
Karl, you will be all right. In those recent
Lessons my heart lifted to your playing.

I know. I see you doing well, invited
In a great chamber in front of the gentry. I
Can see them with their dresses settling in
And bored mouths beneath moustaches sizing
You up as you are, a lout from the canal
With big ears but an angel's tread on the flute.

But you will be all right. Stand in your place
Before them. Remember Johann. Begin with good
Nerve and decision. Do not intrude too much
Into the message you carry and put out.

One last thing, Karl, remember when you enter
The joy of those quick high archipelagoes,
To make to keep your finger-stops as light
As feathers but definite. What can I say more?
Do not be sentimental or in your Art.
I will miss you. Do not expect applause.

ROBERT DUNCAN

"Among my friends love is a great sorrow"

Among my friends love is a great sorrow.
It has become a daily burden, a feast,
a gluttony for fools, a heart's famine.
We visit one another asking, telling one another.
We do not burn hotly, we question the fire.
We do not fall forward with our alive
eager faces looking thru into the fire.
We stare back into our own faces.
We have become our own realities.
We seek to exhaust our lovelessness.

Among my friends love is a painful question.
We seek out among the passing faces
a sphinx-face who will ask its riddle.
Among my friends love is an answer to a question
that has not been askt.
Then ask it.

Among my friends love is a payment.
It is an old debt for a borrowing foolishly spent.

And we go on, borrowing and borrowing
      from each other.

Among my friends love is a wage
that one might have for an honest living.

Often I am Permitted to Return to a Meadow

as if it were a scene made-up by the mind,
that is not mine, but is a made place,

that is mine, it is so near to the heart,
an eternal pasture folded in all thought
so that there is a hall therein

that is a made place, created by light
wherefrom the shadows that are forms fall.

Wherefrom fall all architectures I am
I say are likenesses of the First Beloved
whose flowers are flames lit to the Lady.

She it is Queen Under The Hill
whose hosts are a disturbance of words within words
that is a field folded.

It is only a dream of the grass blowing
east against the source of the sun
in an hour before the sun's going down

whose secret we see in a children's game
of ring a round of roses told.

Often I am permitted to return to a meadow
as if it were a given property of the mind
that certain bounds hold against chaos,

that is a place of first permission,
everlasting omen of what is.

Bending the Bow

We've our business to attend Day's duties,
bend back the bow in dreams as we may
til the end rimes in the taut string
with the sending. Reveries are rivers and flow
where the cold light gleams reflecting the window upon the
    surface of the table,
the presst-glass creamer, the pewter sugar bowl, the litter of
    coffee cups and saucers,
carnations painted growing upon whose surfaces. The whole
composition of surfaces leads into the other
    current disturbing
what I would take hold of. I'd been

in the course of a letter – I am still
in the course of a letter – to a friend,
who comes close in to my thought so that
the day is hers. My hand writing here
there shakes in the currents of . . . of air?
of an inner anticipation of . . .? reaching to touch
ghostly exhilarations in the thought of her.

    At the extremity of this
      design
"there is a connexion working in both directions, as in
    the bow and the lyre" –
only in that swift fulfillment of the wish
    that sleep
   can illustrate my hand
    sweeps the string.

You stand behind the where-I-am.
The deep tones and shadows I will call a woman.
The quick high notes . . . You are a girl there too,

having something of sister and of wife,
　　　　inconsolate,
and I would play Orpheus for you again,

　　　　recall the arrow or song
　　　　to the trembling daylight
　　　　from which it sprang.

The Torso 　　　　*Passages 18*

Most beautiful!　the red-flowering eucalyptus,
　　the madrone, the yew

　　Is he . . .

So thou wouldst smile, and take me in thine arms
The sight of London to my exiled eyes
Is as Elysium to a new-come soul

　　　　If he be Truth
　　　　I would dwell in the illusion of him

His hands unlocking from chambers of my male body

　　　　such an idea in man's image

　　rising tides that sweep me towards him

　　　　. . . *homosexual?*

　　　　　and at the treasure of his mouth

　　　pour forth my soul

　　　　　his soul　　commingling

I thought a Being more than vast, His body leading
　　into Paradise,　his eyes

　　　quickening a fire in me,　　a trembling

　　　hieroglyph:　At the root of the neck

the clavicle, for the neck is the stem of the great artery
        upward into his head that is beautiful

                        At the rise of the pectoral muscle,

the nipples, for the breasts are like sleeping fountains
        of feeling in man, waiting above the beat of his heart,
        shielding the rise and fall of his breath, to be
        awakend

                        At the axis of his mid hriff

the navel, for in the pit of his stomach the chord from
        which first he was fed has its temple

                        At the root of the groin

the pubic hair, for the torso is the stem in which the man
        flowers forth and leads to the stamen of flesh in which
        his seed rises

a wave of need and desire over   taking me

                        cried out my name

        (This was long ago.   It was another life)

                                and said,

        What do you want of me?

I do not know, I said.   I have fallen in love.   He
        has brought me into heights and depths my heart
                would fear   without him.   His look

        pierces my side   •   fire eyes   •

        I have been waiting for you, he said:
                        I know what you desire

                you do not yet know   but through me   •

        And I am with you everywhere.   In your falling

I have fallen from a high place.   I have raised myself

from darkness in your   rising

wherever you are

my hand in your hand   seeking   the locks, the keys

I am there.   Gathering me, you gather

your Self   •

For my Other is not a woman but a man

the King upon whose bosom let me lie.

The Sentinels

Earth owls in ancient burrows clumpt
the dream presents.   I could return to look.
No other fragment remains.   I wanted owls
and brought them back.   The grey-brown earth-
haunted grass and bush and bushy birds
so near to death, silent as a family photograph,
still as if the sound of a rattle were missing,
the owls shifting into the stillness, thicket and hole
alive, impassive witnesses thrive there
as ever – I've but to close my eyes and go.
The rest of that field and the company
I was among in that place are lost – ghost folk,
passing among whom I was a wraith,
awake, studious, writing, the blur
marrd and almost erased,   unmarkt events.
It was night and cold and the light there
was an after-light.   I wrapt my naked body
in my comforter against that wind.   I
do not – I can not – I will not, trying,
recite the rest.   It was grey day in an absence of the sun.
It was a place without a rattling sound,
a deaf waiting room this place is close upon.
The scratching of my pen and my bending thought
move from this margin and return.   Morning shrinks.
The owls shiver down into the secrets of an earth
I began to see when I lookt into the hole I feard
and then saw others in the clump of grass.

I was dreaming and where I dreamt a light had gone out
and in that light they blind their sight and sit
sentinel upon the brooding of owl-thought, counselings
I remember ever mute and alive, hidden in all things.

KEITH DOUGLAS

The Prisoner

Today, Cheng, I touched your face
with two fingers, as a gesture of love;
for I can never prove enough
by sight or sense your strange grace,

but mothwise my hands return
to your fair cheek, as luminous
as a lamp in a paper house,
and touch, to teach love and learn.

I think a hundred hours are gone
that so, like gods, we'd occupy.
But alas, Cheng, I cannot tell why,
today I touched a mask stretched on the stone

person of death. There was the urge
to break the bright flesh and emerge
of the ambitious cruel bone.

Egypt

Aniseed has a sinful taste:
at your elbow a woman's voice
like, I imagine, the voice of ghosts,
demanding food. She has no grace

but, diseased and blind of an eye
and heavy with habitual dolour,
listlessly finds you and I
and the table are the same colour.

The music, the harsh talk, the fine
clash of the drinkseller's tray,
are the same to her, as her own whine;
she knows no variety.

And in fifteen years of living
found nothing different from death
but the difference of moving
and the nuisance of breath.

A disguise of ordure can't hide
her beauty, succumbing in a cloud
of disease, disease, apathy. My God,
the king of this country must be proud.

Cairo Jag

Shall I get drunk or cut myself a piece of cake,
a pasty Syrian with a few words of English
or the Turk who says she is a princess – she dances
apparently by levitation? Or Marcelle, Parisienne
always preoccupied with her dull dead lover:
she has all the photographs and his letters
tied in a bundle and stamped *Décédé* in mauve ink.
All this takes place in a stink of jasmin.

But there are the streets dedicated to sleep
stenches and sour smells, the sour cries
do not disturb their application to slumber
all day, scattered on the pavement like rags
afflicted with fatalism and hashish. The women
offering their children brown-paper breasts
dry and twisted, elongated like the skull,
Holbein's signature. But this stained white town
is something in accordance with mundane conventions –
Marcelle drops her Gallic airs and tragedy
suddenly shrieks in Arabic about the fare
with the cabman, links herself so
with the somnambulists and legless beggars:
it is all one, all as you have heard.

But by a day's travelling you reach a new world
the vegetation is of iron
dead tanks, gun barrels split like celery
the metal brambles have no flowers or berries
and there are all sorts of manure, you can imagine
the dead themselves, their boots, and possessions
clinging to the ground, a man with no head
has a packet of chocolate and a souvenir of Tripoli.

Vergissmeinicht

Three weeks gone and the combatants gone,
returning over the nightmare ground
we found the place again, and found
the soldier sprawling in the sun.

The frowning barrel of his gun
overshadowing. As we came on
that day, he hit my tank with one
like the entry of a demon.

Look. Here in the gunpit spoil
the dishonoured picture of his girl
who has put: *Steffi. Vergissmeinicht*
in a copybook gothic script.

We see him almost with content
abased, and seeming to have paid
and mocked at by his own equipment
that's hard and good when he's decayed.

But she would weep to see today
how on his skin the swart flies move;
the dust upon the paper eye
and the burst stomach like a cave.

For here the lover and killer are mingled
who had one body and one heart.
And death who had the soldier singled
has done the lover mortal hurt.

How to Kill

Under the parabola of a ball,
a child turning into a man,
I looked into the air too long.
The ball fell in my hand, it sang
in the closed fist: *Open Open*
Behold a gift designed to kill.

Now in my dial of glass appears
the soldier who is going to die.
He smiles, and moves about in ways
his mother knows, habits of his.
The wires touch his face: I cry
NOW. Death, like a familiar, hears

and look, has made a man of dust
of a man of flesh. This sorcery
I do. Being damned, I am amused
to see the centre of love diffused
and the waves of love travel into vacancy.
How easy it is to make a ghost.

The weightless mosquito touches
her tiny shadow on the stone,
and with how like, how infinite
a lightness, man and shadow meet.
They fuse. A shadow is a man
when the mosquito death approaches.

Desert Flowers

Living in a wide landscape are the flowers –
Rosenberg I only repeat what you were saying –
the shell and the hawk every hour
are slaying men and jerboas, slaying

the mind: but the body can fill
the hungry flowers and the dogs who cry words
at nights, the most hostile things of all.
But that is not new. Each time the night discards

draperies on the eyes and leaves the mind awake
I look each side of the door of sleep
for the little coin it will take
to buy the secret I shall not keep.

I see men as trees suffering
or confound the detail and the horizon.
Lay the coin on my tongue and I will sing
of what the others never set eyes on.

GWEN HARWOOD

Carnal Knowledge II

Grasshoppers click and whirr.
Stones grow in the field.
Autumnal warmth is sealed
in a gold skin of light
on darkness plunging down
to earth's black molten core.

Earth has no more to yield.
Her blond grasses are dry.
    Nestling my cheek against
    the hollow of your thigh
    I lay cockeyed with love
    in the most literal sense.

Your eyes, kingfisher blue.
This was the season, this
the light, the halcyon air.
Our window framed this place.
If there were music here,
insectile, abstract, bare,

it would bless no human ear.
Shadows lie with the stones.
Bury our hearts, perhaps
they'll strike it rich in earth's
black marrow, crack, take root,
bring forth vines, blossom, fruit.

Roses knocked on the glass.
Wine like a running stream
no evil spell could cross
flowed round the house of touch.
God grant me drunkenness
if this is sober knowledge,

song to melt sea and sky
apart, and lift these hills
from the shadow of what was,
and roll them back, and lie
in naked ignorance
in the hollow of your thigh.

Andante

New houses grasp our hillside,
my favourite walks are fenced.
Still there's the foreshore, still
transparent overlappings
seaward, let there be space
for the demon's timeless patience
with myself and my dying.

Silence fixes our loves.
Let me cultivate silence.
What's my head but a rat's nest
of dubious texts? Let water
ask me, what have you learned?
I tell the plush deeps, nothing.
Nightfall, an old vexed hour.

Why do I have an image
of owls with silver bells
hung from the tarsus, hunting
fieldmice round the new houses?
Hunger, music and death.
And after that the calm
full frontal stare of silence.

Bone Scan

Thou hast searched me and known me. Thou knowest
my downsitting and mine uprising. — Psalm 139

In the twinkling of an eye,
in a moment, all is changed:
on a small radiant screen
(honeydew melon green)
are my scintillating bones.
Still in my flesh I see
the God who goes with me
glowing with radioactive
isotopes. This is what he
at last allows a mortal
eye to behold: the grand
supporting frame complete
(but for the wisdom teeth),
the friend who lives beneath
appearances, alive
with light. Each glittering bone
assures me: you are known.

Cups

They know us by our lips. They know the proverb
about the space between us. Many slip.
They are older than their flashy friends, the glasses.
They held cold water first, are named in scripture.

Most are gregarious. You'll often see them
nestled in snowy flocks on trestle tables
or perched on trolleys. Quite a few stay married
for life in their own home to the same saucer,

and some are virgin brides of quietness
in a parlour cupboard, wearing gold and roses.
Handleless, chipped, some live on in the flour bin,
some with the poisons in the potting shed.

Shattered, they lie in flowerpot, flowerbed, fowlyard.
Fine earth in earth, they wait for resurrection.
Restored, unbreakable, they'll meet our lips
on some bright morning filled with lovingkindness.

Long After Heine

The washing machine was chuffing
  Ja-PAN Ja-PAN Ja-PAN
as she hustled her husband townwards
  and her lonely day began.

The baby screamed with colic
  the windows streamed with rain.
She dreamed of a demon lover
  like Richard Chamberlain.

He towered, austerely perfect
  in samurai brocade,
and hushed the howling baby
  with one swish of his blade.

And then . . . And then she rested,
  stroking his cruel sword
while he recited haiku
  and conjured word by word

a thatch of morning glory,
  a swallow's shadow cast
across the paper shutters;
  a snail stripped to the waist;

a fan seller dispensing
  coolness in summer heat;
a fly under the flyswat
  wringing his hands and feet;

a kingfisher's wet feathers
  catching the setting sun;
a field of summer grasses,
  the warrior's vision gone.

The cherry blossoms leaving
  a world of grief and pain.
A lonely woman sitting
  by glass lacquered with rain.

EDWIN MORGAN

Siesta of a Hungarian Snake

s sz sz SZ sz SZ sz ZS zs ZS zs zs z

A View of Things

what I love about dormice is their size
what I hate about rain is its sneer
what I love about the Bratach Gorm is its unflappability
what I hate about scent is its smell
what I love about newspapers is their etaoin shrdl
what I hate about philosophy is its pursed lip
what I love about Rory is his old grouse
what I hate about Pam is her pinkie
what I love about semi-precious stones is their preciousness
what I hate about diamonds is their mink
what I love about poetry is its ion engine
what I hate about hogs is their setae
what I love about love is its porridge-spoon
what I hate about hate is its eyes
what I love about hate is its salts
what I hate about love is its dog
what I love about Hank is his string vest
what I hate about the twins is their three gloves
what I love about Mabel is her teeter
what I hate about gooseberries is their look, feel, smell, and
    taste
what I love about the world is its shape
what I hate about a gun is its lock, stock, and barrel
what I love about bacon-and-eggs is its predictability
what I hate about derelict buildings is their reluctance to
    disintegrate
what I love about a cloud is its unpredictability
what I hate about you, chum, is your china
what I love about many waters is their inability to quench
    love

Columba's Song

Where's Brude? Where's Brude?
So many souls to be saved!
The bracken is thick, the wildcat is quick,
the foxes dance in the moonlight,
the salmon dance in the waters,
the adders dance in the thick brown bracken.
Where's Brude? Where's man?
There's too much nature here,
eagles and deer,
but where's the mind and where's the soul?
Show me your kings, your women, the man of the plough.
And cry me to your cradles.
It wasn't for a fox or an eagle I set sail!

Itinerary

1

We went to Oldshoremore.
Is the Oldshoremore road still there?
You mean the old shore road?
I suppose it's more an old road than a shore road.
No more! They shored it up, but it's washed away.
So you could sing the old song –
Yes we sang the old song:
    We'll take the old Oldshoremore shore road no more.

2

We passed the Muckle Flugga.
Did you see the muckle flag?
All we saw was the muckle fog.
The flag says ULTIMA FLUGGA WHA'S LIKE US.
Couldn't see flag for fug, sorry.
Ultimately –
    Ultimately we made for Muck and flogged the lugger.

3

Was it bleak at Bowhousebog?
It was black as a hoghouse, boy.
Yes, but bleak?
Look, it was black as a bog and bleak as the Bauhaus!

The Bauhaus wasn't black —
Will you get off my back!
So there were dogs too?
    Dogs, hogs, leaks in the bogs — we never went back.

Cinquevalli

Cinquevalli is falling, falling.
The shining trapeze kicks and flirts free,
solo performer at last.
The sawdust puffs up with a thump,
settles on a tangle of broken limbs.
St Petersburg screams and leans.
His pulse flickers with the gas-jets. He lives.

Cinquevalli has a therapy.
In his hospital bed, in his hospital chair
he holds a ball, lightly, lets it roll round his hand,
or grips it tight, gauging its weight and resistance,
begins to balance it, to feel its life attached to his
by will and knowledge, invisible strings
that only he can see. He throws it
from hand to hand, always different,
always the same, always
different, always the
same.
His muscles learn to think, his arms grow very strong.

Cinquevalli in sepia
looks at me from an old postcard: bundle of enigmas.
Half faun, half military man; almond eyes, curly hair,
conventional moustache; tights, and a tunic loaded
with embroideries, tassels, chains, fringes; hand on hip
with a large signet-ring winking at the camera
but a bull neck and shoulders and a cannon-ball
at his elbow as he stands by the posing pedestal;
half reluctant, half truculent,
half handsome, half absurd,
but let me see you forget him: not to be done.

Cinquevalli is a juggler.
In a thousand theatres, in every continent,
he is the best, the greatest. After eight years perfecting
he can balance one billiard ball on another billiard ball

on top of a cue on top of a third billiard ball
in a wine-glass held in his mouth. To those
who say the balls are waxed, or flattened,
he patiently explains the trick will only work
because the spheres are absolutely true.
There is no deception in him. He is true.

Cinquevalli is juggling with a bowler,
a walking-stick, a cigar, and a coin.
Who foresees? How to please.
The last time round, the bowler
flies to his head, the stick sticks in his hand,
the cigar jumps into his mouth, the coin
lands on his foot – ah, but
is kicked into his eye
and held there as the miraculous monocle
without which the portrait would be incomplete.

Cinquevalli is practising.
He sits in his dressing-room talking to some friends,
at the same time writing a letter with one hand
and with the other juggling four balls.
His friends think of demons, but
"You could do all this," he says,
sealing the letter with a billiard ball.

Cinquevalli is on the high wire in Odessa.
The roof cracks, he is falling, falling
into the audience, a woman breaks his fall,
he cracks her like a flea, but lives.

Cinquevalli broods in his armchair in Brixton Road.
He reads in the paper about the shells whining
at Passchendaele, imagines the mud and the dead.
He goes to the window and wonders through that dark
        evening
what is happening in Poland where he was born.
His neighbours call him a German spy.
"Kestner, Paul Kestner, that's his name!"
"Keep Kestner out of the British music-hall!"
He frowns; it is cold; his fingers seem stiff and old.

Cinquevalli tosses up a plate of soup
and twirls it on his forefinger; not a drop spills.
He laughs, and well may he laugh
who can do that. The astonished table

breathe again, laugh too, think the world
a spinning thing that spills, for a moment, no drop.

Cinquevalli's coffin sways through Brixton
only a few months before the Armistice.
Like some trick they cannot get off the ground
it seems to burden the shuffling bearers, all their arms
cross-juggle that displaced person, that man
of balance, of strength, of delights and marvels,
in his unsteady box at last into the earth.

Sir James Murray

I pick a daimen icker from the thrave
And chew it thoughtfully. I must be brave
And fight for this. My English colleagues frown
But words come skelpin rank and file, and down
They go, the kittle kimmers, they're well caught
And I won't give them up. Who would have thought
A gleg and gangrel Scot like me should barge,
Or rather breenge, like a kelpie at large
In the Cherwell, upon the very palladium
Of anglophilia? My sleekit radium
Is smuggled through the fluttering slips. My shed,
My outhouse with its thousand-plus well-fed
Pigeon-holes, has a northern exposure. Doon
Gaed stumpie in the ink all afternoon,
As Burns and I refreshed the dictionar
With cantrips from his dancing Carrick star!
O lovely words and lovely man! We'll caw
Before us yowes tae knowes; we'll shaw the braw
Auld baudrons by the ingle; we'll comb
Quotations to bring the wild whaup safely home.
Origin obscure? Origin uncertain? Origin unknown?
I love those eldritch pliskies that are thrown
At us from a too playful past, a store
Of splore we should never be blate to semaphore!
Oxford! here is a silent collieshangie
To spike your index-cards and keep them tangy.
Some, though not I, will jib at houghmagandy:
We'll maybe not get that past Mrs Grundy.
– But evening comes. To work, to work! To words!
The bats are turning into bauckie-birds.

The light in my scriptorium flickers gamely.
Pioneers must never labour tamely.
We steam along, we crawl, we pause, we hurtle,
And stir this English porridge with a spurtle.

The Glass

To love you in shadow as in the light
is light itself. In subterranean night
you sow the fields with fireflies of delight.

Lanarkshire holds you, under its grim grass.
But I hold what you were, like a bright glass
I carry brimming through the darkening pass.

RICHARD WILBUR

Parable

I read how Quixote in his random ride
Came to a crossing once, and lest he lose
The purity of chance, would not decide

Whither to fare, but wished his horse to choose.
For glory lay wherever he might turn.
His head was light with pride, his horse's shoes,

Were heavy, and he headed for the barn.

Someone Talking to Himself

Even when first her face,
Younger than any spring,
Older than Pharaoh's grain
And fresh as Phoenix-ashes,
Shadowed under its lashes
Every earthly thing,
There was another place
I saw in a flash of pain:

Off in the fathomless dark
Beyond the verge of love
I saw blind fishes move,
And under a stone shelf
Rode the recusant shark –
Cold, waiting, himself.

Oh, even when we fell,
Clean as a mountain source
And barely able to tell
Such ecstasy from grace,
Into the primal bed
And current of our race,
We knew yet must deny
To what we gathered head:
That music growing harsh,
Trees blotting the sky
Above the roaring course
That in the summer's drought
Slowly would peter out
Into a dry marsh.

Love is the greatest mercy.
A volley of the sun
That lashes all with shade,
That the first day be mended;
And yet, so soon undone,
It is the lover's curse
Till time be comprehended
And the flawed heart unmade.
What can I do but move
From folly to defeat,
And call that sorrow sweet
That teaches us to see
The final face of love
In what we cannot be?

Advice to a Prophet

When you come, as you soon must, to the streets of our city,
Mad-eyed from stating the obvious,
Not proclaiming our fall but begging us
In God's name to have self-pity,

Spare us all word of the weapons, their force and range,
The long numbers that rocket the mind;
Our slow, unreckoning hearts will be left behind,
Unable to fear what is too strange.

Nor shall you scare us with talk of the death of the race.
How should we dream of this place without us? —
The sun mere fire, the leaves untroubled about us,
A stone look on the stone's face?

Speak of the world's own change. Though we cannot
        conceive
Of an undreamt thing, we know to our cost
How the dreamt cloud crumbles, the vines are blackened
        by frost,
How the view alters. We could believe,

If you told us so, that the white-tailed deer will slip
Into perfect shade, grown perfectly shy,
The lark avoid the reaches of our eye,
The jack-pine lose its knuckled grip

On the cold ledge, and every torrent burn
As Xanthus once, its gliding trout
Stunned in a twinkling. What should we be without
The dolphin's arc, the dove's return,

These things in which we have seen ourselves and spoken?
Ask us, prophet, how we shall call
Our natures forth when that live tongue is all
Dispelled, that glass obscured or broken

In which we have said the rose of our love and the clean
Horse of our courage, in which beheld
The singing locust of the soul unshelled,
And all we mean or wish to mean.

Ask us, ask us whether with the worldless rose
Our hearts shall fail us; come demanding
Whether there shall be lofty or long standing
When the bronze annals of the oak-tree close.

Leaving

As we left the garden-party
By the far gate,
There were many loitering on
Who had come late

And a few arriving still.
Though the lawn lay
Like a fast-draining shoal
Of ochre day.

Curt shadows in the grass
Hatched every blade,
And now on pedestals
Of mounting shade

Stood all our friends – iconic,
Now, in mien,
Half-lost in dignities
Till now unseen.

There were the hostess' hands
Held out to greet
The scholar's limp, his wife's
Quick-pecking feet,

And there was wit's cocked head,
And there the sleek
And gaze-enameled look
Of beauty's cheek.

We saw now, loitering there
Knee-deep in night,
How even the wheeling children
Moved in a rite

Or masque, or long charade
Where we, like these,
Had blundered into grand
Identities,

Filling our selves as sculpture
Fills the stone.
We had not played so surely,
Had we known.

Hamlen Brook

At the alder-darkened brink
Where the stream slows to a lucid jet
I lean to the water, dinting its top with sweat,
And see, before I can drink,

A startled inchling trout
Of spotted near-transparency,
Trawling a shadow solider than he.
He swerves now, darting out

To where, in a flicked slew
Of sparks and glittering silt, he weaves
Through stream-bed rocks, disturbing foundered leaves,
And butts then out of view

Beneath a sliding glass
Crazed by the skimming of a brace
Of burnished dragon-flies across its face,
In which deep cloudlets pass

And a white precipice
Of mirrored birch-trees plunges down
Toward where the azures of the zenith drown.
How shall I drink all this?

Joy's trick is to supply
Dry lips with what can cool and slake,
Leaving them dumbstruck also with an ache
Nothing can satisfy.

DONALD DAVIE

Remembering the 'Thirties

I

Hearing one saga, we enact the next.
We please our elders when we sit enthralled;
But then they're puzzled; and at last they're vexed
To have their youth so avidly recalled.

It dawns upon the veterans after all
That what for them were agonies, for us
Are high-brow thrillers, though historical;
And all their feats quite strictly fabulous.

This novel written fifteen years ago,
Set in my boyhood and my boyhood home,
These poems about "abandoned workings", show
Worlds more remote than Ithaca or Rome.

The Anschluss, Guernica – all the names
At which those poets thrilled or were afraid
For me mean schools and schoolmasters and games;
And in the process someone is betrayed.

Ourselves perhaps. The Devil for a joke
Might carve his own initials on our desk,
And yet we'd miss the point because he spoke
An idiom too dated, Audenesque.

Ralegh's Guiana also killed his son.
A pretty pickle if we came to see
The tallest story really packed a gun,
The Telemachiad an Odyssey.

2

Even to them the tales were not so true
As not to be ridiculous as well;
The ironmaster met his Waterloo,
But Rider Haggard rode along the fell.

"Leave for Cape Wrath tonight!" They lounged away
On Fleming's trek or Isherwood's ascent.
England expected every man that day
To show his motives were ambivalent.

They played the fool, not to appear as fools
In time's long glass. A deprecating air
Disarmed, they thought, the jeers of later schools;
Yet irony itself is doctrinaire,

And, curiously, nothing now betrays
Their type to time's derision like this coy
Insistence on the quizzical, their craze
For showing Hector was a mother's boy.

A neutral tone is nowadays preferred.
And yet it may be better, if we must,
To praise a stance impressive and absurd
Than not to see the hero for the dust.

For courage is the vegetable king,
The sprig of all ontologies, the weed
That beards the slag-heap with his hectoring,
Whose green adventure is to run to seed.

Time Passing, Beloved

Time passing, and the memories of love
Coming back to me, carissima, no more mockingly
Than ever before; time passing, unslackening,
Unhastening, steadily; and no more
Bitterly, beloved, the memories of love
Coming into the shore.

How will it end? Time passing and our passages of love
As ever, beloved, blind
As ever before; time binding, unbinding
About us; and yet to remember
Never less chastening, nor the flame of love
Less like an ember.

What will become of us? Time
Passing, beloved, and we in a sealed
Assurance unassailed
By memory. How can it end,
This siege of a shore that no misgivings have steeled,
No doubts defend?

Rodez

Northward I came, and knocked in the coated wall
At the door of a low inn scaled like a urinal
With greenish tiles. The door gave, and I came

Home to the stone north, every wynd and snicket
Known to me wherever the flattened cat
Squirmed home to a hole between housewall and paving.

Known! And in the turns of it, no welcome,
No flattery of the beckoned lighted eye
From a Rose of the rose-brick alleys of Toulouse.

Those more than tinsel garlands, more than masks,
Unfading wreaths of ancient summers, I
Sternly cast off. A stern eye is the graceless

Bulk and bruise that at the steep uphill
Confronts me with its drained-of-colour sandstone
Implacably. The Church. It is Good Friday.

Goodbye to the Middle Ages! Although some
Think that I enter them, those centuries
Of monkish superstition, here I leave them

With their true garlands, and their honest masks,
Every fresh flower cast on the porch and trodden,
Raked by the wind at the Church door on this Friday.

Goodbye to all the centuries. There is
No home in them, much as the dip and turn
Of an honest alley charmingly deceive us.

And yet not quite goodbye. Instead almost
Welcome, I said. Bleak equal centuries
Crowded the porch to be deflowered, crowned.

Epistle. To Enrique Caracciolo Trejo

(Essex)

A shrunken world
Stares from my pages.
What a pellet the authentic is!
My world of poetry,
Enrique, is not large.
Day by day it is smaller.
These poems that you have
Given me, I might
Have made them English once.
Now they are inessential.
The English that I feel in
Fears the inauthentic

Which invades it on all sides
Mortally. The style may die of it,
Die of the fear of it,
Confounding authenticity with essence.

Death, an authentic subject,
Jaime Sabinès has
Dressed with the yew-trees of funereal trope.
It cannot be his fault
If the English that I feel in
Feels itself too poor
Spirited to plant a single cypress.
It is afraid of showing, at the grave-side,
Its incapacity to venerate
Life, or the going of it. These are deaths,
These qualms and horrors shade the ancestral ground.

Sabinès in another
Poem comes down
To the sound of pigeons on a neighbour's tiles,
A manifest of gladness.
Such a descent on clapping wings the English
Contrives to trust
No longer. My own garden
Crawls with a kind of obese
Pigeon from Belgium; they burst through cracking branches
Like frigate-birds.

Still in infested gardens
The year goes round,
A smiling landscape greets returning Spring.
To see what can be said for it, on what
Secure if shallow ground
Of feeling England stands
Unshaken for
Her measure to be taken
Has taken four bad years
Of my life here. And now
I know the ground:
Humiliation, corporate and private,
Not chastens but chastises
This English and this verse.

I cannot abide the new
Absurdities day by day,
The new adulterations.
I relish your condition,
Expatriate! though it be among
A people whose constricted idiom
Cannot embrace the poets you thought to bring them.

The Fountain of Cyanë

I

Her father's brother rapes her!
      In the bright
Ovidian colours all is for delight,
The inadmissible minglings are recounted
With such finesse: the beery ram that mounted
His niece and, hissing "Belt up", had her, is
Hell's grizzly monarch gaunt in tapestries;
The thrashing pallid skivvy under him
A vegetation myth; the stinking slum
Is Enna's field where Phoebus ne'er invades
The tufted fences, nor offends the shades;
And her guffawing Ma assumes the land,
Coarsely divine, cacophonous, gin in hand.
Sky-blue, dark-blue, sea-green, cerulean dyes
Dye into fables what we hoped were lies
And feared were truths. A happy turn, a word,
Says they are both, and nothing untoward.
Coloured by rhetoric, to die of grief
Becomes as graceful as a falling leaf;
No chokings, retchings, not the same as dying
Starved and worn out because you can't stop crying.
Cyanë's fable, that one; how she wept
Herself away, shocked for her girl-friend raped –
"Her varied members to a fluid melt,
A pliant softness in her bones is felt . . ."
Sweet lapse, sweet lapse . . . "till only now remains
Within the channel of her purple veins
A silver liquor . . ." Ah, the master's touch
So suave, mere word-play, that can do so much!
And now at last imperious, in bad taste:
"Nothing to fill love's grasp; her husband chaste
Bathes in that bosom he before embrac'd."

The spring-fed pool that is Cyanë may
Be visited in Sicily today;
And what's to be made of that? Or how excuse
Our intent loitering outside Syracuse?

2

Modesty, I kept saying,
Temperate, temperate . . . Yes,
The papyrus were swaying
Hardly at all, and late,
Late in the season the rings
Widened upon the reedy
Pool, and the beady-eyed frogs
Volleyed out after mayfly.

Fountain? No jet, no spume,
Spew nor spurt . . . Was this
Where Pluto's chariot hurtled
Up out of "gloomy Dis"?
Male contumely for that
First most seminal rape,
Proserpine's, prescribes
Some more vertiginous landscape.

Late, late in that season . . .
Easy, easy the lap
And rustle of blue waters . . .
Wholly a female occasion
This, as Demeter launches
One fish in a silver arc
To signalise her daughter's
Re-entry to the dark.

3

The balked, the aborted vision
Permits of the greater finesse;
The achieved one is fugitive, slighter,
One might almost say, "loose".

And yet the oceanic
Swells of an unencumbered
Metric jiggle the planes
Epiphanies must glow from.

So, though one might almost say "loose",
One mustn't. They like the closed-off
Precincts all right, but never
When those exult in their closures.

The shrine is enclosed from the bare
Fields and, three miles away
Clearly in sight, the high-rise
Shimmering haze of the city.

But the fence is of wire; the warped
Palings give easy access;
No turnstile; and at the pool
Of Cyanë, nothing to pay;

No veil to be rent, no grille,
No holy of holies. The Greek
World, one is made to remember,
Was Christianised quite early.

Epiphanies all around us
Always perhaps. And some
Who missed the flash of a fin
Were keeping their eyes on rhyme-schemes.

4

And so with stanzas . . . moving
From room to room is a habit adapted to winter,
Warm and warming, worship Sunday by Sunday,
And one is glad of it. But when
Now and again I turn the knob and enter
The special chill where my precarious Springs
Hang water-beaded in still air, I hear
A voice announce: "And this is the
Conservatory!" Greenish misted panes
Of mystifying memory conserve
In an unnatural silence nymph and pool;
It is an outside room, at the end of a range of rooms
But still a room, accounted for or even
Entered upon the impatient plans in my
Infidel youth. At that time no
Nymph, and no pool: still, it appears,
Room left for them – and yet
Rooms should have an outside door, I think;
I wilt for lack of it, though my plants do not.

5

Yet there was enough in this –
And it was nothing, nothing at all
   "Happened" – enough in this
   Non-happening to cap
   What Scripture says of the Fall

Which, though it equally may
Not in that sense have happened, is
   A postulate day by day
   Called for, to explain
   Our joys, our miseries.

A fish jumped, silver; small
Frogs took the mayfly; papyrus
   In the Sicilian fall
   Of the leaf was bowing. How
   That weightless weighed with us!

Why, when an unheard air
Stirred in the fronds, did we assume
   An occidental care
   For proximate cause? Egyptian
   Stems abased their plume.

So inattentive we are
We think ourselves unfallen. This
   Pool, when Pluto's car
   Whirled up, was wept by Cyanë
   For her abducted mistress.

One could go round and round
This single and Sicilian less
   Than happening, and ground
   Therein what might suffuse
   Our lives with happiness.

Their Rectitude Their Beauty

"The angels rejoice in
the excellencies of God;
the inferior creatures in
His goodness; sinners only
in His forgiveness."

His polar oppositions;
the habitable zones,
His clemencies; and
His smiling divagations,
uncovenanted mercies,

who turned the hard rock into a standing water
and the flint-stone into a springing well.

The voice of joy and health is in the dwellings of the
       righteous;
my eyes are running with rheum
from looking for that health

in one who has stuck by
His testimonies;
who has delighted in
His regimen; who has run
the circuit of His requirements;
whose songs in the caravanserai
have been about His statutes,

not to deserve nor observe them
(having done neither) but
for the angelic reason:

their rectitude,
their beauty.

PHILIP LARKIN

At Grass

The eye can hardly pick them out
From the cold shade they shelter in,
Till wind distresses tail and mane;
Then one crops grass, and moves about
– The other seeming to look on –
And stands anonymous again.

Yet fifteen years ago, perhaps
Two dozen distances sufficed
To fable them: faint afternoons

Of Cups and Stakes and Handicaps,
Whereby their names were artificed
To inlay faded, classic Junes —

Silks at the start: against the sky
Numbers and parasols: outside,
Squadrons of empty cars, and heat,
And littered grass: then the long cry
Hanging unhushed till it subside
To stop-press columns on the street.

Do memories plague their ears like flies?
They shake their heads. Dusk brims the shadows.
Summer by summer all stole away,
The starting-gates, the crowds and cries —
All but the unmolesting meadows.
Almanacked, their names live; they

Have slipped their names, and stand at ease,
Or gallop for what must be joy,
And not a fieldglass sees them home,
Or curious stop-watch prophesies:
Only the groom, and the groom's boy,
With bridles in the evening come.

Deceptions

*Of course I was drugged, and so heavily I did not regain my consciousness till
the next morning. I was horrified to discover that I had been ruined, and for
some days I was inconsolable, and cried like a child to be killed or sent back
to my aunt.*   Mayhew, *London Labour and the London Poor*

Even so distant, I can taste the grief,
Bitter and sharp with stalks, he made you gulp.
The sun's occasional print, the brisk brief
Worry of wheels along the street outside
Where bridal London bows the other way,
And light, unanswerable and tall and wide,
Forbids the scar to heal, and drives
Shame out of hiding. All the unhurried day
Your mind lay open like a drawer of knives.

Slums, years, have buried you. I would not dare
Console you if I could. What can be said,
Except that suffering is exact, but where
Desire takes charge, readings will grow erratic?
For you would hardly care
That you were less deceived, out on that bed,
Than he was, stumbling up the breathless stair
To burst into fulfilment's desolate attic.

Next, Please

Always too eager for the future, we
Pick up bad habits of expectancy.
Something is always approaching; every day
Till then we say,

Watching from a bluff the tiny, clear,
Sparkling armada of promises draw near.
How slow they are! And how much time they waste,
Refusing to make haste!

Yet still they leave us holding wretched stalks
Of disappointment, for, though nothing balks
Each big approach, leaning with brasswork prinked,
Each rope distinct,

Flagged, and the figurehead with golden tits
Arching our way, it never anchors; it's
No sooner present than it turns to past.
Right to the last

We think each one will heave to and unload
All good into our lives, all we are owed
For waiting so devoutly and so long.
But we are wrong:

Only one ship is seeking us, a black-
Sailed unfamiliar, towing at her back
A huge and birdless silence. In her wake
No waters breed or break.

I Remember, I Remember

Coming up England by a different line
For once, early in the cold new year,
We stopped, and, watching men with number-plates
Sprint down the platform to familiar gates,
"Why, Coventry!" I exclaimed. "I was born here."

I leant far out, and squinnied for a sign
That this was still the town that had been "mine"
So long, but found I wasn't even clear
Which side was which. From where those cycle-crates
Were standing, had we annually departed

For all those family hols? . . . A whistle went:
Things moved. I sat back, staring at my boots.
"Was that," my friend smiled, "where you 'have your
        roots'?"
No, only where my childhood was unspent,
I wanted to retort, just where I started:

By now I've got the whole place clearly charted.
Our garden, first: where I did not invent
Blinding theologies of flowers and fruits,
And wasn't spoken to by an old hat.
And here we have that splendid family

I never ran to when I got depressed,
The boys all biceps and the girls all chest,
Their comic Ford, their farm where I could be
"Really myself". I'll show you, come to that,
The bracken where I never trembling sat,

Determined to go through with it; where she
Lay back, and "all became a burning mist".
And, in those offices, my doggerel
Was not set up in blunt ten-point, nor read
By a distinguished cousin of the mayor,

Who didn't call and tell my father *There
Before us, had we the gift to see ahead* –
"You look as if you wished the place in Hell,"
My friend said, "judging from your face." "Oh well,
I suppose it's not the place's fault," I said.

"Nothing, like something, happens anywhere."

Church Going

Once I am sure there's nothing going on
I step inside, letting the door thud shut.
Another church: matting, seats, and stone,
And little books; sprawlings of flowers, cut
For Sunday, brownish now; some brass and stuff
Up at the holy end; the small neat organ;
And a tense, musty, unignorable silence,
Brewed God knows how long. Hatless, I take off
My cycle-clips in awkward reverence,

Move forward, run my hand around the font.
From where I stand, the roof looks almost new —
Cleaned, or restored? Someone would know: I don't.
Mounting the lectern, I peruse a few
Hectoring large-scale verses, and pronounce
"Here endeth" much more loudly than I'd meant.
The echoes snigger briefly. Back at the door
I sign the book, donate an Irish sixpence,
Reflect the place was not worth stopping for.

Yet stop I did: in fact I often do,
And always end much at a loss like this,
Wondering what to look for; wondering, too,
When churches fall completely out of use
What we shall turn them into, if we shall keep
A few cathedrals chronically on show,
Their parchment, plate and pyx in locked cases,
And let the rest rent-free to rain and sheep.
Shall we avoid them as unlucky places?

Or, after dark, will dubious women come
To make their children touch a particular stone;
Pick simples for a cancer; or on some
Advised night see walking a dead one?
Power of some sort or other will go on
In games, in riddles, seemingly at random;
But superstition, like belief, must die,
And what remains when disbelief has gone?
Grass, weedy pavement, brambles, buttress, sky,

A shape less recognisable each week,
A purpose more obscure. I wonder who
Will be the last, the very last, to seek
This place for what it was; one of the crew

That tap and jot and know what rood-lofts were?
Some ruin-bibber, randy for antique,
Or Christmas-addict, counting on a whiff
Of gown-and-bands and organ-pipes and myrrh?
Or will he be my representative,

Bored, uninformed, knowing the ghostly silt
Dispersed, yet tending to this cross of ground
Through suburb scrub because it held unspilt
So long and equably what since is found
Only in separation – marriage, and birth,
And death, and thoughts of these – for which was built
This special shell? For, though I've no idea
What this accoutred frowsty barn is worth,
It pleases me to stand in silence here;

A serious house on serious earth it is,
In whose blent air all our compulsions meet,
Are recognised, and robed as destinies.
And that much never can be obsolete,
Since someone will forever be surprising
A hunger in himself to be more serious,
And gravitating with it to this ground,
Which, he once heard, was proper to grow wise in,
If only that so many dead lie round.

MCMXIV

Those long uneven lines
Standing as patiently
As if they were stretched outside
The Oval or Villa Park,
The crowns of hats, the sun
On moustached archaic faces
Grinning as if it were all
An August Bank Holiday lark;

And the shut shops, the bleached
Established names on the sunblinds,
The farthings and sovereigns,
And dark-clothed children at play
Called after kings and queens,
The tin advertisements

For cocoa and twist, and the pubs
Wide open all day;

And the countryside not caring:
The place-names all hazed over
With flowering grasses, and fields
Shadowing Domesday lines
Under wheat's restless silence;
The differently-dressed servants
With tiny rooms in huge houses,
The dust behind limousines;

Never such innocence,
Never before or since,
As changed itself to past
Without a word – the men
Leaving the gardens tidy,
The thousands of marriages
Lasting a little while longer:
Never such innocence again.

High Windows

When I see a couple of kids
And guess he's fucking her and she's
Taking pills or wearing a diaphragm,
I know this is paradise

Everyone old has dreamed of all their lives –
Bonds and gestures pushed to one side
Like an outdated combine harvester,
And everyone young going down the long slide

To happiness, endlessly. I wonder if
Anyone looked at me, forty years back,
And thought, *That'll be the life;*
No God any more, or sweating in the dark

About hell and that, or having to hide
What you think of the priest. He
And his lot will all go down the long slide
Like free bloody birds. And immediately

Rather than words comes the thought of high windows:
The sun-comprehending glass,
And beyond it, the deep blue air, that shows
Nothing, and is nowhere, and is endless.

The Trees

The trees are coming into leaf
Like something almost being said;
The recent buds relax and spread,
Their greenness is a kind of grief.

Is it that they are born again
And we grow old? No, they die too.
Their yearly trick of looking new
Is written down in rings of grain.

Yet still the unresting castles thresh
In fullgrown thickness every May.
Last year is dead, they seem to say,
Begin afresh, afresh, afresh.

The Old Fools

What do they think has happened, the old fools,
To make them like this? Do they somehow suppose
It's more grown-up when your mouth hangs open and drools,
And you keep on pissing yourself, and can't remember
Who called this morning? Or that, if they only chose,
They could alter things back to when they danced all night,
Or went to their wedding, or sloped arms some September?
Or do they fancy there's really been no change,
And they've always behaved as if they were crippled or tight,
Or sat through days of thin continuous dreaming
Watching light move? If they don't (and they can't), it's strange:
          Why aren't they screaming?

At death, you break up: the bits that were you
Start speeding away from each other for ever
With no one to see. It's only oblivion, true:
We had it before, but then it was going to end,
And was all the time merging with a unique endeavour

To bring to bloom the million-petalled flower
Of being here. Next time you can't pretend
There'll be anything else. And these are the first signs:
Not knowing how, not hearing who, the power
Of choosing gone. Their looks show that they're for it:
Ash hair, toad hands, prune face dried into lines –
      How can they ignore it?

Perhaps being old is having lighted rooms
Inside your head, and people in them, acting.
People you know, yet can't quite name; each looms
Like a deep loss restored, from known doors turning,
Setting down a lamp, smiling from a stair, extracting
A known book from the shelves; or sometimes only
The rooms themselves, chairs and a fire burning,
The blown bush at the window, or the sun's
Faint friendliness on the wall some lonely
Rain-ceased midsummer evening. That is where they live:
Not here and now, but where all happened once.
      This is why they give

An air of baffled absence, trying to be there
Yet being here. For the rooms grow farther, leaving
Incompetent cold, the constant wear and tear
Of taken breath, and them crouching below
Extinction's alp, the old fools, never perceiving
How near it is. This must be what keeps them quiet:
The peak that stays in view wherever we go
For them is rising ground. Can they never tell
What is dragging them back, and how it will end? Not at night?
Not when the strangers come? Never, throughout
The whole hideous inverted childhood? Well,
      We shall find out.

PATRICIA BEER

The Flood

Noah, looking out of the safe Ark,
Saw, glum as any geographer,
Waterlogged the map of the world sink.
All dry hedges, every crisp park
Were being lowered to their burial, far
Down under the rains, to grow rank.

The sea crept on and upwards with a chill
Giggle over the stomachs of whatever
Could not float. And at length Noah saw
Standing on top of what was the last hill –
A single stepping-stone now with no shore –
The last survivors who had run all the way

Out of their homes and families to be saved:
By height alone for Noah could not stop.
The sea rising stretched them out tall enough
Tiptoe on a rack where they no longer moved,
Taut every neck and every instep
In catapult longing to be up and off.

But this was not the last which Noah saw
Of them. They did not sink with the land. Learners
From desperation, hope happened to them.
Though there was no inch of world left, though
There was no help in sight, or near, or corners
To conceal it, they began to swim.

This was an ignorant way to meet fate,
Hoping. There was not much intelligence
In the eyes now riding level in the water.
Spitting out death and not swallowing it
Was merely postponement, it showed want of sense.
Sooner would have been more sage than later.

But less admirable. There has been some doubt
Among Noah's descendants about hope.
Perhaps because they come from those in the Ark
And not the swimmers, they give hope great weight,
Thinking it not illusion, the final jape,
But the last firework strong and shrewd in the dark.

Middle Age

Middle age at last declares itself
As the time when could-have-been
Is not wishful thinking any more,
Is not, say: I could have been at Oxford
If my parents had been richer
Or if the careers mistress had not thought
Exeter was good enough for me.

It is not misunderstanding either
As when at night in the first year of the war
Bombs could have been thunder
And later on in peace
Thunder could have been bombs.
Sights and sounds are more themselves now.

There have been real alternatives.
They have put on weight and yet faded.

Evening walks go past
Where we could have lived:
The coach-house that the mortgage company
Said had too much charm
And not enough rooms.

Everywhere I look it is the same,
The churchyard or the other side of the bed.
The one who is not lying there
Could have been.

John Milton and My Father

Milton was not my father's favourite poet.
Shakespeare was. And you got marks for that
In the Victorian classroom with the brown
Trusses of the pointed roof and the black fat
Stove with the turtle, and always blowing through it
The smell of clothes muggy with country rain.

Milton came second. You earned marks for that.
My father, a conformist to his death,
Would have believed even at the age of ten
This value judgement to be gospel truth.
But when he spoke of Milton to us, we got
Much more than the right answer from his tone.

Seated on his high Dickensian stool
From puberty to impotence, a clerk,
(The chief clerk in the corner in his glass
Box of authority) he felt that work
And the world were a less smelly school
Where seraphim and angels knew their place.

He tasted hierarchy as Milton did
And was enchanted by it: jewelled stairs
And thrones and powers and principalities.
Each night he knelt but glanced up through his prayers
To the mountain where sat golden almighty God
With nothing over him but empty space.

Ninny's Tomb

I'll meet thee, Pyramus, at Ninny's tomb.
Ninny, you may have laughed in the wrong place
But you are not a noisy spirit. Now
You are as airless as your crop of grass.

It is a quiet night. The sea has lost
Its voice, though it lies plump and blooming
Beyond the monumental arch through which
They brought you in to your dead-serious homing.

You are the founding father of wantwits,
Thesaurus silly-billy, noodle, loon.
Not verb or adjective. You cannot do
Or qualify. You are a proper noun.

Pyramus, Thisbe, Moonshine and the Lion
Come here, and so do I and many another
Whom certainly the good Duke will not ask
To roar again. Ninny, our clone, our brother.

I think you clowned your way into your coffin,
Your feet up where your shoulders ought to go,
Or turned on to your face to get a laugh.
Ninny, please do not ask me how I know.

Ballad of the Underpass

The day I watched them carry her
Along a stony path in Devon,
Black-clothed relations bullied me:
"Now, now, your mother's GONE TO HEAVEN."

Later I went to read her stone.
The churchyard creaked with lumpy graves.
In all that weight I could not see
The feathery souls that Jesus saves.

I travelled. Time looked after me
The seven seas were nothing to it.
I wanted to make money, love
And war. Time showed me how to do it.

I came home like a story book.
The dock had nothing new to say
Tractors and cows strolled down the lane
But now time planned a motorway.

It would be almost out of sight
And in itself do little harm
But the approach road would scoop up
The Church and Farmer Gurney's farm.

The Church sent up some peevish prayers.
The farming lobby stood its ground.
A small mob kicked the Ministry
And an alternative was found:

An underpass. The tunnelled road
Is short, the village is so slight.
Today I drove right underneath
The tombstones in the fading light.

"Now I have really GONE ABOVE,"
My mother said, "though not to Heaven,
Nearer the light, nearer the air.
Set free by half the worms of Devon

My bones hang over you and twitch
Under the rain. Tall as a tree
You used to stand there looking down
And now you must look up at me."

Millennium

A thousand times travelling over these fields,
Shorn as if shamed, the shortest day
Has yellowed and gone, yomping to new year.
From a Wessex window we have watched it.
We mull over the millennium. Not many days now.

This time ten centuries ago
(Romans retired, Normans not ready)
Saxons had come here to settle, not swallow or govern.
Vain in vigour they vowed this hill would suit them.
Wood served these warlords wonderfully for dwelling.
They lived off the land, lopping the trees
That soared again in the same spot, as mead-halls
Where warriors wilted, weapons erect beside them.
They snored, serging and slumping with the verse,
Pleased the poet. They performed his rhythm.
Bats burst in out of a burning night sky
Like stars scorched and scattered over Middle-earth.

At sunrise they would set out to seek more land,
Claiming Cornwall, calling its fields after themselves.
Half-foemen, half farmers, they frisked like centaurs
On the Roman road that rang through Exeter,
Till moors muffled them and mists sent wandering.

Paganism was patchy but powerful nonetheless
Giving new greatness to the goddess Easter.
Kings of Wessex were Christians, counting their years
From the birth. Backsliders, brought home by carols
Each winter, kept Woden but worshipped one God.

Fifty fathers-and-sons fill this place,
Heroes hidden in earth or hoarded offshore
Tombed with their treasures till tides parted them
They left us language and lymph, verse
Made of sibling sounds and strong heartbeats
We have always talked of lasting till Two Thousand.
From January on we could join them, justly,
For now comes Nunc Dimittis, if needed.
It is dispiriting to dodge death for ever.

JAMES K. BAXTER

The Bay

On the road to the bay was a lake of rushes
Where we bathed at times and changed in the bamboos.
Now it is rather to stand and say:
How many roads we take that lead to Nowhere,
The alley overgrown, no meaning now but loss:
Not that veritable garden where everything comes easy.

And by the bay itself were cliffs with carved names
And a hut on the shore beside the Maori ovens.
We raced boats from the banks of the pumice creek
Or swam in those autumnal shallows
Growing cold in amber water, riding the logs
Upstream, and waiting for the taniwha.

So now I remember the bay and the little spiders
On driftwood, so poisonous and quick.
The carved cliffs and the great outcrying surf
With currents round the rocks and the birds rising.
A thousand times an hour is torn across
And burned for the sake of going on living.
But I remember the bay that never was
And stand like stone and cannot turn away.

Morning and Evening Calm

Morning and evening calm: the Lord has spoken
from no devouring whirlwind, but the still
green garden of a world-sustaining Will.
O tenderly by Him the heart is broken,

and Bartimaeus finds in the All-Seeing
his eyes again, grown younger for his pains:
while disparate Love, that else were iron grains
draws meaning from the magnet of His Being.

He has denied my sorrow and my hunger
with voice of wounds, and bleeding I reply
that am content in Him to crave no longer

(dovelike and calm the overarching sky);
and love of flesh to flesh itself shall die
His terrible Compassion being stronger.

Lazarus

After the wake and speeches, when the guests in black
Had with the charm of ordinariness
Dispelled the gross terror of a fellow dead
(Eyelids grown waxen, the body like a sack
Bundled into the tomb) and the women with their mindless
Ritual of grief had murmured abroad all that could be said –

Then, as the world resumed its customary
Mask of civil day, he came, too late to mend
The broken vase (a cracked one could have been mended)
God's image blackened by causality.
And the woman said, "Since he was called your friend,
Why did you not come then? Now it is ended."

And when, the army blanket of grey earth
Put off, Lazarus from the cave mouth stumbled
(Hand, foot and mouth yet bound in mummy cloth)
To the sun's arrow, furnace of rebirth –
What could they do but weep? infirm and humbled
By Love not their love, more to be feared than wrath.

Thief and Samaritan

You, my friend, fallen among thieves,
The parable is harder than we suppose.
Always we say another hand drives
Home the knife, God's malice or the gross
Night-hawking bandit, straddled Apollyon.
We are blinded by the fume of the thieves' kitchen.

To be deceived is human; but till deception end
What hope of a bright inn, Love's oil and wine?
One greasy cloth of comfort I bring, friend
Nailed at the crossroad – I, thief, have seen
The same dawn break in blood and negative fire;
Your night I too could not endure.

Friend, stripped of the double-breasted suit
That left no cold out – if by failing stars
Love come, with ointment for your deadly wound,
Carry you up the steep inn stairs –
What should a thief do, footloose and well,
But rape the landlord's daughter, rummage the till?

Search well the wound, friend: know to the quick
What pain is. Thieves are only taught by pain.
And when, no longer sick,
You sit at table in the bright inn,
Remembering that pain you may sing small, dine
On a little bread, less wine.

The Buried Stream

Tonight our cat, Tahi, who lately lost
One eyebrow, yowls in the bush with another cat;

Our glass Tibetan ghost-trap has caught no ghost
Yet, but jangles suspended in the alcove that

We varnished and enlarged. Unwisely I have read
Sartre on Imagination – very dry, very French,

An old hound with noises in his head
Who dreams the hunt is on, yet fears the stench

Of action – he teaches us that human choice
Is rarely true or kind. My children are asleep.

Something clatters in the kitchen. I hear the voice
Of the buried stream that flows deep, deep,

Through caves I cannot enter, whose watery rope
Tugs my divining rod with the habit some call hope.

from *Jerusalem Sonnets*

Sonnet 36

Brother Ass, Brother Ass, you are full of fancies,
You want this and that – a woman, a thistle,

A poem, a coffeebreak, a white bed, no crabs;
And now you complain of the weight of the Rider

Who will set you free to gallop in the light of the sun!
Ah well, kick Him off then, and see how you go

Lame-footed in the brambles; your disconsolate bray
Is ugly in my ears – long ago, long ago,

The battle was fought and the issue decided
As to who would be King – go on, little donkey

Saddled and bridled by the Master of the world,
Be glad you can distinguish not an inch of the track,

That the stones are sharp, that your hide can itch,
That His true weight is heavy on your back.

Sonnet 37

Colin, you can tell my words are crippled now;
The bright coat of art He has taken away from me

And like the snail I crushed at the church door
My song is my stupidity;

The words of a homely man I cannot speak,
Home and bed He has taken away from me:

Like an old horse turned to grass I lift my head
Biting at the blossoms of the thorn tree;

Prayer of priest or nun I cannot use,
The songs of His house He has taken away from me;

As blind men meet and touch each other's faces
So He is kind to my infirmity;

As the cross is lifted and the day goes dark
Rule over myself He has taken away from me.

Sonnet 38

"I am dying now because I do not die" –
The song of the thief who hangs upon the tree;

"The house where I was born had seven windows
But its door is closed to me;

Whether I robbed or not I have forgotten,
My death has taken hold of me;

There was a woman once who gave me a cup of wine
And her eyes were full of mercy;

There is not even judgement any more
In the place where I have to be;

I cannot turn my head to find out
Who hangs beside me on the other tree;

Let the woman who is standing down below
Say a prayer for him and me."

Sonnet 39

In Auckland it was the twelve days' garland,
Feast with friends and shouting in the streets;

Now it is the apex and the clean flint knife –
Colin, if you meet him, give my love

To Patric Carey, and if you have the time
Once or twice go out to Brighton

To visit my parents – easy to hang
Imperatives on a good friend from a distance,

But I say, "If" – one thing, how can the image come
At all to the centre where the mind is silent

Without being false? I had hoped for fifty sonnets,
But here are thirty-nine, my gift to you, Colin,

From Hiruharama,
From Hemi te tutua.

ALLEN GINSBERG

Howl

For Carl Solomon

I

I saw the best minds of my generation destroyed by madness, starving
    hysterical naked,
dragging themselves through the negro streets at dawn looking for an
    angry fix,
angelheaded hipsters burning for the ancient heavenly connection to
    the starry dynamo in the machinery of night,
who poverty and tatters and hollow-eyed and high sat up smoking in
    the supernatural darkness of cold-water flats floating across the
    tops of cities contemplating jazz,
who bared their brains to Heaven under the El and saw Mohammedan
    angels staggering on tenement roofs illuminated,
who passed through universities with radiant cool eyes hallucinating
    Arkansas and Blake-light tragedy among the scholars of war,
who were expelled from the academies for crazy & publishing obscene
    odes on the windows of the skull,
who cowered in unshaven rooms in underwear, burning their money
    in wastebaskets and listening to the Terror through the wall,
who got busted in their pubic beards returning through Laredo with a
    belt of marijuana for New York,
who ate fire in paint hotels or drank turpentine in Paradise Alley,
    death, or purgatoried their torsos night after night
with dreams, with drugs, with waking nightmares, alcohol and cock
    and endless balls,
incomparable blind streets of shuddering cloud and lightning in the
    mind leaping toward poles of Canada & Paterson, illuminating all
    the motionless world of Time between,
Peyote solidities of halls, backyard green tree cemetery dawns, wine
    drunkenness over the rooftops, storefront boroughs of teahead
    joyride neon blinking traffic light, sun and moon and tree

vibrations in the roaring winter dusks of Brooklyn, ashcan
  rantings and kind king light of mind,
who chained themselves to subways for the endless ride from Battery
  to holy Bronx on benzedrine until the noise of wheels and
  children brought them down shuddering mouth-wracked and
  battered bleak of brain all drained of brilliance in the drear light
  of Zoo,
who sank all night in submarine light of Bickford's floated out and sat
  through the stale beer afternoon in desolate Fugazzi's, listening to
  the crack of doom on the hydrogen jukebox,
who talked continuously seventy hours from park to pad to bar to
  Bellevue to museum to the Brooklyn Bridge,
a lost battalion of platonic conversationalists jumping down the stoops
  off fire escapes off windowsills off Empire State out of the moon,
yacketayakking screaming vomiting whispering facts and memories and
  anecdotes and eyeball kicks and shocks of hospitals and jails and
  wars,
whole intellects disgorged in total recall for seven days and nights with
  brilliant eyes, meat for the Synagogue cast on the pavement,
who vanished into nowhere Zen New Jersey leaving a trail of
  ambiguous picture postcards of Atlantic City Hall,
suffering Eastern sweats and Tangerian bone-grindings and migraines
  of China under junk-withdrawal in Newark's bleak furnished
  room,
who wandered around and around at midnight in the railroad yard
  wondering where to go, and went, leaving no broken hearts,
who lit cigarettes in boxcars boxcars boxcars racketing through snow
  toward lonesome farms in grandfather night,
who studied Plotinus Poe St John of the Cross telepathy and bop
  kabbalah because the cosmos instinctively vibrated at their feet in
  Kansas,
who loned it through the streets of Idaho seeking visionary indian
  angels who were visionary indian angels,
who thought they were only mad when Baltimore gleamed in
  supernatural ecstasy,
who jumped in limousines with the Chinaman of Oklahoma on the
  impulse of winter midnight streetlight smalltown rain,
who lounged hungry and lonesome through Houston seeking jazz or
  sex or soup, and followed the brilliant Spaniard to converse about
  America and Eternity, a hopeless task, and so took ship to Africa,
who disappeared into the volcanoes of Mexico leaving behind nothing
  but the shadow of dungarees and the lava and ash of poetry scat-
  tered in fireplace Chicago,
who reappeared on the West Coast investigating the FBI in beards and
  shorts with big pacifist eyes sexy in their dark skin passing out
  incomprehensible leaflets,

who burned cigarette holes in their arms protesting the narcotic
    tobacco haze of Capitalism,
who distributed Supercommunist pamphlets in Union Square weeping
    and undressing while the sirens of Los Alamos wailed them
    down, and wailed down Wall, and the Staten Island ferry also
    wailed,
who broke down crying in white gymnasiums naked and trembling
    before the machinery of other skeletons,
who bit detectives in the neck and shrieked with delight in policecars
    for committing no crime but their own wild cooking pederasty
    and intoxication,
who howled on their knees in the subway and were dragged off the
    roof waving genitals and manuscripts,
who let themselves be fucked in the ass by saintly motorcyclists, and
    screamed with joy,
who blew and were blown by those human seraphim, the sailors,
    caresses of Atlantic and Caribbean love,
who balled in the morning in the evenings in rosegardens and the grass
    of public parks and cemeteries scattering their semen freely to
    whomever come who may,
who hiccuped endlessly trying to giggle but wound up with a sob
    behind a partition in a Turkish Bath when the blond & naked
    angel came to pierce them with a sword,
who lost their loveboys to the three old shrews of fate the one eyed
    shrew of the heterosexual dollar the one eyed shrew that winks
    out of the womb and the one eyed shrew that does nothing but
    sit on her ass and snip the intellectual golden threads of the crafts-
    man's loom,
who copulated ecstatic and insatiate with a bottle of beer a sweetheart
    a package of cigarettes a candle and fell off the bed, and contin-
    ued along the floor and down the hall and ended fainting on the
    wall with a vision of ultimate cunt and come eluding the last
    gyzym of consciousness,
who sweetened the snatches of a million girls trembling in the sunset,
    and were red eyed in the morning but prepared to sweeten the
    snatch of the sunrise, flashing buttocks under barns and naked in
    the lake,
who went out whoring through Colorado in myriad stolen night-cars,
    N.C., secret hero of these poems, cocksman and Adonis of
    Denver – joy to the memory of his innumerable lays of girls in
    empty lots & diner backyards, moviehouses' rickety rows, on
    mountaintops in caves or with gaunt waitresses in familiar
    roadside lonely petticoat upliftings & especially secret gas-station
    solipsisms of johns, & hometown alleys too,
who faded out in vast sordid movies, were shifted in dreams, woke on
    a sudden Manhattan, and picked themselves up out of basements

hung-over with heartless Tokay and horrors of Third Avenue
      iron dreams & stumbled to unemployment offices,
who walked all night with their shoes full of blood on the snowbank
      docks waiting for a door in the East River to open to a room full
      of steam-heat and opium,
who created great suicidal dramas on the apartment cliff-banks of the
      Hudson under the wartime blue floodlight of the moon & their
      heads shall be crowned with laurel in oblivion,
who ate the lamb stew of the imagination or digested the crab at the
      muddy bottom of the rivers of Bowery,
who wept at the romance of the streets with their pushcarts full of
      onions and bad music,
who sat in boxes breathing in the darkness under the bridge, and rose
      up to build harpsichords in their lofts,
who coughed on the sixth floor of Harlem crowned with flame under
      the tubercular sky surrounded by orange crates of theology,
who scribbled all night rocking and rolling over lofty incantations
      which in the yellow morning were stanzas of gibberish,
who cooked rotten animals lung heart feet tail borsht & tortillas
      dreaming of the pure vegetable kingdom,
who plunged themselves under meat trucks looking for an egg,
who threw their watches off the roof to cast their ballot for Eternity
      outside of Time, & alarm clocks fell on their heads every day for
      the next decade,
who cut their wrists three times successively unsuccessfully, gave up
      and were forced to open antique stores where they thought they
      were growing old and cried,
who were burned alive in their innocent flannel suits on Madison
      Avenue amid blasts of leaden verse & the tanked-up clatter of
      the iron regiments of fashion & the nitroglycerine shrieks of
      the fairies of advertising & the mustard gas of sinister intelligent
      editors, or were run down by the drunken taxicabs of Absolute
      Reality,
who jumped off the Brooklyn Bridge this actually happened and
      walked away unknown and forgotten into the ghostly daze of
      Chinatown soup alleyways & firetrucks, not even one free beer,
who sang out of their windows in despair, fell out of the subway
      window, jumped in the filthy Passaic, leaped on negroes, cried all
      over the street, danced on broken wineglasses barefoot smashed
      phonograph records of nostalgic European 1930s German jazz
      finished the whiskey and threw up groaning into the bloody
      toilet, moans in their ears and the blast of colossal steamwhistles,
who barreled down the highways of the past journeying to each
      other's hotrod-Golgotha jail-solitude watch or Birmingham
      jazz incarnation,

who drove crosscountry seventytwo hours to find out if I had a vision
    or you had a vision or he had a vision to find out Eternity,

who journeyed to Denver, who died in Denver, who came back to
    Denver & waited in vain, who watched over Denver & brooded
    & loned in Denver and finally went away to find out the Time,
    & now Denver is lonesome for her heroes,

who fell on their knees in hopeless cathedrals praying for each other's
    salvation and light and breasts, until the soul illuminated its hair
    for a second,

who crashed through their minds in jail waiting for impossible
    criminals with golden heads and the charm of reality in their
    hearts who sang sweet blues to Alcatraz,

who retired to Mexico to cultivate a habit, or Rocky Mount to tender
    Buddha or Tangiers to boys or Southern Pacific to the black
    locomotive or Harvard to Narcissus to Woodlawn to the daisy-
    chain or grave,

who demanded sanity trials accusing the radio of hypnotism & were
    left with their insanity & their hands & a hung jury,

who threw potato salad at CCNY lecturers on Dadaism and
    subsequently presented themselves on the granite steps of the
    madhouse with shaven heads and harlequin speech of suicide,
    demanding instantaneous lobotomy,

and who were given instead the concrete void of insulin Metrazol
    electricity hydrotherapy psychotherapy occupational therapy
    pingpong & amnesia,

who in humorless protest overturned only one symbolic pingpong
    table, resting briefly in catatonia,

returning years later truly bald except for a wig of blood, and tears and
    fingers, to the visible madman doom of the wards of the
    madtowns of the East,

Pilgrim State's Rockland's and Greystone's foetid halls, bickering with
    the echoes of the soul, rocking and rolling in the midnight
    solitude-bench dolmen-realms of love, dream of life a nightmare,
    bodies turned to stone as heavy as the moon,

with mother finally ******, and the last fantastic book flung out of the
    tenement window, and the last door closed at 4 A.M. and the last
    telephone slammed at the wall in reply and the last furnished
    room emptied down to the last piece of mental furniture, a
    yellow paper rose twisted on a wire hanger in the closet, and
    even that imaginary, nothing but a hopeful little bit of
    hallucination –

ah, Carl, while you are not safe I am not safe, and now you're really in
    the total animal soup of time –

and who therefore ran through the icy streets obsessed with a sudden
    flash of the alchemy of the use of the ellipsis catalogue a variable
    measure and the vibrating plane,

who dreamt and made incarnate gaps in Time & Space through images
  juxtaposed, and trapped the archangel of the soul between 2
  visual images and joined the elemental verbs and set the noun
  and dash of consciousness together jumping with sensation of
  Pater Omnipotens Aeterna Deus
to recreate the syntax and measure of poor human prose and stand
  before you speechless and intelligent and shaking with shame,
  rejected yet confessing out the soul to conform to the rhythm of
  thought in his naked and endless head,
the madman bum and angel beat in Time, unknown, yet putting
  down here what might be left to say in time come after death,
and rose reincarnate in the ghostly clothes of jazz in the goldhorn
  shadow of the band and blew the suffering of America's naked
  mind for love into an eli eli lamma lamma sabacthani saxophone
  cry that shivered the cities down to the last radio
with the absolute heart of the poem of life butchered out of their own
  bodies good to eat a thousand years.

2

What sphinx of cement and aluminum bashed open their skulls and ate
  up their brains and imagination?
Moloch! Solitude! Filth! Ugliness! Ashcans and unobtainable dollars!
  Children screaming under the stairways! Boys sobbing in armies!
  Old men weeping in the parks!
Moloch! Moloch! Nightmare of Moloch! Moloch the loveless! Mental
  Moloch! Moloch the heavy judger of men!
Moloch the incomprehensible prison! Moloch the crossbone soulless
  jail-house and Congress of sorrows! Moloch whose buildings are
  judgment! Moloch the vast stone of war! Moloch the stunned
  governments!
Moloch whose mind is pure machinery! Moloch whose blood is
  running money! Moloch whose fingers are ten armies! Moloch
  whose breast is a cannibal dynamo! Moloch whose ear is a
  smoking tomb!
Moloch whose eyes are a thousand blind windows! Moloch whose
  sky-scrapers stand in the long streets like endless Jehovahs!
  Moloch whose factories dream and croak in the fog! Moloch
  whose smoke-stacks and antennae crown the cities!
Moloch whose love is endless oil and stone! Moloch whose soul is
  electricity and banks! Moloch whose poverty is the specter of
  genius! Moloch whose fate is a cloud of sexless hydrogen!
  Moloch whose name is the Mind!
Moloch in whom I sit lonely! Moloch in whom I dream Angels!
  Crazy in Moloch! Cocksucker in Moloch! Lacklove and manless
  in Moloch!

Moloch who entered my soul early! Moloch in whom I am a
    consciousness without a body! Moloch who frightened me out of
    my natural ecstasy! Moloch whom I abandon! Wake up in
    Moloch! Light streaming out of the sky!
Moloch! Moloch! Robot apartments! invisible suburbs! skeleton
    treasuries! blind capitals! demonic industries! spectral nations!
    invincible madhouses! granite cocks! monstrous bombs!
They broke their backs lifting Moloch to Heaven! Pavements, trees,
    radios, tons! lifting the city to Heaven which exists and is
    everywhere about us!
Visions! omens! hallucinations! miracles! ecstasies! gone down the
    American river!
Dreams! adorations! illuminations! religions! the whole boatload of
    sensitive bullshit!
Breakthroughs! over the river! flips and crucifixions! gone down the
    flood! Highs! Epiphanies! Despairs! Ten years' animal screams
    and suicides! Minds! New loves! Mad generation! down on the
    rocks of Time!
Real holy laughter in the river! They saw it all! the wild eyes! the holy
    yells! They bade farewell! They jumped off the roof! to solitude!
    waving! carrying flowers! Down to the river! into the street!

3

Carl Solomon! I'm with you in Rockland
    where you're madder than I am
I'm with you in Rockland
    where you must feel very strange
I'm with you in Rockland
    where you imitate the shade of my mother
I'm with you in Rockland
    where you've murdered your twelve secretaries
I'm with you in Rockland
    where you laugh at this invisible humor
I'm with you in Rockland
    where we are great writers on the same dreadful typewriter
I'm with you in Rockland
    where your condition has become serious and is reported on the
    radio
I'm with you in Rockland
    where the faculties of the skull no longer admit the worms of the
    senses
I'm with you in Rockland
    where you drink the tea of the breasts of the spinsters of Utica
I'm with you in Rockland
    where you pun on the bodies of your nurses the harpies of the
    Bronx

I'm with you in Rockland
> where you scream in a straightjacket that you're losing the game
> of the actual pingpong of the abyss

I'm with you in Rockland
> where you bang on the catatonic piano the soul is innocent and
> immortal it should never die ungodly in an armed madhouse

I'm with you in Rockland
> where fifty more shocks will never return your soul to its body
> again from its pilgrimage to a cross in the void

I'm with you in Rockland
> where you accuse your doctors of insanity and plot the Hebrew
> socialist revolution against the fascist national Golgotha

I'm with you in Rockland
> where you will split the heavens of Long Island and resurrect your
> living human Jesus from the superhuman tomb

I'm with you in Rockland
> where there are twentyfive thousand mad comrades all together
> singing the final stanzas of the Internationale

I'm with you in Rockland
> where we hug and kiss the United States under our bedsheets the
> United States that coughs all night and won't let us sleep

I'm with you in Rockland
> where we wake up electrified out of the coma by our own souls'
> airplanes roaring over the roof they've come to drop angelic
> bombs the hospital illuminates itself   imaginary walls collapse   O
> skinny legions run outside   O starry-spangled shock of
> mercy the eternal war is here   O victory forget your underwear
> we're free

I'm with you in Rockland
> in my dreams you walk dripping from a sea-journey on the
> highway across America in tears to the door of my cottage in the
> Western night

Fourth Floor, Dawn,
Up All Night Writing Letters

Pigeons shake their wings on the copper church roof
out my window across the street, a bird perched on the cross
surveys the city's blue-gray clouds. Larry Rivers
'll come at 10 a.m. and take my picture. I'm taking
your picture, pigeons. I'm writing you down, Dawn.
I'm immortalizing your exhaust, Avenue A bus.
O Thought, now you'll have to think the same thing forever!

ELIZABETH JENNINGS

Song for a Birth or a Death

Last night I saw the savage world
And heard the blood beat up the stair;
The fox's bark, the owl's shrewd pounce,
The crying creatures – all were there,
And men in bed with love and fear.

The slit moon only emphasised
How blood must flow and teeth must grip.
What does the calm light understand,
The light which draws the tide and ship
And drags the owl upon its prey
And human creatures lip to lip?

Last night I watched how pleasure must
Leap from disaster with its will:
The fox's fear, the watch-dog's lust
Know that all matings mean a kill:
And human creatures kissed in trust
Feel the blood throb to death until

The seed is struck, the pleasure's done,
The birds are thronging in the air;
The moon gives way to widespread sun.
Yes but the pain still crouches where
The young fox and the child are trapped
And cries of love are cries of fear.

My Grandmother

She kept an antique shop – or it kept her.
Among Apostle spoons and Bristol glass,
The faded silks, the heavy furniture,
She watched her own reflection in the brass
Salvers and silver bowls, as if to prove
Polish was all, there was no need of love.

And I remember how I once refused
To go out with her, since I was afraid.
It was perhaps a wish not to be used

Like antique objects. Though she never said
That she was hurt, I still could feel the guilt
Of that refusal, guessing how she felt.

Later, too frail to keep a shop, she put
All her best things in one long narrow room.
The place smelt old, of things too long kept shut,
The smell of absences where shadows come
That can't be polished. There was nothing then
To give her own reflection back again.

And when she died I felt no grief at all,
Only the guilt of what I once refused.
I walked into her room among the tall
Sideboards and cupboards – things she never used
But needed; and no finger-marks were there,
Only the new dust falling through the air.

The Resurrection

I was the one who waited in the garden
Doubting the morning and the early light.
I watched the mist lift off its own soft burden,
Permitting not believing my own sight.

If there were sudden noises I dismissed
Them as a trick of sound, a sleight of hand.
Not by a natural joy could I be blessed
Or trust a thing I could not understand.

Maybe I was a shadow thrown by some
Who, weeping, came to lift away the stone,
Or was I but the path on which the sun,
Too heavy for itself, was loosed and thrown?

I heard the voices and the recognition
And love like kisses heard behind the walls.
Were they my tears which fell, a real contrition?
Or simply April with its waterfalls?

It was by negatives I learnt my place.
The garden went on growing and I sensed
A sudden breeze that blew across my face.
Despair returned but now it danced, it danced.

After a Time

(for a friend dead two years)

I have not stood at this grave nor have I
Been where men come at last to silence when
Death sends them to instinctive ceremony,
Whether in torturing sun or fitting rain,
Whether they stare or cry.

What do I say who never put a wreath
Down for a father or this friend? Someone
Will make the speech for me. O this dear death,
Two years of missing all have been undone,
Yet I am growing with

Spontaneous strengths, blessings I did not claim –
Laughter, a child, knowledge of justice and
Faith like a cross which oddly bears my name,
Falls round my neck. In early hours I stand
Reflecting how I came

To this. What takes me through the corridors
Of grief? Was it the touch of love, that leading thread
Which drew me to glad grief from wrong remorse,
Wiped off the dust and let me see the dead
With new care now, new laws?

Christ Seen by Flemish Painters

Never the loaves and fishes multiplied,
Never the senses loosed, never the full
Attentive crowd, bloat faces set beside
A landscape opulent with sun and whole
Terraces hung with wide

Sweet fruit. Austerity, the grey face drawn,
The body almost spirit on the wood,
The wood like ash. Perhaps two lookers torn
By watching night through with no sleep or food.
Yes, here God is alone.

And man has seen the solitude of spaces,
The no-star air, the soil which hurts the feet,
The puckered pain on hands, the worried faces,
Triumphant anguish just before defeat,
The cool air of hard graces.

The Child's Story

When I was small and they talked about love I laughed
But I ran away and I hid in a tall tree
Or I lay in asparagus beds
But I still listened.
The blue dome sang with the wildest birds
And the new sun sang in the idle noon
But then I heard love, love, rung from the steeples, each belfry,
And I was afraid and I watched the cypress trees
Join the deciduous chestnuts and oaks in a crowd of shadows
And then I shivered and ran and ran to the tall
White house with the green shutters and dark red door
And I cried "Let me in even if you must love me"
And they came and lifted me up and told me the name
Of the near and the far stars,
And so my first love was.

JAMES MERRILL

Swimming by Night

A light going out in the forehead
Of the house by the ocean,
Into warm black its feints of diamond fade.
Without clothes, without caution

Plunging past gravity –
Wait! Where before
Had been floating nothing, is a gradual body
Half remembered, astral with phosphor,

Yours, risen from its tomb
In your own mind,
Haunting nimbleness, glimmerings a random
Spell has kindled. So that, new-limned

By this weak lamp
The evening's alcohol will feed
Until the genie chilling bids you limp
Heavily over stones to bed,

You wear your master's robe
One last time, the far break
Of waves, their length and sparkle, the spinning globe
You wear, and the star running down his cheek.

David's Night in Veliès

Into the flame Godmother put her hand,
Lulling the olive boughs.
Lymph welled from them. I too in her strange house
Kindled and smoked and did not understand.

Followed the Cyclopean meal:
Loaves, rice, hens, goats, gallons of sweet red wine.
I mellowed with the men
Who now waxed crackling, philosophical

– For all I knew – but then
Were on their feet, with flashlights, tramping out
In ancient Air Force overcoats
After the small birds roosting roundabout.

Chains glowing strong
Had bound me to her hearth. Photograph time!
A whole boxful explained in pantomime,
One by one. The string

Retied, warm–hearted questioning
Could start, in mime, about my life.
Each offhand white lie gladdened her, good queen
In whose domain the rueful

Dream was fact. Subdued
Came back her hunters. The lone ortolan,
Head lolling from a sideboard out of Oudry,
Would be my very own to breakfast on.

Bedtime. Inconceivable upper room
Ashiver in lamplight.
Bed clean as ice, heavy as ice
Its layers of coarsely woven pink and white

Woken at once to struggle out from. Bitter
Closet reeking welcome. Wind, moon, frost.
Piebald hindquarters of another guest.
Fowl's nervous titter.

Relieved of wine's last warmth, to lie and freeze . . .
Day would break, never fear;
Rime-sparkling courtesies melt into blue air
Like dew. One hour more? Two? Goodbye! Write please!

The road would climb in bracelets toward the pass,
The sun be high but low,
Each olive tree shed its white thawing shadow
On sallow grass,

Myself become the stranger who remembers
Fire, cold, a smile, a smell,
One tiny plucked form on the embers,
Slow claw raised in blessing or farewell.

Clearing the Title

for D. J.

Because the wind has changed, because I guess
My poem (what to call it though?) is finished,
Because the golden genie chafes within
His smudged-glass bottle and, god help us, you
Have chosen, sight unseen, this tropic rendezvous
Where tourist, outcast and in-groupie gather
Island by island, linked together,
Causeways bridging the vast shallowness –

Through the low ceiling motors rip.
Below me, twisting in the asphalt grip
Of mall and pancake house, boatel and bank,
What's left of Nature here? Those trees five thousand tin
Roofs, like little mirrors in distress,

Would flash up from if the sun were out . . .
Oh for the lucid icebound book of winter
I gave up my rapt place in for this trip!

Such a mistake – past fifty and behaving
As if hope sprang eternal. At the baggage claim
Armed with *The Power and the Glory* (Greene),
I notice, finger-drawn in a soaped pane,
One black sun only, spokes in air
Like feelers of a bug flipped on its back,
Above a clumsy WELLCOME TO THE KEYS
– Then see the open car. You in it, waving.

Couldn't one have gone into the matter
Before succumbing? Easier said than done,
What with this tough white coral skeleton
Beneath a crop of shanties built on blocks,
On air, on edge for, any day,
Water and wind to sweep them clean away.
Meanwhile I'm braced, capricious chatterbox,
Against your blasts of horn and flood of casual patter.

Sales patter? The appalling truth now bores
Into my brain: you've *bought* a house
And pass, en route to it, the peeling white
Five-storey skyscraper in which "our" title
Is being cleared! – activity no more
Thinkable (you park, fling a green-painted door
Open onto a fresh white hall)
Than what the termites do, look! to these floors

Between the muddy varnish of whose lines
(But can you picture *living* here? Expect
Me to swelter, year by sunset year,
Beneath these ceilings? – which at least aren't low.
What about houses elsewhere, rooms already packed
With memories? That chiffonier
Would have to go, or else be painted white . . .)
More brightly with each word the daylight shines.

And fresh as paint the bare rooms, if you please,
Having consumed whatever came before,
Look up unblinking: will *we* bring
Their next meal – table, mirror, bed, lamp, chair?

Serve the ravenous interior
With real-life victuals, voices, vanities
Until it lolls back purring? – like our slum
Garden zonked by milk-bombs from two old bent trees.

Presuming, then, tripod and pendulum
Tell truly, and the freckled county clerk
Completes, adds to the master file
A Gothic-lettered "title" with your name –
What happens next? Behind a latticework
Of deeds no one has time or patience to undo
We cultivate our little lot, meanwhile
Waiting companionably for kingdom come?

Close-ups: hibiscus broad as garden hats.
Large winged but nameless insect excavated
By slaves; the abdomen's deep strata
Primitive-intricate, like macramé.
Then from beneath the house, fee fi fo fum!
Caller the colour of good smoke blown through the years
Into this dumb scarred mug he lifts to say:
"Huh? Not want *me*? Man, the whole world wants cats!"

No. No, no, no. We can't just cast
Three decades' friendships and possessions out.
Who're our friends here? (In fact I recognize
Old ones everywhere I turn my eyes –
Trumpet-vine, cracked pavement, that faint sulphur smell,
Those see-through lizards, quick as a heartbeat . . .)
But people? (Well, the Wilburs live downstreet . . .)
Of course, if shutting doors onto the past

Could damage *it* . . . Wherever that thought led,
Turning the loose knob onto better-late-
Than-never light, we breast its deepening stream
Along with others who've a date
With sunset. Each day's unspent zinc or red brass penny
– Here at land's end not deposited
In winter palisades crowned by antennae,
Fuel for the all-night talk shows of the dead –

Inflates to moidore, melts toward an oblivion
Alone, its gravity unspecified,
The far-off mangrove islet saves
From being wholly formed of air and waves,

Of light and birdcry, as with each step less
Divides the passer-through from, what to call
Such radiance – creative? terminal?
Day's flush of pleasure, knowing its poem done?

Our poem now. It's signed JM, but grew
From life together, grain by coral grain.
Building on it, we let the life cloud over . . .
Time to break through those clouds, for heaven's sake,
And look round. Any place will do
(Remember, later at the discothèque)
And what at first appal precisely are the changes
That everybody is entitled to.

Here at the end's a landing stage swept clean
Of surplus "properties" and "characters".
Gone the thick banyan, the opaque old queen.
Only some flimsiest human veil
Woven of trickster and revivalist,
Musician and snake-charmer (and, yes, us as well)
Pot- and patchouli-scented floats between
The immense warm pink spotlight and the scene.

Here's the Iguana Man, from lands
"Beneath the world". Dragons, withered like him,
Unwinking drape his fishnet singlet. Here
Balloons are straining for release; we pick
A headstrong silver one. And here a clown
Cat-limber, white-lipped with a bright cerulean tear
On one rouged cheek, rides unicycle, hands
Nonchalantly juggling firebrands.

Circles round every act form, or to groans
Disperse. This portion of the dock's been cleared
By the Salvation Army. (They're
Nine strong, a family; beneath the same
Grim visor glowers, babe to grandmother,
The same grim love.) "Y'all give!" our deadpan clown
Yells brandishing a hammer fit for Thor,
"Give or Ah'll clobber yew!" and *grunt* go the trombones.

Though no one does, no thunder strikes. Because –
Say, because a black girl with shaved skull
Sways on the brink: flexed knee and ankle-bell
And eyes that burn back at the fiery ball

Till it relenting tests with one big toe
Its bath, and Archimedean splendours overflow.
As the sun sets, "Let's hear it for the sun!"
Cry voices. Laughter. Bells. Applause

(Think of the dead here, sleeping above ground
– Simpler than to hack a tomb from coral –
In whitewashed hope chests under the palm fronds.
Or think of waking, whether to the quarrel
Of white cat and black crow, those unchanged friends,
Or to a dazzle from below:
Earth visible through floor-cracks, miles – or inches – down,
And spun by a gold key-chain round and round . . .)

Whereupon on high, where all is bright
Day still, blue turning to key lime, to steel
A clear flame-dusted crimson bars,
Sky puts on the face of the young clown
As the balloons, mere hueless dots now, stars
Or periods – although tonight we trust no real
Conclusions will be reached – float higher yet,
Juggled slowly by the changing light.

CHRISTOPHER MIDDLETON

Anasphere: Le torse antique

> *Kami naraba*
> *yurara-sarara-to*
> *ori-tamae!*

I

Among the grains how small you were
Dry in the desert of your image

You did not hear the cries of love as you passed
Down the street, you did not see
The spittle
Fly nor the beads of blood on the axe blade

The naked masked woman
Twice she swung it & once more & high
By its long handle

II

Here we are travelling from place to place

Here I keep you hidden
Held by a great lightness
Body & voice if I could set you free

In my cage a castle rose to its turrets
Only for mice & a flock of ravens
Pure columns unbent by thought

Here they shall flower from our stillness
Voice their future dream
Of being trees

Plant them giving shade in a field
For five cows composing a sign for us
The diagonals of a dice
Or is it the pentagram –
Hidden in a bed the conversation of bodies
Hidden I keep them

And still there is a voice
Whenever in sweet nakedness you nuzzle me
Voice I want you not only to say

A white cow is made of cream & fury

– Hathor

So your face took shape
It was in the boulders uphill before us
A movement of lines to the measure of a dance
A flashing of earth years Egyptian axes and eyes
No time at all in which it happens

One hundred thousand horses
Toppling off the crag were chopped into food
For the hands that peeled leaves of laurel
Out of the flint core
Now in a field of old rain goofily like a fortress
A red horse was planting his hooves
– Look how it is to stand there

Devastation
Marks no tracks of ours
Lightly now through these hidden places we shall walk
Where mouths collect & change to make expressions
Listen
A street with many twistings this one

Lightly you are here you had no weight whatever
Wearing your little cloak over so much nakedness
You leaned against me

III

1

Body of light
    Dwelling in a piss jet
Or particular cherry blossom

    Look, a spirit
Wanted something
    A sign, to be manifest
        In all directions

  Never
Sure, inhaling itself
      A whirlwind

2

    Desire, pressing
On silence
  To lure you, poem
One or two words

  Go
To the southern shore
    One flesh we pursue

3

  One, through Never –
A span, slightest across
     Perdition, horrible
  Deep, the gurgle

It is
Pepper behind my eyes, it fashions
The eye of the hurricane
It fills
With snakes & stars
The liquid cathedral collapsing across
Atolls, Florida keys

4

World, great harp
Built of blood
Now then
What sounds in flight

What muscular forms of breath
Never flow, leap
Up the torrent & restore

To you
Your open tunes

5

One flesh —
Other, another
Horizon, ancient
Unplaceable

Twitter your speech again
Models
Out of oblivion
The bud & the wave & the snowflake

6

Your never is yes,
Out of nowhere the cry
Gone & again
Cupola, welling, spiral, it lifts from

The bird throat

Soon hushed

7

But song in
Some few broken
Tombs

A touched sex

IV

Difficult
    Piecing the life together

        "like a supper in the wind"
How it comes, goes
            Exact from perception
Rhythm

                Not snatching
        It comes in waves
Not knowing me from you
    A spirit cannot be spoken
Or spoken of

Drums drumming the exact measure
Dancer to dancer the flower spray is passed

To build for you a space
    In this drain of being it is I
  Smash the heads & fix famine
A floor strewn with rock-orchid
                Lotus roof

In mid-air, air dangerous with heat
        Carbonic gas, beams of cassia
I have suspended
    A floorspread weighted down with white jades

Margins, like these
    Then at sun up to have leapt into
The blue fragrant living sea

Profit motive melts the poles,
            Paris drowning, Bombay
Alexandria

I have hung strips of flesh at porch & gate
    The flesh of children

The time will not come again
              It will not come again

Saloon with Birds

If someone barefoot stood in a saloon,
His dromedary might be chomping, outside,
That majestic meal. High olive notes
Plucked from a mandolin. Fumes. Leafgreen.

A dark descends. There, with banana palm
Consorts forbidden music. Ugly. Ocean.
Delay it. First a clatter, from the birds.
They wax decrepit. Vocal signatures:

Who could ever have so illuminated them
That the letters, cut from stark air,
Assume no solitary monumental pose,
But wavily ache with the boat hulls?

Certain or not, an urgent finger prodded
Epsilons and wagtailed gammas free
From habit, a peculiar glue. No help. No
Waste. In the saloon each dust spake.

In the saloon the spokes of another
Sunlight, still this ocular companion though,
Rolled afternoons around, like meatballs,
Bubbles of corn sizzling in a crystal pan.

Throaty owls also, they could entertain
Quick, tensile teeth. A joy. Pelican moonlit.
Look at a pine nut. It exists, you know.
Little furred insects inhabit vast smells.

For this the saloon is open. A waft.
A waft is all it takes. A venetian blind
Has wrinkled the wash basin. A cool expounds
Blood orange, air in China, appalling beliefs.

Air wraps the mast. Air singing. Air,
The solo invader who timed anew
Our free objects. The saloon twangs,
Dust swims, a gong letting its hum fly.

Closing never. Least of all on syllables.
A split lemon has released from evil
Any soul what's willing. Get that. Now
Never you move like you were shrunk to be.

Or else forgo the little sorrow. Treasure
The big one. Tell, in the saloon,
Nothing of it. Look up. Long enough
The ocean has delayed. You can breathe again.

FRANK O'HARA

Animals

Have you forgotten what we were like then
when we were still first rate
and the day came fat with an apple in its mouth

it's no use worrying about Time
but we did have a few tricks up our sleeves
and turned some sharp corners

the whole pasture looked like our meal
we didn't need speedometers
we could manage cocktails out of ice and water

I wouldn't want to be faster
or greener than now if you were with me O you
were the best of all my days

Aus Einem April

We dust the walls.
        And of course we are weeping larks
falling all over the heavens with our shoulders clasped
in someone's armpits, so tightly! and our throats are full.
        Haven't you ever fallen down at Christmas

and didn't it move everyone who saw you?
      isn't that what the tree means? the pure pleasure
of making weep those whom you cannot move by your flights!
      It's enough to drive one to suicide.
And the rooftops are falling apart like the applause

of rough, long-nailed, intimate, roughened-by-kisses, hands.
Fingers more breathless than a tongue laid upon the lips
in the hour of sunlight, early morning, before the mist rolls
in from the sea; and out there everything is turbulent and green.

In Memory of My Feelings

To Grace Hartigan

I

My quietness has a man in it, he is transparent
and he carries me quietly, like a gondola, through the streets.
He has several likenesses, like stars and years, like numerals.

My quietness has a number of naked selves,
so many pistols I have borrowed to protect myselves
from creatures who too readily recognize my weapons
and have murder in their heart!
           though in winter
they are warm as roses, in the desert
taste of chilled anisette.
        At times, withdrawn,
I rise into the cool skies
and gaze on at the imponderable world with the simple identification
of my colleagues, the mountains. Manfred climbs to my nape,
speaks, but I do not hear him,
           I'm too blue.
An elephant takes up his trumpet,
money flutters from the windows of cries, silk stretching its mirror
across shoulder blades. A gun is "fired".
           One of me rushes
to window #13 and one of me raises his whip and one of me
flutters up from the center of the track amidst the pink flamingoes,
and underneath their hooves as they round the last turn my lips
are scarred and brown, brushed by tails, masked in dirt's lust,
definition, open mouths gasping for the cries of the bettors for the lungs
of earth.
      So many of my transparencies could not resist the race!

Terror in earth, dried mushrooms, pink feathers, tickets,
a flaking moon drifting across the muddied teeth,
the imperceptible moan of covered breathing,

                                love of the serpent!
I am underneath its leaves as the hunter crackles and pants
and bursts, as the barrage balloon drifts behind a cloud
and animal death whips out its flashlight,

                            whistling
and slipping the glove off the trigger hand. The serpent's eyes
redden at sight of those thorny fingernails, he is so smooth!

                                 My transparent selves
flail about like vipers in a pail, writhing and hissing
without panic, with a certain justice of response
and presently the aquiline serpent comes to resemble the Medusa.

2

The dead hunting
and the alive, ahunted.

                    My father, my uncle,
my grand-uncle and the several aunts. My
grand-aunt, dying for me, like a talisman, in the war,
before I had even gone to Borneo
her blood vessels rushed to the surface
and burst like rockets over the wrinkled
invasion of the Australians, her eyes aslant
like the invaded, but blue like mine.
An atmosphere of supreme lucidity,

                           humanism,
the mere existence of emphasis,

                       a rusted barge
painted orange against the sea
full of Marines reciting the Arabian ideas
which are a proof in themselves of seasickness
which is a proof in itself of being hunted.
A hit? *ergo* swim.

                My 10   my 19,
my 9,   and the several years. My
12 years since they all died, philosophically speaking.
And now the coolness of a mind
like a shuttered suite in the Grand Hotel
where mail arrives for my incognito,

                        whose façade
has been slipping into the Grand Canal for centuries;
rockets splay over a *sposalizio*,

                      fleeing into night

from their Chinese memories, and it is a celebration,
the trying desperately to count them as they die.
But who will stay to be these numbers
when all the lights are dead?

3

The most arid stretch is often richest,
the hand lifting towards a fig tree from hunger
        digging
and there is water, clear, supple, or there
deep in the sand where death sleeps, a murmurous bubbling
proclaims the blackness that will ease and burn.
You preferred the Arabs? but they didn't stay to count
their inventions, racing into sands, converting themselves into
so many,
    embracing, at Ramadan, the tenderest effigies of
themselves with penises shorn by the hundreds, like a camel
ravishing a goat.
     And the mountainous-minded Greeks could speak
of time as a river and step across it into Persia, leaving the pain
at home to be converted into statuary. I adore the Roman copies.
And the stench of the camel's spit I swallow,
and the stench of the whole goat. For we have advanced, France,
together into a new land, like the Greeks, where one feels nostalgic
for mere ideas, where truth lies on its deathbed like an uncle
and one of me has a sentimental longing for number,
as has another for the ball gowns of the Directoire and yet
another for "Destiny, Paris, destiny!"
        or "Only a king may kill a king."

How many selves are there in a war hero asleep in names? under
a blanket of platoon and fleet, orderly. For every seaman
with one eye closed in fear and twitching arm at a sigh for Lord
  Nelson,
he is all dead; and now a meek subaltern writhes in his bedclothes
with the fury of a thousand, violating an insane mistress
who has only herself to offer his multitudes.
       Rising,
he wraps himself in the burnoose of memories against the heat of life
and over the sands he goes to take an algebraic position *in re*
a sun of fear shining not too bravely. He will ask himselves to
vote on fear before he feels a tremor,
      as runners arrive from the mountains
bearing snow, proof that the mind's obsolescence is still capable

of intimacy. His mistress will follow him across the desert
like a goat, towards a mirage which is something familiar about
one of his innumerable wrists,
                          and lying in an oasis one day,
playing catch with coconuts, they suddenly smell oil.

                          4

Beneath these lives
the ardent lover of history hides,
                          tongue out
leaving a globe of spit on a taut spear of grass
and leaves off rattling his tail a moment
to admire this flag.
                  I'm looking for my Shanghai Lil.
Five years ago, enamored of fire-escapes, I went to Chicago,
an eventful trip: the fountains! the Art Institute, the Y
for both sexes, absent Christianity.
                          At 7, before Jane
was up, the copper lake stirred against the sides
of a Norwegian freighter; on the deck a few dirty men,
tired of night, watched themselves in the water
as years before the German prisoners on the *Prinz Eugen*
dappled the Pacific with their sores, painted purple
by a Naval doctor.
                  Beards growing, and the constant anxiety
over looks. I'll shave before she wakes up. Sam Goldwyn
spent $2,000,000 on Anna Sten, but Grushenka left America.
One of me is standing in the waves, an ocean bather,
or I am naked with a plate of devils at my hip.
                                        Grace
to be born and live as variously as possible. The conception
of the masque barely suggests the sordid identifications.
I am a Hittite in love with a horse. I don't know what blood's
in me I feel like an African prince I am a girl walking downstairs
in a red pleated dress with heels I am a champion taking a fall
I am a jockey with a sprained ass-hole I am the light mist
                          in which a face appears
and it is another face of blonde I am a baboon eating a banana
I am a dictator looking at his wife I am a doctor eating a child
and the child's mother smiling I am a Chinaman climbing a mountain
I am a child smelling his father's underwear I am an Indian
sleeping on a scalp
                  and my pony is stamping in the birches,
and I've just caught sight of the *Niña*, the *Pinta* and the *Santa Maria*.

What land is this, so free?
>I watch
the sea at the back of my eyes, near the spot where I think
in solitude as pine trees groan and support the enormous winds,
they are humming *L'Oiseau de feu!*
>They look like gods, these whitemen,
and they are bringing me the horse I fell in love with on the frieze.

>5

And now it is the serpent's turn.
I am not quite you, but almost, the opposite of visionary.
You are coiled around the central figure,
>the heart
that bubbles with red ghosts, since to move is to love
and the scrutiny of all things is syllogistic,
the startled eyes of the dikdik, the bush full of white flags
fleeing a hunter,
>which is our democracy
>but the prey
is always fragile and like something, as a seashell can be
a great Courbet, if it wishes. To bend the ear of the outer world.

>When you turn your head
can you feel your heels, undulating? that's what it is
to be a serpent. I haven't told you of the most beautiful things
in my lives, and watching the ripple of their loss disappear
along the shore, underneath ferns,
>face downward in the ferns
my body, the naked host to my many selves, shot
by a guerrilla warrior or dumped from a car into ferns
which are themselves *journalières*.
>The hero, trying to unhitch his parachute,
stumbles over me. It is our last embrace.
>And yet
I have forgotten my loves, and chiefly that one, the cancerous
statue which my body could no longer contain,
>against my will
>against my love
become art,
>I could not change it into history
and so remember it,
>and I have lost what is always and everywhere
present, the scene of my selves, the occasion of these ruses,
which I myself and singly must now kill
>and save the serpent in their midst.

Ave Maria

Mothers of America
         let your kids go to the movies!
get them out of the house so they won't know what you're up to
it's true that fresh air is good for the body
                   but what about the soul
that grows in darkness, embossed by silvery images
and when you grow old as grow old you must
               they won't hate you
they won't criticize you they won't know
          they'll be in some glamorous
    country
they first saw on a Saturday afternoon or playing hookey
they may even be grateful to you
         for their first sexual experience
which only cost you a quarter
         and didn't upset the peaceful home
they will know where candy bars come from
         and gratuitous bags of
    popcorn
as gratuitous as leaving the movie before it's over
with a pleasant stranger whose apartment is in the Heaven on Earth
    Bldg
near the Williamsburg Bridge
         oh mothers you will have made the little
    tykes
so happy because if nobody does pick them up in the movies
they won't know the difference
         and if somebody does it'll be sheer
    gravy
and they'll have been truly entertained either way
instead of hanging around the yard
         or up in their room
            hating you
prematurely since you won't have done anything horribly mean yet
except keeping them from the darker joys
         it's unforgivable the latter
so don't blame me if you won't take this advice
         and the family breaks up
and your children grow old and blind in front of a TV set
         seeing
movies you wouldn't let them see when they were young

JOHN ASHBERY

"How much longer will I be able to inhabit the divine sepulcher"

How much longer will I be able to inhabit the divine sepulcher
Of life, my great love? Do dolphins plunge bottomward
To find the light? Or is it rock
That is searched? Unrelentingly? Huh. And if some day

Men with orange shovels come to break open the rock
Which encases me, what about the light that comes in then?
What about the smell of the light?
What about the moss?

In pilgrim times he wounded me
Since then I only lie
My bed of light is a furnace choking me
With hell (and sometimes I hear salt water dripping).

I mean it – because I'm one of the few
To have held my breath under the house. I'll trade
One red sucker for two blue ones. I'm
Named Tom. The

Light bounces off mossy rocks down to me
In this glen (the neat villa! which
When he'd had he would not had he of
And jests under the smarting of privet

Which on hot spring nights perfumes the empty rooms
With the smell of sperm flushed down toilets
On hot summer afternoons within sight of the sea.
If you knew why then professor) reads

To his friends: Drink to me only with
And the reader is carried away
By a great shadow under the sea.
Behind the steering wheel

The boy took out his own forehead.
His girlfriend's head was a green bag
Of narcissus stems. "OK you win
But meet me anyway at Cohen's Drug Store

In 22 minutes." What a marvel is ancient man!
Under the tulip roots he has figured out a way to be a religious
     animal
And would be a mathematician. But where in unsuitable heaven
Can he get the heat that will make him grow?

For he needs something or will forever remain a dwarf,
Though a perfect one, and possessing a normal-sized brain
But he has got to be released by giants from things.
And as the plant grows older it realizes it will never be a tree,

Will probably always be haunted by a bee
And cultivates stupid impressions
So as not to become part of the dirt. The dirt
Is mounting like a sea. And we say goodbye

Shaking hands in front of the crashing of the waves
That give our words lonesomeness, and make these flabby hands
     seem ours —
Hands that are always writing things
On mirrors for people to see later —

Do you want them to water
Plant, tear listlessly among the exchangeable ivy —
Carrying food to mouth, touching genitals —
But no doubt you have understood

It all now and I am a fool. It remains
For me to get better, and to understand you so
Like a chair-sized man. Boots
Were heard on the floor above. In the garden the sunlight was still
     purple

But what buzzed in it had changed slightly
But not forever . . . but casting its shadow
On sticks, and looking around for an opening in the air, was quite
     as if it had never refused to exist differently. Guys
In the yard handled the belt he had made

Stars
Painted the garage roof crimson and black
He is not a man
Who can read these signs . . . his bones were stays . . .

And even refused to live
In a world and refunded the hiss
Of all that exists terribly near us
Like you, my love, and light.

For what is obedience but the air around us
To the house? For which the federal men came
In a minute after the sidewalk
Had taken you home? ("Latin . . . blossom . . .")

After which you led me to water
And bade me drink, which I did, owing to your kindness.
You would not let me out for two days and three nights,
Bringing me books bound in wild thyme and scented wild grasses

As if reading had any interest for me, you . . .
Now you are laughing.
Darkness interrupts my story.
Turn on the light.

Meanwhile what am I going to do?
I am growing up again, in school, the crisis will be very soon.
And you twist the darkness in your fingers, you
Who are slightly older . . .

Who are you, anyway?
And it is the color of sand,
The darkness, as it sifts through your hand
Because what does anything mean,

The ivy and the sand? That boat
Pulled up on the shore? Am I wonder,
Strategically, and in the light
Of the long sepulcher that hid death and hides me?

For John Clare

Kind of empty in the way it sees everything, the earth gets to its feet
and salutes the sky. More of a success at it this time than most others it
is. The feeling that the sky might be in the back of someone's mind.
Then there is no telling how many there are. They grace everything –
bush and tree – to take the roisterer's mind off his caroling – so it's like
a smooth switch back. To what was aired in their previous conniption
fit. There is so much to be seen everywhere that it's like not getting
used to it, only there is so much it never feels new, never any different.

You are standing looking at that building and you cannot take it all in, certain details are already hazy and the mind boggles. What will it all be like in five years' time when you try to remember? Will there have been boards in between the grass part and the edge of the street? As long as that couple is stopping to look in that window over there we cannot go. We feel like they have to tell us we can, but they never look our way and they are already gone, gone far into the future – the night of time. If we could look at a photograph of it and say there they are, they never really stopped but there they are. There is so much to be said, and on the surface of it very little gets said.

There ought to be room for more things, for a spreading out, like. Being immersed in the details of rock and field and slope – letting them come to you for once, and then meeting them halfway would be so much easier – if they took an ingenuous pride in being in one's blood. Alas, we perceive them if at all as those things that were meant to be put aside – costumes of the supporting actors or voice trilling at the end of a narrow enclosed street. You can do nothing with them. Not even offer to pay.

It is possible that finally, like coming to the end of a long, barely perceptible rise, there is mutual cohesion and interaction. The whole scene is fixed in your mind, the music all present, as though you could see each note as well as hear it. I say this because there is an uneasiness in things just now. Waiting for something to be over before you are forced to notice it. The pollarded trees scarcely bucking the wind – and yet it's keen, it makes you fall over. Clabbered sky. Seasons that pass with a rush. After all it's their time too – nothing says they aren't to make something of it. As for Jenny Wren, she cares, hopping about on her little twig like she was tryin' to tell us somethin', but that's just it, she couldn't even if she wanted to – dumb bird. But the others – and they in some way must know too – it would never occur to them to want to, even if they could take the first step of the terrible journey toward feeling somebody should act, that ends in utter confusion and hopelessness, east of the sun and west of the moon. So their comment is: "No comment." Meanwhile the whole history of probabilities is coming to life, starting in the upper left-hand corner, like a sail.

Farm Implements and Rutabagas in a Landscape

The first of the undecoded messages read: "Popeye sits in thunder,
Unthought of. From that shoebox of an apartment,
From livid curtain's hue, a tangram emerges: a country."
Meanwhile the Sea Hag was relaxing on a green couch: "How pleasant
To spend one's vacation *en la casa de Popeye*," she scratched
Her cleft chin's solitary hair. She remembered spinach

And was going to ask Wimpy if he had bought any spinach.
"M'love," he intercepted, "the plains are decked out in thunder
Today, and it shall be as you wish." He scratched
The part of his head under his hat. The apartment
Seemed to grow smaller. "But what if no pleasant
Inspiration plunge us now to the stars? *For this is my country*."

Suddenly they remembered how it was cheaper in the country.
Wimpy was thoughtfully cutting open a number 2 can of spinach
When the door opened and Swee'pea crept in. "How pleasant!"
But Swee'pea looked morose. A note was pinned to his bib. "Thunder
And tears are unavailing," it read. "Henceforth shall Popeye's
          apartment
Be but remembered space, toxic or salubrious, whole or scratched."

Olive came hurtling through the window; its geraniums scratched
Her long thigh. "I have news!" she gasped. "Popeye, forced as you
          know to flee the country
One musty gusty evening, by the schemes of his wizened, duplicate
          father, jealous of the apartment
And all that it contains, myself and spinach
In particular, heaves bolts of loving thunder
At his own astonished becoming, rupturing the pleasant

Arpeggio of our years. No more shall pleasant
Rays of the sun refresh your sense of growing old, nor the scratched
Tree-trunks and mossy foliage, only immaculate darkness and
          thunder."
She grabbed Swee'pea. "I'm taking the brat to the country."
"But you can't do that – he hasn't even finished his spinach,"
Urged the Sea Hag, looking fearfully around at the apartment.

But Olive was already out of earshot. Now the apartment
Succumbed to a strange new hush. "Actually it's quite pleasant
Here," thought the Sea Hag. If this is all we need fear from spinach
Then I don't mind so much. Perhaps we could invite Alice the Goon
          over" – she scratched
One dug pensively – "but Wimpy is such a country
Bumpkin, always burping like that." Minute at first, the thunder

Soon filled the apartment. It was domestic thunder,
The color of spinach. Popeye chuckled and scratched
His balls: it sure was pleasant to spend a day in the country.

Pyrography

Out here on Cottage Grove it matters. The galloping
Wind balks at its shadow. The carriages
Are drawn forward under a sky of fumed oak.
This is America calling:
The mirroring of state to state,
Of voice to voice on the wires,
The force of colloquial greetings like golden
Pollen sinking on the afternoon breeze.
In service stairs the sweet corruption thrives;
The page of dusk turns like a creaking revolving stage in Warren,
    Ohio.

If this is the way it is let's leave,
They agree, and soon the slow boxcar journey begins,
Gradually accelerating until the gyrating fans of suburbs
Enfolding the darkness of cities are remembered
Only as a recurring tic. And midway
We meet the disappointed, returning ones, without its
Being able to stop us in the headlong night
Toward the nothing of the coast. At Bolinas
The houses doze and seem to wonder why through the
Pacific haze, and the dreams alternately glow and grow dull.
Why be hanging on here? Like kites, circling,
Slipping on a ramp of air, but always circling?

But the variable cloudiness is pouring it on,
Flooding back to you like the meaning of a joke.
The land wasn't immediately appealing; we built it
Partly over with fake ruins, in the image of ourselves:
An arch that terminates in mid-keystone, a crumbling stone pier
For laundresses, an open-air theater, never completed
And only partially designed. How are we to inhabit
This space from which the fourth wall is invariably missing,
As in a stage-set or dollhouse, except by staying as we are,
In lost profile, facing the stars, with dozens of as yet
Unrealized projects, and a strict sense
Of time running out, of evening presenting
The tactfully folded-over bill? And we fit
Rather too easily into it, become transparent,
Almost ghosts. One day
The birds and animals in the pasture have absorbed
The color, the density of the surroundings,
The leaves are alive, and too heavy with life.

A long period of adjustment followed.
In the cities at the turn of the century they knew about it
But were careful not to let on as the iceman and the milkman
Disappeared down the block and the postman shouted
His daily rounds. The children under the trees knew it
But all the fathers returning home
On streetcars after a satisfying day at the office undid it:
The climate was still floral and all the wallpaper
In a million homes all over the land conspired to hide it.
One day we thought of painted furniture, of how
It just slightly changes everything in the room
And in the yard outside, and how, if we were going
To be able to write the history of our time, starting with today,
It would be necessary to model all these unimportant details
So as to be able to include them; otherwise the narrative
Would have that flat, sandpapered look the sky gets
Out in the middle west toward the end of summer,
The look of wanting to back out before the argument
Has been resolved, and at the same time to save appearances
So that tomorrow will be pure. Therefore, since we have to do
        our business
In spite of things, why not make it in spite of everything?
That way, maybe the feeble lakes and swamps
Of the back country will get plugged into the circuit
And not just the major events but the whole incredible
Mass of everything happening simultaneously and pairing off,
Channeling itself into history, will unroll
As carefully and as casually as a conversation in the next room,
And the purity of today will invest us like a breeze,
Only be hard, spare, ironical: something one can
Tip one's hat to and still get some use out of.

The parade is turning into our street.
My stars, the burnished uniforms and prismatic
Features of this instant belong here. The land
Is pulling away from the magic, glittering coastal towns
To an aforementioned rendezvous with August and December.
The hunch is it will always be this way,
The look, the way things first scared you
In the night light, and later turned out to be,
Yet still capable, all the same, of a narrow fidelity
To what you and they wanted to become:
No sighs like Russian music, only a vast unravelling
Out toward the junctions and to the darkness beyond
To these bare fields, built at today's expense.

What is Poetry

The medieval town, with frieze
Of boy scouts from Nagoya? The snow

That came when we wanted it to snow?
Beautiful images? Trying to avoid

Ideas, as in this poem? But we
Go back to them as to a wife, leaving

The mistress we desire? Now they
Will have to believe it

As we believe it. In school
All the thought got combed out:

What was left was like a field.
Shut your eyes, and you can feel it for miles around.

Now open them on a thin vertical path.
It might give us — what? — some flowers soon?

At North Farm

Somewhere someone is traveling furiously toward you,
At incredible speed, traveling day and night,
Through blizzards and desert heat, across torrents, through
    narrow passes.
But will he know where to find you,
Recognize you when he sees you,
Give you the thing he has for you?

Hardly anything grows here,
Yet the granaries are bursting with meal,
The sacks of meal piled to the rafters.
The streams run with sweetness, fattening fish;
Birds darken the sky. Is it enough
That the dish of milk is set out at night,
That we think of him sometimes,
Sometimes and always, with mixed feelings?

Forgotten Song

O Mary, go and call the cattle home
For I'm sick in my heart and fain would lie down.

As if that wasn't enough, I find this bundle of pain
Left on my doorstep, with a note: "Please raise it as your own."

I don't know. When it grows up will it be like the others,
Able to join in their games, or is it the new person,

As yet indescribable, though existing here and there?
Our caution can't make any sense to it. Meanwhile it erases us

In coming to be what can't possibly be for the time being,
This time we take in and lavish so much affection on

It starts to like us, changeling though it be, and sees
Some point in the way we were made. Death

Always intervenes at that moment, waking avenues
That radiate from the heart of a city whose suburbs

Are its uneasy existence. Put another way, the continual stirring
That we come to recognize as life merely acts blindly,

In pursuit of small, selfish goals, but the repercussions
Are enormous though they concern no one. Growing chooses
          this way

To happen, doesn't mind if a few toes get stepped on,
Though it would hardly have wished things to turn out like this

If it had thought about it for a moment. But it can't – I mean
That's what it is, a sigh of a sleeping giantess

That causes turbulence even in the shy, still unused fields
Stacked to the horizon, not even waiting, secure

In their inertia. A force erupting so violently
We can't witness any of it. Best to leave it alone

And start it all over again, if there's a beginning.
The stalk is withered dry, my love, so will our hearts decay.

Unless we omitted something. And we did. It'll cure it.
It will have to. But I can't whisper that story yet.

Hotel Lautréamont

I

Research has shown that ballads were produced by all of society
working as a team. They didn't just happen. There was no guesswork.
The people, then, knew what they wanted and how to get it.
We see the results in works as diverse as "Windsor Forest" and "The
     Wife of Usher's Well".

Working as a team, they didn't just happen. There was no guesswork.
The horns of elfland swing past, and in a few seconds
We see the results in works as diverse as "Windsor Forest" and "The
     Wife of Usher's Well",
or, on a more modern note, in the finale of the Sibelius violin
     concerto.

The horns of elfland swing past, and in a few seconds
The world, as we know it, sinks into dementia, proving narrative
     passé,
or in the finale of the Sibelius violin concerto.
Not to worry, many hands are making work light again.

The world, as we know it, sinks into dementia, proving narrative
     passé.
In any case the ruling was long overdue.
Not to worry, many hands are making work light again,
so we stay indoors. The quest was only another adventure.

2

In any case, the ruling was long overdue.
The people are beside themselves with rapture
so we stay indoors. The quest was only another adventure
and the solution problematic, at any rate far off in the future.

The people are beside themselves with rapture
yet no one thinks to question the source of so much collective
     euphoria,
and the solution: problematic, at any rate far off in the future.
The saxophone wails, the martini glass is drained.

Yet no one thinks to question the source of so much collective
     euphoria.
In troubled times one looked to the shaman or priest for comfort and
     counsel.
The saxophone wails, the martini glass is drained,
And night like black swansdown settles on the city.

In troubled times one looked to the shaman or priest for comfort and
     counsel
Now, only the willing are fated to receive death as a reward,
and night like black swansdown settles on the city.
If we tried to leave, would being naked help us?

                              3

Now, only the willing are fated to receive death as a reward.
Children twist hula-hoops, imagining a door to the outside.
If we tried to leave, would being naked help us?
And what of older, lighter concerns? What of the river?

Children twist hula-hoops, imagining a door to the outside,
when all we think of is how much we can carry with us.
And what of older, lighter concerns? What of the river?
All the behemoths have filed through the maze of time.

When all we think of is how much we can carry with us
Small wonder that those at home sit, nervous, by the unlit grate.
All the behemoths have filed through the maze of time.
It remains for us to come to terms with *our* commonalty.

Small wonder that those at home sit nervous by the unlit grate.
It was their choice, after all, that spurred us to feats of the imagination.
It remains for us to come to terms with our commonalty
And in so doing deprive time of further hostages.

                              4

It was their choice, after all, that spurred us to feats of the imagination.
Now, silently as one mounts a stair we emerge into the open
and in so doing deprive time of further hostages,
to end the standoff that history long ago began.

Now, silently as one mounts a stair we emerge into the open
but it is shrouded, veiled: we must have made some ghastly error.
To end the standoff that history long ago began
Must we thrust ever onward, into perversity?

But it is shrouded, veiled: we must have made some ghastly error.
You mop your forehead with a rose, recommending its thorns.
Must we thrust ever onward, into perversity?
Only night knows for sure; the secret is safe with her.

You mop your forehead with a rose, recommending its thorns.
Research has shown that ballads were produced by all of society;
Only night knows for sure. The secret is safe with her:
the people, then, knew what they wanted and how to get it.

CHARLES TOMLINSON

More Foreign Cities

"Nobody wants any more poems about foreign cities . . ."
(From a recent disquisition on poetics)

> Not forgetting Ko–jen, that
> Musical city (it has
> Few buildings and annexes
> Space by combating silence),
> There is Fiordiligi, its sun–changes
> Against walls of transparent stone
> Unsettling all preconception – a city
> For architects (they are taught
> By casting their nets
> Into those moving shoals); and there is
> Kairouan, whose lit space
> So slides into and fits
> The stone masses, one would doubt
> Which was the more solid
> Unless, folding back
> Gold segments out of the white
> Pith globe of a quartered orange,
> One may learn perhaps
> To read such perspectives. At Luna
> There is a city of bridges, where
> Even the inhabitants are mindful
> Of a shared privilege: a bridge
> Does not exist for its own sake.
> It commands vacancy.

Prometheus[1]

Summer thunder darkens, and its climbing
   Cumulae, disowning our scale in the zenith,
Electrify this music: the evening is falling apart.
   Castles-in-air; on earth: green, livid fire.
The radio simmers with static to the strains
   Of this mock last-day of nature and of art.

We have lived through apocalypse too long:
   Scriabin's dinosaurs! Trombones for the transformation
That arrived by train at the Finland Station,
   To bury its hatchet after thirty years in the brain
Of Trotsky. Alexander Nikolayevitch, the events
   Were less merciful than your mob of instruments.

Too many drowning voices cram this waveband.
   I set Lenin's face by yours –
Yours, the fanatic ego of eccentricity against
   The systematic son of a schools inspector
Tyutchev on desk – for the strong man reads
   Poets as the antisemite pleads: "A Jew was my friend."

Cymballed firesweeps. Prometheus came down
   In more than orchestral flame and Kérensky fled
Before it. The babel of continents gnaws now
   And tears at the silk of those harmonies that seemed
So dangerous once. You dreamed an end
   Where the rose of the world would go out like a close in
      music.

Population drags the partitions down
   And we are a single town of warring suburbs:
I cannot hear such music for its consequence:
   Each sense was to have been reborn
Out of a storm of perfumes and light
   To a white world, an in-the-beginning.

In the beginning, the strong man reigns:
   Trotsky, was it not then you brought yourself
To judgement and to execution, when you forgot
   Where terror rules, justice turns arbitrary?
Chromatic Prometheus, myth of fire,
   It is history topples you in the zenith.

---

1. "Prometheus" refers to the tone-poem by Scriabin and to his hope of transforming the
world by music and rite.

Blok, too, wrote The Scythians
  Who should have known: he who howls
With the whirlwind, with the whirlwind goes down.
  In this, was Lenin guiltier than you
When, out of a merciless patience grew
  The daily prose such poetry prepares for?

Scriabin, Blok, men of extremes,
  History treads out the music of your dreams
Through blood, and cannot close like this
  In the perfection of anabasis. It stops. The trees
Continue raining though the rain has ceased
  In a cooled world of incessant codas:

Hard edges of the houses press
  On the after-music senses, and refuse to burn,
Where an ice cream van circulates the estate
  Playing Greensleeves, and at the city's
Stale new frontier even ugliness
  Rules with the cruel mercy of solidities.

Against Extremity

Let there be treaties, bridges,
  Chords under the hands, to be spanned
Sustained: extremity hates a given good
  Or a good gained. That girl who took
Her life almost, then wrote a book
  To exorcise and to exhibit the sin,
Praises a friend there for the end she made
  And each of them becomes a heroine.
The time is in love with endings. The time's
  Spoiled children threaten what they will do,
And those they cannot shake by petulance
  They'll bribe out of their wits by show.
Against extremity, let there be
  Such treaties as only time itself
Can ratify, a bond and test
  Of sequential days, and like the full
Moon slowly given to the night,
  A possession that is not to be possessed.

After a Death

A little ash, a painted rose, a name.
   A moonshell that the blinding sky
Puts out with winter blue, hangs
   Fragile at the edge of visibility. That space
Drawing the eye up to its sudden frontier
   Asks for a sense to read the whole
Reverted side of things. I wanted
   That height and prospect such as music brings –
Music or memory. Neither brought me here.
   This burial place straddles a green hill,
Chimneys and steeples plot the distances
   Spread vague below: only the sky
In its upper reaches keeps
   An untarnished January colour. Verse
Fronting that blaze, that blade,
   Turns to retrace the path of its dissatisfactions,
Thought coiled on thought, and only certain that
   Whatever can make bearable or bridge
The waste of air, a poem cannot.
   The husk of moon, risking the whole of space,
Seemingly sails it, fraily launched
   To its own death and fulness. We buried
A little ash. Time so broke you down,
   Your lost eyes, dry beneath
Their matted lashes, a painted rose
   Seems both to memorialize and mock
What you became. It picks your name out
   Written on the roll beside a verse –
Obstinate words: measured against the blue,
   They cannot conjure with the dead. Words,
Bringing that space to bear, that air
   Into each syllable we speak, bringing
An earnest to us of the portion
   We must inherit, what thought of that would give
The greater share of comfort, greater fear –
   To live forever, or to cease to live?
The imageless unnaming upper blue
   Defines a world, all images
Of endeavours uncompleted. Torn levels
   Of the land drop, street by street,
Pitted and pooled, its wounds
   Cleansed by a light, dealt out
With such impartiality you'd call it kindness,
   Blindly assuaging where assuagement goes unfelt.

For Danton

"Bound to the fierce Metropolis . . ."
The Prelude, Book X

In the autumn of 1793 – the year in which he had instituted the Revolutionary
Tribunal – Danton went back to his birthplace, Arcis-sur-Aube. After his return
in November, he was to be arrested, tried and condemned.

Who is the man that stands against this bridge
And thinks that he and not the river advances?
Can he not hear the links of consequence
Chiming his life away? Water is time.
Not yet, not yet. He fronts the parapet
Drinking the present with unguarded sense:

The stream comes on. Its music deafens him
To other sounds, to past and future wrong.
The beat is regular beneath that song.
He hears in it a pulse that is his own;
He hears the year autumnal and complete.
November waits for him who has not done

With seeings, savourings. Grape-harvest brings
The south into the north. This parapet
Carries him forward still, a ship from Rheims,
From where, in boyhood and on foot, he'd gone
"To see," he said, "the way a king is made,"
The king that he himself was to uncrown –

Destroyed and superseded, then secure
In the possession of a perfect power
Returned to this: to river, town and plain,
Walked in the fields and knew what power he'd lost,
The cost to him of that metropolis where
He must come back to rule and Robespierre.

Not yet. This contrary perfection he
Must taste into a life he has no time
To live, a lingered, snatched maturity
Before he catches in the waterchime
The measure and the chain a death began,
And fate that loves the symmetry of rhyme
Will spring the trap whose teeth must have a man.

Weather Report

for Brian Cox

First snow comes in on lorries from the north,
   Whitens their loads – an earnest of that threat
Cromarty, Mull, Fair Isle and Fasnet
   Have weathered already. It has passed
Down the Pennine chain and choked Shap Fell;
   The Snake is lost and every moor
In Derbyshire under a deep, advancing pile.
   It covers the county, dwindling south,
But the wind that carries it, overshoots,
   The frontier snow has mapped. It is the wind
Seems to be blowing the sunlight out
   As it roams the length of the whole land,
Freezing the fingers of tillers and of trees,
   Until it curls back the tides off Cornwall
Telling the snowless shires they too must freeze,
   In this turbulence that began as Swedish air
And has turned in the translated atmosphere
   To the weather of the one nation we suddenly are.

THOMAS KINSELLA

Soft, to Your Places

Soft, to your places, animals,
Your legendary duty calls.
   It is, to be
Lucky for my love and me.
   And yet we have seen that all's
A fiction that is heard of love's difficulty.

And what if the simple primrose show
That mighty work went on below
   Before it grew
A moral miracle for us two?
   Since of ourselves we know
Beauty to be an easy thing, this will do.

But O when beauty's brought to pass
Will Time set down his hour-glass
    And rest content,
His hand upon that monument?
    Unless it is so, alas
That the heart's calling is but to go stripped and diffident.

Soft, to your places, love; I kiss
Because it is, because it is.

Another September

Dreams fled away, this country bedroom, raw
With the touch of the dawn, wrapped in a minor peace,
Hears through an open window the garden draw
Long pitch black breaths, lay bare its apple trees,
Ripe pear trees, brambles, windfall-sweetened soil,
Exhale rough sweetness against the starry slates.
Nearer the river sleeps St John's, all toil
Locked fast inside a dream with iron gates.

Domestic Autumn, like an animal
Long used to handling by those countrymen,
Rubs her kind hide against the bedroom wall
Sensing a fragrant child come back again
– Not this half-tolerated consciousness,
Its own cold season never done,
But that unspeaking daughter, growing less
Familiar where we fell asleep as one.

Wakeful moth-wings blunder near a chair,
Toss their light shell at the glass, and go
To inhabit the living starlight. Stranded hair
Stirs on the still linen. It is as though
The black breathing that billows her sleep, her name,
Drugged under judgment, waned and – bearing daggers
And balances – down the lampless darkness they came,
Moving like women: Justice, Truth, such figures.

The Laundress

Her chair drawn to the door,
A basket at her feet,
She sat against the sun
And stitched a linen sheet.
Over harrowed Flanders
August moved the wheat.

Poplars sharing the wind
With Saxony and France
Dreamed at her gate,
Soared in a Summer trance.
A cluck in the cobbled yard:
A shadow changed its stance.

As a fish disturbs the pond
And sinks without a stain
The heels of ripeness fluttered
Under her apron. Then
Her heart grew strained and light
As the shell that shields the grain.

Bluntly through the doorway
She stared at shed and farm,
At yellow fields unstitching
About the hoarded germ,
At land that would spread white
When she had reached her term.

The sower plumps his acre,
Flanders turns to the heat,
The winds of Heaven winnow
And the wheels grind the wheat.
She searched in her basket
And fixed her ruffled sheet.

Downstream

Drifting to meet us on the darkening stage
A pattern shivered; whorling in its place
Another held us in a living cage
Then broke to its reordered phase of grace.

*

Again in the mirrored dusk the paddles sank.
   We thrust forward, swaying both as one.
   The ripples widened to the ghostly bank

Where willows, with their shadows half undone,
   Hung to the water, mowing like the blind.
   The current seized our skiff. We let it run

Grazing the reeds, and let the land unwind
   In stealth on either hand. Dark woods: a door
   Opened and shut. The clear sky fell behind,

The channel shrank. Thick slopes from shore to shore
   Lowered a matted arch. I thought of roots
   Crawling full of pike on the river-floor

To cage us in, sensed the furred night-brutes
   Halt in their trails, twitching their tiny brushes.
   What plopped in the reeds and stirred between the shoots?

Then I remembered how among those bushes
   A man one night fell sick and left his shell
   Collapsed, half eaten, like a rotted thrush's

To frighten stumbling children. "You could tell,"
   My co-shadow murmured, "by the hands
   He died in terror." And the cold of hell,

A limb-lightness, a terror in the glands,
   Pierced again as when that story first
   Froze my blood: the soil of other lands

Drank lives that summer with a body thirst;
   Nerveless by the European pit
   – Ourselves through seven hundred years accurst –

We saw the barren world obscurely lit
   By tall chimneys flickering in their pall,
   The haunt of swinish man – each day a spit

That, turning, sweated war, each night a fall
   Back to the evil dream where rodents ply,
   Man-rumped, sow-headed, busy with whip and maul

Among nude herds of the damned. It seemed that I,
   Coming to conscience on that lip of dread,
   Still dreamed, impervious to calamity,

Imagining a formal drift of the dead
   Stretched calm as effigies on velvet dust,
   Scattered on starlit slopes with arms outspread

And eyes of silver – when that story thrust
   Pungent horror and an actual mess
   Into my very face, and taste I must.

Then hungry joy and sickening distress
   Fumbled together by the brimming flood,
   And night consumed a hopeless loneliness.

Like mortal jaws, the alleys of the wood
   Fell-to behind us. At its heart, a ghost
   Glimmered briefly with my gift of blood

– Spreadeagled on a rack of leaves, almost
   Remembering. It looked full at the sky,
   Calmly encountering the starry host,

Meeting their silver eyes with silver eye.
   An X of wavering flesh, a skull of light,
   Extinguished in our wake without a sigh.

Then the current shuddered in its flight
   And swerved on pliant muscle; we were sped
   Through sudden peace into a pit of night:

The Mill-Hole, whose rocky fathoms fed
   On moss and pure depth and the cold fin
   Turning in its heart. The river bed

Called to our flesh. Across the watery skin,
   Breathless, our shell trembled. The abyss . . .
   We shipped our oars in dread. Now, deeper in,

Something shifted in sleep, a quiet hiss
   As we slipped by. Adrift . . . A milk-white breast . . .
   A shuffle of wings betrayed with a feathery kiss

A soul of white with darkness for a nest.
   The creature bore the night so tranquilly
   I lifted up my eyes. There without rest

The phantoms of the overhanging sky
   Occupied their stations and descended;
   Another moment, to the starlit eye,

The slow, downstreaming dead, it seemed, were blended
   One with those silver hordes, and briefly shared
   Their order, glittering. And then impended

A barrier of rock that turned and bared
   A varied barrenness as toward its base
   We glided – blotting heaven as it towered –

Searching the darkness for a landing place.

Brotherhood

   I stretched out
   my hand to you. Brother.

   The reason for the impulse
   was unclear:

   your behaviour and your work
   are incomprehensible to me.

   But I had offered my hand.
   We were joined by the soft leather of palms.

   The matter resolved itself.
   A voice whispered:

   it is Spring
   and no time for kindness;

   we must bear in mind
   the quality of the Fall.

   I dropped your hand.

Talent and Friendship

Neither is simple
and neither is handed down.

Either persisted in without change
grows ridiculous

and either at any time
may fail.

If it fail in part
it is made good only in part

and if it come to final failure
accept – but prepare for a difficult widow:

that fig-bodied stone devil
on your sanctuary wall

gross mouth open
to all comers

or, as I remember,
a still youthful witch

moving off sick to death
among the graves and the old men

in sharp argument with her pale son,
he muttering in sharp answer,

deadly familiar,
so unlike.

*

There is no mantle
and it does not descend.

A Portrait of the Artist

We might have guessed it would end in argument
and the personal. Those acid exchanges
hoarse in the hall: An architect
is an artist! His first duty is beauty!
Finding our way down the steps in the small hours
and walking up the terrace in relief.

A movement of memory over on the far side.
They had reached the canal bank
and, turning from their course,
a pair of ghosts came on by the trees,
the other side of the Canal. About there.
Two figures tangled in argument. The one,
in crisis, nagging beauty to her place
among the senses. And the fool
lending a quick ear, sniggering:

What is beauty?

– The fugitive, exact in its accident:
a jewel of process turned around on the fingers.

My fingers framed your throat in the night air.

*

A car prowled over the Bridge and turned around
in a slow curve under the lamp, then back again
across the Canal. Another came exactly
in the same track, the tail lights pulsing rose.

A silent soul bestirred herself to meet them
in red and black leatherette, another waiting
against the railings in a tiny skirt,
her cigarette-tip pointing in the night
– her eyes hidden, wet to my senses,
and her oyster mouth.

BURNS SINGER

Still and All

I give my word on it. There is no way
Other than this. There is no other way
Of speaking. I am my name. I find my place
Empty without a word, and my word is
Given again. It is nothing less than all
Given away again, and all still truly
Returned on a belief. Believe me now.
There is no other. There is no other way.

These words run vertical in their slim green tunnels
Without any turning away. They turn into
The first flower and speak from a silent bell.
But underneath it is as always still
Truly awakening, slowly and slowly turning
About a shadow scribbled down by sunlight
And turning about my name. I am in my
Survival's hands. I am my shadow's theme.

My shadow's ground feeds me with roots, and rhymes
My statement over. Its radius feeds my flames
Into a cool tunnel. And I who find your ways
About me (In every part I find your ways
Of speech.) pierce ground and shadow still. The light
Is struck. Its definition makes me my quiet
Survival's answer. All still and all so truly
Wakening underneath me and turning slowly.

It's all so truly still. I'll take you into
The first statement. I'll take you along cool tunnels
That channelled light and petalled an iridescent
Symmetry over my bruised shadow. And yes
I'll take you, and your word will follow me,
Till definitions gather distilled honey
And make their mark the fingerprints of light.
I am, believe me then, the name I write.

I lie here still. Yes, truly still. And all
My deliberate identities have fallen
Away with the word given. I find my place
In every place, in every part of speech,

And lie there still. I let my statements go.
A cool green tunnel has stepped in the light of my shadow
There is no way round it. It leads to the flower
Bell – that swings slowly and slowly over.

Your Words, My Answers

Then what is it I am
To make of what I mean?
What words will take it down
Through the disputed realm
Where you and I across
An oblique imperative
Meet one another's loss?
Let that fierce statute give
Us new authority
Which takes away our claim
To saying what we mean:
Like the two limbs of a cross
Your words, my answers lie
Together in the place
Where all our meanings die.

Corner Boy's Farewell

In the yellow room among the grey furniture I sit sorrowfully
Already sour with the wisdom of age and bitterly complaining.
Outside the evening sulks away.
The garden vegetation curls up like a cat.
The hillside tumbles a snug green wall.
Why do they keep coming back, the days we have spent together?
They come in their long lines but dancing and deep in the sun,
Deep in the sun, black and engraved in shadows.
Why do they keep coming back with such regular purpose?

First in the club-room,
The grumbling inconsequent people
Arguing art over stale tea-bread . . .
And I very young was greatly impressed.
You hardly saw me through their foggy heads.
Bluebottles clung to the damp flycatcher. My eyes were glued on
    your face.
You hardly saw me. Then you went away.

Between parting and our second meeting
Months passed and many things happened.
During that time my heart and mind were hid.
The twins of the wood were hid from woodcutters'
Eyes, from the temptations of the house of sugar.
I hid them alive in the shape of a drunken bout.
I put them to sleep in the dugs of a dried-up whore.
I silvered round in tinfoil cartons, talked them into the noisy drugs,
To hide from my grand accusers, from the huge scenery of your
      great disciples.
And yet when we finally met again,
You, half mad with your own problems:
I, an absconded schoolboy:
Our laughter was green in the London pubs
And a sympathy somehow occurred that was not to be laughed at.

And after that time the occasions of meeting gather:
From the ends of this country, from the cramped edges of
      experience
They trek in a single direction that makes us separate ever.
I cannot quite remember all the dates and places
But we have stood at corners, sat together
Between apprisal and dismissal,
Arrival and departure,
Between anticipation and delight,
Boisterous days and the long memory.
We have stood at corners and waited together.
What I remember best is saying goodbye
For that is most in the nature of friendship.

A week ago in this selfsame city
We said farewell and did not know we said it.
And I was left to revile in this rainy place.
O my poems, be against this city:
Its people badly dressed and without good manners,
The simplest necessities of life made lewd and tortuous.
Let them be things of a day.
Let my poems have bees' blood in them,
Let them be sharp but sensitive to honey.
For I still think of life as once of mist in Cornwall
Man-high and from the sea subsiding gently
Over the ploughed fields, brown, with scarce green growth,
But hidden under field-grey all that day,
Woven to one opacity.
Then on my eyesight the slant light broke
Of a single mist-drop narrowly slung to a cobweb

And each, the mist, through which my senses travelled
Broke at that sun-reflecting signal to its own:
The watered air grew bright with single claws:
So on the fine web spun from something stronger
One man can hold, precarious, complete
His own self's light that never is repeated
But acts as orrery to all the lights of others:
And that same web grows finer with its function,
More beautiful to praise with each drop held
In that peculiar tension once forever.

That's how I think of you and your calm discourse,
And thinking too the knowledge of a minute,
Planet's discovery or the seed of tree,
A new tree in a new place, something
To come, to grow gradually actual,
Thinking of this and that and all together
You grow so bright I sometimes seem to see
Walking between you and the direct sun
My evening-shadow struggling like a breeze
Until it climbs against it, smothers light
And drowns the sun out down beneath your face.

For that is the special human knowledge,
Knowledge of genesis
Of a brightness other than that of the day sun,
Outstaring and outstripping.
And this is human too
– Though valid more than for humanity,
Humanity its instrument – this knowledge
That I have hit on since you went
Of going further out than light can follow, rooted and separate,
Into America, my mind or sea.
This I prepare for and communicate
In the anticipation of my lifelong voyage
Of seeing what has always been most loved grow dim and disappear
Into perfection's prodigies of peace.

Into the sacrifice bitterly endless of all that man means
In terms of bones, breath, skin and brain,
Of his achievements, even the love humility achieved.
Love he can only like a beggar take
From the kind hand of passage hidden in his heart,
The hand that could be merciless as he,
Deny as he denies.

Love he is given, he who, like a beggar,
Squats where the virtues congregate their outpour,
He who is hasty when a dime of knowledge
Drops in his cap
To run and spend it in the nearest brothel
And then come howling back to the mercy and lucky
    downpouring.
This knowledge then of leaving all behind
All, that by wailing meanly, may attend my vigil.

IAIN CRICHTON SMITH

Old Woman

And she, being old, fed from a mashed plate
as an old mare might droop across a fence
to the dull pastures of its ignorance.
Her husband held her upright while he prayed

to God who is all-forgiving to send down
some angel somewhere who might land perhaps
in his foreign wings among the gradual crops.
She munched, half dead, blindly searching the spoon.

Outside, the grass was raging. There I sat
imprisoned in my pity and my shame
that men and women having suffered time
should sit in such a place, in such a state

and wished to be away, yes, to be far away
with athletes, heroes, Greek or Roman men
who pushed their bitter spears into a vein
and would not spend an hour with such decay.

"Pray God," he said, "we ask you, God," he said.
The bowed back was quiet. I saw the teeth
tighten their grip around a delicate death.
And nothing moved within the knotted head

but only a few poor veins as one might see
vague wishless seaweed floating on a tide
of all the salty waters where had died
too many waves to mark two more or three.

from *Deer on the High Hills*

1

A deer looks through you to the other side,
and what it is and sees is an inhuman pride.

2

Yesterday three deer stood at the roadside.
It was icy January and there they were
like debutantes on a smooth ballroom floor.

They stared at us out of that French
arrogant atmosphere, like Louis the Sixteenth
sustained in twilight on a marble plinth.

They wore the inhuman look of aristocrats
before a revolution comes, and the people
blaspheme the holy bells in the high steeple.

Before the ice breaks, and heroes in spring
come up like trees with bursting wrongs in their arms
and feed the nobles to the uniform worms.

So were these deer, balanced on delicate logic,
till suddenly they broke from us and went
outraged and sniffing into the dark wind.

Difficult to say where they go to
in the harsh weather when the mountains stand
like judging elders, tall on either hand.

Except that they know the ice is breaking now.
They take to the hills pursued by darkness and lie
beneath the starry metaphysical sky.

Sometimes in a savage winter they'll come down
and beg like fallen nobles for their bread.
They'd rather live in poverty than be dead.

Nevertheless there's something dangerous
in a deer's head. He might suddenly open your belly
with his bitter antlers to the barren sky.

Especially in winter when tormented
by loneliness they descend to this road
with great bounding leaps like the mind of God.

In summer they can be ignored. They crop so gently
among the hills that no one notices
their happy heads sunk in the feeding cresses.

But beware of them now when ice is on the ground.
A beggared noble can conceal a sword
next to his skin for the aimless and abhorred

tyrants who cannot dance but throw stones,
tyrants who can crack the finest bones:
tyrants who do not wear but break most ancient crowns.

3

One would be finished with these practical things
in order to return as deer do
to the tall mountain springs.

Nevertheless one should not so return
till soldier of the practical or doer
one wholly learns to learn

a real contempt, a fine hard-won disdain
for these possessions, marbles of unripe children,
as, again,

a deer might walk along a sweating street,
stare in a cramped window and then go
back to the hills but not on ignorant feet.

4

Forget these purple evenings and these poems
that solved all or took for myth
the pointed sail of Ulysses enigmatic.

There was Hector with his child in his arms.
Where is that other Hector
who wore the internal shield, the inner sword?

Ulysses scurries, like a rat trapped in a maze.
He wears the sharp look of a business magnate.
Late from the office he had a good excuse.

Ideas clash on the mountain tops.
By the appalled peaks the deer roar.
Simply a question of rutting, these cloudy systems

or as yesterday we saw a black cloud
become the expression of a tall mountain.
And that was death, the undertaker, present.

And all became like it for that moment,
assumption of anguish, and the hollow waters
the metaphysics of an empty country

deranged, deranged, a land of rain and stones
of stones and rain, of the huge barbarous bones,
plucked like a loutish harp their harmonies.

5

You must build from the rain and stones,
from the incurable numbers: the grasses
innumerable on the many hills.

Not to geometry or algebra,
or an inhuman music, but
in the hollow roar of the waterfall,

you must build from there and not be
circumvented by sunlight or a taste of love
or intuitions from the sky above

the deadly rock. Or even history,
Prince Charles in a gay Highland shawl,
or mystery in a black Highland coffin.

You must build from the rain and stones
till you can make
a stylish deer on the high hills,
and let its leaps be unpredictable!

6

Duncan Ban McIntyre, the poet,
knew them intimately, was one of them.
They had waxen hides, they were delicate dancers.

They evolved their own music which became
his music: they elected him
their poet laureate.

It was a kind of Eden these days
with something Cretan in his eulogy.
Nevertheless he shot them also.

Like shooting an image or a vivid grace.
Brutality and beauty danced together
in a silver air, incorruptible.

And the clean shot did not disturb his poems.
Nor did the deer kneel in a pool of tears.
The stakes were indeed high in that game.

And the rocks did not weep with sentiment.
They were simply there: the deer were simply there.
The witty gun blazed from his knowing hand.

The Exiles

(*translated from the author's own Gaelic*)

The many ships that left our country
with white wings for Canada.
They are like handkerchiefs in our memories
and the brine like tears
and in their masts sailors singing
like birds on branches.
That sea of May running in such blue,
a moon at night, a sun at daytime,
and the moon like a yellow fruit,
like a plate on a wall
to which they raise their hands
like a silver magnet
with piercing rays
streaming into the heart.

Listen

Listen, I have flown through darkness towards joy,
I have put the mossy stones away from me,
and the thorns, the thistles, the brambles.
I have swum upward like a fish

through the black wet earth, the ancient roots
which insanely fight with each other
in a grave which creates a treasure house
of light upward-springing leaves.

Such joy, such joy! Such airy drama
the clouds compose in the heavens,
such interchange of comedies,
disguises, rhymes, denouements.

I had not believed that the stony heads
would change to actors and actresses,
and that the grooved armour of statues
would rise and walk away

into a resurrection of villages,
townspeople, citizens, dead exiles,
who sing with the salt in their mouths,
winged nightingales of brine.

THOM GUNN

Tamer and Hawk

I thought I was so tough,
But gentled at your hands,
Cannot be quick enough
To fly for you and show
That when I go I go
At your commands.

Even in flight above
I am no longer free:
You seeled me with your love,
I am blind to other birds –
The habit of your words
Has hooded me.

As formerly, I wheel
I hover and I twist,
But only want the feel,
In my possessive thought,
Of catcher and of caught
Upon your wrist.

You but half civilize,
Taming me in this way.
Through having only eyes
For you I fear to lose,
I lose to keep, and choose
Tamer as prey.

The Allegory of the Wolf Boy

The causes are in Time; only their issue
Is bodied in the flesh, the finite powers.
And how to guess he hides in that firm tissue
Seeds of division? At tennis and at tea
Upon the gentle lawn, he is not ours,
But plays us in a sad duplicity.

Tonight the boy, still boy open and blond,
Breaks from the house, wedges his clothes between
Two moulded garden urns, and goes beyond
His understanding, through the dark and dust:
Fields of sharp stubble, abandoned by machine
To the whirring enmity of insect lust.

As yet ungolden in the dense, hot night
The spikes enter his feet: he seeks the moon,
Which, with the touch of its infertile light,
Shall loose desires hoarded against his will
By the long urging of the afternoon.
Slowly the hard rim shifts above the hill.

White in the beam he stops, faces it square,
And the same instant leaping from the ground
Feels the familiar itch of close dark hair;
Then, clean exception to the natural laws,
Only to instinct and the moon being bound,
Drops on four feet. Yet he has bleeding paws.

In Santa Maria del Popolo

Waiting for when the sun an hour or less
Conveniently oblique makes visible
The painting on one wall of this recess
By Caravaggio, of the Roman School,
I see how shadow in the painting brims
With a real shadow, drowning all shapes out
But a dim horse's haunch and various limbs,
Until the very subject is in doubt.

But evening gives the act, beneath the horse
And one indifferent groom, I see him sprawl,
Foreshortened from the head, with hidden face,
Where he has fallen, Saul becoming Paul.
O wily painter, limiting the scene
From a cacophony of dusty forms
To the one convulsion, what is it you mean
In that wide gesture of the lifting arms?

No Ananias croons a mystery yet,
Casting the pain out under name of sin.
The painter saw what was, an alternate
Candour and secrecy inside the skin.
He painted, elsewhere, that firm insolent
Young whore in Venus' clothes, those pudgy cheats,
Those sharpers; and was strangled, as things went,
For money, by one such picked off the streets.

I turn, hardly enlightened, from the chapel
To the dim interior of the church instead,
In which there kneel already several people,
Mostly old women: each head closeted
In tiny fists holds comfort as it can.
Their poor arms are too tired for more than this
– For the large gesture of solitary man,
Resisting, by embracing, nothingness.

Touch

You are already
asleep. I lower
myself in next to
you, my skin slightly

numb with the restraint
of habits, the patina of
self, the black frost
of outsideness, so that even
unclothed it is
a resilient chilly
hardness, a superficially
malleable, dead
rubbery texture.

You are a mound
of bedclothes, where the cat
in sleep braces
its paws against your
calf through the blankets,
and kneads each paw in turn.

Meanwhile and slowly
I feel a is it
my own warmth surfacing or
the ferment of your whole
body that in darkness beneath
the cover is stealing
bit by bit to break
down that chill.

              You turn and
hold me tightly, do
you know who
I am or am I
your mother or
the nearest human being to
hold on to in a
dreamed pogrom.

What I, now loosened,
sink into is an old
big place, it is
there already, for
you are already
there, and the cat
got there before you, yet
it is hard to locate.
What is more, the place is
not found but seeps
from our touch in

continuous creation, dark
enclosing cocoon round
ourselves alone, dark
wide realm where we
walk with everyone.

The Idea of Trust

The idea of trust, or,
the thief. He
was always around,
"pretty" Jim.
Like a lilac bush or
a nice picture on the wall.
Blue eyes of an
intense vagueness
and the well-arranged
bearing of an animal.
Then one day he
said something!
             he said
that trust is
an intimate conspiracy.

What did that
mean? Anyway next day
he was gone, with
all the money and dope
of the people he'd lived with.

I begin
to understand. I see him
picking through their things
at his leisure, with
a quiet secret smile
choosing and taking,
having first discovered
and set up his phrase to
scramble
that message of
enveloping trust.

He's getting
free. His eyes
are almost transparent.
He has put on
gloves. He fingers
the little privacies of those
who acted as if there
should be no privacy.

They took that
risk.
    Wild lilac
chokes the garden.

The Hug

It was your birthday, we had drunk and dined
   Half of the night with our old friend
      Who'd showed us in the end
   To a bed I reached in one drunk stride.
      Already I lay snug,
And drowsy with the wine dozed on one side.

I dozed, I slept. My sleep broke on a hug,
      Suddenly, from behind,
In which the full lengths of our bodies pressed:
      Your instep to my heel,
   My shoulder-blades against your chest.
   It was not sex, but I could feel
   The whole strength of your body set,
      Or braced, to mine,
     And locking me to you
   As if we were still twenty-two
   When our grand passion had not yet
      Become familial.
   My quick sleep had deleted all
   Of intervening time and place.
      I only knew
The stay of your secure firm dry embrace.

The Man with Night Sweats

I wake up cold, I who
Prospered through dreams of heat
Wake to their residue,
Sweat, and a clinging sheet.

My flesh was its own shield:
Where it was gashed, it healed.

I grew as I explored
The body I could trust
Even while I adored
The risk that made robust,

A world of wonders in
Each challenge to the skin.

I cannot but be sorry
The given shield was cracked
My mind reduced to hurry,
My flesh reduced and wrecked.

I have to change the bed,
But catch myself instead

Stopped upright where I am
Hugging my body to me
As if to shield it from
The pains that will go through me,

As if hands were enough
To hold an avalanche off.

ADRIENNE RICH

"I Am in Danger – Sir – "

"Half-cracked" to Higginson, living,
afterward famous in garbled versions,
your hoard of dazzling scraps a battlefield,
now your old snood

mothballed at Harvard
and you in your variorum monument
equivocal to the end –
who are you?

Gardening the day-lily,
wiping the wine-glass stems,
your thought pulsed on behind
a forehead battered paper-thin,

you, woman, masculine
in single-mindedness,
for whom the word was more
than a symptom –

a condition of being.
Till the air buzzing with spoiled language
sang in your ears
of Perjury

and in your half-cracked way you chose
silence for entertainment,
chose to have it out at last
on your own premises.

The Burning of Paper Instead of Children

*I was in danger of verbalizing my moral
impulses out of existence.
– Daniel Berrigan, on trial in Baltimore.*

1. My neighbor, a scientist and art-collector, telephones me in a state of
violent emotion. He tells me that my son and his, aged eleven and
twelve, have on the last day of school burned a mathematics textbook
in the backyard. He has forbidden my son to come to his house for a
week, and has forbidden his own son to leave the house during that
time. "The burning of a book," he says, "arouses terrible sensations in
me, memories of Hitler; there are few things that upset me so much as
the idea of burning a book."

Back there: the library, walled
with green Britannicas
Looking again
in Dürer's *Complete Works*
for MELANCOLIA, the baffled woman

the crocodiles in Herodotus
the Book of the Dead
the *Trial of Jeanne d'Arc* so blue
I think, It is her color

and they take the book away
because I dream of her too often

love and fear in a house
knowledge of the oppressor
I know it hurts to burn

2. To imagine a time of silence
or few words
a time of chemistry and music

the hollows above your buttocks
traced by my hand
or, *hair is like flesh*, you said

an age of long silence

relief

from this tongue   this slab of limestone
or reinforced concrete
fanatics and traders
dumped on this coast wildgreen clayred
that breathed once
in signals of smoke
sweep of the wind

knowledge of the oppressor
this is the oppressor's language

yet I need it to talk to you

3. *People suffer highly in poverty and it takes dignity and intelligence to over-
come this suffering. Some of the suffering are: a child did not had dinner last
night: a child steal because he did not have money to buy it: to hear a mother
say she do not have money to buy food for her children and to see a child with-
out cloth it will make tears in your eyes.*

            (the fracture of order
            the repair of speech
            to overcome this suffering)

4. We lie under the sheet
after making love, speaking
of loneliness
relieved in a book
relived in a book
so on that page
the clot and fissure
of it appears
words of a man
in pain
a naked word
entering the clot
a hand grasping
through bars:

deliverance

What happens between us
has happened for centuries
we know it from literature

still it happens

sexual jealousy
outflung hand
beating bed

dryness of mouth
after panting

there are books that describe all this
and they are useless

You walk into the woods behind a house
there in that country
you find a temple
built eighteen hundred years ago
you enter without knowing
what it is you enter

so it is with us

no one knows what may happen
though the books tell everything

burn the texts   said Artaud

5. I am composing on the typewriter late at night, thinking of today. How well we all spoke. A language is a map of our failures. Frederick Douglass wrote an English purer than Milton's. People suffer highly in poverty. There are methods but we do not use them. Joan, who could not read, spoke some peasant form of French. Some of the suffering are: it is hard to tell the truth; this is America; I cannot touch you now. In America we have only the present tense. I am in danger. You are in danger. The burning of a book arouses no sensation in me. I know it hurts to burn. There are flames of napalm in Catonsville, Maryland. I know it hurts to burn. The typewriter is overheated, my mouth is burning, I cannot touch you and this is the oppressor's language.

Diving into the Wreck

First having read the book of myths,
and loaded the camera,
and checked the edge of the knife-blade,
I put on
the body-armor of black rubber
the absurd flippers
the grave and awkward mask.
I am having to do this
not like Cousteau with his
assiduous team
aboard the sun-flooded schooner
but here alone.

There is a ladder.
The ladder is always there
hanging innocently
close to the side of the schooner.
We know what it is for,
we who have used it.
Otherwise
it's a piece of maritime floss
some sundry equipment.

I go down.
Rung after rung and still
the oxygen immerses me
the blue light
the clear atoms
of our human air.
I go down.

My flippers cripple me,
I crawl like an insect down the ladder
and there is no one
to tell me when the ocean
will begin.

First the air is blue and then
it is bluer and then green and then
black I am blacking out and yet
my mask is powerful
it pumps my blood with power
the sea is another story
the sea is not a question of power
I have to learn alone
to turn my body without force
in the deep element.

And now: it is easy to forget
what I came for
among so many who have always
lived here
swaying their crenellated fans
between the reefs
and besides
you breathe differently down here.

I came to explore the wreck.
The words are purposes.
The words are maps.
I came to see the damage that was done
and the treasures that prevail.
I stroke the beam of my lamp
slowly along the flank
of something more permanent
than fish or weed

the thing I came for:
the wreck and not the story of the wreck
the thing itself and not the myth
the drowned face always staring
toward the sun
the evidence of damage
worn by salt and sway into this threadbare beauty
the ribs of the disaster
curving their assertion
among the tentative haunters.

This is the place.
And I am here, the mermaid whose dark hair
streams black, the merman in his armored body
We circle silently
about the wreck
we dive into the hold.
I am she: I am he

whose drowned face sleeps with open eyes
whose breasts still bear the stress
whose silver, copper, vermeil cargo lies
obscurely inside barrels
half-wedged and left to rot
we are the half-destroyed instruments
that once held to a course
the water-eaten log
the fouled compass

We are, I am, you are
by cowardice or courage
the one who find our way
back to this scene
carrying a knife, a camera
a book of myths
in which
our names do not appear.

Splittings

I

My body opens over San Francisco like the day-
light raining down   each pore crying the change of light
I am not with her   I have been waking off and on
all night to that pain   not simply absence but
the presence of the past   destructive
to living here and now   Yet if I could instruct
myself, if we could learn to learn from pain
even as it grasps us   if the mind, the mind that lives
in this body could refuse   to let itself be crushed
in that grasp   it would loosen   Pain would have to stand
off from me and listen   its dark breath still on me
but the mind could begin to speak to pain
and pain would have to answer:

We are older now
we have met before   these are my hands before your eyes

my figure blotting out   all that is not mine
I am the pain of division   creator of divisions
it is I who blot your lover from you
and not the time-zones nor the miles
It is not separation calls me forth   but I
who am separation   And remember
I have no existence   apart from you

2

I believe I am choosing something new
not to suffer uselessly   yet still to feel
Does the infant memorize the body of the mother
and create her in absence?   or simply cry
primordial loneliness?   does the bed of the stream
once diverted   mourning   remember wetness?
But we, we live so much in these
configurations of the past   I choose
to separate her   from my past we have not shared
I choose not to suffer uselessly
to detect primordial pain as it stalks toward me
flashing its bleak torch in my eyes   blotting out
her particular being   the details of her love
I will not be divided   from her or from myself
by myths of separation
while her mind and body in Manhattan are more with me
than the smell of eucalyptus coolly burning   on these hills

3

The world tells me I am its creature
I am raked by eyes   brushed by hands
I want to crawl into her for refuge   lay my head
in the space   between her breast and shoulder
abnegating power for love
as women have done   or hiding
from power in her love   like a man
I refuse these givens   the splitting
between love and action   I am choosing
not to suffer uselessly   and not to use her
I choose to love   this time   for once
with all my intelligence

Delta

If you have taken this rubble for my past
raking through it for fragments you could sell
know that I long ago moved on
deeper into the heart of the matter

If you think you can grasp me, think again:
my story flows in more than one direction
a delta springing from the riverbed
with its five fingers spread

Amends

Nights like this: on the cold apple-bough
a white star, then another
exploding out of the bark:
on the ground, moonlight picking at small stones

as it picks at greater stones, as it rises with the surf
laying its cheek for moments on the sand
as it licks the broken ledge, as it flows up the cliffs,
as it flicks across the tracks

as it unavailing pours into the gash
of the sand-and-gravel quarry
as it leans across the hangared fuselage
of the crop-dusting plane

as it soaks through cracks into the trailers
tremulous with sleep
as it dwells upon the eyelids of the sleepers
as if to make amends

Late Ghazal

Footsole to scalp alive facing the window's black mirror.
First rains of the winter   morning's smallest hour.

Go back to the ghazal then   what will you do there?
Life always pulsed harder than the lines.

Do you remember the strands that ran from eye to eye?
The tongue that reached everywhere, speaking all the parts?

Everything there was cast in an image of desire.
The imagination's cry is a sexual cry.

I took my body anyplace with me.
In the thickets of abstraction my skin ran with blood.

Life was always stronger . . . the critics couldn't get it.
Memory says the music always ran ahead of the words.

KAMAU BRATHWAITE

The Journeys

I

E-
gypt
in Af-
rica
Mesopo-
tamia
Mero-
ë

the
Nile
silica
glass
and brittle
Sa-
hara, Tim-
buctu, Gao
the hills of
Ahafo, winds
of the Ni-
ger, Kumasi
and Kiver
down the
coiled Congo
and down
that black river
that tides us to hell

Hell
in the water
brown
boys of Bushongo
drowned in the
blue and the bitter
salt of the wave-gullied
Ferdinand's sea
Soft winds
to San Salvador, Christoph-
er, Christ, and no Noah
or dove to promise us, grim
though it was, the simple sal-
vation of love. And so it was Little
Rock, Dall-
as, New Orleans, Santiago
De Cuba, the miles
of unfortunate islands: the

Saints and the Virgins, L'Ouverture's Haiti
ruined by greed and the slow
growing green of its freedom; golden Guiana:
Potaro
leaping in light liquid amber
in Makonaima's perpetual falls. And as if
the exhaustion of this wasn't all – Egypt,
Meroë, the Congo and all –
in the fall we reached De-
troit, Chicago and Den-
ver; and then it was New
York, selling news-
papers in Brooklyn and Harlem.
Then Capetown and Rio; remember how we
took Paris by storm: Sartre, Camus, Picasso and all?

But where are the dreams
of that bug happy, trash-
holstered tropical bed
when Uncle Tom lived
and we cursed him? This
the new deal for we black
grinning jacks? Lights
big like bubbies but we
still in shacks?

2

Tall, with slow
dignity

(so
goes the saying

so
went the dream)

the negro
steps his way among the follies.

With well-cut wood-cut head,
with subtle tie

and fashionably
faun exterieur

he needs no clowning
to assert himself: no boot

black smile, no warm humility:
no hanging

one-hand from his strength, playing
the black baboon.

He plays his own
game here and plays it

hard: and whether
gentleman or gigolo or

both, he holds himself
aloof from minor glitters

and does not wink
at mouching, long-haired, well-

upholstered fillies, soft in public sweaters,
or turn distracted

head to watch the carefully
arranged and ready nylon

ladies' legs along
the boulevard. His glance

is only for *la femme*
exceptionnelle: the leading-

lady with no dissonance
in view: the rich-lipped generous

ewe, returning reconnoitre'd
stare for candid *coup*

d'oeil: the ariadne clue
that tries to trick him, trap him,

track him down and lead him
to himself, the minotaur.

There
he abides: himself, coursing his own

man-
oeuvres: jives calmly, merely nods

his head and keeps
his potent subterranean power

for this his victim lover,
who through the artful

glance
the sacrificial

dance,
delivers him his chance.

Meanwhile he keeps
himself, asking no favours

and expecting
none: taking

his chance
among the dead-

ly follies with this
nonchalance

of shoulder and this
urbane head.

                    3
So went the black
hatted zoot-
suited watch-
chained dream
of the Panama boys
and the hoods
from Chicago.

Yeah man!
the real ne-
gro, man, real
cool.

Broad back
big you know what
black sperm spews
negritude.

Yeah man!
so went the
mud hut, hole-
hatted glorious

dream. Harlem
was heaven
and Paris a palace
for all.

Yeah man!
and the old man gone
old Uncle Tom gone
rain making souse

of his balls in the soil,
But he's real cool,
man, while we sweat
in this tin trunk'd house

that we rent from the rat
to share with the mouse:

Castries' Conway and Brixton in London,
Port of Spain's jungle

and Kingston's dry Dungle
Chicago Smethwick and Tiger Bay.

4

Never seen
a man
travel more
seen more
lands
than this poor
path-
less harbour-
less spade.

Calypso

1

The stone had skidded arc'd and bloomed into islands:
Cuba and San Domingo
Jamaica and Puerto Rico
Grenada Guadeloupe Bonaire

curved stone hissed into reef
wave teeth fanged into clay
white splash flashed into spray
Bathsheba Montego Bay

bloom of the arcing summers . . .

2

The islands roared into green plantations
ruled by silver sugar cane
sweat and profit
cutlass profit
islands ruled by sugar cane

And of course it was a wonderful time
a profitable hospitable well-worth-your-time
when captains carried receipts for rices
letters spices wigs
opera glasses swaggering asses
debtors vices pigs

O it was a wonderful time
an elegant benevolent redolent time –
and young Mrs. P.'s quick irrelevant crime
at four o'clock in the morning . . .

3

But what of black Sam
with the big splayed toes
and the shoe black shiny skin?

He carries bucketfuls of water
'cause his Ma's just had another daughter.

And what of John with the European name
who went to school and dreamt of fame
his boss one day called him a fool
and the boss hadn't even been to school . . .

4

Steel drum steel drum
hit the hot calypso dancing
hot rum hot rum
who goin' stop this bacchanalling?

For we glance the banjo
dance the limbo
grow our crops by maljo

have loose morals
gather corals
father our neighbour's quarrels

perhaps when they come
with their cameras and straw
hats: sacred pink tourists from the frozen Nawth

we should get down to those
white beaches
where if we don't wear breeches

it becomes an island dance
Some people doin' well
while others are catchin' hell

o the boss gave our Johnny the sack
though we beg him please
please to take 'im back

so the boy now nigratin' overseas . . .

Caliban

the flesh of dark
    into which i have carved no holy place
    the lightning of scars
    my flash illuminated by the writhing of death
    by the ideals of eels
    the gum tree writing its tears

i have become lost in this forest of singing wires
    of grasshopper gossip
    of syphilitic cities of no night
    touch my hand   .   it is a plank of wood floating away
    call my name   .   it is answered by the spittle of lizards
    the pathways are burning to dragons

into the square now a phalanx of xecutioners
    halt. pre*sent* spite pre*sent* envy fire
    tirade of hate echoing out of the iron wells of my flesh
    the crystal water slowing upwards to drench me
    its sibilance devouring my eyes
    like a train drinking speed along the rails of its tongue

    alive through the withering trees
    there is a butterfly of light
    there is a silence of humming birds
    monkeys of limestone water that would contain my thirst

but the cockpit is burst in a mabrak of madness
    the coal xplodes inwards to furnace of darkness
    the cup of the skull cracks.   wracking ichor and incense
    no goblet no damp/ness
    trash trash trampled windmills no harvest

And i caliban
    blind

and i caliban
    tortured

and i caliban
    twisted & bent

    victim of the cities' victory
    victim of the cities' skin and trinkets
    wilderness of wind and shellac
    wilderness of papernapkins soiled with sperm
    wilderness of howls of caves of eyes.   consumers' virtuses

      the flash of dark
          into which i have carved no holy place
          the lightning of these scars
      xposed xposed
      cowhead glut skeletone

ELAINE FEINSTEIN

At Seven a Son

In cold weather on a
garden swing, his legs
in wellingtons rising over
the winter rose trees

he sits serenely
smiling like a Thai
his coat open, his gloves
sewn to the flapping sleeves

his thin knees working
with his arms
folded about the
metal struts

as he flies up
(his hair like long
black leaves) he
lies back freely

astonished in
sunshine as serious
as a stranger he is
a bird in his own thought.

Mother Love

You eat me, your
nights eat me.
Once you took
haemoglobin and bone
out of my blood,

now my head
sleeps forward on my neck
holding you.

In the morning my
skin shines hot
and you are happy
banging your fat hands.

I kiss your
soft feet mindless:
delicately

your shit slides out
yellow and
smelling of curd cheese.

The Magic Apple Tree

Sealed in rainlight one
November sleepwalking afternoon streets
I remembered Samuel Palmer's garden
Waterhouse in Shoreham, and at once
I knew: that the chill of wet
brown streets was no more literal
than the yellow he laid there against
his unnatural blue   because
together they worked upon me like
an icon   infantine

he called his vision   so it was
with the early makers of icons, who
worked humbly, choosing wood without resin.
They stilled their spirits before using the gold
and while the brightness held under the *kvass*
their colours too induced
the peculiar joy of abandoning restlessness

and now in streets where only white
mac or car metal catches the failing
light, if we sing of
the red and the blue and the texture of goat hair,
there is no deceit in our prophecy:
for even now our brackish waters can
be sweetened by a strange tree.

Bathroom

My legs shimmer like fish
my hair floats on the water:
tonight I observe that my
skin is no longer smooth
that blue veins show
in my arms that my
breasts are smaller

and lie seeing still water
meeting a white sky
(my elbows swim for me)
waiting for those
queer trails of thought
that move toward sleep

to where
the unforgiven words are
stored in circuits
of cells that hold
whatever shape there is
of the lost days

Getting Older

The first surprise: I like it.
Whatever happens now, some things
that used to terrify have not:

I didn't die young, for instance. Or lose
my only love. My three children
never had to run away from anyone.

Don't tell me this gratitude is complacent.
We all approach the edge of the same blackness
which for me is silent.

Knowing as much sharpens
my delight in January freesia,
hot coffee, winter sunlight. So we say

as we lie close on some gentle occasion:
every day won from such
darkness is a celebration.

Lazarus' Sister

On hot nights now, in the smell of trees and water,
you beg me to listen and your words enter my spirit.

Your descriptions unmake me; I am like wood
that thought has wormed; even the angels

that report our innermost wish must be kinder.
And yet, when your face is grey in the pillow, I wake you

gently, kissing your eyes, my need for you
stronger than the hope of love. I carry your body

where the hillside flickers: olive cypress ash.
But nothing brings relief. All our days

are numbered in a book. I try to imagine
a way our story can end without a magician.

Prayer

The windows are black tonight. The lamp
at my bedside peering with its yellow
40 watt light can hardly make out the chair.
Nothing is stranger than the habit of prayer.

The face of God as seen on this planet
is rarely gentle: the young gazelle is food
for the predator; filmy shapes
that need little more than carbon and water,

evolve like patterns on Dawkins'
computer; the intricate miracles
of eye and wing respond to the same
logic. I accept the evidence.

God is the wish to live. Everywhere,
as carnivores lick their young with
tenderness, in the human struggle
nothing is stranger than the habit of prayer.

ROY FISHER

Toyland

Today the sunlight is the paint on lead soldiers
Only they are people scattering out of the cool church

And as they go across the gravel and among the spring streets
They spread formality: they know, we know, what they have been
        doing,

The old couples, the widowed, the staunch smilers,
The deprived and the few nubile young lily-ladies,

And we know what they will do when they have opened the doors
        of their houses and walked in:
Mostly they will make water, and wash their calm hands and eat.

The organ's flourishes finish; the verger closes the doors;
The choirboys run home, and the rector goes off in his motor.

Here a policeman stalks, the sun glinting on his helmet-crest;
Then a man pushes a perambulator home; and somebody posts a
    letter.

If I sit here long enough, loving it all, I shall see the District Nurse
    pedal past,
The children going to Sunday School and the strollers strolling;

The lights darting on in different rooms as night comes in;
And I shall see washing hung out, and the postman delivering
    letters.

I might by exception see an ambulance or the fire brigade
Or even, if the chance came round, street musicians (singing and
    playing).

For the people I've seen, this seems the operation of life:
I need the paint of stillness and sunshine to see it that way.

The secret laugh of the world picks them up and shakes them like
    peas boiling;
They behave as if nothing happened; maybe they no longer notice.

I notice. I laugh with the laugh, cultivate it, make much of it,
But I still don't know what the joke is, to tell them.

As He Came Near Death

As he came near death things grew shallower for us:
We'd lost sleep and now sat muffled in the scent of tulips, the medical
    odours, and the street sounds going past, going away;
And he, too, slept little, the morphine and the pink light the curtains
    let through floating him with us,
So that he lay and was worked out on to the skin of his life and left
    there,
And we had to reach only a little way into the warm bed to scoop
    him up.

A few days, slow tumbling escalators of visitors and cheques, and
    something like popularity;
During this time somebody washed him in a soap called *Narcissus* and
    mounted him, frilled with satin, in a polished case.

Then the hole: this was a slot punched in a square of plastic grass rug,
    a slot lined with white polythene, floored with dyed green
    gravel.
The box lay in it; we rode in the black cars round a corner, got out
    into our coloured cars and dispersed in easy stages.

After a time the grave got up and went away.

The Thing About Joe Sullivan

The pianist Joe Sullivan,
jamming sound against idea

hard as it can go
florid and dangerous

slams at the beat, or hovers,
drumming, along its spikes;

in his time almost the only
one of them to ignore

the chance of easing down,
walking it leisurely,

he'll strut, with gambling shapes,
underpinning by James P.,

amble, and stride over
gulfs of his own leaving, perilously

toppling octaves down to where
the chords grow fat again

and ride hard-edged, most lucidly
voiced, and in good inversions even when

the piano seems at risk of being
hammered the next second into scrap.

For all that, he won't swing
like all the others;

disregards mere continuity,
the snakecharming business,

the "masturbator's rhythm"
under the long variations:

Sullivan can gut a sequence
in one chorus –

– approach, development, climax, discard –
and sound magnanimous.

The mannerism of intensity
often with him seems true,

too much to be said, the mood
pressing in right at the start, then

running among stock forms
that could play themselves

and moving there with such
quickness of intellect

that shapes flaw and fuse,
altering without much sign,

concentration
so wrapped up in thoroughness

it can sound bluff, bustling,
just big-handed stuff –

belied by what drives him in
to make rigid, display,

shout and abscond, rather
than just let it come, let it go –

And that thing is his mood:
a feeling violent and ordinary

that runs in among standard forms so
wrapped up in clarity

that fingers following his
through figures that sound obvious

find corners everywhere,
marks of invention, wakefulness;

the rapid and perverse
tracks that ordinary feelings

make when they get driven
hard enough against time.

The Least

The least, the meanest,
goes down to less;
there's never an end.

And you can learn
looking for less
and again, less;
your eyes don't get sharper.

For there is less
eyesight;
and no end to that.

There is you,
there is less-you:
the merest trace –
less-eyes will find it.

Occasional Poem 7.1.72

The poets are dying because they are told to die.
What kind of dirt is that? Whose hand
jiggles the nerve, what programme demands it,
what death-train are we on? Not poetry:
some of us drink,
some take the wrong kind of walk
or get picked up in canteens
by killer lays – it's all
tasteless to talk about.
Taste is what death has for the talented. Then
the civilization is filth, its taste

the scum on filth. Then the poets
are going to be moving on out past talent,
out past taste. If taste
gets its gift wrappers on death – well –
out past that, too. There are courts
where nobody ought to testify.

The Supposed Dancer

Jumping out of the straw,
jumping out of the straw,
his cheeks alive with bristles,
jumping out –
     you've got him!
He'll ruin the lot of you,
jumping out:
  two drums
  tied up in this
jumping
  and the joy and the
jumping
  bitchery of art, the men
  with warm hard
  hearts
    out of the straw –
Got him!
   Alive with bristles,
jumping with his cheeks
out of the straw alive
with bristles, his cheeks
  ready to jump
the cameraman's guitar, the guitarist's
  camera;
    alive with
jumping out of the
jumping out of the straw.

TED HUGHES

Wind

This house has been far out at sea all night,
The woods crashing through darkness, the booming hills,
Winds stampeding the fields under the window
Floundering black astride and blinding wet

Till day rose; then under an orange sky
The hills had new places, and wind wielded
Blade-light, luminous black and emerald,
Flexing like the lens of a mad eye.

At noon I scaled along the house-side as far as
The coal-house door. Once I looked up –
Through the brunt wind that dented the balls of my eyes
The tent of the hills drummed and strained its guyrope,

The fields quivering, the skyline a grimace,
At any second to bang and vanish with a flap:
The wind flung a magpie away and a black-
Back gull bent like an iron bar slowly. The house

Rang like some fine green goblet in the note
That any second would shatter it. Now deep
In chairs, in front of the great fire, we grip
Our hearts and cannot entertain book, thought,

Or each other. We watch the fire blazing,
And feel the roots of the house move, but sit on,
Seeing the window tremble to come in,
Hearing the stones cry out under the horizons.

Snowdrop

Now is the globe shrunk tight
Round the mouse's dulled wintering heart.
Weasel and crow, as if moulded in brass,
Move through an outer darkness
Not in their right minds,

With the other deaths. She, too, pursues her ends,
Brutal as the stars of this month,
Her pale head heavy as metal.

Her Husband

Comes home dull with coal-dust deliberately
To grime the sink and foul towels and let her
Learn with scrubbing brush and scrubbing board
The stubborn character of money.

And let her learn through what kind of dust
He has earned his thirst and the right to quench it
And what sweat he has exchanged for his money
And the blood-weight of money. He'll humble her

With new light on her obligations.
The fried, woody chips, kept warm two hours in the oven,
Are only part of her answer.
Hearing the rest, he slams them to the fire back

And is away round the house-end singing
"Come back to Sorrento" in a voice
Of resounding corrugated iron.
Her back has bunched into a hump as an insult.

For they will have their rights.
Their jurors are to be assembled
From the little crumbs of soot. Their brief
Goes straight up to heaven and nothing more is heard of it.

Full Moon and Little Frieda

A cool small evening shrunk to a dog bark and the clank
    of a bucket –

And you listening.
A spider's web, tense for the dew's touch.
A pail lifted, still and brimming – mirror
To tempt a first star to a tremor.

Cows are going home in the lane there, looping the hedges with
    their warm wreaths of breath –
A dark river of blood, many boulders,
Balancing unspilled milk.

"Moon!" you cry suddenly, "Moon! Moon!"

The moon has stepped back like an artist gazing amazed at a work

That points at him amazed.

Wodwo

What am I? Nosing here, turning leaves over
Following a faint stain on the air to the river's edge
I enter water. What am I to split
The glassy grain of water looking upward I see the bed
Of the river above me upside down very clear
What am I doing here in mid-air? Why do I find
this frog so interesting as I inspect its most secret
interior and make it my own? Do these weeds
know me and name me to each other have they
seen me before, do I fit in their world? I seem
separate from the ground and not rooted but dropped
out of nothing casually I've no threads
fastening me to anything I can go anywhere
I seem to have been given the freedom
of this place what am I then? And picking
bits of bark off this rotten stump gives me
no pleasure and it's no use so why do I do it
me and doing that have coincided very queerly
But what shall I be called am I the first
have I an owner what shape am I what
shape am I am I huge if I go
to the end on this way past these trees and past these trees
till I get tired that's touching one wall of me
for the moment if I sit still how everything
stops to watch me I suppose I am the exact centre
but there's all this what is it roots
roots roots roots and here's the water
again very queer but I'll go on looking

Crow and the Birds

When the eagle soared clear through a dawn distilling of emerald.
When the curlew trawled in seadusk through a chime of wineglasses
When the swallow swooped through a woman's song in a cavern
And the swift flicked through the breath of a violet

When the owl sailed clear of tomorrow's conscience
And the sparrow preened himself of yesterday's promise
And the heron laboured clear of the Bessemer upglare
And the bluetit zipped clear of lace panties
And the woodpecker drummed clear of the rotovator and the
    rose-farm
And the peewit tumbled clear of the laundromat

While the bullfinch plumped in the apple bud
And the goldfinch bulbed in the sun
And the wryneck crooked in the moon
And the dipper peered from the dewball

Crow spraddled head-down in the beach-garbage, guzzling a
    dropped ice-cream.

Crow's Last Stand

Burning
        burning
            burning
                there was finally something
The sun could not burn, that it had rendered
Everything down to – a final obstacle
Against which it raged and charred

And rages and chars

Limpid among the glaring furnace clinkers
The pulsing blue tongues and the red and the yellow
The green lickings of the conflagration

Limpid and black –

Crow's eye-pupil, in the tower of its scorched fort.

Bones

Bones is a crazy pony.
Moon-white – star-mad.
All skull and skeleton.

Her hooves pound. The sleeper awakes with a cry.

Who has broken her in?
Who has mounted her and come back
Or kept her?

She lifts under them, the snaking crest of a bullwhip.

Hero by hero they go –
Grimly get astride
And their hair lifts.

She laughs, smelling the battle – their cry comes back.

Who can live her life?
Every effort to hold her or turn her falls off her
Like rotten harness.

Their smashed faces come back, the wallets and the watches.

And this is the stunted foal of the earth –
She that kicks the cot
To flinders and is off.

That Morning

We came where the salmon were so many
So steady, so spaced, so far-aimed
On their inner map, England could add

Only the sooty twilight of South Yorkshire
Hung with the drumming drift of Lancasters
Till the world had seemed capsizing slowly.

Solemn to stand there in the pollen light
Waist-deep in wild salmon swaying massed
As from the hand of God. There the body

Separated, golden and imperishable,
From its doubting thought – a spirit-beacon
Lit by the power of the salmon

That came on, came on, and kept on coming
As if we flew slowly, their formations
Lifting us toward some dazzle of blessing

One wrong thought might darken. As if the fallen
World and salmon were over. As if these
Were the imperishable fish

That had let the world pass away –

There, in a mauve light of drifted lupins,
They hung in the cupped hands of mountains

Made of tingling atoms. It had happened.
Then for a sign that we were where we were
Two gold bears came down and swam like men

Beside us. And dived like children.
And stood in deep water as on a throne
Eating pierced salmon off their talons.

So we found the end of our journey.

So we stood, alive in the river of light
Among the creatures of light, creatures of light.

DEREK WALCOTT

The Schooner Flight

1 Adios, Carenage

In idle August, while the sea soft,
and leaves of brown islands stick to the rim
of this Caribbean, I blow out the light
by the dreamless face of Maria Concepcion
to ship as a seaman on the schooner *Flight*.
Out in the yard turning grey in the dawn,
I stood like a stone and nothing else move

but the cold sea rippling like galvanize
and the nail holes of stars in the sky roof,
till a wind start to interfere with the trees.
I pass me dry neighbour sweeping she yard
as I went downhill, and I nearly said:
"Sweep soft, you witch, 'cause she don't sleep hard,"
but the bitch look through me like I was dead.
A route taxi pull up, park-lights still on.
The driver size up my bags with a grin:
"This time, Shabine, like you really gone!"
I ain't answer the ass, I simply pile in
the back seat and watch the sky burn
above Laventille pink as the gown
in which the woman I left was sleeping,
and I look in the rearview and see a man
exactly like me, and the man was weeping
for the houses, the streets, that whole fucking island.

Christ have mercy on all sleeping things!
From that dog rotting down Wrightson Road
to when I was a dog on these streets;
if loving these islands must be my load,
out of corruption my soul takes wings,
But they had started to poison my soul
with their big house, big car, big-time bohbohl,
coolie, nigger, Syrian, and French Creole,
so I leave it for them and their carnival –
I taking a sea-bath, I gone down the road.
I know these islands from Monos to Nassau,
a rusty head sailor with sea-green eyes
that they nickname Shabine, the patois for
any red nigger, and I, Shabine, saw
when these slums of empire was paradise.
I'm just a red nigger who love the sea,
I had a sound colonial education,
I have Dutch, nigger, and English in me,
and either I'm nobody, or I'm a nation.

But Maria Concepcion was all my thought
watching the sea heaving up and down
as the port side of dories, schooners, and yachts
was painted afresh by the strokes of the sun
signing her name with every reflection;
I knew when dark-haired evening put on
her bright silk at sunset, and, folding the sea,
sidled under the sheet with her starry laugh,

that there'd be no rest, there'd be no forgetting.
Is like telling mourners round the graveside
about resurrection, they want the dead back,
so I smile to myself as the bow rope untied
and the *Flight* swing seaward: "Is no use repeating
that the sea have more fish. I ain't want her
dressed in the sexless light of a seraph,
I want those round brown eyes like a marmoset, and
till the day when I can lean back and laugh,
those claws that tickled my back on sweating
Sunday afternoons, like a crab on wet sand."
As I worked, watching the rotting waves come
past the bow that scissor the sea like silk,
I swear to you all, by my mother's milk,
by the stars that shall fly from tonight's furnace,
that I loved them, my children, my wife, my home;
I loved them as poets love the poetry
that kills them, as drowned sailors the sea.

You ever look up from some lonely beach
and see a far schooner? Well, when I write
this poem, each phrase go be soaked in salt;
I go draw and knot every line as tight
as ropes in this rigging; in simple speech
my common language go be the wind,
my pages the sails of the schooner *Flight*.
But let me tell you how this business begin.

2 *Raptures of the Deep*

Smuggled Scotch for O'Hara, big government man,
between Cedros and the Main, so the Coast Guard couldn't
    touch us,
and the Spanish pirogues always met us halfway,
but a voice kept saying: "Shabine, see this business
of playing pirate?" Well, so said, so done!
That whole racket crash. And I for a woman,
for her laces and silks, Maria Concepcion.
Ay, ay! Next thing I hear, some Commission of Enquiry
was being organized to conduct a big quiz,
with himself as chairman investigating himself.
Well, I knew damn well who the suckers would be,
not that shark in shark skin, but his pilot fish,
khaki-pants red niggers like you and me.
What worse, I fighting with Maria Concepcion,
plates flying and thing, so I swear: "Not again!"
It was mashing up my house and my family.

I was so broke all I needed was shades and a cup
or four shades and four cups in four-cup Port of Spain;
all the silver I had was the coins on the sea.

You saw them ministers in *The Express*,
guardians of the poor – one hand at their back,
and one set o' police only guarding their house,
and the Scotch pouring in through the back door.
As for that minister-monster who smuggled the booze,
that half-Syrian saurian, I got so vex to see
that face thick with powder, the warts, the stone lids
like a dinosaur caked with primordial ooze
by the lightning of flashbulbs sinking in wealth,
that I said: "Shabine, this is shit, understand!"
But he get somebody to kick my crutch out his office
like I was some artist! That bitch was so grand,
couldn't get off his high horse and kick me himself.
I have seen things that would make a slave sick
in this Trinidad, the Limers' Republic.

I couldn't shake the sea noise out of my head,
the shell of my ears sang Maria Concepcion,
so I start salvage diving with a crazy Mick,
name O'Shaughnessy, and a limey named Head;
but this Caribbean so choke with the dead
that when I would melt in emerald water,
whose ceiling rippled like a silk tent,
I saw them corals: brain, fire, sea-fans,
dead-men's-fingers, and then, the dead men.
I saw that the powdery sand was their bones
ground white from Senegal to San Salvador,
so, I panic third dive, and surface for a month
in the Seamen's Hostel. Fish broth and sermons.
When I thought of the woe I had brought my wife,
when I saw my worries with that other woman,
I wept under water, salt seeking salt,
for her beauty had fallen on me like a sword
cleaving me from my children, flesh of my flesh!

There was this barge from St Vincent, but she was too deep
to float her again. When we drank, the limey
got tired of my sobbing for Maria Concepcion.
He said he was getting the bends. Good for him!
The pain in my heart for Maria Concepcion,
the hurt I had done to my wife and children,
was worse than the bends. In the rapturous deep

there was no cleft rock where my soul could hide
like the boobies each sunset, no sandbar of light
where I could rest, like the pelicans know,
so I got raptures once, and I saw God
like a harpooned grouper bleeding, and a far
voice was rumbling, "Shabine, if you leave her,
if you leave her, I shall give you the morning star."
When I left the madhouse I tried other women
but, once they stripped naked, their spiky cunts
bristled like sea-eggs and I couldn't dive.
The chaplain came round. I paid him no mind.
Where is my rest place, Jesus? Where is my harbour?
Where is the pillow I will not have to pay for,
and the window I can look from that frames my life?

3 *Shabine Leaves the Republic*

I had no nation now but the imagination.
After the white man, the niggers didn't want me
when the power swing to their side.
The first chain my hands and apologize, "History";
the next said I wasn't black enough for their pride.
Tell me, what power, on these unknown rocks –
a spray-plane Air Force, the Fire Brigade,
the Red Cross, the Regiment, two, three police dogs
that pass before you finish bawling "Parade!"?
I met History once, but he ain't recognize me,
a parchment Creole, with warts
like an old sea-bottle, crawling like a crab
through the holes of shadow cast by the net
of a grille balcony; cream linen, cream hat.
I confront him and shout, "Sir, is Shabine!
They say I'se your grandson. You remember Grandma,
your black cook, at all?" The bitch hawk and spat.
A spit like that worth any number of words.
But that's all them bastards have left us: words.

I no longer believed in the revolution.
I was losing faith in the love of my woman.
I had seen that moment Aleksandr Blok
crystallize in *The Twelve*. Was between
the Police Marine Branch and Hotel Venezuelana
one Sunday at noon. Young men without flags
using shirts, their chests waiting for holes.
They kept marching into the mountains, and
their noise ceased as foam sinks into sand.
They sank in the bright hills like rain, every one

with his own nimbus, leaving shirts in the street,
and the echo of power at the end of the street.
Propeller-blade fans turn over the Senate;
the judges, they say, still sweat in carmine,
on Frederick Street the idlers all marching
by standing still, the Budget turns a new leaf.
In the 12:30 movies the projectors best
not break down, or you go see revolution. Aleksandr Blok
enters and sits in the third row of pit eating choc-
olate cone, waiting for a spaghetti West-
ern with Clint Eastwood and featuring Lee Van Cleef.

4 The Flight, *Passing Blanchisseuse*

Dusk. The *Flight* passing Blanchisseuse.
Gulls wheel like from a gun again,
and foam gone amber that was white,
lighthouse and star start making friends,
down every beach the long day ends,
and there, on that last stretch of sand,
on a beach bare of all but light,
dark hands start pulling in the seine
of the dark sea, deep, deep inland.

5 *Shabine Encounters the Middle Passage*

Man, I brisk in the galley first thing next dawn,
brewing li'l coffee; fog coil from the sea
like the kettle steaming when I put it down
slow, slow, 'cause I couldn't believe what I see:
where the horizon was one silver haze,
the fog swirl and swell into sails, so close
that I saw it was sails, my hair grip my skull,
it was horrors, but it was beautiful.
We float through a rustling forest of ships
with sails dry like paper, behind the glass
I saw men with rusty eyeholes like cannons,
and whenever their half-naked crews cross the sun,
right through their tissue, you traced their bones
like leaves against the sunlight; frigates, barkentines,
the backward-moving current swept them on,
and high on their decks I saw great admirals,
Rodney, Nelson, de Grasse, I heard the hoarse orders
they gave those Shabines, and the forest
of masts sail right through the *Flight*,
and all you could hear was the ghostly sound
of waves rustling like grass in a low wind

and the hissing weeds they trailed from the stern;
slowly they heaved past from east to west
like this round world was some cranked water wheel,
every ship pouring like a wooden bucket
dredged from the deep; my memory revolve
on all sailors before me, then the sun
heat the horizon's ring and they was mist.

Next we pass slave ships. Flags of all nations,
our fathers below deck too deep, I suppose,
to hear us shouting. So we stop shouting. Who knows
who his grandfather is, much less his name?
Tomorrow our landfall will be the Barbados.

6 The Sailor Sings Back to the Casuarinas

You see them on the low hills of Barbados
bracing like windbreaks, needles for hurricanes,
trailing, like masts, the cirrus of torn sails;
when I was green like them, I used to think
those cypresses, leaning against the sea,
that take the sea-noise up into their branches,
are not real cypresses but casuarinas.
Now captain just call them Canadian cedars.
But cedars, cypresses, or casuarinas,
whoever called them so had a good cause,
watching their bending bodies wail like women
after a storm, when some schooner came home
with news of one more sailor drowned again.
Once the sound "cypress" used to make more sense
than the green "casuarinas", though, to the wind
whatever grief bent them was all the same,
since they were trees with nothing else in mind
but heavenly leaping or to guard a grave;
but we live like our names and you would have
to be colonial to know the difference,
to know the pain of history words contain,
to love those trees with an inferior love,
and to believe: "Those casuarinas bend
like cypresses, their hair hangs down in rain
like sailors' wives. They're classic trees, and we,
if we live like the names our masters please,
by careful mimicry might become men."

7 *The* Flight *Anchors in Castries Harbor*

When the stars self were young over Castries,
I loved you alone and I loved the whole world.
What does it matter that our lives are different?
Burdened with the loves of our different children?
When I think of your young face washed by the wind
and your voice that chuckles in the slap of the sea?
The lights are out on La Toc promontory,
except for the hospital. Across at Vigie
the marina arcs keep vigil. I have kept my own
promise, to leave you the one thing I own,
you whom I loved first: my poetry.
We here for one night. Tomorrow, the *Flight* will be gone.

8 *Fight with the Crew*

It had one bitch on board, like he had me mark –
that was the cook, some Vincentian arse
with a skin like a gommier tree, red peeling bark,
and wash-out blue eyes; he wouldn't give me a ease,
like he feel he was white. Had an exercise book,
this same one here, that I was using to write
my poetry, so one day this man snatch it
from my hand, and start throwing it left and right
to the rest of the crew, bawling out, "Catch it,"
and start mincing me like I was some hen
because of the poems. Some case is for fist,
some case is for tholing pin, some is for knife –
this one was for knife. Well, I beg him first,
but he keep reading, "O my children, my wife,"
and playing he crying, to make the crew laugh;
it move like a flying fish, the silver knife
that catch him right in the plump of his calf,
and he faint so slowly, and he turn more white
than he thought he was. I suppose among men
you need that sort of thing. It ain't right
but that's how it is. There wasn't much pain,
just plenty blood, and Vincie and me best friend,
but none of them go fuck with my poetry again.

9 *Maria Concepcion & the Book of Dreams*

The jet that was screeching over the *Flight*
was opening a curtain into the past.
"Dominica ahead!"
                    "It still have Caribs there."
"One day go be planes only, no more boat."

"Vince, God ain't make nigger to fly through the air."
"Progress, Shabine, that's what it's all about.
Progress leaving all we small islands behind."
I was at the wheel, Vince sitting next to me
gaffing. Crisp, bracing day. A high-running sea.
"Progress is something to ask Caribs about.
They kill them by millions, some in war,
some by forced labour dying in the mines
looking for silver, after that niggers; more
progress. Until I see definite signs
that mankind change, Vince, I ain't want to hear.
Progress is history's dirty joke.
Ask that sad green island getting nearer."
Green islands, like mangoes pickled in brine.
In such fierce salt let my wound be healed,
me, in my freshness as a seafarer.

That night, with the sky sparks frosty with fire,
I ran like a Carib through Dominica,
my nose holes choked with memory of smoke;
I heard the screams of my burning children,
I ate the brains of mushrooms, the fungi
of devil's parasols under white, leprous rocks;
my breakfast was leaf mould in leaking forests,
with leaves big as maps, and when I heard noise
of the soldiers' progress through the thick leaves,
though my heart was bursting, I get up and ran
through the blades of balisier sharper than spears;
with the blood of my race, I ran, boy, I ran
with moss-footed speed like a painted bird;
then I fall, but I fall by an icy stream under
cool fountains of fern, and a screaming parrot
catch the dry branches and I drowned at last
in big breakers of smoke; then when that ocean
of black smoke pass, and the sky turn white,
there was nothing but Progress, if Progress is
an iguana as still as a young leaf in sunlight.
I bawl for Maria, and her *Book of Dreams*.

It anchored her sleep, that insomniac's Bible,
a soiled orange booklet with a cyclops' eye
center, from the Dominican Republic.
Its coarse pages were black with the usual
symbols of prophecy, in excited Spanish;
an open palm upright, sectioned and numbered
like a butcher chart, delivered the future.

One night, in a fever, radiantly ill,
she say, "Bring me the book, the end has come."
She said: "I dreamt of whales and a storm,"
but for that dream, the book had no answer.
A next night I dreamed of three old women
featureless as silkworms, stitching my fate,
and I scream at them to come out my house,
and I try beating them away with a broom,
but as they go out, so they crawl back again,
until I start screaming and crying, my flesh
raining with sweat, and she ravage the book
for the dream meaning, and there was nothing;
my nerves melt like a jellyfish – that was when I broke –
they found me round the Savannah, screaming:

All you see me talking to the wind, so you think I mad.
Well, Shabine has bridled the horses of the sea;
you see me watching the sun till my eyeballs seared,
so all you mad people feel Shabine crazy,
but all you ain't know my strength, hear? The coconuts
standing by in their regiments in yellow khaki,
they waiting for Shabine to take over these islands,
and all you best dread the day I am healed
of being a human. All you fate in my hand,
ministers, businessmen, Shabine have you, friend,
I shall scatter your lives like a handful of sand,
I who have no weapon but poetry and
the lances of palms and the sea's shining shield!

10 *Out of the Depths*

Next day, dark sea. A arse-aching dawn.
"Damn wind shift sudden as a woman mind."
The slow swell start cresting like some mountain range
with snow on the top.
                    "Ay, Skipper, sky dark!"
"This ain't right for August."
                    "This light damn strange,
this season, sky should be clear as a field."

A stingray steeplechase across the sea,
tail whipping water, the high man-o'-wars
start reeling inland, quick, quick an archery
of flying fish miss us! Vince say: "You notice?"
and a black-mane squall pounce on the sail
like a dog on a pigeon, and it snap the neck
of the *Flight* and shake it from head to tail.

"Be Jesus, I never see sea get so rough
so fast! That wind come from God back pocket!"
"Where Cap'n headin? Like the man gone blind!"
"If we's to drong, we go drong, Vince, fock-it!"
"Shabine, say your prayers, if life leave you any!"

I have not loved those that I loved enough.
Worse than the mule kick of Kick-'Em-Jenny
Channel, rain start to pelt the *Flight* between
mountains of water. If I was frighten?
The tent poles of water spouts bracing the sky
start wobbling, clouds unstitch at the seams
and sky water drench us, and I hear myself cry,
"I'm the drowned sailor in her *Book of Dreams*."
I remembered them ghost ships, I saw me corkscrewing
to the sea-bed of sea-worms, fathom pass fathom,
my jaw clench like a fist, and only one thing
hold me, trembling, how my family safe home.
Then a strength like it seize me and the strength said:
"I from backward people who still fear God."
Let Him, in His might, heave Leviathan upward
by the winch of His will, the beast pouring lace
from his sea-bottom bed; and that was the faith
that had fade from a child in the Methodist chapel
in Chisel Street, Castries, when the whale-bell
sang service and, in hard pews ribbed like the whale,
proud with despair, we sang how our race
survive the sea's maw, our history, our peril,
and now I was ready for whatever death will.
But if that storm had strength, was in Cap'n face,
beard beading with spray, tears salting the eyes,
crucify to his post, that nigger hold fast
to that wheel, man, like the cross held Jesus,
and the wounds of his eyes like they crying for us,
and I feeding him white rum, while every crest
with Leviathan-lash make the *Flight* quail
like two criminal. Whole night, with no rest,
till red-eyed like dawn, we watch our travail
subsiding, subside, and there was no more storm.
And the noon sea get calm as Thy Kingdom come.

11 *After the Storm*

There's a fresh light that follows a storm
while the whole sea still havoc; in its bright wake
I saw the veiled face of Maria Concepcion
marrying the ocean, then drifting away

in the widening lace of her bridal train
with white gulls her bridesmaids, till she was gone.
I wanted nothing after that day.
Across my own face, like the face of the sun,
a light rain was falling, with the sea calm.

Fall gently, rain, on the sea's upturned face
like a girl showering; make these islands fresh
as Shabine once knew them! Let every trace,
every hot road, smell like clothes she just press
and sprinkle with drizzle. I finish dream;
whatever the rain wash and the sun iron:
the white clouds, the sea and sky with one seam,
is clothes enough for my nakedness.
Though my *Flight* never pass the incoming tide
of this inland sea beyond the loud reefs
of the final Bahamas, I am satisfied
if my hand gave voice to one people's grief.
Open the map. More islands there, man,
than peas on a tin plate, all different size,
one thousand in the Bahamas alone,
from mountains to low scrub with coral keys,
and from this bowsprit, I bless every town,
the blue smell of smoke in hills behind them,
and the one small road winding down them like twine
to the roofs below; I have only one theme:

The bowsprit, the arrow, the longing, the lunging heart –
the flight to a target whose aim we'll never know,
vain search for one island that heals with its harbour
and a guiltless horizon, where the almond's shadow
doesn't injure the sand. There are so many islands!
As many islands as the stars at night
on that branched tree from which meteors are shaken
like falling fruit around the schooner *Flight*.
But things must fall, and so it always was,
on one hand Venus, on the other Mars;
fall, and are one, just as this earth is one
island in archipelagoes of stars.
My first friend was the sea. Now, is my last.
I stop talking now. I work, then I read,
cotching under a lantern hooked to the mast.
I try to forget what happiness was,
and when that don't work, I study the stars.
Sometimes is just me, and the soft-scissored foam

as the deck turn white and the moon open
a cloud like a door, and the light over me
is a road in white moonlight taking me home.
Shabine sang to you from the depths of the sea.

GEOFFREY HILL

Genesis

I

Against the burly air I strode
Crying the miracles of God.

And first I brought the sea to bear
Upon the dead weight of the land;
And the waves flourished at my prayer,
The rivers spawned their sand.

And where the streams were salt and full
The tough pig-headed salmon strove,
Ramming the ebb, in the tide's pull,
To reach the steady hills above.

2

The second day I stood and saw
The osprey plunge with triggered claw,
Feathering blood along the shore,
To lay the living sinew bare.

And the third day I cried: "Beware
The soft-voiced owl, the ferret's smile,
The hawk's deliberate stoop in air,
Cold eyes, and bodies hooped in steel,
Forever bent upon the kill."

3

And I renounced, on the fourth day,
This fierce and unregenerate clay,
Building as a huge myth for man
The watery Leviathan,

And made the long-winged albatross
Scour the ashes of the sea
Where Capricorn and Zero cross,
A brooding immortality –
Such as the charmed phoenix has
In the unwithering tree.

4

The phoenix burns as cold as frost;
And, like a legendary ghost,
The phantom-bird goes wild and lost,
Upon a pointless ocean tossed.

So, the fifth day, I turned again
To flesh and blood and the blood's pain.

5

On the sixth day, as I rode
In haste about the works of God,
With spurs I plucked the horse's blood.

By blood we live, the hot, the cold,
To ravage and redeem the world:
There is no bloodless myth will hold.

And by Christ's blood are men made free
Though in close shrouds their bodies lie
Under the rough pelt of the sea;

Though Earth has rolled beneath her weight
The bones that cannot bear the light.

Ovid in the Third Reich

non peccat, quaecumque potest peccasse negare,
solaque famosam culpa professa facit.
                        (*Amores*, III, xiv)

I love my work and my children. God
Is distant, difficult. Things happen.
Too near the ancient troughs of blood
Innocence is no earthly weapon.

I have learned one thing: not to look down
So much upon the damned. They, in their sphere,
Harmonize strangely with the divine
Love. I, in mine, celebrate the love-choir.

September Song

born 19.6.32 – deported 24.9.42

Undesirable you may have been, untouchable
you were not. Not forgotten
or passed over at the proper time.

As estimated, you died. Things marched,
sufficient, to that end.
just so much Zyklon and leather, patented
terror, so many routine cries.

(I have made
an elegy for myself it
is true)

September fattens on vines. Roses
flake from the wall. The smoke
of harmless fires drifts to my eyes.

This is plenty. This is more than enough.

The Pentecost Castle

It is terrible to desire and not possess,
and terrible to possess and not desire.
                    W. B. Yeats

What we love in other human beings
is the hoped-for satisfaction of our desire.
We do not love their desire. If what we
loved in them was their desire, then
we should love them as ourself.
                    Simone Weil

1

They slew by night
upon the road
Medina's pride
Olmedo's flower

shadows warned him
not to go
not to go
along that road

weep for your lord
Medina's pride
Olmedo's flower
there in the road

2

Down in the orchard
I met my death
under the briar rose
I lie slain

I was going
to gather flowers
my love waited
among the trees

down in the orchard
I met my death
under the briar rose
I lie slain

3

You watchers on the wall
grown old with care
I too looked from the wall
I shall look no more

tell us what you saw
the lord I sought to serve
caught in the thorn grove
his blood on his brow

you keepers of the wall
what friend or enemy
sets free the cry
of the bell

4

At dawn the Mass
burgeons from stone
a Jesse tree
of resurrection

budding with candle
flames the gold
and the white wafers
of the feast

and ghosts for love
void a few tears
of wax upon
forlorn altars

5

Goldfinch and hawk
and the grey aspen tree
I have run to the river
mother call me home

the leaves glint in the wind
turning their quiet song
the wings flash and are still
I sleep in the shade

when I cried out you
made no reply
tonight I shall pass by
without a sound

6

Slowly my heron flies
pierced by the blade
mounting in slow pain
strikes the air with its cries

goes seeking the high rocks
where no man can climb
where the wild balsam stirs
by the little stream

the rocks the high rocks
are brimming with flowers
there love grows and there love
rests and is saved

7

I went out early
to the far field
ermine and lily
and yet a child

Love stood before me
in that place
prayers could not lure me
to Christ's house

Christ the deceiver
took all I had
his darkness ever
my fair reward

8

And you my spent heart's treasure
my yet unspent desire
measurer past all measure
cold paradox of fire

as seeker so forsaken
consentingly denied
your solitude a token
the sentries at your side

fulfilment to my sorrow
indulgence of your prey
the sparrowhawk the sparrow
the nothing that you say

9

This love will see me dead
he has the place in mind
where I am free to die
be true at last true love

my love meet me half-way
I bear no sword of fear
where you dwell I
dwell also says my lord

dealing his five wounds
so cunning and so true
of love to rouse this death
I die to sleep in love

10

St James and St John
bless the road she has gone
St John and St James
a rosary of names

child-beads of fingered bread
never-depleted heart's food
the nominal the real
subsistence past recall

bread we shall never break
love-runes we cannot speak
scrolled effigy of a cry
our passion its display

11

If the night is dark
and the way short
why do you hold back
dearest heart

though I may never
see you again
touch me I will shiver
at the unseen

the night is so dark
the way so short
why do you not break
o my heart

12

Married and not for love
you of all women
you of all women
my soul's darling my love

faithful to my desire
lost in the dream's grasp where
shall I find you everywhere
unmatched in my desire

each of us dispossessed
so richly in my sleep
I rise out of my sleep
crying like one possessed

13

Splendidly-shining darkness
proud citadel of meekness
likening us our unlikeness
majesty of our distress

emptiness ever thronging
untenable belonging
how long until this longing
end in unending song

and soul for soul discover
no strangeness to dissever
and lover keep with lover
a moment and for ever

14

As he is wounded
I am hurt
he bleeds from pride
I from my heart

as he is dying
I shall live
in grief desiring
still to grieve

as he is living
I shall die
sick of forgiving
such honesty

15

I shall go down
to the lovers' well
and wash this wound
that will not heal

beloved soul
what shall you see
nothing at all
yet eye to eye

depths of non-being
perhaps too clear
my desire dying
as I desire

Tenebrae

He was so tired that he was scarcely able to
hear a note of the songs: he felt imprisoned
in a cold region where his brain was numb
and his spirit was isolated.

I

Requite this angel whose
flushed and thirsting face
stoops to the sacrifice
out of which it arose.
This is the lord Eros
of grief who pities
no one; it is
Lazarus with his sores.

2

And you, who with your soft but searching voice
drew me out of the sleep where I was lost,
who held me near your heart that I might rest
confiding in the darkness of your choice:
possessed by you I chose to have no choice,
fulfilled in you I sought no further quest.
You keep me, now, in dread that quenches trust,
in desolation where my sins rejoice.
As I am passionate so you with pain
turn my desire; as you seem passionless
so I recoil from all that I would gain,
wounding myself upon forgetfulness,
false ecstasies, which you in truth sustain
as you sustain each item of your cross.

3

Veni Redemptor, but not in our time.
Christus Resurgens, quite out of this world.
"Ave" we cry; the echoes are returned.
Amor Carnalis is our dwelling-place.

4

O light of light, supreme delight;
grace on our lips to our disgrace.
Time roosts on all such golden wrists;
our leanness is our luxury.
Our love is what we love to have;
our faith is in our festivals.

5

Stupefying images of grief-in-dream,
succubae to my natural grief of heart,
cling to me, then; you who will not desert
your love nor lose him in some blank of time.
You come with all the licence of her name
to tell me you are mine. But you are not
and she is not. Can my own breath be hurt
by breathless shadows groaning in their game?
It can. The best societies of hell
acknowledge this, aroused by what they know:
consummate rage recaptured there in full
as faithfulness demands it, blow for blow,
and rectitude that mimics its own fall
reeling with sensual abstinence and woe.

6

This is the ash-pit of the lily-fire,
this is the questioning at the long tables,
this is true marriage of the self-in-self,
this is a raging solitude of desire,
this is the chorus of obscene consent,
this is a single voice of purest praise.

7

He wounds with ecstasy. All
the wounds are his own.
He wears the martyr's crown.
He is the Lord of Misrule.
He is the Master of the Leaping Figures,
the motley factions.
Revelling in auguries
he is the Weeper of the Valedictions.

8

Music survives, composing her own sphere,
Angel of Tones, Medusa, Queen of the Air,
and when we would accost her with real cries
silver on silver thrills itself to ice.

SYLVIA PLATH

Soliloquy of the Solipsist

I?
I walk alone;
The midnight street
Spins itself from under my feet;
When my eyes shut
These dreaming houses all snuff out;
Through a whim of mine
Over gables the moon's celestial onion
Hangs high.

I
Make houses shrink
And trees diminish
By going far; my look's leash

Dangles the puppet-people
Who, unaware how they dwindle,
Laugh, kiss, get drunk,
Nor guess that if I choose to blink
They die.

I
When in good humor,
Give grass its green
Blazon sky blue, and endow the sun
With gold;
Yet, in my wintriest moods, I hold
Absolute power
To boycott color and forbid any flower
To be.

I
Know you appear
Vivid at my side,
Denying you sprang out of my head,
Claiming you feel
Love fiery enough to prove flesh real,
Though it's quite clear
All your beauty, all your wit, is a gift, my dear,
From me.

The Manor Garden

The fountains are dry and the roses over.
Incense of death. Your day approaches.
The pears fatten like little buddhas.
A blue mist is dragging the lake.

You move through the era of fishes,
The smug centuries of the pig –
Head, toe and finger
Come clear of the shadow. History

Nourishes these broken flutings,
These crowns of acanthus,
And the crow settles her garments.
You inherit white heather, a bee's wing,

Two suicides, the family wolves,
Hours of blankness. Some hard stars
Already yellow the heavens.
The spider on its own string

Crosses the lake. The worms
Quit their usual habitations.
The small birds converge, converge
With their gifts to a difficult borning.

Morning Song

Love set you going like a fat gold watch.
The midwife slapped your footsoles, and your bald cry
Took its place among the elements.

Our voices echo, magnifying your arrival. New statue.
In a drafty museum, your nakedness
Shadows our safety. We stand round blankly as walls.

I'm no more your mother
Than the cloud that distills a mirror to reflect its own slow
Effacement at the wind's hand.

All night your moth-breath
Flickers among the flat pink roses. I wake to listen:
A far sea moves in my ear.

One cry, and I stumble from bed, cow-heavy and floral
In my Victorian nightgown.
Your mouth opens clean as a cat's. The window square

Whitens and swallows its dull stars. And now you try
Your handful of notes;
The clear vowels rise like balloons.

The Bee Meeting

Who are these people at the bridge to meet me? They are the
        villagers –
The rector, the midwife, the sexton, the agent for bees.
In my sleeveless summery dress I have no protection,

And they are all gloved and covered, why did nobody tell me?
They are smiling and taking out veils tacked to ancient hats.

I am nude as a chicken neck, does nobody love me?
Yes, here is the secretary of bees with her white shop smock,
Buttoning the cuffs at my wrists and the slit from my neck to my
    knees.
Now I am milkweed silk, the bees will not notice.
They will not smell my fear, my fear, my fear.

Which is the rector now, is it that man in black?
Which is the midwife, is that her blue coat?
Everybody is nodding a square black head, they are knights in
    visors,
Breastplates of cheesecloth knotted under the armpits.
Their smiles and their voices are changing. I am led through a
    beanfield.

Strips of tinfoil winking like people,
Feather dusters fanning their hands in a sea of bean flowers,
Creamy bean flowers with black eyes and leaves like bored hearts.
Is it blood clots the tendrils are dragging up that string?
No, no, it is scarlet flowers that will one day be edible.

Now they are giving me a fashionable white straw Italian hat
And a black veil that molds to my face, they are making me one of
    them.
They are leading me to the shorn grove, the circle of hives.
Is it the hawthorn that smells so sick?
The barren body of hawthorn, etherizing its children.

Is it some operation that is taking place?
It is the surgeon my neighbors are waiting for,
This apparition in a green helmet,
Shining gloves and white suit.
Is it the butcher, the grocer, the postman, someone I know?

I cannot run, I am rooted, and the gorse hurts me
With its yellow purses, its spiky armory.
I could not run without having to run forever.
The white hive is snug as a virgin,
Sealing off her brood cells, her honey, and quietly humming.

Smoke rolls and scarves in the grove.
The mind of the hive thinks this is the end of everything.
Here they come, the outriders, on their hysterical elastics.

If I stand very still, they will think I am cow-parsley,
A gullible head untouched by their animosity,

Not even nodding, a personage in a hedgerow.
The villagers open the chambers, they are hunting the queen.
Is she hiding, is she eating honey? She is very clever.
She is old, old, old, she must live another year, and she knows it.
While in their fingerjoint cells the new virgins

Dream of a duel they will win inevitably,
A curtain of wax dividing them from the bride flight,
The upflight of the murderess into a heaven that loves her.
The villagers are moving the virgins, there will be no killing.
The old queen does not show herself, is she so ungrateful?

I am exhausted, I am exhausted –
Pillar of white in a blackout of knives.
I am the magician's girl who does not flinch.
The villagers are untying their disguises, they are shaking hands.
Whose is that long white box in the grove, what have they
      accomplished, why am I cold.

Lady Lazarus

I have done it again.
One year in every ten
I manage it –

A sort of walking miracle, my skin
Bright as a Nazi lampshade,
My right foot

A paperweight,
My face a featureless, fine
Jew linen.

Peel off the napkin
O my enemy.
Do I terrify? –

The nose, the eye pits, the full set of teeth?
The sour breath
Will vanish in a day.

Soon, soon the flesh
The grave cave ate will be
At home on me

And I a smiling woman.
I am only thirty.
And like the cat I have nine times to die.

This is Number Three.
What a trash
To annihilate each decade.

What a million filaments.
The peanut-crunching crowd
Shoves in to see

Them unwrap me hand and foot –
The big strip tease.
Gentlemen, ladies

These are my hands
My knees.
I may be skin and bone,

Nevertheless, I am the same, identical woman.
The first time it happened I was ten.
It was an accident.

The second time I meant
To last it out and not come back at all.
I rocked shut

As a seashell.
They had to call and call
And pick the worms off me like sticky pearls.

Dying
Is an art, like everything else.
I do it exceptionally well.

I do it so it feels like hell.
I do it so it feels real.
I guess you could say I've a call.

It's easy enough to do it in a cell.
It's easy enough to do it and stay put.
It's the theatrical

Comeback in broad day
To the same place, the same face, the same brute
Amused shout:

"A miracle!"
That knocks me out.
There is a charge

For the eyeing of my scars, there is a charge
For the hearing of my heart –
It really goes.

And there is a charge, a very large charge
For a word or a touch
Or a bit of blood

Or a piece of my hair or my clothes.
So, so, Herr Doktor.
So, Herr Enemy.

I am your opus,
I am your valuable,
The pure gold baby

That melts to a shriek.
I turn and burn.
Do not think I underestimate your great concern.

Ash, ash –
You poke and stir.
Flesh, bone, there is nothing there –

A cake of soap,
A wedding ring,
A gold filling.

Herr God, Herr Lucifer
Beware
Beware.

Out of the ash
I rise with my red hair
And I eat men like air.

PETER SCUPHAM

The Nondescript

I am plural. My intents are manifold:
I see through many eyes. I am fabulous.

I assimilate the suffering of monkeys:
Tiger and musk-ox are at my disposal.

My ritual is to swallow a pale meat
Prepared by my ignorant left hand.

It is my child's play to untie a frog,
Humble further the worm and dogfish.

When I comb the slow pond,
I shake out a scurf of tarnished silver;

When I steer the long ship to the stones,
A brown sickness laps at the cliff's foot.

Shreds of fur cling to my metalled roads,
Old plasters seeping a little blood.

I dress and powder the wide fields:
They undergo my purgatorial fires.

Come with me. I will shake the sky
And watch the ripe birds tumble.

It requires many deaths to ease
The deep cancer in my marrowbones.

I have prepared a stone inheritance.
It flourishes beneath my fertile tears.

Birthday Triptych

I

Birth days: as of the spirit.
She cannot dissemble.
We break a fiery bread.

How should we navigate
The waves' coarse turmoil
Without appointed stars?

A luminary day, then.
Light of the first magnitude,
Confirm our chosen course.

Tides, in their slow recession,
Delay about your fingers
A light sweet freight of shells.

When fresh seas break,
May that beached miraculous wrack
Still hold its water lights.

On this your name day,
Under Janus, God of thresholds,
Past and future both become you.

2

The true gift claims us.
Look! The flowered paper
Spills and crinkles.

A drift of white tissue:
Snow wreaths in May
We missed last winter.

And the small sign disclosed
Says in a new voice:
I tell of love in the world

To steady and delight you.
A long draught fills our horn;
We cannot exhaust her.

We read a common language
Runed in each offered hand.
Here, riddles are their answers.

Eyes rehearse tender cues.
All images compose and celebrate
The selves we have become.

3

None can walk safely.
The roads are dark, unsigned,
The sky precariously blue.

We must endure
Flowers, the rain's refreshment,
Each beautiful absurdity:

Accept with clear laughter
The dissonance of white hair,
Pain at the source.

A tree shakes at your window
Her brilliance of leafwork,
Admiration heals us.

Our vulnerability preserves.
To counter such a strength
Time's tactics have no skill.

Love sustains. By this avowal
We cancel fear, whatever tremors
Approach us from the bowed horizon.

Pompeii: Plaster Casts

It seemed to Pliny, stationed at Misenum,
A trembling pine stood from the distant peak.
When Vulcan beat new armour out for Rome

The vines that healed the landscape told green lies,
Skeined cupids hooded their toy bacchanals
And sparkling Venus dimmed her tesserae.

Those who in tremor fled the glinting pall
By an Ovidian sleight-of-hand renew
The loves and foliage of the littoral;

But here, where ashen faces tell the tale,
Cold anchorites pressed from retaining cells
Still fend off skies that neither pass nor fall.

Under the cockled ruins and stubbed columns
Glass coffins sequestrate a finer dust;
A long girl bares her lips against your kisses.

Conspiring years blurred out her skeleton;
Earth took the contours of her cooling flesh,
Saving a few stained teeth, a cranial bone,

And to that last of gestures – "I must die",
Some dark enclosure kept a secret faith.
Annealed to shredded togas, sandal ties,

She and her fellows lie composed in fury,
Haunting the vault, their own substantial ghosts.
Air twists in pain, thickens to effigy.

The Beach

And Langland told how heaven could not keep love;
It overflowed that room, took flesh, became
Light as a linden-leaf, sharp as a needle.

Today, the stone pavilion throws a window
Into the morning, that great strength of silver
Shawled from the climbing sun, and on four children
Alive to rippled beach and rippled water
Swaying their metalled lights in amity.

Hands build an airy house of meetings, partings,
Over a confluence of the elements
Here, where there is neither sex nor name,
Only the skirmishes of dark and bright,
Clear surfaces replenished and exchanged.

Black dancing in a hall of spacious mirrors,
Far voices, and the hush of sea on sand
Light as a linden-leaf, sharp as a needle.

After Ovid, Tristia

Deeper the drifts now, rain and sun won't ease
This crabbed and crusty land a north wind scours,
Each snowfall hard upon another's heels
And summer elbowed from the frozen year –
These Arctic gales brew up a special fury,
Whipping the tall towers down, whirling our roofs off.
We shivering men, in pelts and galligaskins,
Put no more than a bold face to the world:
Each hair's an icicle, a shaken tinkle,
And blanching frost makes all beards venerable.
Our wine becomes its jar, stone-cold and sober
It stands its round; we break our drinks off piecemeal.
More news? How rivers lie in manacles,
And how we quarry water from the lake?
Our feet trudge in the wake of summer boats;
Our horses' hooves ring hard against each wave-crest.
Over new trackways bridging secret currents
The Russian oxen tug their simple carts.

The Key

Neither leaving, nor wishing that they were staying,
   They stood at the gate,
Cinnabars on the ragwort, the wind crossing
   Swords in the bents, the light
   Moving about.

There was nothing else much that needed doing,
   The key under the stone,
The stone under the grass, the grass blowing
   Under time gone,
   The fences down.

And already the rooms were changing, the ochre curtains
   Fading to blue,
The carpet figuring out a forgotten pattern,
   Leaves learning to grow
   As they used to.

Cows grazing their shadows, a clock ticking,
  A pause to share
The hour with anything else that needed saying.
  A note lay under the door
  To be read last year.

They stood there still, as if time, the grass tossing,
  The white stone,
The key to the blistered door that was always missing
  Could ask the two of them in,
  Or wish them gone.

Service

Hearing the organ stray,
Wambling slow time away
In sit and stand,
A candle-bracket cold to hand,

Watching the shadows pass
Under this burning-glass:
One bright eye
Of lapis lazuli

Over an old saint's head,
A running maze of lead.
Robes of blood,
And little understood

But the high lancet's blue
Which makes the whole tale true
And is definite,
Shifting its weight of light

As afternoon lies dying,
The trebles following,
Stone gone dim,
God down to his last hymn.

R. F. LANGLEY

Mariana

And, looking out, she might
have said, "We could have all
of this," and would have meant
the serious ivy
on the thirteen trunks, the
ochre field behind, soothed
passage of the cars, slight
pressure of the sparrow's
chirps – just what the old glass
gently tested, bending,
she would have meant, and not
a dream ascending.

And, looking in, she might
have seen the altering
cream of unemphatic
light across the bevel
of the ceiling's beam, and,
shaken by the flare of
quiet wings around the
room as martins hovered
at the guttering, she
might have soon settled for
these things, without the need
for certainties elsewhere.

So, "Please", she would have said.
"We could", she would have said,
and "Maybe", mildly. Then,
selling out, buying in,
the drawling light and the
quiet squall of martins'
wings again, again, she
might have soon discerned her
self, seeing them. Not things,
but seeing things. And with
such care, it would be like
being shown what was not there.

It was the old glass cooled
the colours and transposed
them in a different key. It
chastened most of what the
sparrow said, and made an
affilatura of
the tree. She would have known
the consolation that
it gave, and smiled to see
the unthought-of tricks she
needed, and the sort of
liar she was, or might soon be.

As things came in, and as
they spread and sprayed, she could
have tilted up her face
in the soft fuss they made,
encouraging the cheat
with shivering lashes,
tremulo, fermo, wide
or tight, intending
to confuse her sight until,
perhaps, she dared to make
a try – to find her own
cupid in her own eye.

To such a scene, amongst
such possibilities –
the downright, matter of
fact determination
of ivy on the trees,
wriggling queerly under
the examination
of the glass, the steady
sunlit room, fluttered by
each martin as it made
its pass – to all of this
she might have deftly given

a lash, until there were
sequins in the air and
surreptitious cupids
glancing everywhere. They
pricked their wings. Their arrows
spun away with thinnest
silver chirruping. They

were miraculous, picked
by her to be beyond
belief – believing them –
the lie she told to throw
the truth into relief.

Into the pure relief
of ordinary light.
But now she must have all
of this, compelled to see
by possibility
just what the glass finds real
enough to bend, jolted
by tilting shadows that
the martins send, seized by
the amorini, who,
being unreal, demand
her head for what they steal.

Jack's Pigeon

The coffee bowl called Part of Poland bursts
on the kitchen tiles like twenty thousand
souls. It means that much. By the betting shop,
Ophelia, the pigeon squab, thuds to
the gutter in convulsions, gaping for
forty thousand brothers. So much is such.
Jack leans on the wall. He says it's true or
not; decides that right on nine is time for
the blue bee to come to the senna bush,
what hope was ever for a bowl so round,
so complete, in an afternoon's best light,
and even where the pigeon went, after
she finished whispering goodnight. Meanwhile,
a screw or two of bloody paper towel
and one dead fledgling fallen from its nest
lie on Sweet Lady Street, and sharp white shards
of Arcopal, swept up with fluff and bits
of breadcrust, do for charitable prayers.
The bee came early. Must have done. It jumped
the gun. Jill and the children hadn't come.

How hard things are. Jack sips his vinegar
and sniffs the sour dregs in each bottle in
the skip. Some, as he dumps them, jump back with
a shout of "Crack!" He tests wrapping paper
and finds crocodiles. The bird stretched up its
head and nodded, opening its beak. It
tried to speak. I hope it's dead. Bystanders
glanced, then neatly changed the name of every
street. Once this was Heaven's Hill, but now the
clever devils nudge each other on the
pavement by the betting shop. Jill hurried
the children off their feet. Jack stood and shook.
He thought it clenched and maybe moved itself
an inch. No more. Not much. He couldn't bring
himself to touch. And then he too had gone.
He's just another one who saw, the man
who stopped outside the door, then shrugged, and checked
his scratchcard, and moved on. Nothing about
the yellow senna flowers when we get home.
No Jack. No bee. We leave it well alone.

Jack built himself a house to hide in and
take stock. This is his property in France.
First, in the middle of the table at
midday, the bowl. Firm, he would say, as rock.
The perfect circle on the solid block.
Second, somewhere, there is an empty sack.
Third, a particular angry dormouse,
in the corner of a broken shutter,
waiting a chance to run, before the owl
can get her. The kick of the hind legs of
his cat, left on the top step of a prance.
The bark of other peoples' dogs, far off,
appropriately. Or a stranger's cough.
His cows' white eyelashes. Flies settled at
the roots of tails. What is it never fails?
Jack finds them, the young couple dressed in black,
and, sitting at the front, they both look up.
Her thin brown wrist twists her half open hand
to indicate the whole show overhead.
Rotating fingernails are painted red.

Who is the quiet guard with his elbow
braced against the pillar, thinking his thoughts
close to the stone? He is hard to make out,

and easy for shadows to take away.
Half gone in *la nef lumineuse et rose*.
A scarlet cardinal, Jack rather hoped.
A tired cyclist in a vermilion
anorak. Could anyone ever know?
Sit down awhile. Jill reads the posy in
her ring and then she smiles. The farmer owns
old cockerels which peck dirt. But he is
standing where he feels the swallows' wings flirt
past him as they cut through the shed to reach
the sunlit yard, bringing a distant blue
into the comfortable gold. How much
can all this hold? To lie and eat. To kill
and worry. To toss and milk and kiss and
marry. To wake. To keep. To sow. Jack meets
me and we go to see what we must do.
The bird has turned round once, and now it's still.

There's no more to be done. No more be done.
And what there was, was what we didn't do.
It needed two of us to move as one,
to shake hands with a hand that's shaking, if
tint were to be tant, and breaking making.
Now, on the terrace, huddled in my chair,
we start to mend a bird that isn't there,
fanning out feathers that had never grown
with clever fingers that are not our own;
stroking the lilac into the dove grey,
hearing the croodle that she couldn't say.
Night wind gives a cool hoot in the neck of
Jack's beer bottle, open on the table.
Triggered by this, the dormouse shoots along
the sill, illuminated well enough
for us to see her safely drop down through
the wriggling of the walnut tree to find
some parings of the fruit we ate today,
set out on the white concrete, under the
full presentation of the Milky Way.

GILLIAN CLARKE

St Thomas's Day

It's the darkest morning of the year.
Day breaks in water runnels
In the yard: a flutter
Of light on a tiled roof;
The loosening of night's
Stonehold on tap and bolt.

Rain on my face wakes me
From recent sleep. I cross
The yard, shovel bumping
In the barrow, fingers
Stiff as hinges. Catrin
Brings bran and fresh hay.

A snort in the dark, a shove
For supremacy.
My hands are warmed
In the steam of his welcome.
Midwinter, only here
Do the fields still summer,
Thistlehead and flower
Powdered by hoof and tooth.

Les Grottes

I

Rouffignac

In the forest overhead
summer fruit is falling
like the beat of a drum.

Hold your breath and you hear
millennia of water
sculpting limestone.

The river runs in the heat
of the sun. We are walking
in its grave, imagine

a throat choking with water.
Vast cupolas
prove its turbulence.

I am not deceived
by the nursery frieze
of mammoth. The circus act

brings on the bison,
black and ochre
ponies on terra cotta.

The Vézère is a ghost,
its footprints everywhere.
Even the kitchen taps

run cloudy into the palms
of our hands, fill our mouths
with chalk.

2

Font de Gaume

Fourteen thousand years make little difference.
Some of us, finding smooth places in the rough
must carve there, using old water marks.
A stalactite for a horse's thigh, its eye
a fault, or where the river fingered a whorl
a vortex turned the doorways of the skull.
Sinews of calcite, muscles run and slack,
the belly droops, a boulder marbles bone.

The imagination's caverns cry for symbols,
shout to the hot sun in the present tense.
We walk again in the afternoon,
watch out for vipers lazy on their stones.
Two tractors are towing home the harvest.
Tobacco saps evaporate in rows.
The glittering Vézère is at its work,
its inexhaustible calligraphy.

Brother, grinding your colours by tallow light,
I hear your heart beat under my collarbone.

Border

It crumbles
where the land forgets its name
and I'm foreign in my own country.
Fallow, pasture, ploughland
ripped from the hill
beside a broken farm.

The word's exactness
slips from children's tongues.
Saints fade in the parishes.
Fields blur between the scar
of hedgerow and new road.
History forgets itself.

At the garage they're polite.
"Sorry love, no Welsh."
At the shop I am slapped
by her hard "What!"
They came for the beauty
but could not hear it speak.

Overheard in County Sligo

I married a man from County Roscommon
and I live in the back of beyond
with a field of cows and a yard of hens
and six white geese on the pond.

At my door's a square of yellow corn
caught up by its corners and shaken,
and the road runs down through the open gate
and freedom's there for the taking.

I had thought to work on the Abbey stage
or have my name in a book,
to see my thought on the printed page,
or still the crowd with a look.

But I turn to fold the breakfast cloth
and to polish the lustre and brass,
to order and dust the tumbled rooms
and find my face in the glass.

I ought to feel I'm a happy woman
for I lie in the lap of the land,
and I married a man from County Roscommon
and I live at the back of beyond.

Lament

For the green turtle with her pulsing burden,
in search of the breeding-ground.
For her eggs laid in their nest of sickness.

For the cormorant in his funeral silk,
the veil of iridescence on the sand,
the shadow on the sea.

For the ocean's lap with its mortal stain.
For Ahmed at the closed border.
For the soldier in his uniform of fire.

For the gunsmith and the armourer,
the boy fusilier who joined for the company,
the farmer's sons, in it for the music.

For the hook-beaked turtles,
the dugong and the dolphin,
the whale struck dumb by the missile's thunder.

For the tern, the gull and the restless wader,
the long migrations and the slow dying,
the veiled sun and the stink of anger.

For the burnt earth and the sun put out,
the scalded ocean and the blazing well.
For vengeance, and the ashes of language.

TONY HARRISON

Heredity

How you became a poet's a mystery!
Wherever did you get your talent from?
I say: I had two uncles, Joe and Harry —
one was a stammerer, the other dumb.

On Not being Milton

For Sergio Vieira and Armando Guebuza (Frelimo)

Read and committed to the flames, I call
these sixteen lines that go back to my roots
my *Cahier d'un retour au pays natal,*
my growing black enough to fit my boots.

The stutter of the scold out of the branks
of condescension, class and counter-class
thickens with glottals to a lumpen mass
of Ludding morphemes closing up their ranks.
Each swung cast-iron Enoch[1] of Leeds stress
clangs a forged music on the frames of Art,
the looms of owned language smashed apart!

Three cheers for mute ingloriousness!

Articulation is the tongue-tied's fighting.
In the silence round all poetry we quote
Tidd the Cato Street conspirator who wrote:

Sir, I Ham a very Bad Hand at Righting.

---

1. An "Enoch" is an iron sledge-hammer used by the Luddites to smash the
frames which were also made by the same Enoch Taylor of Marsden. The cry
was: "Enoch made them, Enoch shall break them!"

National Trust

Bottomless pits. There's one in Castleton,
and stout upholders of our law and order
one day thought its depth worth wagering on
and borrowed a convict hush-hush from his warder
and winched him down; and back, flayed, grey, mad, dumb.

Not even a good flogging made him holler!

O gentlemen, a better way to plumb
the depths of Britain's dangling a scholar,
say, here at the booming shaft at Towanroath,
now National Trust, a place where they got tin,
those gentlemen who silenced the men's oath
and killed the language that they swore it in.

The dumb go down in history and disappear
and not one gentleman's been brought to book:

Mes den hep lavas a-gollas y dyr

(Cornish) –
            "the tongueless man gets his land took."

Timer

Gold survives the fire that's hot enough
to make you ashes in a standard urn.
An envelope of coarse official buff
contains your wedding ring which wouldn't burn.

Dad told me I'd to tell them at St James's
that the ring should go in the incinerator.
That "eternity" inscribed with both their names is
his surety that they'd be together, "later".

I signed for the parcelled clothing as the son,
the cardy, apron, pants, bra, dress –

the clerk phoned down: *6–8–8–3–1?*
Has she still her ring on? (Slight pause) *Yes!*

It's on my warm palm now, your burnished ring!

I feel your ashes, head, arms, breasts, womb, legs,
sift through its circle slowly, like that thing
you used to let me watch to time the eggs.

Art & Extinction

*"When I hear of the destruction of a species I feel as if all
the works of some great writer had perished."*
Theodore Roosevelt, 1899

1 The Birds of America

(I) *John James Audubon (1785–1851)*

The struggle to preserve once spoken words
from already too well-stuffed taxonomies
is a bit like Audubon's when painting birds,
whose method an admirer said was this:
Kill 'em, wire 'em, paint 'em, kill a fresh 'un!

The plumage even of the brightest faded.
The artist had to shoot in quick succession
till all the feathers were correctly shaded.

Birds don't pose for pictures when alive!
Audubon's idea of restraint,
doing the Pelican, was 25
dead specimens a day for *one* in paint.

By using them do we save words or not?

As much as Audubon's art could save a,
say, godwit, or a grackle, which he shot
and then saw "multiplied by Havell's graver".

(II) *Weeki Wachee*

Duds doomed to join the dodo: the dugong,
talonless eagles, croc, gimp manatee,
here, courtesy Creation's generous strong,
the losers of thinned jungle and slicked sea.

Many's the proud chieftain used to strut
round shady clearings of dark festooned teak
with twenty cockatoo tails on his nut,
macaw plumes à la mode, rainforest chic.

Such gladrag gaudies safe in quarantine
and spared at least their former jungle fate
of being blowpiped for vain primitives to preen
now race a tightrope on one roller skate.

A tanned sophomore, these ghettoed birds' Svengali,
shows glad teeth, evolved for smiling, as macaws
perform their deft Darwinian finale
by hoisting the Stars and Stripes for our applause.

(III) *Standards*

in hopeful anticipation of the bicentenary of the national emblem of the
United States of America, *Haliaaetus falco leucocephalus,* 1782–1982.

*"The bald eagle is likewise a large, strong, and very active bird, but an execrable
tyrant: he supports his assumed dignity and grandeur by rapine and violence,
extorting unreasonable tribute and subsidy from the feathered nations."*
                                        William Bartram, *Travels,* 1791

"Our standard with the eagle stands for us.
It waves in the breeze in almost every clime."

(The flag, not *Falco leucocephalus*
poised in its dying on the brink of time!)

Rejecting Franklin's turkey for a bird that *flies*
Congress chose the soaring eagle, called,
for its conspicuous white head, "the bald".

Now the turkey's thriving and the eagle dies!

When the last stinks in its eyrie, or falls slow,
when the very last bald eagle goes the way
of all the unique fauna, it won't know
the Earth it plummets to 's the USA.

But will still wing over nations as the ghost
on money, and the mountainous US Post,

much as sunlight shining through the British pound
showed PEACE with her laurels, white on a green ground.

2 *Loving Memory*

For Teresa Stratas

The fosses where Caractacus fought Rome
blend with grey bracken and become a blur
above the Swedish Nightingale's last home.

Somehow my need for you makes me seek her.

The Malverns darken as the dusk soaks in.
The rowan berries' dark red glaze grows dull.
The harvest moon's scraped silver and bruised tin
is only one night off from being full.

Death keeps all hours, but graveyards close at nights.
I hurry past the Malvern Hospital
where a nurse goes round small wards and puts on lights
and someone there's last night begins to fall.

"The oldest rocks this earth can boast," these hills,
packed with extinction, make me burn for you.

I ask two women leaving with dead daffodils:
Where's Jenny Lind's grave, please? They both say: *Who?*

3 *Looking Up*

*For Philip, Terry and Will Sharpe and the bicentenary of the
birth of Peter Mark Roget (1779–1869)*

All day till it grows dark I sit and stare
over Herefordshire hills and into Wales.
Reflections of red coals thrown on the air
blossom to brightness as the daylight fails.

An uncharred cherry flaunts a May of flames.
Like chaffinches and robins tongues of fire
flit with the burden of Creation's names
but find no new apostles to inspire.

Bar a farm house TV aerial or two,
the odd red bus, the red Post Office van,
this must have been exactly Roget's view,
good Dr Roget, the *Thesaurus* man.

Roget died here, but 90 when he died
of natural causes, twice as old as me.

Of his six synonyms for suicide
I set myself alight with safe suttee.

4 *Killing Time*

Among death-protected creatures in a case,
'The Earth's Endangered Species' on display
at a jam-packed terminal at JFK,
killing time again, I see my face
with Hawksbill Turtle, scrimshawed spermwhale bone,
the Margay of the family *Felidae*,
that, being threatened, cost the earth to buy.

And now with scientists about to clone
the long-haired mammoth back from Soviet frost,
my reflection's on the species the World's lost,
or will be losing in a little while,
which, as they near extinction, grow in worth,
the leopard, here a bag and matching purse,
the dancing shoes that were Nile crocodile,

the last *Felis pardalis* left on Earth,

the poet preserved beneath deep permaverse.

5 *Dark Times*

That the *Peppered Moth* was white and now is dark 's
a lesson in survival for Mankind.

Around the time Charles Darwin had declined
the dedication of *Das Kapital* by Marx
its predators could spot it on the soot,
but Industrial Revolution and Evolution taught
the moth to black its wings and not get caught
where all of Nature perished, or all but.

When lichens lighten some old smoke-grimed trees
and such as Yorkshire's millstacks now don't burn
and fish nose waters stagnant centuries,
can *Biston carbonaria* relearn,

if Man's awakened consciousness succeeds
in turning all these tides of blackness back
and diminishing the need for looking black,

to flutter white again above new Leeds?

6 T' Ark

Silence and poetry have their own reserves.
The numbered creatures flourish less and less.
A language near extinction best preserves
the deepest grammar of our nothingness.

Not only dodo, oryx and great auk
waddled on their tod to t'monster ark,
but "leg", "night", "origin" in crushed people's talk,
tongues of fire last witnessed mouthing: *dark!*

Now when the future couldn't be much darker,
there being fewer epithets for sun,
and Cornish and the Togoland *Restsprache*
name both the animals and hunter's gun,
celebrate before things go too far
Papua's last reported manucode,
the pygmy hippo of the Côte d'Ivoire,
and Upper Guinea's oviparous toad –

(or mourn in Latin their imminent death,
then translate these poems into *cynghanedd*).

7 *The Birds of Japan*

Campi Phlegraei, Lake Nyos of Wum,
their sulphur could asphyxiate whole flocks
but combustibility had not yet come
to the femto-seconds of the *Fiat Nox*:
men made magma, flesh made fumaroles,
first mottled by the flash to brief mofettes
and Hiroshima's fast pressurizing souls
hissed through the fissures in mephitic jets.

Did the birds burst into song as they ignited
above billowing waves of cloud up in the sky,
hosannahs too short-lived to have alighted
on a Bomb-Age Bashō, or a Hokusai?

Apostles of that pinioned Pentecaust
of chirrupings cremated on the wing
will have to talk their ghosts down, or we're lost.
Until we know what they sang, who can sing?

8 *The Poetry Lesson*

Its proboscis probes the basking monster's eye.
The *Flambeau*, whose ambrosia's salt dew
and nectars sucked from caymans' *lacrimae*,
survives on saurian secretions in Peru.

The blue fritillary of north Brazil
I saw uncurl the watchspring of its tongue
and, by syphoning or licking, have its fill
of goodnesses discarded in man's dung.
The question mark (complete with added dot)
crapped on the pavement in full public view
by cane-hooch-smashed emaciate was steaming hot
but ambrosia not shit to browsing Blue.

Both lessons in survival for fine words
to look for fodder where they've not yet looked –
be lepidoptera that browse on turds
or delicately drain the monster's duct.

LES MURRAY

An Absolutely Ordinary Rainbow

The word goes round Repins,
the murmur goes round Lorenzinis.
At Tattersalls, men look up from sheets of numbers,
the Stock Exchange scribblers forget the chalk in their hands
and men with bread in their pockets leave the Greek Club:
There's a fellow crying in Martin Place. They can't stop him.

The traffic in George Street is banked up for half a mile
and drained of motion. The crowds are edgy with talk
and more crowds come hurrying. Many run in the back streets
which minutes ago were busy main streets, pointing:
There's a fellow weeping down there. No one can stop him.

The man we surround, the man no one approaches
simply weeps, and does not cover it, weeps
not like a child, not like the wind, like a man
and does not declaim it, nor beat his breast, nor even
sob very loudly – yet the dignity of his weeping

holds us back from his space, the hollow he makes about him
in the midday light, in his pentagram of sorrow,
and uniforms back in the crowd who tried to seize him
stare out at him, and feel, with amazement, their minds
longing for tears as children for a rainbow.

Some will say, in the years to come, a halo
or force stood around him. There is no such thing.
Some will say they were shocked and would have stopped
    him
but they will not have been there. The fiercest manhood,
the toughest reserve, the slickest wit amongst us

trembles with silence, and burns with unexpected
judgements of peace. Some in the concourse scream
who thought themselves happy. Only the smallest children
and such as look out of Paradise come near him
and sit at his feet, with dogs and dusty pigeons.

Ridiculous, says a man near me, and stops
his mouth with his hands, as if it uttered vomit –
and I see a woman, shining, stretch her hand
and shake as she receives the gift of weeping;
as many as follow her also receive it

and many weep for sheer acceptance, and more
refuse to weep for fear of all acceptance,
but the weeping man, like the earth, requires nothing,
the man who weeps ignores us, and cries out
of his writhen face and ordinary body

not words, but grief, not messages, but sorrow
hard as the earth, sheer, present as the sea –
and when he stops, he simply walks between us
mopping his face with the dignity of one
man who has wept, and now has finished weeping.

Evading believers, he hurries off down Pitt Street.

The Broad Bean Sermon

Beanstalks, in any breeze, are a slack church parade
without belief, saying *trespass against us* in unison,
recruits in mint Air Force dacron, with unbuttoned leaves.

Upright with water like men, square in stem-section
they grow to great lengths, drink rain, keel over all ways,
kink down and grow up afresh, with proffered new greenstuff.

Above the cat-and-mouse floor of a thin bean forest
snails hang rapt in their food, ants hurry through several dimensions:
spiders tense and sag like little black flags in their cordage.

Going out to pick beans with the sun high as fence-tops, you find
plenty, and fetch them. An hour or a cloud later
you find shirtfulls more. At every hour of daylight

appear more that you missed: ripe, knobbly ones, fleshy-sided,
thin-straight, thin-crescent, frown-shaped, bird-shouldered,
        boat-keeled ones,
beans knuckled and single-bulged, minute green dolphins at suck,

beans upright like lecturing, outstretched like blessing fingers
in the incident light, and more still, oblique to your notice
that the noon glare or cloud-light or afternoon slants will uncover

till you ask yourself Could I have overlooked so many, or
do they form in an hour? unfolding into reality
like templates for subtly broad grins, like unique caught expressions,

like edible meanings, each sealed around with a string
and affixed to its moment, an unceasing colloquial assembly,
the portly, the stiff, and those lolling in pointed green slippers . . .

Wondering who'll take the spare bagfulls, you grin with happiness
– it is your health – you vow to pick them all
even the last few, weeks off yet, misshapen as toes.

The Quality of Sprawl

Sprawl is the quality
of the man who cut down his Rolls Royce
into a farm utility truck, and sprawl
is what the company lacked when it made repeated efforts
to buy the vehicle back and repair its image.

Sprawl is doing your farming by aeroplane, roughly,
or driving a hitchhiker that extra hundred miles home.
It is the rococo of being your own still centre.
It is never lighting cigars with ten-dollar notes:
that's idiot ostentation and murder of starving people.
Nor can it be bought with the ash of million-dollar deeds.

Sprawl lengthens the legs; it trains greyhounds on liver and beer.
Sprawl almost never says Why not? with palms comically raised
nor can it be dressed for, not even in running shoes worn
with mink and a nose ring. That is Society. That's Style.
Sprawl is more like the thirteenth banana in a dozen
or anyway the fourteenth.

Sprawl is Hank Stamper in *Never Give an Inch*
bisecting an obstructive official's desk with a chain saw.
Not harming the official. Sprawl is never brutal
though it's often intransigent. Sprawl is never Simon de Montfort
at a town-storming: Kill them all! God will know his own.
Knowing the man's name this was said to might be sprawl.

Sprawl occurs in art. The fifteenth to twenty-first
lines in a sonnet, for example. And in certain paintings;
I have sprawl enough to have forgotten which paintings.
Turner's glorious *Burning of the Houses of Parliament*
comes to mind, a doubling bannered triumph of sprawl –
except, he didn't fire them.

Sprawl gets up the nose of many kinds of people
(every kind that comes in kinds) whose futures don't include it.
Some decry it as criminal presumption, silken-robed Pope
    Alexander
dividing the new world between Spain and Portugal.
If he smiled *in petto* afterwards, perhaps the thing did have sprawl.

Sprawl is really classless, though. It's John Christopher Frederick
    Murray
asleep in his neighbours' best bed in spurs and oilskins
but not having thrown up:
sprawl is never Calum who, in the loud hallway of our house,
reinvented the Festoon. Rather
it's Beatrice Miles going twelve hundred ditto in a taxi,
No Lewd Advances, No Hitting Animals, No Speeding,
on the proceeds of her two-bob-a-sonnet Shakespeare readings.
An image of my country. And would that it were more so.

No, sprawl is full-gloss murals on a council-house wall.
Sprawl leans on things. It is loose-limbed in its mind.
Reprimanded and dismissed
it listens with a grin and one boot up on the rail
of possibility. It may have to leave the Earth.
Being roughly Christian, it scratches the other cheek
and thinks it unlikely. Though people have been shot for sprawl.

Satis Passio

Elites, levels, proletariat:
the uniting cloth crowns
of Upper and Lower Egypt
suggest theories of poetry
which kindness would accept
to bestow, like Heaven, dignity
on the inept and the ept,
one Papuan warrior's phallocrypt
the soaring equal of its fellowcrypt.

By these measures, most knowledge
in our heads is poetry,
varied crystals of detail, chosen
by dream-interest, and poured spirally
from version to myth, with spillage,
from theory to history
and, with toppings-up, to story,
not metered, lined or free
but condensed by memory
to roughly vivid essences:
most people's poetry is now this.
Some of it is made by poets.

God bless the feral poetries,
littératures and sensibilities,
theory, wonder, the human gamut
leaping cheerfully or in heavy earnest
– but there is this quality to art
which starts, rather than ends, at the gist.
Not the angle, but the angel.

Art is what can't be summarised:
it has joined creation from our side,
entered Nature, become a fact
and acquired presence,
more like ourselves or any subject
swirled around, about, in and out,
than like the swirling poetries.

Art's best is a standing miracle
at an uncrossable slight distance,
an anomaly, finite but inexhaustible,
unaltered after analysis
as an ancient face.

Not the portrait of one gone
merely, no pathos of the bygone
but a section, of all that exist,
a passage, a whole pattern
that has shifted the immeasurable
first step into Heaven.
A first approximation.
Where is heaven? Down these roads.

The fine movement of art's face
before us is a motionless traffic
between here and remote Heaven.
It is out through this surface,
we may call it the Unfalling Arrow,
this third mode, and perhaps by art first
that there came to us the dream-plan
of equality and justice,
long delayed by the poetries –

but who was the more numinous,
Pharaoh or the hunted Nile heron?
more splendid, the iris or Solomon?
Beauty lives easily with equities
more terrible than theory dares mean.

Of the workers set free to break stone
and the new-cracked stone, which is more luminous?

God bless the general poetries?
This is how it's done.

It Allows a Portrait in Line Scan at Fifteen

He retains a slight "Martian" accent, from the years of single phrases.
He no longer hugs to disarm. It is gradually allowing him affection.
It does not allow proportion. Distress is absolute, shrieking, and runs
    him at frantic speed through crashing doors.
He likes cyborgs. Their taciturn power, with his intonation.
It still runs him around the house, alone in the dark, cooing and
    laughing.
He can read about soils, populations and New Zealand. On neutral
    topics he's illiterate.
Arnie Schwarzenegger is an actor. He isn't a cyborg really, is he, Dad?
He lives on forty acres, with animals and trees, and used to draw it
    continually.
He knows the map of Earth's fertile soils, and can draw it freehand.
He can only lie in a panicked shout *SorrySorryIdidn'tdoit!* warding off
    conflict with others and himself.
When he ran away constantly it was to the greengrocers to worship
    stacked fruit.
His favourite country was the Ukraine: it is nearly all deep fertile soil.
Giggling, he climbed all over the dim Freudian psychiatrist who told
    us how autism resulted from "refrigerator" parents.
When asked to smile, he photographs a rictus-smile on his face.
It long forbade all naturalistic films. They were Adult movies.
If they (that is, he) *are bad the police will put them in hospital.*
He sometimes drew the farm amid Chinese or Balinese rice terraces.
When a runaway, he made uproar in the police station, playing at
    three times adult speed.
Only animated films were proper. *Who Framed Roger Rabbit* then
    authorised the rest.
Phrases spoken to him he would take as teaching, and repeat,
When he worshipped fruit, he screamed as if poisoned when it was fed
    to him.
A one-word first conversation: *Blane. —Yes! Plane, that's right, baby! —*
    Blane.
He has forgotten nothing, and remembers the precise quality of
    experiences.
It requires rulings: *Is stealing very playing up, as bad as murder?*

He counts at a glance, not looking. And he has never been lost.
When he ate only nuts and dried fruit, words were for dire
    emergencies.
He knows all the breeds of fowls, and the counties of Ireland.
He'd begun to talk, then returned to babble, then silence. It withdrew
    speech for years.
Is that very autistic, to play video games in the day?
He is anger's mirror, and magnifies any near him, raging it down.
It still won't allow him fresh fruit, or orange juice with bits in it.
He swam in the midwinter dam at night. It had no rules about cold.
He was terrified of thunder and finally cried as if in explanation
    It – angry!
He grilled an egg he'd broken into bread. Exchanges of soil-knowledge
    are called landtalking.
He lives in objectivity. I was sure Bell's palsy would leave my face only
    when he said it had begun to.
Don't say word! when he was eight forbade the word "autistic" in his
    presence.
Bantering questions about girlfriends cause a terrified look and blocked
    ears.
He sometimes centred the farm in a furrowed American midwest.
Eye contact, Mum! means he truly wants attention. It dislikes I–contact.
He is equitable and kind, and only ever a little jealous. It was a relief
    when that little arrived.
He surfs, bowls, walks for miles. For many years he hasn't trailed his left
    arm while running.
I gotta get smart! looking terrified into the years. *I gotta get smart!*

Burning Want

From just on puberty, I lived in funeral:
mother dead of miscarriage, father trying to be dead,
we'd boil sweat-brown cloth; cows repossessed the garden.
Lovemaking brought death, was the unuttered principle.

I met a tall adopted girl some kids thought aloof,
but she was intelligent. Her poise of white-blonde hair
proved her no kin to the squat tanned couple who loved her.
Only now do I realise she was my first love.

But all my names were fat-names, at my new town school.
Between classes, kids did erocide: destruction of sexual morale.
Mass refusal of unasked love; that works. Boys cheered as seventeen-
year-old girls came on to me, then ran back whinnying ridicule.

The slender girl came up on holidays from the city
to my cousins' farm. She was friendly and sane.
Whispers giggled round us. A letter was written as from me
and she was there, in mid-term, instantly.

But I called people "the humans" not knowing it was rage.
I learned things sidelong, taking my rifle for walks,
recited every scene of *From Here to Eternity*, burned paddocks
and soldiered back each Monday to that dawning Teen age.

She I admired, and almost relaxed from placating,
was gnawed by knowing what she came from, not who.
Showing off was my one social skill, oddly never with her
but I dissembled feelings, till mine were unknown to me too

and I couldn't add my want to her shortfall of wantedness.
I had forty more years, with one dear remission,
of a white paralysis: she's attracted it's not real nothing is enough
she's mistaken she'll die go now! she'll tell any minute she'll laugh –

Whether other hands reached out to Marion, or didn't,
at nineteen in her training ward she had a fatal accident
alone, at night, they said, with a lethal injection
and was spared from seeing what my school did to the world.

The Last Hellos

Don't die, Dad –
but they die.

This last year he was wandery:
took off a new chainsaw blade
and cobbled a spare from bits.
Perhaps if I lay down
my head'll come better again.
His left shoulder kept rising
higher in his cardigan.

He could see death in a face.
Family used to call him in
to look at sick ones and say.
At his own time, he was told.

The knob found in his head
was duck-egg size. Never hurt.
Two to six months, Cecil.

I'll be right, he boomed
to his poor sister on the phone
I'll do that when I finish dyin.

                    *

Don't die, Cecil.
But they do.

Going for last drives
in the bush, odd massive
board-slotted stumps bony white
in whipstick second growth.
I could chop all day.

*I could always cash
a cheque, in Sydney or anywhere.
Any of the shops.*

Eating, still at the head
of the table, he now missed
food on his knife's side.

*Sorry, Dad, but like
have you forgiven your enemies?
Your father and all of them?*
All his lifetime of hurt.

I must have (grin). *I don't
think about that now.*

                    *

People can't say goodbye
any more. They say last hellos.

Going fast, over Christmas,
he'd still stumble out
of his room, where his photos
hang over the other furniture,
and play host to his mourners.

The courage of his bluster,
firm big voice of his confusion.

Two last days in the hospital:
his long forearms were still
red mahogany. His hands
gripped steel frame. *I'm dyin.*

On the second day:
You're bustin to talk
but I'm too busy dyin.

*

Grief ended when he died,
the widower like soldiers who
won't live life their mates missed.

Good boy Cecil! No more Bluey dog.
No more cowtime. No more stories.
We're still using your imagination,
it was stronger than all ours.

Your grave's got littler
somehow, in the three months.
More pointy as the clay's shrivelled,
like a stuck zip in a coat.

Your cricket boots are in
the State museum! Odd letters
still come. Two more's died since you:
Annie, and Stewart. Old Stewart.

On your day there was a good crowd,
family, and people from away.
But of course a lot had gone
to their own funerals first.

Snobs mind us off religion
nowdays, if they can.
Fuck thém. I wish you God.

SEAMUS HEANEY

The Peninsula

When you have nothing more to say, just drive
For a day all round the peninsula.
The sky is tall as over a runway,
The land without marks so you will not arrive

But pass through, though always skirting landfall.
At dusk, horizons drink down sea and hill,
The ploughed field swallows the whitewashed gable
And you're in the dark again. Now recall

The glazed foreshore and silhouetted log,
That rock where breakers shredded into rags,
The leggy birds stilted on their own legs,
Islands riding themselves out into the fog

And drive back home, still with nothing to say
Except that now you will uncode all landscapes
By this: things founded clean on their own shapes,
Water and ground in their extremity.

Anahorish

My "place of clear water",
the first hill in the world
where springs washed into
the shiny grass

and darkened cobbles
in the bed of the lane.
Anahorish, soft gradient
of consonant, vowel-meadow,

after-image of lamps
swung through the yards
on winter evenings.
With pails and barrows

those mound-dwellers
go waist-deep in mist
to break the light ice
at wells and dunghills.

Westering

In California

I sit under Rand McNally's
"Official Map of the Moon" –
The colour of frogskin,
Its enlarged pores held

Open and one called
"Pitiscus" at eye level –
Recalling the last night
In Donegal, my shadow

Neat upon the whitewash
From her bony shine,
The cobbles of the yard
Lit pale as eggs.

Summer had been a free fall
Ending there,
The empty amphitheatre
Of the west. Good Friday

We had started out
Past shopblinds drawn on the afternoon,
Cars stilled outside still churches,
Bikes tilting to a wall;

We drove by,
A dwindling interruption,
As clappers smacked
On a bare altar

And congregations bent
To the studded crucifix.
What nails dropped out that hour?
Roads unreeled, unreeled

Falling light as casts
Laid down
On shining waters.
Under the moon's stigmata

Six thousand miles away,
I imagine untroubled dust,
A loosening gravity,
Christ weighing by his hands.

Mossbawn: Two Poems in Dedication

For Mary Heaney

1 Sunlight

There was a sunlit absence.
The helmeted pump in the yard
heated its iron,
water honeyed

in the slung bucket
and the sun stood
like a griddle cooling
against the wall

of each long afternoon.
So, her hands scuffled
over the bakeboard,
the reddening stove

sent its plaque of heat
against her where she stood
in a floury apron
by the window.

Now she dusts the board
with a goose's wing,
now sits, broad-lapped,
with whitened nails

and measling shins:
here is a space
again, the scone rising
to the tick of two clocks.

And here is love
like a tinsmith's scoop
sunk past its gleam
in the meal-bin.

2 *The Seed Cutters*

They seem hundreds of years away. Breughel,
You'll know them if I can get them true.
They kneel under the hedge in a half-circle
Behind a windbreak wind is breaking through.
They are the seed cutters. The tuck and frill
Of leaf-sprout is on the seed potatoes
Buried under that straw. With time to kill,
They are taking their time. Each sharp knife goes
Lazily halving each root that falls apart
In the palm of the hand: a milky gleam,
And, at the centre, a dark watermark.
O calendar customs! Under the broom
Yellowing over them, compose the frieze
With all of us there, our anonymities.

The Guttural Muse

Late summer, and at midnight
I smelt the heat of the day:
At my window over the hotel car park
I breathed the muddied night airs off the lake
And watched a young crowd leave the discothèque.

Their voices rose up thick and comforting
As oily bubbles the feeding tench sent up
That evening at dusk – the slimy tench
Once called the "doctor fish" because his slime
Was said to heal the wounds of fish that touched it.

A girl in a white dress
Was being courted out among the cars:
As her voice swarmed and puddled into laughs
I felt like some old pike all badged with sores
Wanting to swim in touch with soft-mouthed life.

The Harvest Bow

As you plaited the harvest bow
You implicated the mellowed silence in you
In wheat that does not rust
But brightens as it tightens twist by twist
Into a knowable corona,
A throwaway love-knot of straw.

Hands that aged round ashplants and cane sticks
And lapped the spurs on a lifetime of game cocks
Harked to their gift and worked with fine intent
Until your fingers moved somnambulant:
I tell and finger it like braille,
Gleaning the unsaid off the palpable.

And if I spy into its golden loops
I see us walk between the railway slopes
Into an evening of long grass and midges,
Blue smoke straight up, old beds and ploughs in hedges,
An auction notice on an outhouse wall –
You with a harvest bow in your lapel,

Me with the fishing rod, already homesick
For the big lift of these evenings, as your stick
Whacking the tips off weeds and bushes
Beats out of time, and beats, but flushes
Nothing: that original townland
Still tongue-tied in the straw tied by your hand.

The end of art is peace
Could be the motto of this frail device
That I have pinned up on our deal dresser –
Like a drawn snare
Slipped lately by the spirit of the corn
Yet burnished by its passage, and still warm.

The Haw Lantern

The wintry haw is burning out of season,
crab of the thorn, a small light for small people,
wanting no more from them but that they keep
the wick of self-respect from dying out,
not having to blind them with illumination.

But sometimes when your breath plumes in the frost
it takes the roaming shape of Diogenes
with his lantern, seeking one just man;
so you end up scrutinized from behind the haw
he holds up at eye-level on its twig,
and you flinch before its bonded pith and stone,
its blood-prick that you wish would test and clear you,
its pecked-at ripeness that scans you, then moves on.

Seeing Things

I

Inishbofin on a Sunday morning.
Sunlight, turfsmoke, seagulls, boatslip, diesel.
One by one we were being handed down
Into a boat that dipped and shilly-shallied
Scaresomely every time. We sat tight
On short cross-benches, in nervous twos and threes,
Obedient, newly close, nobody speaking
Except the boatmen, as the gunwales sank
And seemed they might ship water any minute.
The sea was very calm but even so,
When the engine kicked and our ferryman
Swayed for balance, reaching for the tiller,
I panicked at the shiftiness and heft
Of the craft itself. What guaranteed us –
That quick response and buoyancy and swim –
Kept me in agony. All the time
As we went sailing evenly across
The deep, still, seeable-down-into water,
It was as if I looked from another boat
Sailing through air, far up, and could see
How riskily we fared into the morning,
And loved in vain our bare, bowed, numbered heads.

2

Claritas. The dry-eyed Latin word
Is perfect for the carved stone of the water
Where Jesus stands up to his unwet knees
And John the Baptist pours out more water
Over his head: all this in bright sunlight
On the façade of a cathedral. Lines
Hard and thin and sinuous represent

The flowing river. Down between the lines
Little antic fish are all go. Nothing else.
And yet in that utter visibility
The stone's alive with what's invisible:
Waterweed, stirred sand-grains hurrying off,
The shadowy, unshadowed stream itself.
All afternoon, heat wavered on the steps
And the air we stood up to our eyes in wavered
Like the zig-zag hieroglyph for life itself.

ROBERT PINSKY

Braveries

Once, while a famous town lay torn and burning
A woman came to childbed, and lay in labor
While all around her people cursed and screamed
In desperation, and soldiers raged insanely –
So that the child came out, the story says,
In the loud center of every horror of war.
And looking on that scene, just halfway out,
The child retreated backward, to the womb:
And chose to make those quiet walls its urn.

"*Brave infant of Saguntum,*" a poet says –
As though to embrace a limit might show courage.
(Although the word is more like *bravo*, the glory,
Of a great tenor, the swagger of new clothes:
The infant as a brilliant moral performer
Defying in its retreat the bounds of life.)

Denial of limit has been the pride, or failing,
Well-known to be shared by all this country's regions,
Races, and classes; which all seem to challenge
The idea of sufficiency itself . . .
And while it seems that in the name of limit
Some people are choosing to have fewer children,
Or none, that too can be a gesture of freedom –
A way to deny or brave the bounds of time.

A boundary is a limit. How can I
Describe for you the boundaries of this place
Where we were born: where Possibility spreads

And multiplies and exhausts itself in growing,
And opens yawning to swallow itself again?
What pictures are there for that limitless grace
Unrealized, those horizons ever dissolving?

A field house built of corrugated metal,
The frosted windows tilted open inward
In two lines high along the metal walls;
Inside, a horse-ring and a horse called Yankee
Jogging around the ring with clouds of dust
Rising and settling in the still, cold air
Behind the horse and rider as they course
Rhythmically through the bars of washed-out light
That fall in dim arcades all down the building.

The rider, a girl of seven or eight called Rose,
Concentrates firmly on her art, her body,
Her small, straight back and shoulders as they rise
Together with the alternate, gray shoulders
Of the unweary horse. Her father stands
And watches, in a business suit and coat,
Watching the child's face under the black serge helmet,
Her yellow hair that bounces at her nape
And part-way down her back. He feels the cold
Of the dry, sunless earth up through the soles
Of his thin, inappropriate dress shoes.

He feels the limit of that simple cold,
And braves it, concentrating on the progress
Of the child riding in circles around the ring.
She is so charming that he feels less mortal.
As from the bravery of a fancy suit,
He takes crude courage from the ancient meaning
Of the horse, as from a big car or a business:
He feels as if the world had fewer limits.
The primitive symbols of the horse and girl
Seem goods profound and infinite, as clear
As why the stuffs of merchants are called, "goods".

The goods of all the world seem possible
And clear in that brave spectacle, the rise
Up from the earth and onto the property
Of horses and the history of riding.

In his vague yearning, as he muses on goods
Lost and confused as chivalry, he might
Dream anything: as from the Cavalier
One might dream up the Rodeo, or the Ford,
Or some new thing the country waited for –
Some property, some consuming peasant dream
Of horses and walls; as though the Rodeo
And Ford were elegiac gestures: as though
Invented things gave birth to long-lost goods.

The country, boasting that it cannot see
The past, waits dreaming ever of the past,
Or all the plural pasts: the way a fetus
Dreams vaguely of heaven – waiting, and in its courage
Willing, not only to be born out into
The Actual (with its ambiguous goods),
But to retreat again and be born backward
Into the gallant walls of its potential,
Its sheltered circle . . . willing to leave behind,
It might be, carnage.
                        What shall we keep open –
Where shall we throw our courage, where retreat?

White settlers disembarked here, to embark
Upon a mountain-top of huge potential –
Which for the disembarking slaves was low:
A swamp, or valley of dry bones, where they lay
In labor with a brilliant, strange slave-culture –
All emigrants, ever disembarking. *Shall these
Bones live?* And in a jangle of confusion
And hunger, from the mountains to the valleys,
They rise; and breathe; and fall in the wind again.

Shirt

The back, the yoke, the yardage. Lapped seams,
The nearly invisible stitches along the collar
Turned in a sweatshop by Koreans or Malaysians

Gossiping over tea and noodles on their break
Or talking money or politics while one fitted
This armpiece with its overseam to the band

Of cuff I button at my wrist. The presser, the cutter,
The wringer, the mangle. The needle, the union,
The treadle, the bobbin. The code. The infamous blaze

At the Triangle Factory in nineteen-eleven.
One hundred and forty-six died in the flames
On the ninth floor, no hydrants, no fire escapes –

The witness in a building across the street
Who watched how a young man helped a girl to step
up to the windowsill, then held her out

Away from the masonry wall and let her drop.
And then another. As if he were helping them up
To enter a streetcar, and not eternity.

A third before he dropped her put her arms
Around his neck and kissed him, Then he held
Her into space, and dropped her. Almost at once

He stepped to the sill himself, his jacket flared
And fluttered up from his shirt as he came down,
Air filling up the legs of his gray trousers –

Like Hart Crane's Bedlamite, "shrill shirt ballooning".
Wonderful how the pattern matches perfectly
Across the placket and over the twin bar-tacked

Corners of both pockets, like a strict rhyme
Or a major chord. Prints, plaids, checks,
Houndstooth, Tattersall, Madras. The clan tartans

Invented by mill-owners inspired by the hoax of Ossian,
To control their savage Scottish workers, tamed
By a fabricated heraldry: MacGregor,

Bailey, MacMartin. The kilt, devised for workers
To wear among the dusty clattering looms.
Weavers, carders, spinners. The loader,

The docker, the navvy. The planter, the picker, the sorter
Sweating at her machine in a litter of cotton
As slaves in calico headrags sweated in fields:

George Herbert, your descendant is a Black
Lady in South Carolina, her name is Irma
And she inspected my shirt. Its color and fit

And feel and its clean smell have satisfied
Both her and me. We have culled its cost and quality
Down to the buttons of simulated bone,

The buttonholes, the sizing, the facing, the characters
Printed in black on neckband and tail. The shape,
The label, the labor, the color, the shade. The shirt.

From the Childhood of Jesus

One Saturday morning he went to the river to play.
He modeled twelve sparrows out of the river clay

And scooped a clear pond, with a dam of twigs and mud.
Around the pond he set the birds he had made,

Evenly as the hours. Jesus was five. He smiled,
As a child would who had made a little world

Of clear still water and clay beside a river.
But a certain Jew came by, a friend of his father,

And he scolded the child and ran at once to Joseph,
Saying, "Come see how your child has profaned the Sabbath,

Making images at the river on the Day of Rest."
So Joseph came to the place and took his wrist

And told him, "Child, you have offended the Word."
Then Jesus freed the hand that Joseph held

And clapped his hands and shouted to the birds
To go away. They raised their beaks at his words

And breathed and stirred their feathers and flew away.
The people were frightened. Meanwhile, another boy,

The son of Annas the scribe, had idly taken
A branch of driftwood and leaning against it had broken

The dam and muddied the little pond and scattered
The twigs and stones. Then Jesus was angry and shouted,

"Unrighteous, impious, ignorant, what did the water
Do to harm you? Now you are going to wither

The way a tree does, you shall bear no fruit
And no leaves, you shall wither down to the root."

At once, the boy was all withered. His parents moaned,
The Jews gasped, Jesus began to leave, then turned

And prophesied, his child's face wet with tears:
"Twelve times twelve times twelve thousands of years

Before these heavens and this earth were made,
The Creator set a jewel in the throne of God

With Hell on the left and Heaven to the right,
The Sanctuary in front, and behind, an endless night

Endlessly fleeing a Torah written in flame.
And on that jewel in the throne, God wrote my name."

Then Jesus left and went into Joseph's house.
The family of the withered one also left the place,

Carrying him home. The Sabbath was nearly over.
By dusk, the Jews were all gone from the river.

Small creatures came from the undergrowth to drink
And foraged in the shadows along the bank.

Alone in his cot in Joseph's house, the Son
Of Man was crying himself to sleep. The moon

Rose higher, the Jews put out their lights and slept,
And all was calm and as it had been, except

In the agitated household of the scribe Annas,
And high in the dark, where unknown even to Jesus

The twelve new sparrows flew aimlessly through the night,
Not blinking or resting, as if never to alight.

DEREK MAHON

Consolations of Philosophy

(for Eugene Lambe)

When we start breaking up in the wet darkness
And the rotten boards fall from us, and the ribs
Crack under the constriction of tree-roots
And the seasons slip from the fields unknown to us,

Oh, then there will be the querulous complaining
From citizens who had never dreamt of this –
Who, shaken to the bone in their stout boxes
By the latest bright cars, will not inspect them

And, kept awake by the tremors of new building,
Will not be there to comment. When the broken
Wreath bowls are speckled with rain-water
And the grass grows wild for want of a caretaker,

There will be time to live through in the mind
The lives we might have lived, and get them right;
To lie in silence listening to the wind
Mourn for the living through the livelong night.

The Snow Party

(for Louis Asekoff)

Bashō, coming
To the city of Nagoya,
Is asked to a snow party.

There is a tinkling of china
And tea into china;
There are introductions.

Then everyone
Crowds to the window
To watch the falling snow.

Snow is falling on Nagoya
And farther south
On the tiles of Kyōto.

Eastward, beyond Irago,
It is falling
Like leaves on the cold sea.

Elsewhere they are burning
Witches and heretics
In the boiling squares,

Thousands have died since dawn
In the service
Of barbarous kings;

But there is silence
In the houses of Nagoya
And the hills of Ise.

A Disused Shed in Co. Wexford

Let them not forget us, the weak souls among the asphodels.
  – Seferis, *Mythistorema*, tr. Keeley and Sherrard

(for J. G. Farrell)

Even now there are places where a thought might grow –
Peruvian mines, worked out and abandoned
To a slow clock of condensation,
An echo trapped for ever, and a flutter
Of wild-flowers in the lift-shaft,
Indian compounds where the wind dances
And a door bangs with diminished confidence,
Lime crevices behind rippling rain-barrels,
Dog corners for bone burials;
And in a disused shed in Co. Wexford,

Deep in the grounds of a burnt-out hotel,
Among the bathtubs and the washbasins
A thousand mushrooms crowd to a keyhole.
This is the one star in their firmament
Or frames a star within a star.
What should they do there but desire?
So many days beyond the rhododendrons
With the world waltzing in its bowl of cloud,
They have learnt patience and silence
Listening to the rooks querulous in the high wood.

They have been waiting for us in a foetor
Of vegetable sweat since civil war days,
Since the gravel-crunching, interminable departure
Of the expropriated mycologist.
He never came back, and light since then
Is a keyhole rusting gently after rain.
Spiders have spun, flies dusted to mildew
And once a day, perhaps, they have heard something –
A trickle of masonry, a shout from the blue
Or a lorry changing gear at the end of the lane.

There have been deaths, the pale flesh flaking
Into the earth that nourished it;
And nightmares, born of these and the grim
Dominion of stale air and rank moisture.
Those nearest the door grow strong –
"Elbow room! Elbow room!"
The rest, dim in a twilight of crumbling
Utensils and broken pitchers, groaning
For their deliverance, have been so long
Expectant that there is left only the posture.

A half century, without visitors, in the dark –
Poor preparation for the cracking lock
And creak of hinges. Magi, moonmen,
Powdery prisoners of the old regime,
Web-throated, stalked like triffids, racked by drought
And insomnia, only the ghost of a scream
At the flash-bulb firing-squad we wake them with
Shows there is life yet in their feverish forms.
Grown beyond nature now, soft food for worms,
They lift frail heads in gravity and good faith.

They are begging us, you see, in their wordless way,
To do something, to speak on their behalf
Or at least not to close the door again.
Lost people of Treblinka and Pompeii!
"Save us, save us," they seem to say,
"Let the god not abandon us
Who have come so far in darkness and in pain.
We too had our lives to live.
You with your light meter and relaxed itinerary,
Let not our naive labours have been in vain!"

Going Home

Pure, bracing ventilation they must have up there at all times, indeed:
one may guess the power of the north wind . . . by a range of gaunt
thorns all stretching their limbs one way, as if craving alms of the sun.
                    Emily Brontë, *Wuthering Heights*

(*for John Hewitt*)

I am saying goodbye to the trees,
The beech, the cedar, the elm,
The mild woods of these parts
Misted with car exhaust
And sawdust, and the last
Gasps of the poisoned nymphs.

I have watched girls walking
And children playing under
Lilac and rhododendron,
And me flicking my ash
Into the rose bushes
As if I owned the place;

As if the trees responded
To my ignorant admiration
Before dawn when the branches
Glitter at first light,
Or later on when the finches
Disappear for the night;

And often thought if I lived
Long enough in this house
I would turn into a tree
Like somebody in Ovid
– A small tree certainly
But a tree nevertheless –

Perhaps befriend the oak,
The chestnut and the yew,
Become a home for birds,
A shelter for the nymphs,
And gaze out over the downs
As if I belonged here too.

But where I am going the trees
Are few and far between.
No richly forested slopes,
Not for a long time,
And few winking woodlands.
There are no nymphs to be seen.

Out there you would look in vain
For a rose bush; but find,
Rooted in stony ground,
A last stubborn growth
Battered by constant rain
And twisted by the sea-wind

With nothing to recommend it
But its harsh tenacity
Between the blinding windows
And the forests of the sea,
As if its very existence
Were a reason to continue.

Crone, crow, scarecrow,
Its worn fingers scrabbling
At a torn sky, it stands
On the edge of everything
Like a burnt-out angel
Raising petitionary hands.

Grotesque by day, at twilight
An almost tragic figure
Of anguish and despair,
it merges into the funeral
Cloud-continent of night
As if it belongs there.

The Hunt by Night

Uccello, 1465

Flickering shades,
Stick figures, lithe game,
Swift flights of bison in a cave
Where man the maker killed to live;
But neolithic bush became
The midnight woods

Of nursery walls,
   The ancient fears mutated
To play, horses to rocking-horses
Tamed and framed to courtly uses,
   Crazed no more by foetid
     Bestial howls

   But rampant to
   The pageantry they share
And echoes of the hunting horn
At once peremptory and forlorn.
   The mild herbaceous air
     Is lemon-blue,

   The glade aglow
   With pleasant mysteries,
Diuretic depots, pungent prey;
And midnight hints at break of day
   Where, among sombre trees,
     The slim dogs go

   Wild with suspense
   Leaping to left and right,
Their cries receding to a point
Masked by obscurities of paint –
   As if our hunt by night,
     So very tense,

   So long pursued,
   In what dark cave begun
And not yet done, were not the great
Adventure we suppose but some elaborate
   Spectacle put on for fun
     And not for food.

JOHN PECK

"Vega over the rim of the Val Verzasca"

Vega over the rim of the Val Verzasca
and a mountain heaped from night with house light in it
   make a vast cave over man.

I have mislaid Rome, and the long house of Greece
has slipped my grasp, I am motionless.

In the eye's cavern, in the ear's dripping chamber . . .
    hunters brushed at wet space
    arching them overhead:
    endless, those recessions.

And on a mountain, when the last evening
    trades fuzzy dusk for totality
and stone ledges are everywhere our door,
    and we are set free in the house
to run, loll, knock over the ochre pots
    where bloods of gift achingly flower —

    yet as it was with the commanding
      Florentine, so even now:
      the color of all this
      has passed when I feel it come home,
      and even it, while it speaks,
      has not yet witnessed the end.

Anti-dithyrambics

He only wanted to sleep, that wakeful
professor among the ridgey pastures,
    he only wanted to lie down
    and snore like the hired hand sprawled
wholly this side of a searing command.

Through the car's headlights, a grey crone
    pushing a milk can on wheels:
    what Zarathustra caught in his high beams
was at first merely an old man of the woods
but at last the greybeard voltage that sizzled him.

    Under the sweep of headlights
      the flank of a red thresher
still chewing, across the dark field:
behind, virtues churning sightlessly,
ahead, the massed clans of black grasses.

The inconceivable marriage was here consummated:
    the lonely one with his thunder eggs
      and a milky wraith off the peaks.
But their children are not our lame wolves in lamb's fur,
their terrible bairns do not clamber back into old forms.

Campagna

Wavering blue floor
of a skiff in the field's river
softens a gash of red
down the slant wreck of brick,
marks the air's gatherings
where a language sank and still murmurs.
Columns, tasks, burnt sisterings
of hands torn away, towering
on the lip of sunny dust,
shag of spurting grasses,
mud of the breeding bank.
When I was struck from that tiller
it was in service, the overmastering
pulled me from it
into these alien hours
beyond a downsuck that men
much better have not beaten.
Blue fluency that I'll not
fathom, from that city
I have come back to pray you
never to bear my body
towards your beachings again
unless you set me down
with the other blinking survivors
beside the blooded stone.

End of July

Of longing, Termia, the sharp specifics know
no end, and down its progress the sharp days
lose no edge, the hours
crumbling streambeds to strand
the source deeper in summer. Orchard ladders
lean into the moist sheen of dark globes.

Near Baden under swallows, one
belltower cut through vineyards, banners out,
when the wish fixed me, rash
as blind archery, to lift
one clean impulse streaking out of the ruck
even if it landed wide of your touch

while quarter-hour strokes
through worn maroon face rings rounded
on their gold mark.

   Slow tones, swelling
things to a lightness – but if
that shivered me, it wasn't from forgetting
how separateness the cold angel converts us
to our fixities,
nor from denying she turns
each of us in her fire
like hickory seasoned for a torch,
nor from ceasing to share in her trade
of thrust, chill, thrust, the injustices
giving and taking justice in good time,
no one shouts the recognition,
it will not cry out in us,
yet they rang out, bronze
minutes, the bronze years,
with blunt frayed rope those changes
threading the spin of one swallow
who still climbed slabs of vapor thickening
over vine and crest, then
targeted down through harvest,
his poverty with ours
uncancelled yet his riches
plunging, sounding there
while bolted counterweights
thudding inside their dry tower argued
you could not hear, and claimed no one could tell you
how they made medley, before the orisons
of Roman candles and rocket wails
broke from streets below:
Unification Eve.

Archeus Terrae

rear ruth as the seat, rear her ureaus, cart cheer there
char the rat's tree, sear the cause, hate the rest
he, she errs, thee erreth, eaters at the heart
earth, aster, tar, hut, star are hers
use, re-use tears, her rarest chart
star's heat teases the archer's reach
thus true care, the scar, rehurts, reheats us
ear sure at the hatch, seer at such heat as

rush sheer arches thru the scare – thereat, the rue, the hurt:
rust ate these earths at the heart's rate
at us, teacher, the art tears; steer us
each search reaches the hearts there

Monologue of the Magdalene

I am not myself, I am my sisters,
yet not utterly, I am their unbound hair
in hands which, resettling it not after love
but recognition, not after tented
tastings and feedings, but after gazing
to the garden's end bringing
lightnings, lifted and were gone.

Thus, though she only
set kasha and the wine,
and then stood with back turned in the pantry
while the two men grew quiet
as the third one, the hooded stranger, gathered
them and time and blood's beat
                              and her also
into his low speaking, I took her
chill hand, stroked her hot cheek
while she held as a bell does its own deafened
expanding center.

And so with others at the window near dawn
in a palace, and by the gusty
bridge rail over a barge's wake.
So too they needed
me, having been me.

It was because they hung there that they
went on, because they guttered that they flared.
So that in my heart I can see, sleeping
to pain and the past, waking
to that something more, escaping yet always here,
which gathers at last to the mist
which is the heart:
from unstill waves,
from tugged silk of the waters,
mounts the moon.

From the Viking Museum

I eat with them at table,
I wear a suit, I walk
in step, and when I'm able
I listen to them talk . . .

I is also far,
the tedium of its noise
dwindles, tweetering star
turns asteroid, redeploys.

Monster of adaptation!
This man was once a child.
Shaping his daily nation
he ruled, he was reconciled.

The man I call myself
entered a pine-walled room,
came to a glassed-in shelf
with its hoard from a little tomb

and tried to assemble it:
corroded axe head, pin
of braided iron crudded
sea-deep, still feminine,

tiny wave-crumpled knife,
and a bronze fibula
that clasped the hair from a life
cut off soon, *regula*

deorum of Finland yet
also the Eastern Cross's
chained there with bronze, to set
Russia in Finnish moss.

Thor's hammer was not there
but might have been: the smiths
poured it and the cross as a pair
in one mold, lapping the myths.

But who was seeing this?
Where was that child? Where, and who?
Wherever I reached, I missed.
Looking, I saw through.

Vision huddling darker
shields fire behind its doors
from the obtuse world. Worker
in metal, it grasps and pours.

Contrary admirations
disperse its sweat, they are not
hybrid invigorations,
strife's alloys in one spot,

but strife and love themselves
have fled what they make of us
even as we heap the shelves
of schist, marl, tumulus.

The compromise I am,
a fluid mixture more
convenience than sham,
funneled in with a roar

down a lane super-dense
all quiet, through the gate
of this or that present tense
into bronze cooling: fate,

yet there I could cry for life
God hold him and God take
him spouse who never took wife
and O God pour me awake.

LOUISE GLÜCK

The Edge

Time and again, time and again I tie
My heart to that headboard
While my quilted cries
Harden against his hand. He's bored —
I see it. Don't I lick his bribes, set his bouquets
In water? Over Mother's lace I watch him drive into the gored
Roasts, deal slivers in his mercy . . . I can feel his thighs

Against me for the children's sakes. Reward?
Mornings, crippled with this house,
I see him toast his toast and test
His coffee, hedgingly. The waste's my breakfast.

Firstborn

The weeks go by. I shelve them,
They are all the same, like peeled soup cans . . .
Beans sour in their pot. I watch the lone onion
Floating like Ophelia, caked with grease:
You listless, fidget with the spoon.
What now? You miss my care? Your yard ripens
To a ward of roses, like a year ago when staff nuns
Wheeled me down the aisle . . .
You couldn't look. I saw
Converted love, your son,
Drooling under glass, starving . . .

We are eating well.
Today my meatman turns his trained knife
On veal, your favorite. I pay with my life.

The Magi

Toward world's end, through the bare
beginnings of winter, they are traveling again.
How many winters have we seen it happen,
watched the same sign come forward as they pass
cities sprung around this route their gold
engraved on the desert, and yet
held our peace, these
being the Wise, come to see at the accustomed hour
nothing changed: roofs, the barn
blazing in darkness, all they wish to see.

Nativity Poem

It is the evening
of the birth of god.
Singing &
with gold instruments
the angels bear down
upon the barn, their wings
neither white
wax nor marble. So
they have been recorded:
burnished,
literal in the composed air,
they raise their harps above
the beasts likewise gathering,
the lambs & all the startled
silken chickens . . . And Joseph,
off to one side, has touched
his cheek, meaning
he is weeping –

But how small he is, withdrawn
from the hollow of his mother's life,
the raw flesh bound
in linen as the stars yield
light to delight his sense
for whom there is no ornament.

The Letters

It is night for the last time.
For the last time your hands
gather on my body.

Tomorrow it will be autumn.
We will sit together on the balcony
watching the dry leaves drift over the village
like the letters we will burn,
one by one, in our separate houses.

Such a quiet night.
Only your voice murmuring
You're wet, you want to
and the child
sleeps as though he were not born.

In the morning it will be autumn.
We will walk together in the small garden
among stone benches and the shrubs
still sheeted in mist
like furniture left for a long time.

Look how the leaves drift in the darkness.
We have burned away
all that was written on them.

Illuminations

1

My son squats in the snow in his blue snowsuit.
All around him stubble, the brown
degraded bushes. In the morning air
they seem to stiffen into words.
And, between, the white steady silence.
A wren hops on the airstrip
under the sill, drills
for sustenance, then spreads
its short wings, shadows
dropping from them.

2

Last winter he could barely speak.
I moved his crib to face the window:
in the dark mornings
he would stand and grip the bars
until the walls appeared,
calling *light, light,*
that one syllable, in
demand or recognition.

3

He sits at the kitchen window
with his cup of apple juice.
Each tree forms where he left it,
leafless, trapped in his breath.
How clear their edges are,
no limb obscured by motion,
as the sun rises
cold and single over the map of language.

Happiness

A man and woman lie on a white bed.
It is morning. I think
Soon they will waken.
On the bedside table is a vase
of lilies; sunlight
pools in their throats.
I watch him turn to her
as though to speak her name
but silently, deep in her mouth —
At the window ledge,
once, twice,
a bird calls.
And then she stirs; her body
fills with his breath.

I open my eyes; you are watching me.
Almost over this room
the sun is gliding.
Look at your face, you say,
holding your own close to me
to make a mirror.
How calm you are. And the burning wheel
passes gently over us.

Hawk's Shadow

Embracing in the road
for some reason I no longer remember
and then drawing apart, seeing
that shape ahead — how close was it?
We looked up to where the hawk
hovered with its kill; I watched them
veering toward West Hill, casting
their one shadow in the dirt, the all-inclusive
shape of the predator —
Then they disappeared. And I thought:
one shadow. Like the one we made,
you holding me.

Lamium

This is how you live when you have a cold heart.
As I do: in shadows, trailing over cool rock,
under the great maple trees.

The sun hardly touches me.
Sometimes I see it in early spring, rising very far away.
Then leaves grow over it, completely hiding it. I feel it
glinting through the leaves, erratic,
like someone hitting the side of a glass with a metal spoon.

Living things don't all require
light in the same degree. Some of us
make our own light: a silver leaf
like a path no one can use, a shallow
lake of silver in the darkness under the great maples.

But you know this already.
You and the others who think
you live for truth and, by extension, love
all that is cold.

Vespers

I don't wonder where you are anymore.
You're in the garden; you're where John is,
in the dirt, abstracted, holding his green trowel.
This is how he gardens: fifteen minutes of intense effort,
fifteen minutes of ecstatic contemplation. Sometimes
I work beside him, doing the shade chores,
weeding, thinning the lettuces; sometimes I watch
from the porch near the upper garden until twilight makes
lamps of the first lilies: all this time,
peace never leaves him. But it rushes through me,
not as sustenance the flower holds
but like bright light through the bare tree.

MICHAEL PALMER

from *Series*

Prose 22

Plan of the City of O. The great square
curves down toward the cathedral. The
water runs out into night where the patron
saint still maintains his loft. He enters
from the lower level and pulls up the ladder
after him. The women and children and
most of the old men spend their time painting
pictures of the ladder. The rest lay the
three kinds of stone or type the performance
for the eastern quarter. There the first
colony left its box-shaped mark. But
the sun always goes down in several places,
so the clocks serve as maps. And at the
end of the nearest mountain stands the
larger and less perfect box.

Prose 31

The Logic of Contradictions

A logical principle is said to be an empty
or formal proposition because it can add
nothing to the premises of the argument it
governs. This leads to the logic of contra-
dictions. It is an anacoluthon to say that
a proposition is impossible because it is
self-contradictory. (It is also ambiguous.)
The definition of the possible as that which
in a given state of information (real or
pretended) we do not know not to be true
conceals another anacoluthon.

Sonnet

Now I see them

Now I see them sitting me before a mirror.
There's noise and laughter. Somebody
mentions that hearing is silver
before we move on to Table One
with the random numbers. I look down
a long street containing numbers.
A white four leans against the fence
and disappears. In the doorway
is the seven, then the x
painted red so you can find it
more easily. Five goes by
without its cap. My father wears
the second x. He has a grey cloud
for a face, and dark lines for arms.

Ninth Symmetrical Poem

(after Southwell)

It's November the thirty-third
of an actual November
and the children sleep in the crystal world
turning their heads from the fire that burns them

The burning children are invisible
but the carriers of wounded thought
are everywhere visible
as letters strung along a word

whose economies
work backward from speech
Mirrored we reflect such things
as they've seen

Seven Forbidden Words

"Mon chat sur le carreau cherchant une litière"
Baudelaire, "Spleen"

Who peered from the invisible world
toward a perfectly level field. Terms
will be broken here (have been broken here).
Should a city of blue tile appear
no one will be listening there.
He stood up, walked across the room
and broke his nose against the door.
A was the face of a letter
reflected in the water below.
He watched cross-eyed
learning a few words at a time.
The sun rose behind your shoulder
and told me to act casual
while striking an attitude of studied repose.
You grew these flowers yourself
so how could you forget their names.
The yellow one is said to be uncommon
and the heart tastes as expected, tender
and bitter like an olive
but less violent. It has been summer for a day
or part of a day
with shades drawn. The fires were deliberately set
and the inhabitants welcomed them.

The Theory of the Flower

I will read a few of these to see if they exist
(We will translate logos as logos)

He swam in the rock
I am here from a distance

"Now kiss her cunt"
"Now take his cock in your hand"

The film is of a night garden
There is nothing meaningful about the text

There is nothing meaningful about a text
She

brushed away the sand
She brushed away the hand

This is Paradise, an unpunctuated book
and this a sequence of laws

in which the night sky is lost
and the flower of theory is a black spot

upon the foxglove
(These words have all been paid for)

He turns then to shade his eyes from the sun
She edges closer to the fallen log

This is Paradise, a mildewed book
left too long in the house

Now say the words you had meant to
Now say the words such words mean

The car is white but does not run
It fits in a pocket

He slept inside the rock,
a flower that was almost blue

Such is order
which exenterates itself

The islands will be a grave for their children
after they are done

You may use the paper with my name on it
to say whatever you want

I promise not to be so boring next time
never again to laugh and weep so much

which is how spring comes
to the measured center of the eye

The mind is made up
but you forget who it was first spoke

The mind is made up
and then and then

This is the paradise of emptiness
and this the blank picture in a book

I've looked over the photographs and they all are of you
just as we'd been warned

How strange
The winged figure in tuxedo is bending from the waist

The metalion addresses the mirror
and the music of the shattered window

falls unheard past the window below
How strange

but not so strange as speech
mistaken for a book

The phrase "for a moment" is popular in the world
yet not really meant to be said

That is the third or the fourth world
where you can step into a tremor with your tongue

I do not drink of it myself
but intend a different liquid

clear as the glass in which it's held,
the theory of the flower and so on

or the counter-terror of this valley
the fog gradually fills

just as we've been warned
It isn't true but must be believed

and the leaves of the sound of such belief
form a paradise

(pronounced otherwise)
from which we fall toward a window

Autobiography 2 (hellogoodby)

The Book of Company which
I put down and can't pick up

The Trans-Siberian disappearing,
the Blue Train and the Shadow Train

Her body with ridges like my skull
Two children are running through the Lion
     Cemetery

Five travelers are crossing the Lion Bridge
A philosopher in a doorway insists

that there are no images
He whispers instead: Possible Worlds

The Mind-Body Problem
The Tale of the Color Harpsichord

Skeleton of the World's Oldest Horse
The ring of O dwindles

sizzling round the hole until gone
False spring is laughing at the snow

and just beyond each window
immense pines weighted with snow

A philosopher spread-eagled in the snow
holds out his Third Meditation

like a necrotic star. He whispers:
archery is everywhere in decline,

photography the first perversion of our time
Reach to the milky bottom of this pond

to know the feel of bone,
a knuckle from your grandfather's thumb,

the maternal clavicle, the familiar
arch of a brother's brow

He was your twin, no doubt,
forger of the unicursal maze

My dearest Tania, When I get a good position
        in the courtyard
I study their faces through the haze

Dear Tania, Don't be annoyed,
please, at these digressions

They are soldering the generals
back onto their pedestals

EAVAN BOLAND

The Black Lace Fan My Mother Gave Me

It was the first gift he ever gave her,
buying it for five francs in the Galeries
in pre-war Paris. It was stifling.
A starless drought made the nights stormy.

They stayed in the city for the summer.
They met in cafés. She was always early.
He was late. That evening he was later.
They wrapped the fan. He looked at his watch.

She looked down the Boulevard des Capucines.
She ordered more coffee. She stood up.
The streets were emptying. The heat was killing.
She thought the distance smelled of rain and lightning.

These are wild roses, appliqued on silk by hand,
darkly picked, stitched boldly, quickly.
The rest is tortoiseshell and has the reticent,
clear patience of its element. It is

a worn-out, underwater bullion and it keeps,
even now, an inference of its violation.
The lace is overcast as if the weather
it opened for and offset had entered it.

The past is an empty café terrace.
An airless dusk before thunder. A man running.
And no way now to know what happened then –
none at all – unless, of course, you improvise:

The blackbird on this first sultry morning,
in summer, finding buds, worms, fruit,
feels the heat. Suddenly she puts out her wing –
the whole, full, flirtatious span of it.

The Achill Woman

She came up the hill carrying water.
She wore a half-buttoned, wool cardigan,
a tea-towel round her waist.

She pushed the hair out of her eyes with
her free hand and put the bucket down.

The zinc-music of the handle on the rim
tuned the evening. An Easter moon rose.
In the next-door field a stream was
a fluid sunset; and then, stars.

I remember the cold rosiness of her hands.
She bent down and blew on them like broth.
And round her waist, on a white background,
in coarse, woven letters, the words "glass cloth".

And she was nearly finished for the day.
And I was all talk, raw from college –
week-ending at a friend's cottage
with one suitcase and the set text
of the Court poets of the Silver Age.

We stayed putting down time until
the evening turned cold without warning.
She said goodnight and started down the hill.

The grass changed from lavender to black.
The trees turned back to cold outlines.
You could taste frost

but nothing now can change the way I went
indoors, chilled by the wind
and made a fire
and took down my book
and opened it and failed to comprehend

the harmonies of servitude,
the grace music gives to flattery
and language borrows from ambition -

and how I fell asleep
oblivious to

the planets clouding over in the skies,
the slow decline of the Spring moon,
the songs crying out their ironies.

What We Lost

It is a winter afternoon.
The hills are frozen. Light is failing.
The distance is a crystal earshot.
A woman is mending linen in her kitchen.

She is a countrywoman.
Behind her cupboard doors she hangs sprigged,
stove-dried lavender in muslin.
Her letters and mementoes and memories

are packeted in satin at the back with
gaberdine and worsted and
the cambric she has made into bodices;
the good tobacco silk for Sunday Mass.

She is sewing in the kitchen.
The sugar-feel of flax is in her hands.
Dusk. And the candles brought in then.
One by one. And the quiet sweat of wax.

There is a child at her side.
The tea is poured, the stitching put down.
The child grows still, sensing something of importance.
The woman settles and begins her story.

Believe it, what we lost is here in this room
on this veiled evening.
The woman finishes. The story ends.
The child, who is my mother, gets up, moves away.

In the winter air, unheard, unshared,
the moment happens, hangs fire, leads nowhere.
The light will fail and the room darken,
the child fall asleep and the story be forgotten.

The fields are dark already.
The frail connections have been made and are broken.
The dumb-show of legend has become language,
is becoming silence and who will know that once

words were possibilities and disappointments,
were scented closets filled with love-letters
and memories and lavender hemmed into muslin,
stored in sachets, aired in bed-linen;

and travelled silks and the tones of cotton
tautened into bodices, subtly shaped by breathing;
were the rooms of childhood with their griefless peace,
their hands and whispers, their candles weeping brightly?

Distances

The radio is playing downstairs in the kitchen.
The clock says eight and the light says
winter. You are pulling up your hood against a bad morning.

Don't leave, I say. Don't go without telling me
the name of that song. You call it back to me from the stairs:
"I Wish I Was In Carrickfergus"

and the words open out with emigrant grief the way the
        streets
of a small town open out in
memory: salt-loving fuchsias to one side and

a market in full swing on the other with
linen for sale and tacky apples and a glass and wire hill
of spectacles on a metal tray. The front door bangs

and you're gone. I will think of it all morning while a fine
drizzle closes in, making the distances
fiction: not of that place but this and of how

restless we would be, you and I, inside the perfect
music of that basalt and sandstone
coastal town. We would walk the streets in

the scentless afternoon of a ballad measure,
longing to be able
to tell each other that the starched lace and linen of

adult handkerchiefs scraped your face and left your tears
falling; how the apples were mush inside the crisp sugar
shell and the spectacles out of focus.

That the Science of Cartography is Limited

– and not simply by the fact that this shading of
forest cannot show the fragrance of balsam,
the gloom of cypresses
is what I wish to prove.

When you and I were first in love we drove
to the borders of Connacht
and entered a wood there.

Look down you said: this was once a famine road.

I looked down at ivy and the scutch grass
rough-cast stone had
disappeared into as you told me
in the second winter of their ordeal, in

1847, when the crop had failed twice,
Relief Committees gave
the starving Irish such roads to build.

Where they died, there the road ended
and ends still and when I take down
the map of this island, it is never so
I can say here is
the masterful, the apt rendering of

the spherical as flat, nor
an ingenious design which persuades a curve
into a plane,
but to tell myself again that

the line which says woodland and cries hunger
and gives out among sweet pine and cypress,
and finds no horizon

will not be there.

Love

Dark falls on this mid-western town
where we once lived when myths collided.
Dusk has hidden the bridge in the river
which slides and deepens
to become the water
the hero crossed on his way to hell.

Not far from here is our old apartment.
We had a kitchen and an Amish table.
We had a view. And we discovered there
love had the feather and muscle of wings
and had come to live with us,
a brother of fire and air.

We had two infant children one of whom
was touched by death in this town
and spared: and when the hero
was hailed by his comrades in hell
their mouths opened and their voices failed and
there is no knowing what they would have asked
about a life they had shared and lost.

I am your wife.
It was years ago.
Our child was healed. We love each other still.
Across our day-to-day and ordinary distances
we speak plainly. We hear each other clearly.

And yet I want to return to you
on the bridge of the Iowa river as you were,
with snow on the shoulders of your coat
and a car passing with its headlights on:

I see you as a hero in a text –
the image blazing and the edges gilded –
and I long to cry out the epic question
my dear companion:
Will we ever live so intensely again?
Will love come to us again and be
so formidable at rest it offered us ascension
even to look at him?

But the words are shadows and you cannot hear me.
You walk away and I cannot follow.

The Huguenot Graveyard at the Heart of the City

It is the immodesty we bring to these
names which have eased into ours, and
their graves in the alcove of twilight,
which shadows their exile:

There is a flattery in being a destination.
There is a vanity in being the last resort.
They fled the Edict of Nantes –
hiding their shadows on the roads from France –

and now under brambles and granite
faith lies low with the lives it
dispossessed, and the hands it emptied out,
and the sombre dances they were joined in.

The buses turn right at Stephen's Green.
Car exhausts and sirens fill the air. See
the planted wildness of their rest and
grant to them the least love asks of

the living. Say: *they had another life once.*
And think of them as they first heard of us:
huddled around candles and words failing as
the stubborn tongue of the South put

oo and *an* to the sounds of Dublin,
and of their silver fingers at the windowsill
in the full moon as they leaned out
to breathe the sweet air of Nîmes

for the last time, and the flame
burned down in a dawn agreed upon
for their heart-broken leave-taking. And,
for their sakes, accept in that moment,

this city with its colours of sky and day –
and which is dear to us and particular –
was not a place to them: merely
the one witty step ahead of hate which

is all that they could keep. Or stay.

Story

Two lovers in an Irish wood at dusk
are hiding from an old and vengeful king.

The wood is full of sycamore and elder.
And set in that nowhere which is anywhere:

And let the woman be slender. As I was at twenty.
And red-haired. As I was until recently.

They cling together listening to his hounds
get nearer in the twilight and the spring

thickets fill with the sound of danger.
Blossoms are the colour of blood and capture.

We can be safe, they say. We can start
a rumour in the wood to reach the king –

that she has lost her youth. That her mouth is
cold. That this woman is growing older.

They do not know. They have no idea
how much of this: the ocean-coloured peace

of the dusk, and the way legend stresses it,
depend on her to be young and beautiful.

They start the rumour in the last light.
But the light changes. The distance shudders.

And suddenly what is happening is not
what happens to the lovers in the wood

or an angry king and his frantic hounds –
and the tricks and kisses he has planned.

But what is whispering out of sycamores.
And over river-noise. And by-passes harebells

and blue air. And is overheard by the birds
which are the elements of logic in an early

spring. And is travelling to enter a suburb
at the foothills of the mountains in Dublin.

And a garden with jasmine and poplars. And
a table at which I am writing. I am writing

a woman out of legend. I am thinking
how new it is – this story. How hard it will be to tell.

DAVID CONSTANTINE

"You are distant, you are already leaving"

You are distant, you are already leaving
You will have seemed here only between trains
And we are met here in the time of waiting
And what you last want is our eyes on you.

We shall have said nothing, we shall have done
Nothing in all that meantime there will
Have been not one gift pleasing us
You will have looked away and only behind
The pane of glass taking your seat with strangers
Being conveyed from here and when there is
No stay of parting you will smile perhaps
And give your face then the small mercy of weeping.

Watching for Dolphins

In the summer months on every crossing to Piraeus
One noticed that certain passengers soon rose
From seats in the packed saloon and with serious
Looks and no acknowledgement of a common purpose
Passed forward through the small door into the bows
To watch for dolphins. One saw them lose

Every other wish. Even the lovers
Turned their desires on the sea, and a fat man
Hung with equipment to photograph the occasion
Stared like a saint, through sad bi-focals; others,
Hopeless themselves, looked to the children for they
Would see dolphins if anyone would. Day after day

Or on their last opportunity all gazed
Undecided whether a flat calm were favourable
Or a sea the sun and the wind between them raised
To a likeness of dolphins. Were gulls a sign, that fell
Screeching from the sky or over an unremarkable place
Sat in a silent school? Every face

After its character implored the sea.
All, unaccustomed, wanted epiphany,
Praying the sky would clang and the abused Aegean
Reverberate with cymbal, gong and drum.
We could not imagine more prayer, and had they then
On the waves, on the climax of our longing come

Smiling, snub-nosed, domed like satyrs, oh
We should have laughed and lifted the children up
Stranger to stranger, pointing how with a leap
They left their element, three or four times, centred
On grace, and heavily and warm re-entered,
Looping the keel. We should have felt them go

Further and further into the deep parts. But soon
We were among the great tankers, under their chains
In black water. We had not seen the dolphins
But woke, blinking. Eyes cast down
With no admission of disappointment the company
Dispersed and prepared to land in the city.

Lasithi

Lasithi: notable for windmills. Summits are
    The petals of Lasithi and their snow
Streams underground. Ten thousand mills, sailing like toys,
    Crank it to surface into troughs. At dawn
The families come down to a lake of mist. Women
    In black unmoor and swivel the bare crosses
To feel the wind. The rods blossom and in its throat
    A well reaches for water like a man

Strangling. It mounts like birdsong then – oh lovely work
   Of slowly scooping sails – it fills the reed,
The wells respire, the cisterns wait like mares and when
   In leaps, crashing like laughter, water comes,
A full wellbeing ascends and wets the walls and brims and
   Down the runnels like amusement overflows
Under the leaves, along the root-courses, and men
   Go about with hoes gently conducting it.
After the evaporation of the mist, under
   The sheer sun, under descending eagles,
Rimmed with snow, veined silvery with water and laced
   With childish flowers, the plateau works. The mills
Labour like lilies of the field, they toil and spin
   Like quivering cherry trees in one white orchard.

"He arrived, towing a crowd, and slept"

He arrived, towing a crowd, and slept
That night at the house of Simon
The leper, in Bethany, three miles out.
We know the rest. But Simon adds
A leper is good company for
A christ, each in his skin
So lonely and viewing the ordinary loves and trades
From a star through frozen lashes
(Simon whose face
Shines in a certain light like mother-of-pearl
Or a silver-fish). And when he blew
On lepers and pushed them gently
Back into the camp this only whitened him
The more. He was the cold
Blood-brother of Lazarus anointed by
A whore out of alabaster. His feet
Felt heavy in her net of hair
Like twins
Like bastards drowned.

JEFFREY WAINWRIGHT

Thomas Müntzer

for David Spooner

Thomas Müntzer was a Protestant reformer in the early years of the German Reformation. He was a radical and a visionary both in theo-logy and politics for whom religious thought and experience became integrated with ideas and movements towards social revolution.

Travelling through Germany, preaching and writing, continually in trouble with the authorities, he came to support and lead struggles by common people against the monopolies of wealth and learning. In 1525, in the Peasant War, he led an army against the princes which was heavily defeated at Frankenhausen. Müntzer was subsequently captured and executed.

> *Doubt is the Water, the movement to good and evil. Who swims on the water without a saviour is between life and death.*
>
> Müntzer

> *I have seen in my solitude very clear things that are not true.*
>
> Machado

1

Just above where my house sits on the slope
Is a pond, a lodge when the mine was here,
Now motionless, secretive, hung in weeds.

Sometimes on clear nights I spread my arms wide
And can fly, stiff but perfect, down
Over this pond just an inch above the surface.

When I land I have just one, two drops of water
On my beard. I am surprised how quick
I have become a flier, a walker on air.

2

I see my brother crawling in the woods
To gather snails' shells. *This is not
A vision.* Look carefully and you can tell

How he is caught in the roots of a tree
Whose long branches spread upwards bearing as
Fruit gardeners and journeymen, merchants

And lawyers, jewellers and bishops,
Cardinals chamberlains nobles princes
Branch by branch kings pope and emperor.

3

I feel the very earth is against me.
Night after night she turns in my sleep
And litters my fields with stones.

I lie out all summer spread like a coat
Over the earth one night after another
Waiting to catch her. And then

She is mine and the rowan blooms –
His black roots swim out and dive to subdue her –
His red blood cracks in the air and saves me.

4

How many days did I search in my books
For such power, crouched like a bird under
My roof and lost to the world?

Scholars say God no longer speaks with us
Men – as though he has grown dumb, lost his tongue,
(Cut out for stealing a hare or a fish?)

Now I explode – out of this narrow house,
My mind lips hands skin my whole body
Cursing them for their flesh and their learning –

5

dran dran dran we have the sword – the purity
Of metal – the beauty of blood falling.
Spilt it is refreshed, it freshens also

The soil which when we turn it will become
Paradise for us once rid of these maggots
And their blind issue. They will seek about

And beg you: "Why is this happening to us?
Forgive us Forgive us", pleading now for
Mercy a new sweet thing they've found a taste for.

6

So you see from this how I am – Müntzer:
"O bloodthirsty man" breathing not air
But fire and slaughter, a true phantasist –

"A man born for heresy and schism",
"This most lying of men", "a mad dog",
And all because I speak and say: God made

All men free with His own blood shed.
Hold everything in common. Share evil.
And I find I am a god, like all men.

7

He teaches the gardener from his trees
And the fisherman from his catch, even
The goldsmith from the testing of his gold.

In the pond the cold thick water clothes me.
I live with the timorous snipe, beetles
And skaters, the pike smiles and moves with me.

We hold it in common without jealousy.
Touch your own work and the simple world.
In these unread creatures sings the real gospel.

8

I have two guilders for a whole winter.
I ask for company and food from beggars,
The very poorest, those I fancy most

Blessed . . . I am in love with a girl
And dare not tell her so . . . she makes me
Like a boy again – sick and dry-mouthed.

How often have I told you God comes only
In your apparent abandonment. This is
The misery of my exile – I was elected to it.

9

My son will not sleep. The noise
And every moving part of the world
Shuttles round him, making him regard it,

Giving him – only four years old! – no peace.
He moves quietly in his own purposes
Yet stays joyless. There is no joy to be had,

And he knows that and is resigned to it.
At his baptism we dressed him in white
And gave him salt as a symbol of this wisdom.

10

I am white and broken. I can hardly gasp out
What I want to say, which is: *I believe in God* . . .
At Frankenhausen His promised rainbow

Did bloom in the sky, silky and so bold
No one could mistake it. Seeing it there
I thought I could catch their bullets in my hands.

An article of faith. I was found in bed
And carried here for friendly
Interrogation. They ask me *what I believe*.

11

Their horsemen ride over our crops kicking
The roots from the ground. They poison wells
And throw fire down the holes where people hide.

An old woman crawls out. She is bleeding
And screaming so now they say they are sorry
And would like to bandage her. She won't

Go with them. She struggles free. *I see it*
I see it – she is bound to die . . .
This is the glittering night we wake in.

12

I lie here for a few hours yet, clothed still
In my external life, flesh I have tried
To render pure, and a scaffold of bones.

I would resign all interest in it.
To have any love for my own fingered
Body and brain is a luxury.

History, which is Eternal Life, is what
We need to celebrate. Stately tearful
Progress . . . you've seen how I have wept for it.

The Apparent Colonnades

I

Across the red cliff, dotted in, stand the apparent colonnades.
The sun will know the truth of them,
How far they resemble distant basilicas or market-halls,
Whether an entrance might be concealed.
He will march through them fearlessly, knowing there is nothing
    behind him, not even blackness,
For he never sees darkness,
Cannot conceive of shadow,
Has no need even to imagine a smudge.
He is where all such knowledge starts,
Semplice lume, somma luce,
All hues in all proportions,
Undivided and in no need of difference to see.

2

Compare the painter's muddle:
"The *apparent* colonnades";
The locomotive all at sea with steam and dusk, the firebox over-
    dramatised upon the viaduct;
The fancy that at evening the walls and trees themselves dispense
    the light;
That it was the artist's intuition that devised the still trapezist's
    shadow on the wall.

Nor, given a subject, can any two of them agree just how it was:
Christ lies pinkly, greyly, austerely blind;
Christ poses spotlit among the shavings, like a five-year-old at a
    party;
Christ folded into linen in so many different tombs;
Christ scrawny, ragg'd with spines, observing his armpit;
Christ in a dab of shadow, often a full poultice-paste of blackness,
    light only allowed across his brow and the buffed shine of the
    black cuirass.
Somewhere, perhaps, a Christ sorry for himself, hiding under a
    table, a little boy after all.

And, especially in executions, so much obscurity:
Who is this dark-furred judge presiding?
Who is this "dead father", as wasted as by months entombed, roped
    to a tree?
Does the curly-headed archer – foreground illuminated –
Think his shaded mark is Death itself?

3

But sunny Apollo falls upon all this evenly,
No sunkenness or hollowing,
Everything is there.
Thus he can pick out the unfinished hands of he who pulled a knife
    in a robbery,
He who shot the man kneeling by the safe in *Kwik-Save*.
To that curve in the brain, the sickle shape of *vanitas* within the
    male-factor's skull he penetrates,
And thus reassures the People's headsman,
Puts the felon to rasp brazilwood,
To the rope, the bull's pizzle, the hundred lashes,
To work the drowning cell —
Burning and grim he is, his eyes a domino of flame —
And so she should go down and dangle,
Peroxide bitch!

4

An argument should be approaching now
But only a cadence comes.
It rises to conclude that
We are all of us like painters and their kin,
All inside the light,
Only knowing what we know by darkness
And its feats of shadow.

It is a weak procedure for showing ourselves the world,
And still more for drawing out of our own heads such things as Justice —
That which we know we need but don't know the look of
Beyond that it is everything that is due,
And is strife, not vision (if we are tough enough),
And its every smudge is Tragedy,
All that is spilt, that could not become capable of solution, what makes
    us gasp, terror —
Though we can turn that to advantage and wangle beauty from it,
The *chiaroscuro* Apollo has not a glimmer of,
A mood where we can ponder
Who is the cross-hatched old man sagging at the mark?
Does the dark-furred judge doubt he knows the facts?
Is the curly-headed archer praying "Christ, Apollo, tell me this is right!"?

And what of the boy beneath the table
Who fears both the friends outside and friendlessness,
Fears both any kind of love and this solitude he seeks,
Who wants to be away, untouched in there, his own ragged splotch
    of life

Untamed by wisdom as she is practised?
He pulls the cloth down against the shiny afternoon,
Thinking he can keep it out, that he will not be seen,
And he is not.
He shoots the man he has kneeling by the safe in *Kwik-Save*.
This is where the argument and poem end.
How he would love simple, perfect light.

WENDY COPE

Waste Land Limericks

I

In April one seldom feels cheerful;
Dry stones, sun and dust make me fearful;
Clairvoyantes distress me,
Commuters depress me –
Met Stetson and gave him an earful.

2

She sat on a mighty fine chair,
Sparks flew as she tidied her hair;
She asks many questions,
I make few suggestions –
Bad as Albert and Lil – what a pair!

3

The Thames runs, bones rattle, rats creep;
Tiresias fancies a peep –
A typist is laid,
A record is played –
Wei la la. After this it gets deep.

4

A Phoenician called Phlebas forgot
About birds and his business – the lot,
Which is no surprise,
Since he'd met his demise
And been left in the ocean to rot.

5

No water. Dry rocks and dry throats,
Then thunder, a shower of quotes
From the Sanskrit and Dante.
Da. Damyata. Shantih.
I hope you'll make sense of the notes.

On Finding an Old Photograph

Yalding, 1912. My father
in an apple orchard, sunlight
patching his stylish bags;

three women dressed in soft,
white blouses, skirts that brush the grass;
a child with curly hair.

If they were strangers
it would calm me – half-drugged
by the atmosphere – but it does more –

eases a burden
made of all his sadness
and the things I didn't give him.

There he is, happy, and I am unborn.

Rondeau Redoublé

There are so many kinds of awful men –
One can't avoid them all. She often said
She'd never make the same mistake again:
She always made a new mistake instead.

The chinless type who made her feel ill-bred;
The practised charmer, less than charming when
He talked about the wife and kids and fled –
There are so many kinds of awful men.

The half-crazed hippy, deeply into Zen,
Whose cryptic homilies she came to dread;
The fervent youth who worshipped Tony Benn –
"One can't avoid them all," she often said.

The ageing banker, rich and overfed,
Who held forth on the dollar and the yen –
Though there were many more mistakes ahead,
She'd never make the same mistake again.

The budding poet, scribbling in his den
Odes not to her but to his pussy, Fred;
The drunk who fell asleep at nine or ten –
She always made a new mistake instead.

And so the gambler was at least unwed
And didn't preach or sneer or wield a pen
Or hoard his wealth or take the Scotch to bed.
She'd lived and learned and lived and learned but then
There are so many kinds.

Bloody Men

Bloody men are like bloody buses –
You wait for about a year
And as soon as one approaches your stop
Two or three others appear.

You look at them flashing their indicators,
Offering you a ride.
You're trying to read the destinations,
You haven't much time to decide.

If you make a mistake, there is no turning back.
Jump off, and you'll stand there and gaze
While the cars and the taxis and lorries go by
And the minutes, the hours, the days.

I Worry

I worry about you –
So long since we spoke.
Love, are you downhearted,
Dispirited, broke?

I worry about you.
I can't sleep at night.
Are you sad? Are you lonely?
Or are you all right?

They say that men suffer,
As badly, as long.
I worry, I worry,
In case they are wrong.

BILL MANHIRE

On Originality

Poets, I want to follow them all,
out of the forest into the city
or out of the city into the forest.

The first one I throttle.
I remove his dagger
and tape it to my ankle in a shop doorway.
Then I step into the street
picking my nails.

I have a drink with a man
who loves young women.
Each line is a fresh corpse.

There is a girl with whom we make friends.
As he bends over her body
to remove the clothing
I slip the blade between his ribs.

Humming a melody, I take his gun.
I knot his scarf carelessly at my neck, and

I trail the next one into the country.
On the bank of a river I drill
a clean hole in his forehead.

Moved by poetry
I put his wallet in a plain envelope
and mail it to the widow.

I pocket his gun.
This is progress.
For instance, it is nearly dawn.

Now I slide a gun into the gun
and go out looking.

It is a difficult world.
Each word is another bruise.

This is my nest of weapons.
This is my lyrical foliage.

The Distance Between Bodies

Sheets on the floor, a stick
of lipstick on the table,
bits of coastline almost visible at the window.

The distance between bodies
is like the distance between two photographs.
The star on the boy's chest.
The girl's head resting on the star.

Brazil

I

All night Brazil approached you through the dark.
The light behind mountains
was the light in the silver-merchant's eyes
two villages down river, was the blade
his father's father gave him, years ago,
to help him strike a deal with strangers.
His great right arm struck you
once, struck you twice,
because you had no money.
He watched you walk towards Brazil.

Brazil was women buying food from men,
the directions water followed.
Brazil was stars above the water-raft,
the parchment and the livestock where you slept,
and in the morning you woke and travelled on,
Brazil was where you were going.

Years later, a thousand miles away,
the place was still Brazil,
was still a single-minded journey,
the turmoil of a single coin ungiven,
the silver there in your hand.

2

The people of the second river
announced themselves by clapping;
you entered every village to applause.
You filmed their dances, the bodies
moving to the sound of waterfalls
a little way downstream. You watched
their life go on by word of mouth.
The dance of men with cattle,
of manioc and chicken, the dance of Elvis,
the dance of cattletrucks and pastry.

* * *

The boy turned to the Senator.
One thousand feet below the copter
you could see the white flashing of water
mixed with the bright grins of bandits.
"Bad country," he said. "Poisonous spiders."

3

Papers on a desk, a river,
and around each bend in the river
Brazil replaced Brazil.
It was a funny idea, she thought:
tampons in the jungle.

Papers on a desk safeguarded the desk.
You sat in a chair while the man there
told you his problems: no village,
no machinery, no available women.

* * *

The captain sat in his chair while the man
told him his problems. Outside
engines shunted in the yard.
Brazil was several photographs of feathers.
Brazil was urgent measures, which ended

when we disappeared from sight. And around
each bend in the river, Brazil replaced Brazil.
You looked at your ticket: the picture
of birds, the single word, *Brazil*.

4

Take-offs and delays.

Brazil was a rough airstrip in the jungle.
Near the runway, parrots chattered on a log.
He watched the woman spray her hammock
with insecticide, and sat beside her as she slept.
She tossed and turned in the black waters
and white waters of her sleep, imagining
an angel made of bricks. The colonel
came down the path towards them,
already screwing the top off the bottle.
This was more like it! Manioc and chicken
and, if they were lucky, ice-cold lager.

The suitcase was filled with batteries.
Mr Sunday sang on the radio,
a girl waved her Davy Crockett hat.
The explorers sprayed their hammocks
hoping to get a good night's sleep.
Short powerful men demanded cigarettes.
Nose flutes, necklaces of teeth.
She kept glancing at their genitals.
What would she do with so many nose flutes?

She sprayed her hammock with insecticide.
This time, surely, a good night's sleep.
"I'll just knock on the door," he said.
The senator himself answered, delighted to see them.
Before they were seated, he had taken
the top off the brandy.

5

The secret tribe knew a secret tribe
but would not say. "Do you mean deeper
in the jungle?" he demanded, beginning to get angry.

But they would not say. The woman
swam, anyway, not caring about the crocodiles.

Butterflies settled on the old Vauxhall Velox.
The word for the snakes was viridescent.
She worried about their driver's bandaged hands.

6

God floated above the Amazon.
He dreamed of Europe under sail.
He thought of the pre-Columbian sky,
and Portugal with cities in its stomach.
He placed a conference of spiders on the track.

* * *

Brazil, he wrote, was tribe after tribe
attached to stone, windows which rose
above the poverty of beef, everyone eating.

And everything you admired, the people
gave you. This child, this river,
all these trees.

7

"So many birds and I yearn to see seagulls."
She wrote such things in her diary.

Brazil was the way
her memories all deserted her
and then came back, frightened,
full of apology, asking to stay.

* * *

Oh her eyes are black, far down,
like stones below a bridge.
Her hair is long, or short,
the way hair is . . .

* * *

"Can you imagine
this place?" said the young American,
who already thought he would stay.

He turned off the radio.
"It's like there are 500 words for jungle
and only one for flame."

The man at the FUNAI post nodded.
He went on reading Shakespeare.

8

Brazil would watch the jungle murder sleep
and then perhaps sing on.
Brazil was happy, Brazil
was the great intolerable lines of song
a peasant offered on a piece of stone.

* * *

Look! They watched
the canoe sing on through the foaming waters.
God was on fire above the Amazon.

* * *

"There is a place," sang Mr Sunday,
"beyond the barricades of stars . . . "

* * *

He turned off the radio
and gave the boy the two batteries.
Muito obrigado. He spoke some Portuguese,

but probably he would never understand
the music he held there, just for a moment,
in the palm of his hand.

9

We filled the suitcase with cigarettes.
The Indians ran towards us.
The Amazon flamed and we shielded our eyes.
The water foamed, it wandered
like the edges of lace, it travelled across
the high wide cheekbones of our race.

* * *

"Help, look at the time," said the missionary.
He turned on his heel and was gone.
So this was Brazil.
He stepped out of Brazil, or into Brazil.
He stepped out of the half-built cathedral
and simply vanished into the jungle.

VERONICA FORREST-THOMSON

Michaelmas

daisy:
> garden aster of a shrubby habit

October:
> bearing masses of small purplish flowers

blackbird:
> the ring ouzel

crocus:
> the autumn crocus

moon:
> the
> harvest
> moon

Michaelse maesse her on lande wunode
se eorl syththan oth thet ofer sce
in 1123
> masses of small purplish flowers
> the ring ouzel
> the autumn crocus
> the
> harvest
> moon

tide:
> time

spring:
> Indian Summer

term:
> a term or session of the High Court of Justice
> in England and also of Oxford,
> Cambridge

the kinges power and is ost wende vorth
to Oxenforde aboute mielmasse
in 1297
> time
> Indian Summer
> also of Oxford, Cambridge
> at the gret cowrtes at Mykelmas the year
> in 1453

Trinity
Nevile's
Queens'
and
bearing masses of small purplish flowers
the harvest
moon.

(All quotations from the OED.)

Phrase-Book

Words are a monstrous excrescence.
Everything green is extended. It
is apricot, orange, lemon, olive and cherry,
and other snakes in the linguistic grass;
also a white touch of marble which evokes
no ghosts, the taste of squid, the . . .
Go away. I shall call a policeman.
Acrocorinth which evokes no
goats under the lemon blossom.

World is a monstrous excrescence;
he is following me everywhere, one
Nescafé and twenty Athenes, everything
green; I am not responsible for it.
I don't want to speak to you.
Leave me alone. I shall stay here.
I refuse a green extension. Beware.
I have paid you. I have paid you
enough, sea, sun, and octopodi.
It is raining cats and allomorphs.

"Where" is the British Embassy.

Pfarr-Schmerz (Village-Anguish)

Making love & omelettes
        For every poem ought to contain
        at least one zeugma
we may discern a very
palpable corner of a
sheet. Like love it

It ought to; and since "is"
may be derived from "ought",
the sheet, the situation and
ourselves exist (see *Proc. Arist. Soc.*
supp. vol. XCCCI)

is like the palpable
light set square
in wooden tapestry

stained glass (see La Sainte Chapelle)

like irony discerned
in fan-vaulting.
Interlocking rings
of glazed perception
turn in our eyes &
fingers, to be unravelled, Chinese

It was, therefore, quite right
of Chiang Hen to write down
the text only. For if the student
concentrates and uses his mind
he will discover the process
between the lines (see, *The
Unwobbling Pivot*, trans E.P.)

puzzles. Have you
seen the minnows
in the steel-dust,
the rose, the magnet
leaves, in the mere?

Irony as an acceptance of limitation
is our natural approach to the divine
(see, Elizabeth David, *French Provincial
Cooking*)

If we are going
to get up we ought
to get up, and

Thus we are derived from "ought"

eat our glazed
perceptions in
the form of
croissants, leaving
the palpable corner
to the sheet.

To seek mysteries in the obscure, poking into magic and commit-
      ting
eccentricities in order to be talked about later – This I do not.

Sonnet

My love, if I write a song for you
To that extent you are gone
For, as everyone says, and I know it's true:
We are all always alone.

Never so separate trying to be two
And the busy old fool is right.
To try and finger myself from you
Distinguishes day from night.

If I say "I love you" we can't but laugh
Since irony knows what we'll say.
If I try to free myself by my craft
You vary as night from day.

So, accept the wish for the deed my dear.
Words were made to prevent us near.

JOHN ASH

Them/There

to the memory of Erik Satie

What are the people like there? How do they live? . . . I'll admit I've never been there, but that won't stop me telling you all about it.

The people there weep often, alone in rooms with candles and old books. In their terrible Augusts they make black entries in their diaries. Their songs are doleful but the dances at funerals can be very lively, – danced to the rhythm of whips, gourds and snares – and the colour of mourning is ochre . . . They are fervently religious yet their government is atheist: to discourage worship the roofs have been removed from all their churches. But any government is provisional. Each summer, and sometimes during bad winters there are riots in the streets of their windswept and lacustrine capital. There are so many informers, however, that the police always know in advance the exact time and place. Thus everything is done properly: vendors may set up their stalls, street musicians choose their stands, and respectable families gather in perfect safety to watch the instructive spectacle . . . Tobacco and sheep are the basis of the economy. Out of patriotic duty everyone there chain smokes at incredible speed: they regard the medical reports with furious disdain, and their ceilings are stained a deep, yellowish-brown (like papyrus scrolls from the cemeteries of Fayyum). Their sheep are, without question, the shaggiest and most unkempt in the world, – each animal a mobile continent colonised by vast tribes of ticks . . . They are always washing things in water so soapy it is barely fluid, and yet nothing ever seems clean. And they think of themselves as Hellenes! Arbiters! . . . In their typical symphonic music a huge, squelching adagio like a sea-slug is followed by epileptic dances, catastrophic marches, – the whole concluding in a welter of chromatic swoons. Their orchestras are very large. They play everything *fortissimo*. (And – horrors! – they re-orchestrate Mozart!) Their national anthem is an arrangement of the mastodon-trumpet theme from Scriabin's "Poem of Ecstasy". (When the massed bands of the Republic begin to play this it is difficult to persuade them to stop . . .) And yet, strange to relate, they possess singing voices of an exceptional and haunting beauty . . . Their buildings are either hen-coops or Piranesi dungeons, Nissen huts or Sammarran mausoleums . . . Their poets write constantly of their failed marriages, failing health, unhappy childhoods and – for variety – the apostrophes to stars of laundresses and cabmen . . . It rains often, yet the vegetation is sparse in many areas and the summers can be oppressively hot. Steam rises in great clouds from their low roofs, and from the many balconies where drenched furs are hung to dry. Steam rises and moisture drips ceaselessly onto their unsurfaced streets in which a score of jeeps and hay-carts have their wheels stuck fast. Their flags hang always at half mast. As if ashamed their rivers vanish underground . . . In the south of the country there are extensive lakes of warm, grey mud . . . The train there moves in fantastic, slow loops, – a baroque embroidery expressing an infinite reluctance to arrive. They think, with good reason, that the world is forgetting them . . . They greet each dawn with a chorus of deafening expectorations.

Poor Boy: Portrait of a Painting

Difficult to say what all of this is all about.
Being young. Or simply arrogance, lack of patience –

a misunderstanding about what the word maturity
can mean when exchanged among "real" adults . . .

I don't know what kind of plant that is, but it
is green and has a small red flower

and the glass it strives towards is latticed,
yellowish and cracked. Beyond it

roofs are bunched together like boats
in a popular harbour
and through it the inevitable light falls . . .

And the light is art! It is arranged *so*,
over the bed and the pale dead boy,
his astonishing red hair, the shirt rumpled like sculpture,

the breeches . . . The breeches are a problem:
no one can decide whether they are blue
or mauve. Versions differ. But the light

is faultless. It can hit anything
whatever the distance, –
for example, the squashed triangle of white lining
to the stiff, mulberry coloured dressing-gown,
the torn-up sheets of poems or pornography,
the oriental blade of pallor above
the boy's large, left eye-lid or even the small, brown
dope bottle lying on the scrubbed floor
almost at the bottom of the picture. Of course

much depends on the angle. Much remains
obscure, but this only enhances
these significant islands of brilliance,
exposed and absolutely
vulnerable to our interpretation:

there is nowhere he can hide the hand that rests
just above his stomach as if he still felt horribly ill.

Ferns and the Night

Und wir hörten sie noch von ferne
Trotzig singen im Wald.

This is the sort of place you might arrive at after a long journey
involving the deaths of several famous monsters,
only to be disappointed almost to the point of grief.

Heavy clouds hang in a clump above a wide, perfectly level plain
which is the image of a blank mind. Night is falling.
There is a wooden house, a lighted porch: it is a scene of
    "marvellous simplicity". –

too marvellous perhaps: the very grain of the wood offers itself
for our admiration, and the light has such "warmth"
it is hard to restrain tears. The clouds are now distinctly purple,
agitated, – a kind of frantically stirred borsch, suitable backdrop
for some new opera's Prelude of Foreboding, but not for this
        ambiguous scene
of severity tempered by domestic tenderness, in which we find
the "young mother" looking for her child . . . He has run off
into deep woods nearby, leaving his blue train crashed on the lawn.
She calls his name, but after the third call it becomes difficult or
        exotic music,
a series in retrograde inversion, an entry in the catalogue of unknown
        birds:
she is already elsewhere, her torch illuminating the pure,
chlorophyll-green ferns of a forest, and the torch itself, a flame . . .

She finds that her bare feet are wet and that she is looking into a
        puddle,
Seeing the clouds reflected and her face (the moon also). She calls
        again
but has forgotten where she is, or whose name she is calling. Her
        own perhaps?
The wooden house, the lighted porch seem unreachable, –
artfully lit, a glassed-in exhibit in some future museum of the human.
Ferns and the night conceal the child whose laughter distantly
        reaches her.

Desert Song

And so, as in the opening of a *quasida*
I address the remains of a campfire, –

the one we shared in the waterless outer precincts
of the riot-torn city . . . Beloved! O
moon among flickering lanterns, I am on my way, –

my light skiff negotiates with ease
the rusting hulks and gun-boats of the port,

and soon I am well advanced along the Grand Canal,
passing the Green Mosque,
skirting the Tower Of The Winds until

I disembark at the Square Of The Souks, –
famed in history and travelogue . . .

And here is something to mock the visitor,
for at the centre of the square lies
a massive compass-star drawn in white mosaic
on a ground of dull, red stone, –

and a compass is what you will need
(and of course you didn't think to bring one)
for it is easy to lose your way in this place

amidst the din
of metal workers and public address systems,
amidst the scent of grilling meats and burning charcoal,

among the roses and grottoes of the Monteverdi Gardens,
in the sound of rebecs, ouds, tramcars, telephones,
cavalry, and shells exploding along the besieged corniche!

Here are numberless distractions and alarms:
sometimes a man swaying under the weight of a fluttering totem
of lottery tickets will fall at your feet, smiling

as if death, or a woman with a scar across her throat
will call out confused words from the dim porch of an alley
(and she, you at once recognise, is a visitant
from another poem, not this one you are living)

– indeed, in no other city is panic so likely
to attack the stranger, and yet considerations
of religious taboo and military strategy
forbid the publication of maps. But courage,

oh my star! for I am still on my way,
clutching grimly at my water-flask, eyes fixed
on the exposed mechanism of the casino's clock tower, –

which is like our hearts, like the rich and complex feelings
that should be coming into play at this moment, amidst
the striking of bells and the ululations of muezzins,

if only I could find you. But, as is inevitable,
the sky begins to darken as if an immense shutter were sliding into
        place,
a fog rises from the canals and a swarm of starving people
stumbles through the narrow streets.

I am thrown aside into the crumbling pavilion
of a disused public fountain, and fear,
like a line of ants, begins to crawl up my spine.

Malicious birds, carriers of disease, have devoured the crumbs I left
        as a trail,
and examination of my pockets reveals that I carry
no note of your address. The crowd thickens
and begins to chant in unison words
my phrase book does not record; they begin to lacerate their faces
with their nails; they begin to strike out at one another
confusedly with branches.
I dare not emerge from my hiding place,
and I am still on my way. Forever now.

Following a Man

I was following a man
with a handsome, intelligent face
(the cheekbones high, the nose straight, the lips
sufficiently full), and judging by the shape
of his neck (an unfailingly reliable
indicator in my experience) a lithe, athletic
figure; or, to be more exact, he and I were merely walking
in the same direction along Seventh Avenue,
having earlier stood side by side in the Old Chelsea Post Office:
the day was Friday, June 9th, the time late afternoon,
and after only two or three blocks,
each full of its particular events and distractions
(such as dogs, clouds, paupers, hydrants, hairdressers),
I began to feel that I was almost in love with this man,
that, like a song, I would follow him anywhere . . .

Something about the way he slicked back his hair
delighted me, and I admired his beautiful raincoat
which so enhanced the easy masculine grace
of his movements. I was concentrating hard,
trying to take in all these details without giving
any cause for embarrassment (either on my part
or his) when he swerved into a newspaper store
between 16th Street and 15th, and I could think of no
plausible excuse for following him into that meagre space
where, surely, our eyes would have been forced to meet,
and I would have blushed (he being protected by a light tan).

In all likelihood he is lost to me, as
he would have been had that door been
the door to an elevator in an apartment building
bigger than all the pyramids combined.
Even if he should prove to be my near-neighbour
I doubt that I will ever see him again,
since in New York there are always too many
neighbours to keep track of (you hear
their footsteps, their voices and their music,
but it is difficult to attach these attributes
to a particular person, in much the same way
that an archaeologist may uncover the fragments
of a mirror but will never know the face
that, day by day, was reflected there)
but it is not as if he were dead. He exists
and will continue to do so for some time, perhaps
for many years, and as I walked without hesitation
directly past the store he had entered I was overcome
with a sudden feeling of elation at the thought
that it was within my power to record this incident
which is unexceptional
as the budding of pear trees in their season,
unrepeatable as the first sight of a great city.

JAMES FENTON

A German Requiem

It is not what they built. It is what they knocked down.
It is not the houses. It is the spaces between the houses.
It is not the streets that exist. It is the streets that no longer exist.
It is not your memories which haunt you.
It is not what you have written down.
It is what you have forgotten, what you must forget.
What you must go on forgetting all your life.
And with any luck oblivion should discover a ritual.
You will find out that you are not alone in the enterprise.
Yesterday the very furniture seemed to reproach you.
Today you take your place in the Widow's Shuttle.

*

The bus is waiting at the southern gate
To take you to the city of your ancestors
Which stands on the hill opposite, with gleaming pediments,
As vivid as this charming square, your home.
Are you shy? You should be. It is almost like a wedding,
The way you clasp your flowers and give a little tug at your veil. Oh,
The hideous bridesmaids, it is natural that you should resent them
Just a little, on this first day.
But that will pass, and the cemetery is not far.
Here comes the driver, flicking a toothpick into the gutter,
His tongue still searching between his teeth.
See, he has not noticed you. No one has noticed you.
It will pass, young lady, it will pass.

*

How comforting it is, once or twice a year,
To get together and forget the old times.
As on those special days, ladies and gentlemen,
When the boiled shirts gather at the graveside
And a leering waistcoat approaches the rostrum.
It is like a solemn pact between the survivors.
The mayor has signed it on behalf of the freemasonry.
The priest has sealed it on behalf of all the rest.
Nothing more need be said, and it is better that way –

*

The better for the widow, that she should not live in fear of surprise,
The better for the young man, that he should move at liberty
        between the armchairs,
The better that these bent figures who flutter among the graves
Tending the nightlights and replacing the chrysanthemums
Are not ghosts,
That they shall go home.
The bus is waiting, and on the upper terraces
The workmen are dismantling the houses of the dead.

*

But when so many had died, so many and at such speed,
There were no cities waiting for the victims.
They unscrewed the name-plates from the shattered doorways
And carried them away with the coffins.
So the squares and parks were filled with the eloquence of young
        cemeteries:
The smell of fresh earth, the improvised crosses
And all the impossible directions in brass and enamel.

*

"Doctor Gliedschirm, skin specialist, surgeries 14–16 hours or by
    appointment."
Professor Sargnagel was buried with four degrees, two associate
    memberships
And instructions to tradesmen to use the back entrance.
Your uncle's grave informed you that he lived on the third floor, left.
You were asked please to ring, and he would come down in the lift
To which one needed a key . . .

*

Would come down, would ever come down
With a smile like thin gruel, and never too much to say.
How he shrank through the years.
How you towered over him in the narrow cage.
How he shrinks now . . .

*

But come. Grief must have its term? Guilt too, then.
And it seems there is no limit to the resourcefulness of recollection.
So that a man might say and think:
When the world was at its darkest,
When the black wings passed over the rooftops
(And who can divine His purposes?) even then
There was always, always a fire in this hearth.
You see this cupboard? A priest-hole!
And in that lumber-room whole generations have been housed and fed.
Oh, if I were to begin, if I were to begin to tell you
The half, the quarter, a mere smattering of what we went through!

*

His wife nods, and a secret smile,
Like a breeze with enough strength to carry one dry leaf
Over two pavingstones, passes from chair to chair.
Even the enquirer is charmed.
He forgets to pursue the point.
It is not what he wants to know.
It is what he wants not to know.
It is not what they say.
It is what they do not say.

The Skip

I took my life and threw it on the skip,
Reckoning the next-door neighbours wouldn't mind
If my life hitched a lift to the council tip
With their dry rot and rubble. What you find

With skips is – the whole community joins in.
Old mattresses appear, doors kind of drift
Along with all that won't fit in the bin
And what the bin-men can't be fished to shift.

I threw away my life, and there it lay
And grew quite sodden. "What a dreadful shame,"
Clucked some old bag and sucked her teeth: "The way
The young these days . . . no values . . . me, I blame . . ."

But I blamed no one. Quality control
Had loused it up, and that was that. 'Nough said.
I couldn't stick at home. I took a stroll
And passed the skip, and left my life for dead.

Without my life, the beer was just as foul,
The landlord still as filthy as his wife,
The chicken in the basket was an owl,
And no one said: "Ee, jim-lad, whur's thee life?"

Well, I got back that night the worse for wear,
But still just capable of single vision;
Looked in the skip; my life – it wasn't there!
Some bugger'd nicked it – *without* my permission.

Okay, so I got angry and began
To shout, and woke the street. Okay. *Okay*!
And I was sick all down the neighbour's van.
And I disgraced myself on the par-*kay*.

And then . . . you know how if you've had a few
You'll wake at dawn, all healthy, like sea breezes,
Raring to go, and thinking: "Clever you!
You've got away with it." And then, oh Jesus,

It hits you. Well, that morning, just at six
I woke, got up and looked down at the skip.
There lay my life, still sodden, on the bricks;
There lay my poor old life, arse over tip.

Or was it mine? Still dressed, I went downstairs
And took a long cool look. The truth was dawning.
Someone had just exchanged my life for theirs.
Poor fool, I thought – I should have left a warning.

Some bastard saw my life and thought it nicer
Than what he had. Yet what he'd had seemed fine.
He'd never caught his fingers in the slicer
The way I'd managed in that life of mine.

His life lay glistening in the rain, neglected,
Yet still a decent, an authentic life.
Some people I can think of, I reflected
Would take that thing as soon as you'd say Knife.

It seemed a shame to miss a chance like that.
I brought the life in, dried it by the stove.
It looked so fetching, stretched out on the mat.
I tried it on. It fitted, like a glove.

And now, when some local bat drops off the twig
And new folk take the house, and pull up floors
And knock down walls and hire some kind of big
Container (say, a skip) for their old doors,

I'll watch it like a hawk, and every day
I'll make at least – oh – half a dozen trips.
I've furnished an existence in that way.
You'd not believe the things you find on skips.

The Possibility

The lizard on the wall, engrossed,
The sudden silence from the wood
Are telling me that I have lost
The possibility of good.

I know this flower is beautiful
And yesterday it seemed to be.
It opened like a crimson hand.
It was not beautiful to me.

I know that work is beautiful.
It is a boon. It is a good.
Unless my working were a way
Of squandering my solitude.

And solitude was beautiful
When I was sure that I was strong.
I thought it was a medium
In which to grow, but I was wrong.

The jays are swearing in the wood.
The lizard moves with ugly speed.
The flower closes like a fist.
The possibility recedes.

Jerusalem

1

Stone cries to stone,
Heart to heart, heart to stone,
And the interrogation will not die
For there is no eternal city
And there is no pity
And there is nothing underneath the sky
No rainbow and no guarantee –
There is no covenant between your God and me.

2

It is superb in the air.
Suffering is everywhere
And each man wears his suffering like a skin.
My history is proud.
Mine is not allowed.
This is the cistern where all wars begin,
The laughter from the armoured car.
This is the man who won't believe you're what you are.

3

This is your fault.
This is a crusader vault.
The Brook of Kidron flows from Mea She'arim.
I will pray for you.
I will tell you what to do.

I'll stone you. I shall break your every limb.
   Oh I am not afraid of you
But maybe I should fear the things you make me do.

4

   This is not Golgotha.
   This is the Holy Sepulchre,
The Emperor Hadrian's temple to a love
   Which he did not much share.
   Golgotha could be anywhere.
Jerusalem itself is on the move.
   It leaps and leaps from hill to hill
And as it makes its way it also makes its will.

5

   The city was sacked.
   Jordan was driven back.
The pious Christians burned the Jews alive.
   This is a minaret.
   I'm not finished yet.
We're waiting for reinforcements to arrive.
   What was your mother's real name?
Would it be safe today to go to Bethlehem?

6

   This is the Garden Tomb.
   No, *this* is the Garden Tomb.
I'm an Armenian. I am a Copt.
   This is Utopia.
   I came here from Ethiopia.
This hole is where the flying carpet dropped
   The Prophet off to pray one night
And from here one hour later he resumed his flight.

7

   Who packed your bag?
   I packed my bag.
Where was your uncle's mother's sister born?
   Have you ever met an Arab?
   Yes I am a scarab.
I am a worm. I am a thing of scorn.
   I cry Impure from street to street
And see my degradation in the eyes I meet.

8

I am your enemy.
This is Gethsemane.
The broken graves look to the Temple Mount.
Tell me now, tell me when
When shall we all rise again?
Shall I be first in that great body count?
When shall the tribes be gathered in?
When, tell me, when shall the Last Things begin?

9

You are in error.
This is terror.
This is your banishment. This land is mine.
This is what you earn.
This is the Law of No Return.
This is the sour dough, this the sweet wine.
This is my history, this my race
And this unhappy man threw acid in my face.

10

Stone cries to stone,
Heart to heart, heart to stone.
These are the warrior archaeologists.
This is us and that is them.
This is Jerusalem.
These are the dying men with tattooed wrists.
Do this and I'll destroy your home.
I have destroyed your home. You have destroyed my home.

JORIE GRAHAM

Tennessee June

This is the heat that seeks the flaw in everything
and loves the flaw.
Nothing is heavier than its spirit,
nothing more landlocked than the body within it.
Its daylilies grow overnight, our lawns
bare, then falsely gay, then bare again. Imagine
your mind wandering without its logic,
your body the sides of a riverbed giving in . . .

In it, no world can survive
having more than its neighbors;
in it, the pressure to become forever less is the pressure
to take forevermore
to get there. Oh

let it touch you . . .
The porch is sharply lit – little box of the body –
and the hammock swings out easily over its edge.
Beyond, the hot ferns bed, and fireflies gauze
the fat tobacco slums,
the crickets boring holes into the heat the crickets fill.
Rock out into that dark and back to where
the blind moths circle, circle,
back and forth from the bone-white house to the creepers
        unbraiding.
Nothing will catch you.
Nothing will let you go.
We call it blossoming –
the spirit breaks from you and you remain.

History

Into whose ear the deeds are spoken. The only
listener. So I believed
he would remember everything, the murmuring trees,
the sunshine's zealotry, its deep
unevenness. For history
is the opposite
of the eye
for whom, for instance, six million bodies in portions
of hundreds and
the flowerpots broken by a sudden wind stand as
equivalent. What more
is there
than fact? *I'll give ten thousand dollars to the man*
who proves the holocaust really
occurred said the exhausted solitude
in San Francisco
in 1980. Far in the woods
in a faded photograph
in 1942 the man with his own
genitalia in his mouth and hundreds of
slow holes

a pitchfork has opened
over his face
grows beautiful. The ferns and deepwood
lilies catch
the eye. Three men in ragged uniforms
with guns keep laughing
nervously. They share the day
with him. A bluebird
sings. The feathers of the shade touch every inch
of skin – the hand holding down the delicate gun,
the hands holding down the delicate
hips. And the sky
is visible between the men, between
the trees, a blue spirit
enveloping
anything. Late in the story, in northern Italy,
a man cuts down some trees for winter
fuel. We read this in the evening
news. Watching the fire burn late
one night, watching it change and change, a hand
　　　grenade,
lodged in the pulp the young tree
grew around, explodes, blinding the man, killing
his wife. Now who
will tell the children
fairytales? The ones where simple
crumbs over the forest
floor endure
to help us home?

The Region of Unlikeness

You wake up and you don't know who it is there breathing
　　beside you (the world is a different place from what it
seems)
　　and then you do.
The window is open, it is raining, then it has just
　　ceased. What is the purpose of poetry, friend?
And you, are you one of those girls?
　　The floor which is cold touching your instep now,

is it more alive for those separate instances it crosses
　　up through your whole stalk into your mind?

Five, six times it gets let in, step, step, across to the
  window.
Then the birdcall tossing quick cuts your way,

a string strung a thousand years ago still taut . . . .
  He turns in his sleep.
You want to get out of here.
  The stalls going up in the street below now for market.
Don't wake up. Keep this in black and white. It's

Rome. The man's name . . .? The speaker
  thirteen. Walls bare. Light like a dirty towel.
It's *Claudio*. He will overdose before the age of
  thirty someone told me time
ago. In the bar below, the counterterrorist police

(three of them for this neighborhood) (the Old Ghetto)
  take coffee. You hear them laugh.
When you lean out you see the butts
  of the machineguns shake
in the doorway.
  You wake up from what? Have you been there?
What of this loop called *being* beating against the ends
of things?
  The shutters, as you lean out to push them, creak.
Three boys seen from above run fast down the narrows,
  laughing.
A black dog barks. Was it more than

one night? Was it all right? Where are
  the parents? Dress and get to the door. (Repeat after me.)
Now the cold edge of the door crosses her body
  into the field where it will grow. Now the
wrought-iron banister – three floors of it – now the *clack*

clack of her sandals on stone –
  each a new planting – different from all the others –
each planted fast, there, into that soil,
  and the thin strip of light from the heavy street-door,
and the other light after her self has slipped through.
  Later she will walk along and name them, one by

one – the back of the girl in the print dress carrying bread,
  the old woman seen by looking up suddenly.
Later she will walk along, a word in

each moment, to slap them down onto the plantings,
to keep them still.
  But now it's the hissing of cars passing,

and Left into Campo dei Fiori –
  And though it should be through flames dear god,
it's through clarity,
  through the empty thing with minutes clicking in it,
right through it no resistance,
  running a bit now, the stalls filling all round,
cats in the doorways,
  the woman with artichokes starting it up

– this price then that price –
  right through it, it not burning, not falling, no
piercing sound –
  just the open, day pushing through it, any story pushing through.
Do you want her to go home now? do you want her late for school?
  Here is her empty room,

a trill of light on the white bedspread. This is
  exactly
how slow it moves.
  The women are all in the stalls now.
The one behind the rack of flowers is crying
  – put that in the field for later – into

captivity –
  If I am responsible, it is for what? the field at the
end? the woman weeping in the row of colors? the exact
  shades of color? the actions of the night before?
Is there a way to move through which makes it hard
  enough – thorny, re-

membered? Push. Push through with this girl
  recalled down to the last bit of cartilage, ash, running along the
river now, then down to the bridge, then quick,
  home. Twenty years later

  it's 9:15, I go for a walk, the butterflies are hatching,
(that minute has come),
  and she is still running down the Santo Spirito, and I push her
to go faster, faster, little one, fool, push her, but I'm
  in the field near Tie Siding, the new hatchlings

everywhere – they're drying in the grasses – they lift their wings up
    into the
groundwind – so many –
I kick them gently to make them make room –
    clusters lift with each step –

    and below the women leaning, calling the price out, handling
each fruit, shaking the dirt off. Oh wake up, wake
    up, something moving through the air now, something in the
        ground that
waits.

The Surface

It has a hole in it. Not only where I
                concentrate.
The river still ribboning, twisting up,
          into its re-
arrangements, chill enlightenments, tight-knotted
                   quickenings
and loosenings – whispered messages dissolving
               the messengers –
the river still glinting-up into its handfuls, heapings,
             glassy
forgettings under the river of
my attention –
and the river of my attention laying itself down –
               bending,
reassembling – over the quick leaving-offs and windy
              obstacles –
and the surface rippling under the wind's attention –
rippling over the accumulations, the slowed-down drifting
            permanences
of the cold
bed.
I say *iridescent* and I look down.
The leaves very still as they are carried.

PAUL MULDOON

The Electric Orchard

The early electric people had domesticated the wild ass.
They knew all about falling off.
Occasionally, they would have fallen out of the trees.
Climbing again, they had something to prove
To their neighbours. And they did have neighbours.
The electric people lived in villages
Out of their need of security and their constant hunger.
Together they would divert their energies

To neutral places. Anger to the banging door,
Passion to the kiss.
And electricity to earth. Having stolen his thunder
From an angry god, through the trees
They had learned to string his lightning.
The women gathered random sparks into their aprons,
A child discovered the swing
Among the electric poles. Taking everything as given,

The electric people were confident, hardly proud.
They kept fire in a bucket,
Boiled water and dry leaves in a kettle, watched the lid
By the blue steam lifted and lifted.
So that, where one of the electric people happened to fall,
It was accepted as an occupational hazard.
There was something necessary about the thing. The North Wall
Of the Eiger was notorious for blizzards,

If one fell there his neighbour might remark, Bloody fool.
All that would have been inappropriate,
Applied to the experienced climber of electric poles.
I have achieved this great height?
No electric person could have been that proud,
Thirty or forty feet. Perhaps not that,
If the fall happened to be broken by the roof of a shed.
The belt would burst, the call be made,

The ambulance arrive and carry the faller away
To hospital with a scream.
There and then the electric people might invent the railway,
Just watching the lid lifted by the steam.

Or decide that all laws should be based on that of gravity,
Just thinking of the faller fallen.
Even then they were running out of things to do and see.
Gradually, they introduced legislation

Whereby they nailed a plaque to every last electric pole.
They would prosecute any trespassers.
The high up, singing and live fruit liable to shock or kill
Were forbidden. Deciding that their neighbours
And their neighbours' innocent children ought to be stopped
For their own good, they threw a fence
Of barbed wire round the electric poles. None could describe
Electrocution, falling, the age of innocence.

The Narrow Road to the Deep North

A Japanese soldier
Has just stumbled out of the forest.
The war has been over
These thirty years, and he has lost

All but his ceremonial sword.
We offer him an American cigarette.
He takes it without a word.
For all this comes too late. Too late

To break the sword across his knee,
To be right or wrong.
He means to go back to his old farm

And till the land. Though never to deny
The stone its sling,
The blade of grass its one good arm.

Mules

Should they not have the best of both worlds?

Her feet of clay gave the lie
To the star burned in our mare's brow.
Would Parsons' jackass not rest more assured
That cross wrenched from his shoulders?

We had loosed them into one field.
I watched Sam Parsons and my quick father
Tense for the punch below their belts,
For what was neither one thing or the other.

It was as though they had shuddered
To think, of their gaunt, sexless foal
Dropped tonight in the cowshed.

We might yet claim that it sprang from earth
Were it not for the afterbirth
Trailed like some fine, silk parachute,
That we would know from what heights it fell.

Gathering Mushrooms

The rain comes flapping through the yard
like a tablecloth that she hand-embroidered.
My mother has left it on the line.
It is sodden with rain.
The mushroom shed is windowless, wide,
its high-stacked wooden trays
hosed down with formaldehyde.
And my father has opened the Gates of Troy
to that first load of horse manure.
Barley straw. Gypsum. Dried blood. Ammonia.
Wagon after wagon
blusters in, a self-renewing gold-black dragon
we push to the back of the mind.
We have taken our pitchforks to the wind.

All brought back to me that September evening
fifteen years on. The pair of us
tripping through Barnett's fair demesne
like girls in long dresses
after a hail-storm.
We might have been thinking of the fire-bomb
that sent Malone House sky-high
and its priceless collection of linen
sky-high.
We might have wept with Elizabeth McCrum.
We were thinking only of psilocybin.
You sang of the maid you met on the dewy grass –

And she stooped so low gave me to know
it was mushrooms she was gathering O.

He'll be wearing that same old donkey-jacket
and the sawn-off waders.
He carries a knife, two punnets, a bucket.
He reaches far into his own shadow.
We'll have taken him unawares
and stand behind him, slightly to one side.
He is one of those ancient warriors
before the rising tide.
He'll glance back from under his peaked cap
without breaking rhythm:
his coaxing a mushroom – a flat or a cup –
the nick against his right thumb;
the bucket then, the punnet to left or right,
and so on and so forth till kingdom come.

We followed the overgrown towpath by the Lagan.
The sunset would deepen through cinnamon
to aubergine,
the wood-pigeon's concerto for oboe and strings,
allegro, blowing your mind.
And you were suddenly out of my ken, hurtling
towards the ever-receding ground,
into the maw
of a shimmering green-gold dragon.
You discovered yourself in some outbuilding
with your long-lost companion, me,
though my head had grown into the head of a horse
that shook its dirty-fair mane
and spoke this verse:

Come back to us. However cold and raw, your feet
were always meant
to negotiate terms with bare cement.
Beyond this concrete wall is a wall of concrete
and barbed wire. Your only hope
is to come back. If sing you must, let your song
tell of treading your own dung,
let straw and dung give a spring to your step.
If we never live to see the day we leap
into our true domain,
lie down with us now and wrap
yourself in the soiled grey blanket of Irish rain
that will, one day, bleach itself white.
Lie down with us and wait.

Long Finish

Ten years since we were married, since we stood
under a chuppah of pine-boughs
in the middle of a little pinewood
and exchanged our wedding-vows.
Save me, good thou,
a piece of marchpane, while I fill your glass with Simi
Chardonnay as high as decency allows,
and then some.

Bear with me now as I myself must bear
the scrutiny of a bottle of wine
that boasts of hints of plum and pear,
its muscadine
tempered by an oak backbone. I myself have designs
on the willow-boss
of your breast, on all your waist confines
between longing and loss.

The wonder is that we somehow have withstood
the soars and slumps in the Dow
of ten years of marriage and parenthood,
its summits and its sloughs –
that we've somehow
managed to withstand an almond-blossomy
five years of bitter rapture, five of blissful rows,
(and then some

if we count the one or two to spare
when we've been firmly on cloud nine).
Even now, as you turn away from me with your one bare
shoulder, the veer of your neckline,
I glimpse the all-but-cleared-up eczema-patch on your spine
and it brings to mind not the Schloss
that stands, transitory, tra la, Triestine,
between longing and loss

but a crude
hip-trench in a field, covered with pine-boughs
in which two men in masks and hoods
who have themselves taken vows
wait for a farmer to break a bale for his cows
before opening fire with semi-
automatics, cutting him off slightly above the eyebrows,
and then some.

It brings to mind another, driving out to care
for six white-faced kine
finishing on heather and mountain-air,
another who'll shortly divine
the precise whereabouts of a landmine
on the road between Beragh and Sixmilecross,
who'll shortly know what it is to have breasted the line
between longing and loss.

Such forbearance in the face of vicissitude
also brings to mind the little "there, theres" and "now, nows"
of two sisters whose sleeves are imbued
with the constant douse and souse
of salt-water through their salt-house
in *Matsukaze* (or "Pining Wind"), by Zeami,
the salt-house through which the wind soughs and soughs,
and then some

of the wind's little "now, nows" and "there, theres"
seem to intertwine
with those of Pining Wind and Autumn Rain, who must
        forbear
the dolor of their lives of boiling down brine.
For the double meaning of "pine"
is much the same in Japanese as English, coming across
both in the sense of "tree" and the sense we assign
between "longing" and "loss"

as when the ghost of Yukihira, the poet–courtier who wooed
both sisters, appears as a ghostly pine, pining among pine-
        boughs.
Barely have Autumn Rain and Pining Wind renewed
their vows
than you turn back towards me and your blouse,
while it covers the all-but-cleared-up patch of eczema,
falls as low as decency allows,
and then some.

Princess of Accutane, let's no more try to refine
the pure drop from the dross
than distinguish, good thou, between mine and thine,
between longing and loss,
but rouse
ourselves each dawn, here on the shore at Suma,
with such force and fervor as spouses may yet espouse,
and then some.

MARK DOTY

The Ware Collection of Glass Flowers
and Fruit, Harvard Museum

Strange paradise, complete with worms,
monument of an obsessive will to fix forms;
every apricot or yellow spot's seen so closely,
in these blown blooms and fruit, that exactitude

is not quite imitation. Leaf and root,
the sweet flag's flaring bud already,
at the tip, blackened: it's hard to remember
these were ballooned and shaped by breath.

They're lovely because they *seem*
to decay: blue spots on bluer plums,
mold tarring a striped rose. I don't want to admire
the glassblower's academic replica,

his copies correct only to a single sense.
And why did a god so invested in permanence
choose so fragile a medium, the last material
he might expect to last? Better prose

to tell the forms of things, or illustration.
Though there's something seductive in this impossibility:
transparent color telling the live mottle of peach,
the blush or tint of crab, englobed,

gorgeous, edible. How else match that flush?
He's built a perfection out of hunger,
fused layer upon layer, swirled until
what can't be tasted, won't yield,

almost satisifies, an art
mouthed to the shape of how soft things are,
how good, before they disappear.

A Letter from the Coast

All afternoon the town readied for storm,
    men in the harbor shallows hauling in small boats
      that rise and fall on the tide. Pleasure,

one by our house is called. I didn't think
    the single man who tugged her in could manage
      alone, though he pushed her up high enough,

he must have hoped, to miss the evening's
    predicted weather: a huge freight of rain
      tumbling up the coast. There's another storm

in town, too, a veritable cyclone
    of gowns and wigs: men in dresses here for a week
      of living the dream of crossing over.

All afternoon they braved the avenue
    fronting the harbor, hats set against the wind,
      veils seedpearled with the first rain,

accessoried to the nines. The wardrobes
    in their rented rooms must glitter,
      opened at twilight when they dress

for the evening, sequin shimmer
    leaping out of the darkness . . . Their secret's
      visible here, public, as so many are,

and in that raw weather I loved
    the flash of red excess, the cocktail dress
      the fur hat, the sheer pleasure

of stockings and gloves.
    I'm writing to tell you this:
      what was left of the hurricane arrived by ten.

All night I heard, under the steep-pitched shallows
    of our sleep, the shoulders of the sea flashing,
      loaded, silvering with so much broken cargo:

shell and rusted metal, crabclaw and spine,
    kelp and feathers and the horseshoe carapace,
      and threading through it all the foghorns'

double harmony of warning, one note layered
  just over and just after the other. *Safety*,
    they said, or *shelter*, two inexact syllables

repeated precisely all night, glinting
  through my dream the way the estuaries
    shone before sunup, endless

invitation and promise, till dawn
  beat the whole harbor to pewter.
    Pleasure was unmoved and burnished a cobalt

the exact shade of a mussel's hinge,
  and every metal shone in the sea: platinum,
    sterling, tarnished chrome.

The law of the tide is accumulation, *More*,
  and our days here are layered detail,
    the shore's grand mosaic of detritus:

tumbled beach glass, endless bits
  of broken china, as if whole nineteenth-century kitchens
    went down in the harbor and lie scattered

at our feet, the tesserae of Byzantium.
  Those syllables sounded all night,
    their meaning neither completed nor exhausted.

What was it I meant to tell you?
  All I meant to do this storm-rinsed morning,
    which has gone brilliant and uncomplicated

as silk, that same watery sheen?
  How the shore's a huge armoire
    full of gowns, all its drawers packed

and gleaming? Something about pleasure
  and excess: thousands of foamy veils,
    a tidal wrack of emerald, glamor

of froth-decked, dashed pearl bits.
  A million earrings rinsed in the dawn.
    I wish you were here.

Homo Will Not Inherit

Downtown anywhere and between the roil
of bathhouse steam – up there the linens of joy
and shame must be laundered again and again,

all night – downtown anywhere
and between the column of feathering steam
unknotting itself thirty feet above the avenue's

shimmered azaleas of gasoline,
between the steam and the ruin
of the Cinema Paree (marquee advertising

its own milky vacancy, broken showcases sealed,
ticketbooth a hostage wrapped in tape
and black plastic, captive in this zone

of blackfronted bars and bookstores
where there's nothing to read
but longing's repetitive texts,

where desire's unpoliced, or nearly so)
someone's posted a xeroxed headshot
of Jesus: permed, blonde, blurred at the edges

as though photographed through a greasy lens,
and inked beside him, in marker strokes:
HOMO WILL NOT INHERIT. *Repent & be saved.*

I'll tell you what I'll inherit: the margins
which have always been mine, downtown after hours
when there's nothing left to buy,

the dreaming shops turned in on themselves,
seamless, intent on the perfection of display,
the bodegas and offices lined up, impenetrable:

edges no one wants, no one's watching. Though
the borders of this shadow-zone (mirror and dream
of the shattered streets around it) are chartered

by the police, and they are required,
some nights, to redefine them. But not now, at twilight,
permission's descending hour, early winter darkness

pillared by smoldering plumes. The public city's
ledgered and locked, but the secret city's boundless;
from which do these tumbling towers arise?

I'll tell you what I'll inherit: steam,
and the blinding symmetry of some towering man,
fifteen minutes of forgetfulness incarnate.

I've seen flame flicker around the edges of the body,
pentecostal, evidence of inhabitation.
And I have been possessed of the god myself,

I have been the temporary apparition
salving another, I have been his visitation, I say it
without arrogance, I have been an angel

for minutes at a time, and I have for hours
believed – without judgement, without condemnation –
that in each body, however obscured or recast,

is the divine body – common, habitable –
the way in a field of sunflowers
you can see every bloom's

the multiple expression
of a single shining idea,
which is the face hammered into joy.

I'll tell you what I'll inherit:
stupidity, erasure, exile
inside the chalked lines of the police,

who must resemble what they punish,
the exile you require of me,
you who's posted this invitation

to a heaven nobody wants.
You who must be patrolled,
who adore constraint, I'll tell you

what I'll inherit, not your pallid temple
but a real palace, the anticipated
and actual memory, the moment flooded

by skin and the knowledge of it,
the gesture and its description
– do I need to say it? –

the flesh *and* the word. And I'll tell you,
you who can't wait to abandon your body,
what you want me to, maybe something

like you've imagined, a dirty story:
Years ago, in the baths,
a man walked into the steam,

the gorgeous deep indigo of him gleaming,
solid tight flanks, the intricately ridged abdomen –
and after he invited me to his room,

nudging his key toward me,
as if perhaps I spoke another tongue
and required the plainest of gestures,

after we'd been, you understand,
worshipping a while in his church,
he said to me, *I'm going to punish your mouth.*

I can't tell you what that did to me.
My shame was redeemed then;
I won't need to burn in the afterlife.

It wasn't that he hurt me,
more than that: the spirit's transactions
are enacted now, here – no one needs

your eternity. This failing city's
radiant as any we'll ever know,
paved with oily rainbow, charred gates

jeweled with tags, swoops of letters
over letters, indecipherable as anything
written by desire. I'm not ashamed

to love Babylon's scrawl. How could I be?
It's written on my face as much as on
these walls. This city's inescapable,

gorgeous, and on fire. I have my kingdom.

Aubade: Opal and Silver

First snow, unrolling scrim, my dogs running
through a continuously descending voile

of little white darts, heaven's
heavy silver blushed to lavender

at the rim: what opera is this,
the curtain falling all morning,

its figured ripple airy and endless?

Two hurriers, just after dawn,
one black and one golden: the new dog,

the one my lover's asked for
in the last month of his life

racing unbridled now, abandoning himself
to the arc of his transit

through these brilliant strokes
crosshatching the bay's pewter.

First snow, opal and silver,
evidence and demonstration:

from the magician's secret wardrobes
emerge whole realms of costume,

not one of them ever worn twice.
Here's enough antique lace

to sew a bodice for the harbor,
its silver-skinned breathing

dotted now with little flowers of ice.

Here a dreaming princess decked
in forty bolts of eyelet,

a wicked mandarin whose lunar silks
are flecked with ashen butterflies:

apparitions of time – who'll play,
and wreck, each character in the comedy.

That's the nature of the trick:
time animates what it kills.

Two arcs, one black and one golden,
racing ahead till they're only

quick strokes on the page
the shore's become, under a sky

intimate and iridescent
as the interior of a gem. Time's

not the enemy, nothing
as simple as that; our old enchanter

— dressmaker to reality —

works these fierce and delicate effects
from somewhere in the wings.

From nowhere, shifting tableaux
— for our instruction

and delight? meant to confound us? —
come looming through the morning's

steadily unfolding screen,
the silken undulation

between this life and the next,
now and *ever*. A lip of sun

— unpredictable appearance —
and the snowy billow's overshot

with gold like Favrile glass; this fabric's
spun of such insubstantial stuff

it doesn't quite conceal the other world.
Can't we see into it already, a little? Look,

there: two gestures, one black
and one golden, racing into the veil.

ANDREW MOTION

Anne Frank Huis

Even now, after twice her lifetime of grief
and anger in the very place, whoever comes
to climb these narrow stairs, discovers how
the bookcase slides aside, then walks through
shadow into sunlit rooms, can never help

but break her secrecy again. Just listening
is a kind of guilt: the Westerkirk repeats
itself outside, as if all time worked round
towards her fear, and made each stroke
die down on guarded streets. Imagine it –

three years of whispering and loneliness
and plotting, day by day, the Allied line
in Europe with a yellow chalk. What hope
she had for ordinary love and interest
survives her here, displayed above the bed

as pictures of her family; some actors;
fashions chosen by Princess Elizabeth.
And those who stoop to see them find
not only patience missing its reward,
but one enduring wish for chances

like my own: to leave as simply
as I do, and walk at ease
up dusty tree-lined avenues, or watch
a silent barge come clear of bridges
settling their reflections in the blue canal.

One Life

Up country, her husband is working late
on a high cool veranda. His radio plays
World Service News, but he does not listen,
and does not notice how moonlight fills
the plain below, with its ridge of trees
and shallow river twisting to Lagos
a whole night's journey south. What holds

him instead are these prizes that patience
and stealthy love have caught: *papilio
dardanus* – each with the blacks and whites
of simple absolutes he cannot match.

She understands nothing of this.
Away in her distant room, she lies
too sick to see the bar-sign steadily print
its purple letters again and again on her wall.
Too tired to care when the silence breaks
and this stranger, her friend, leans over the bed.
There is just one implausible thought
that haunts her as clear and perfect as ever –
the delicate pottery bowl she left
forgotten at home, still loaded with apples
and pears she knows by their English names.

Close

The afternoon I was killed
I strolled up the beach from the sea
where the big wave had hit me,
helped my wife and kids
pack up their picnic things,
then took my place in the car
for the curving journey home
through almost-empty lanes.

I had never seen the country
looking so beautiful –
furnace red in the poppies
scribbled all over the fields;
a darker red in the rocks
which sheltered the famous caves;
and pink in the western sky
which bode us well for tomorrow.

Nobody spoke about me
or how I was no longer there.
It was odd, but I understood why:
when I had drowned I was only
a matter of yards out to sea
(not *too far out* – too close),
still able to hear the talk
and have everything safe in view.

My sunburned wife, I noticed,
was trying to change for a swim,
resting her weight on one leg
as if she might suddenly start
to dance, or jump in the air,
but in fact snaking out of her knickers –
as shy as she was undressing
the first time we went to bed.

Reading the Elephant

For Ted Hughes

I won't say much about it now, except that she got
bored, or I did, at any rate someone left someone,
there was a leaving, and quite by chance
I had this friend of a friend who said why not
run away for a bit, it won't seem like running,
it won't when you say it's to Africa, God no,
that sounds like choice. So I did. I went like a shot.

And the next thing I knew was this place
marooned in the trees – that is: in the hills,
except it was trees I could see, no two the same
and swarming right up to the house – one with a face
in its trunk like a skinny-jawed Rackham witch,
one a cedar of some sort though really like clouds,
slabs of green cloud which boiled straight up into space.

It had people there too, of course, but they left me
as well, or rather I chose to stay put. Come morning
they'd clatter out into the jeep with their hampers,
their cameras, their hip-flasks, and set off to see
whatever strayed into their paths (one day a lion
shagged out on a comfortable branch, the next a croc
rip-roaring a bambi, just like they do on TV).

I'd walk round in circles indoors and wait until no one
was looking – in circles, but never unhappy, just
turning time back on itself. You know how it is.
Then I'd slither away to a spot where the sun
splayed down through those trees I was talking about
like a bicycle tyre, and set myself square to the world
as though everything in it had only that moment begun.

I mean: as though never till then had the daylight
come razoring over that silver-grey scrub,
never till then had the dust of that infinite landscape
been glued into cones of such a miraculous height
by ants with such staggering brains, never till then
had leaves been shelter or simply the things that they were –
pure pattern, pure beauty, pure pleasure in living, pure sight.

They never last long, these moments. With half a chance
we drop back to life as it is. I understand that.
I'm not quite a fool. So to keep myself airborne I always
snapped open some book (some parachute) just as my trance
was ending – which meant on the day that I'm thinking about
I'd turned to Pierre and was hearing how Moscow must fall
this month, what with the winter, what with the French advance.

Soldiers fanned out on the steppes. Feathers of smoke
flapped above burnt-out farms. An immense chandelier
reflected bare shoulders and medals revolving in miniature,
time and again, as the string quartet for a joke
performed by a wide-open window for Boney to hear,
each note struck fierce and hard and long on the dark
like stones sent skittering out on a windless lake –

like something inside me, yet outside as well,
a fracture, a cracking, which made me whisk round,
heart jumping, and find there not ten yards behind,
stock still in the African day I could no longer tell
was real – an elephant. Elephant.
Huge as a hill, creased where the weather runs down,
grave-grey in the haze of its dry-grass-pissed-on smell

and staring me out. That lasted I don't know how long –
the eyes not blinking no matter how busily flies
kept fussing and dabbling, the ragged-edged ears
traced with lugubrious veins, the bristly thong
of its tail twitched side to side, and me just sitting
not thinking at all – at least, me thinking that never
would one of the several worlds I was living among

connect with another, that soon I would just disappear
as the elephant would, its baggy-skinned legs
slow-pumping, its tentative feet squashing down
on their silent compressors, and leaving the air
disturbed for only a moment, no more, as I did myself
when I saw that enough was enough, and escaped
from the trees into unbroken sunlight with everything clear.

ROBERT MINHINNICK

Twenty-Five Laments for Iraq

The muezzin voices break the night
Telling us of what we are composed:
Coffee grits; a transparency of sugar;
The ghost of the cardamom in the cup's mosque.

*

These soldiers will not marry.
They are wed already
To the daughters of uranium.

*

Scheherazade sits
In heat and dust
Watching her bucket fill.
This is the first story.

*

Before hunger
       Thirst.
Before prayer
       Thirst.
Before money
       Thirst.
Before thirst.
       Water.

*

Boys of Watts and Jones County
Build cookfires on the ramparts of Ur.
But the desert birds are silent
And all the wolves of the province
Fled to the north.

*

While we are filming the sick child
The sick child behind us
Dies. And as we turn our camera
The family group smartens itself
As if grieving might offend.

*

Red and gold
The baldaquins
Beneath the Baghdad moon,
Beneath the Pepsi globe.

*

Since the first Caliph
There has been the *suq* –
These lemons, this fish:
And hunched over the stone
The women in their black –
Four dusty aubergines.

*

My daughter, he says,
Stroking the Sony DV Cam,
Its batteries hot, the tally light red.
My daughter.

But his daughter, 12, keeps to her cot,
Woo, woo wooing like the hoopoe
Over the British cemetery.

*

What are children here
But olivestones under our shoes?
Reach instead for the date
Before its brilliance tarnishes.

*

Back and forth
Back and forth
The Euphrates kingfisher,
The ferryman's rope.

*

The ice seller waits
Beneath his thatch of palm,
His money running in the gutter's tilth.

*

Over the searchlights
And machine gun nests on Rashid Street
The bats explode like tracer fire.

*

Yellow as dates these lizards
Bask on the basilica.
Our cameraman removes his shoes,
Squats down to pray.

*

Radiant,
With the throat of a shark,
The angel who came to the hundreds
Sheltered in Amariya.

*

In the hotel carpark
One hundred and fifty brides and grooms
Await the photographer.
All night I lie awake
Listening to their cries.

*

This first dollar peeled off the wad
Buys a stack of dinars higher than my heart.

*

A heron in white
And a woman in black
Knee deep together
In the green Tigris.

*

Her two pomegranates lie beside the bed
But they have carried the child away.

*

She alights from the bus
In a cloud of black,
The moon and stars upon her skirt,
And painted across her breast
The Eye that Sees All Things.

*

The vermilion on his toenails
    Is almost worn away,
This child of the bazaar
Who rolls my banknote to a tube
And scans through its telescope
The ruins of Babylon.

*

Four billion years
Until the uranium
That was spilled at Ur
Unmakes itself.
Easier to wait for the sun to die.

*

In the Ministry of Information
Computers are down, the offices dark;
But with me in the corridor
A secret police of cockroaches.

*

Moths, I say.
No. Look again, she suggests.
Fused to the ceiling are the black hands
Of the children of Amariya.

*

    Sometimes
The certainties return:
These cushions, a pipe,
And the sweet Basran tea
Stewed with limes.

CAROL ANN DUFFY

Foreign

Imagine living in a strange, dark city for twenty years.
There are some dismal dwellings on the east side
and one of them is yours. On the landing, you hear
your foreign accent echo down the stairs. You think
in a language of your own and talk in theirs.

Then you are writing home. The voice in your head
recites the letter in a local dialect; behind that
is the sound of your mother singing to you,
all that time ago, and now you do not know
why your eyes are watering and what's the word for this.

You use the public transport. Work. Sleep. Imagine one night
you saw a name for yourself sprayed in red
against a brick wall. A hate name. Red like blood.
It is snowing on the streets, under the neon lights,
as if this place were coming to bits before your eyes.

And in the delicatessen, from time to time, the coins
in your palm will not translate. Inarticulate,
because this is not home, you point at fruit. Imagine
that one of you says *Me not know what these people mean.*
It like they only go to bed and dream. Imagine that.

Girlfriends

derived from Verlaine
for John Griffith

That hot September night, we slept in a single bed,
naked, and on our frail bodies the sweat
cooled and renewed itself. I reached out my arms
and you, hands on my breasts, kissed me. Evening of amber.

Our nightgowns lay on the floor where you fell to your knees
and became ferocious, pressed your head to my stomach,
your mouth to the red gold, the pink shadows; except
I did not see it like this at the time, but arched

my back and squeezed water from the sultry air
with my fists. Also I remembered hearing, clearly
but distantly, a siren some streets away – *de*

da de da de da – which mingled with my own
absurd cries, so that I looked up, even then,
to see my fingers counting themselves, dancing.

Small Female Skull

With some surprise, I balance my small female skull in my hands.
What is it like? An ocarina? Blow in its eye.
It cannot cry, holds my breath only as long as I exhale,
mildly alarmed now, into the hole where the nose was,
press my ear to its grin. A vanishing sigh.

For some time, I sit on the lavatory seat with my head
in my hands, appalled. It feels much lighter than I'd thought;
the weight of a deck of cards, a slim volume of verse,
but with something else, as though it could levitate. Disturbing.
So why do I kiss it on the brow, my warm lips to its papery bone,

and take it to the mirror to ask for a gottle of geer?
I rinse it under the tap, watch dust run away, like sand
from a swimming-cap, then dry it – firstborn – gently
with a towel. I see the scar where I fell for sheer love
down treacherous stairs, and read that shattering day like braille.

Love, I murmur to my skull, then, louder, other grand words,
shouting the hollow nouns in a white-tiled room.
Downstairs they will think I have lost my mind. No. I only weep
into these two holes here, or I'm grinning back at the joke, this is
a friend of mine. See, I hold her face in trembling, passionate hands.

The Grammar of Light

Even barely enough light to find a mouth,
and bless both with a meaningless O, teaches,
spells out. The way a curtain opened at night
lets in neon, or moon, or a car's hasty glance,
and paints for a moment someone you love, pierces.

And so many mornings to learn; some
when the day is wrung from damp, grey skies
and rooms come on for breakfast
in the town you are leaving early. The way
a wasteground weeps glass tears at the end of a street.

Some fluent, showing you how the trees
in the square think in birds, telepathise. The way
the waiter balances light in his hands, the coins
in his pocket silver, and a young bell shines
in its white tower ready to tell.

Even a saucer of rain in a garden at evening
speaks to the eye. Like the little fires
from allotments, undressing in veils of mauve smoke
as you walk home under the muted lamps,
perplexed. The way the shy stars go stuttering on.

And at midnight, a candle next to the wine
slurs its soft wax, flatters. Shadows
circle the table. The way all faces blur
to dreams of themselves held in the eyes.
The flare of another match. The way everything dies.

Prayer

Some days, although we cannot pray, a prayer
utters itself. So, a woman will lift
her head from the sieve of her hands and stare
at the minims sung by a tree, a sudden gift.

Some nights, although we are faithless, the truth
enters our hearts, that small familiar pain;
then a man will stand stock-still, hearing his youth
in the distant Latin chanting of a train.

Pray for us now. Grade I piano scales
console the lodger looking out across
a Midlands town. Then dusk, and someone calls
a child's name as though they named their loss.

Darkness outside. Inside, the radio's prayer –
Rockall. Malin. Dogger. Finisterre.

SUJATA BHATT

Muliebrity

I have thought so much about the girl
who gathered cow-dung in a wide, round basket
along the main road passing by our house
and the Radhavallabh temple in Maninagar.
I have thought so much about the way she
moved her hands and her waist
and the smell of cow-dung and road-dust and wet canna lilies,
the smell of monkey breath and freshly washed clothes
and the dust from crows' wings which smells different –
and again the smell of cow-dung as the girl scoops
it up, all these smells surrounding me separately
and simultaneously – I have thought so much
but have been unwilling to use her for a metaphor,
for a nice image – but most of all unwilling
to forget her or to explain to anyone the greatness
and the power glistening through her cheekbones
each time she found a particularly promising
mound of dung –

A Different History

I

Great Pan is not dead;
he simply emigrated
        to India.
Here, the gods roam freely,
disguised as snakes or monkeys;
every tree is sacred
and it is a sin
to be rude to a book.
It is a sin to shove a book aside
        with your foot,
a sin to slam books down
      hard on a table,
a sin to toss one carelessly
      across a room.
You must learn how to turn the pages gently
without disturbing Sarasvati,
without offending the tree
from whose wood the paper was made.

2

Which language
has not been the oppressor's tongue?
Which language
truly meant to murder someone?
And how does it happen
that after the torture,
after the soul has been cropped
with a long scythe swooping out
of the conqueror's face –
the unborn grandchildren
grow to love that strange language.

Understanding *the* Ramayana

When they bowed
to us in their sparkling robes
I didn't want them to leave –

that day felt scorched
from the beginning;
unbearably hot
as if it were perpetually noon.

No cool imlee scented
                    Poona breeze,
so we had retreated
into the shadows cast
                    by our house.

We were tired, almost bored
when we saw them unfasten the latch
to the gate like thieves and slip through
into our garden before
anyone could stop them.

We were only children then
still we admired the fitted
yet comfortable sleeves
partly covering their furry arms –
arms which were a slightly different
                    brown from ours.

And I envied the tailor
who had stitched such earnest
headdresses – a tailor who
I thought was privileged to be
designing clothes for such creatures.

Sita, I stare at
        the longest.
She was so refined,
the way she folded up
her hands for *namaste*, while the slant
of her neck told us everything
about a disciplined suffering.
And the swift darting of her eyes
between Rama and Lakshman
required no words.

So it didn't matter
that none of them could speak.
We could even have done without
the whiny drone of the narrator
who also directed them, waving
his hands about with such force
as if that would sharpen
Sita's emotions.

It didn't matter
that now and then we glimpsed
a looped up tail
motionless as if drugged to sleep
beneath their costumes.

Their tails were fanned by swishing hems
when they leaped –
Sita flying away in fear;
Rama flying in for a fight
        to save her.

Bright pink and orange frills
speckled with blue-green sequins
and outlined with silver
threads, zig-zagging stars –
bright frills would flutter up
revealing the quiet tail – its power
dormant and forbidden to take any part
in the actions of Prince Rama
            or Princess Sita.

We felt relieved to know
the narrator hadn't chopped off
or even shortened
the glorious question marks
curling behind their backs.

Only Hanuman
allowed to use his tail
was the most joyous
and felt perfectly cast.

Monkeys more humane
              than anyone –
But it relieved me to see
a flash of pride, of anger
cut through their meek faces.
Or was it only acting?

Where had they been found?
And how had they learnt
the meaning of the *Ramayana*
              that well?

So absorbed were we
as if we had never heard
this saga before,
that we didn't mind
the withered, small-pox
              scarred face
of the man who owned them;
we didn't pay much attention
to the chains around the delicate
              monkey feet – preventing them
from jumping very far.

In the end our only regret
was that we couldn't join them
when they were dragged away
by their worn out master.

We stood in the middle
              of the garden
watching them leave –
our hands hanging limp
              by our sides.

They seemed to disappear
into haloes of swirling dust.

The gate clanged shut
        and the heat
descended like a curtain
forcing us back
        into the shade.

White Asparagus

Who speaks of the strong currents
streaming through the legs, the breasts
of a pregnant woman
in her fourth month?

She's young, this is her first time,
she's slim and the nausea has gone.
Her belly's just starting to get rounder
her breasts itch all day,

and she's surprised that what she wants
is *him*
        inside her again.
Oh come like a horse, she wants to say,
move like a dog, a wolf,
                become a suckling lion-cub −

Come here, and here, and here −
but swim fast and don't stop.

Who speaks of the green coconut uterus
the muscles sliding, a deeper undertow
and the green coconut milk that seals
her well, yet flows so she is wet
from his softest touch?

Who understands the logic
behind this desire?

Who speaks of the rushing tide
        that awakens
her slowly increasing blood − ?

And the hunger
          raw obsessions beginning
with the shape of asparagus:
sun-deprived white and purple-shadow-veined,
she buys three kilos
of the fat ones, thicker than anyone's fingers,
she strokes the silky heads,
some are so jauntily capped . . .
          even the smell pulls her in –

The Stinking Rose

Everything I want to say
is in that name
for these cloves of garlic – they shine
like pearls still warm from a woman's neck.

My fingernail nudges and nicks
the smell open, a round smell
          that spirals up. Are you hungry?
Does it burn through your ears?

Did you know some cloves were planted
near the coral-coloured roses
to provoke the petals
into giving stronger perfume . . .

Everything is in that name
          for garlic:
Roses and smells
          and the art of naming . . .

What's in a name? that which we call a rose,
By any other name would smell as sweet . . .

But that which we call garlic
smells sweeter, more
vulnerable, even delicate
if we call it *The Stinking Rose.*

The roses on the table, the garlic in the salad
and the salt teases our ritual
tasting to last longer.
You who dined with us tonight,

this garlic will sing to your heart
to your slippery muscles – will keep
your nipples and your legs from sleeping.

Fragrant blood full of garlic –
yes, they noted it reeked under the microscope.

His fingers tired after peeling and crushing
the stinking rose, the sticky cloves –
Still, in the middle of the night his fingernail
nudges and nicks her very own smell
        her prism open –

MICHAEL HOFMANN

By Forced Marches

Who knows what would happen if you stopped?
The autobiography draws out, lengthens
towards the end. Life stays in one place,
often Rome; and to compensate, you cut up
your time in many pieces. Rations are halved,
then quartered. The emergency is acute.
Now it is one lump of sugar per day.

Eclogue

Industry undressing in front of Agriculture –
not a pretty sight. The subject for one
of those allegorical Victorian sculptures.
An energetic mismatch. But Pluto's hell-holes
terminate in or around the flower-meadows
and orchards of Proserpine. Ceres's poor daughter
is whisked away by the top-hatted manufacturer
on his iron horse . . . Brick huts in the fields,
barred mine entrances from the last century,
narrow-gauge railways, powdery cement factories.
A quarry is an inverted cathedral: witchcraft,
a steeple of air sharpened and buried in the ground.
– All around these dangerous sites, sheep graze,
horned and bleating like eminent Victorians.

Pastorale

for Beat Sterchi

Where the cars razored past on the blue highway,
I walked, unreasonably, *contre-sens*,

the slewed census-taker on the green verge,
noting a hedgehog's defensive needle-spill,

the bullet-copper and bullet-steel of pheasants,
henna ferns and a six-pack of Feminax,

indecipherable cans and the cursive snout and tail
of a flattened rat under the floribund ivy,

the farmer's stockpiled hayrolls and his flocks,
ancillary, bacillary blocks of anthrax.

Postcard from Cuernavaca

to Ralph Manheim

Picture me
sitting between the flying buttresses of Cuernavaca Cathedral
reading Lawrence on the clitoral orgasm, and (more!)
his notion of replacing the Virgin Mary,
the one enduringly popular foreigner,
with Cortez' translator, later mistress, La Malinche,
the one enduringly unpopular – because xenophile – Mexican . . .

The night wind
blows the clouds over from the direction of his old palace,
a rather gloomy, conglomerate affair, pirated from an old pyramid,
and studded with red volcanic tufa in heart-sized pieces.
It's an even-handed museum now: offensively large statue of Cortez –
revisionist Rivera mural. (Or you turn away from both,
and look to where the volcanoes used to be.)

Out in front,
there are forests of helium balloons glittering under the fresno trees
where sociable black grackles natter and scream.
Hawkers trailing by in profile like matadors, trailing – in one case a
    hawk.
A Mariachi trumpeter, wearing just his old pesos,

trilling drily into the gutter. Ostensible Aztecs
stitching their silver Roman-style tunics *im Schneidersitz*.

There's a band
hidden in Eiffel's unilluminated iron snowdrop bandstand –
bought by the Austrians here to cheer them up
when Maximilian left the scene – giving it some humpity.
The rondure and Prussian gleam of the horns –
I sit and listen in the Café Viena.
Anything north of here goes, and most things east.

My room is both.
A steel door, pasteboard panelling,
and so high it makes me dizzy.
The toilet paper dangles inquiringly from the window cross.
A light bulb's skull tumbles forlornly into the room.
Outside there is a chained monkey who bites. He lives,
as I do, on Coke and bananas, which he doesn't trouble to peel.

GWYNETH LEWIS

Six Poems on Nothing

1 *Midwinter Marriage*

After autumn's fever and its vivid trees,
infected with colour as the light died back,
we've settled to greyness: fields behind gauze,

hedges feint in tracing-paper mists,
the sun diminished to a midday moon
and daylight degraded to the monochrome

of puritan weather. This healing cold
holds us to pared-down simplicities.
Now is the worst-case solstice time,

acutest angle of the shortest day,
a time to condemn the frippery of leaves
and know that trees stand deltas to the sky

producing nothing. A time to take your ease
in not knowing, in blankness, in vacuity.
This is the season that has married me.

2 *Annunciation*

When first he painted the Virgin the friar filled
the space around her with angels' wings,
scalloped and plated, with skies of gold,

heavy with matter. He thought that he knew
that heaven was everywhere. He grew
older, wiser and found that he drew

more homely rooms with pots and beds,
but lavished his art on soft furnishings
and the turn of the waiting angel's wings

(still gorgeous with colour and precious dust).
Much later, he sensed that his God had withdrawn,
was spacious. On smaller frescoes he painted less,

let wall be wall, but drew in each lawn
the finer detail of sorrel and weed.
Still later, he found his devotion drawn

to nothing – shadows hinted at hidden rooms,
at improbable arches, while the angel's news
shattered the Virgin, who became a view

as open as virtue, her collapsing planes
easy and vacant as the evening breeze
that had brought a plain angel to his grateful knees.

3

I've made friends with nothing and have found
it is a husband. See these wedding rings?
Two eyes through which I see everything

but not as I used to. Importance leaves me cold,
as does all information that is classed as "news".
I like those events that the centre ignores:

small branches falling, the slow decay
of wood into humus, how a puddle's eye
silts up slowly, till, eventually,

the birds can't bathe there. I admire the edge;
the sides of roads where the ragwort blooms
low but exotic in the traffic fumes;

the scruffy ponies in a scrubland field
like bits of a jigsaw you can't complete;
the colour of rubbish in a stagnant leat.

These are rarest enjoyments, for connoisseurs
of blankness, an acquired taste,
once recognised, impossible to shake,

this thirst for the lovely commonplace.
It's offered me freedom, so I choose to stay.
And I thought my heart had been given away.

4

He started to transform himself in sixty-three,
though few of us knew it at the very start
or suspected his goal was transparency.

We only noticed that he'd disappear
from time to time off the factory floor.
We covered, but his absences grew longer

till, for all our lying, he was finally caught
by the foreman in the locker room,
tied up in a clear chrysalis of thought.

Nothing would shift him, so he got the sack,
but took it quite calmly. When I walked him home
he explained that there was no turning back

from his self-translation. The scales of a butterfly
aren't coloured at all, but are shingles of white
which simply accept the prismatics of light

in spectacular patterns. That humility
was what he was after. I met him often
and watched his skin's translucency

deepen with practice, so that his derm
and epidermis were transmogrified.
He was able to earn some cash on the side

as a medical specimen while muscles and veins
were still visible and then even more
for the major organs as he became pure

through his praying (this after his wife
had sued him for lack of comfort and joy
in their marriage) but by then his life

was simply reflective. I could only discern
his shape in the sunshine, so purged was he
of his heaviness and opacity.

He knew he was nothing. Through him I saw
colours shades deeper than ever before
and detail: the ratchets on a snail's rough tongue,

the way light bruises, how people fall
to weakness through beauty and when we came
to him for vision, he accepted us all,

made us more real, gave us ourselves
redeemed in the justice of his paraphrase,
the vivid compassion of his body's gaze.

5 *"A Calm"*[1]

Nothing is happening everywhere,
if only we knew it. Take these clouds,
our most expensive purchase to date,

five million for a fleet becalmed
off the coast of nowhere. I like the restraint
that chose this lack of action in paint,

this moment of poise between travel and rain –
cumulonimbus in a threatening sky,
horizon, cumulonimbus again

as water gives the air its rhyme
and the pressure keeps dropping. An oily tide
buoys up a barrel by the coaster's side,

emptied, no doubt, by the sailors on board
waiting, tipsy, for their lives to begin
again with the weather. The clouds close in

but this boredom's far richer than anything
that can happen inside it – than the wind, than a port,
or the storm that will wipe out this moment of nought.

1. *A Calm*: a painting by Jan van de Capelle, acquired by the
National Museum of Wales.

6

The monk says nothing, finger to his lips
and day begins inside his silences.
First dawn then birdsong fill the gaps

his love has left them. He's withdrawn
to let things happen. His humility
has allowed two kinds of ordinary –

sparrows and starlings – to fight it out
over the fruit of a backyard tree
and against the blackbirds. His nonentity

is a fertile garden, fed from the well
of a perfect cipher, and the water's cool,
most nourishing. He drinks his fill

and cities happen in his fissured mind,
motorways, roadblocks. He is host
to ecosystems that sustain us all,

for our lives depend on his emptiness.
His attention flickers. He turns away
to something and destroys our day.

Herod's Palace

It seemed a simple case of opulence,
when diggers discovered the marble pool
still edged in lapis lazuli and gold
with dolphin mosaics under a portico,
all placed so the swimmer would seem to dive
into the wealth of the valley below.

But mercy's a mystery and takes time to see:
They found another pool outside the gates,
its bottom cluttered with unclaimed lamps
knocked over by lepers as they shuffled, late,
to bathe there in secret, never thinking that now
we see them immersing themselves in pure light.

Walking with the God

This Mahādeva is a great white dog
who sets out with me on a winter walk
in snowy mountains, though he never stays.
He is also the god who suddenly appears
to herd men's souls, a palindrome, a way

of moving, though the world withdraws
from us in mist, as faith draws back from words,
to leave us groping. Hear him pant behind,
circling my path then passing, pulled ahead
by smells that say this is his land

though I keep to the path, as farmers shoot for rain
and other creatures. In the fields around
the melt is making continents of snow
and slopes are shading into mackerel skies
that hide him from me. Now as I go

rain brings down mist and I find that I wear
thousands of diamonds on clothes and hair
and now it's white-out and behind I hear
that Mahādeva the wolf is here,
hungry for wonder, thirsting for fear.

GLYN MAXWELL

Mild Citizen

Sunday is wringing its discoloured hands.
The elms are rinsed of light and greenness, birds
shit and circle over these charlatans
who haggle in the field. I do my work,
    scotching the short words
I really want, the ragged and berserk,
in favour of a point of view. I lean
into the vertical, out of the murk
which pulls and changes what it didn't say
    and didn't know, but mean,
and I'm ready. Ever younger people play
there or near, as the adult town of men
fills up with us, and yellow yesterday

in its sheets, smells. When it gets late
    I walk, mild citizen
of what's suggested, what's appropriate
because it saves my neck. Only, again,
I see the pale, shock-headed Delegate
emerging from the Chamber, and I hear
    the moaning on the lane,
where the mild citizens keep moving, where
empty musicians play in endless rain.

Poisonfield

We went to vote in our democracy,
    and saw a poisoned field behind a fence.
Dangerous for children, I think I said,

but those behind me disagreed at once,
    pointing out the great wire that the field had
wound itself in. They asked if I could see.

It's safe, they said. We reached the yellow wood
    where we thought the voting gates would be
but no – there was a map, moving with ants

and my best mate shuddered, lost his melody
    around the gatepost, changed his fingerprints.
There was a black cow and a lightning rod:

voortrekkers in the sky, doing the rounds
    of wagons, holiness, and the brown lid
banging out a song for me and thee.

We tried to vote, and were told to thank God
    we weren't the winged things we could clearly see
eating out of half a poor man's hands.

We thanked. We stopped at a dance-hall for tea,
    discussing politics, and our new friends
we couldn't shake off. Then I think I said

Is it time to move to a vote? And the dance
    failed, the disapproving children heard
apologies that sidled out of me . . .

*   *   *

It seems to last forever. In my bed
   I sulk and spoil the paper. Tyranny
is mine. I miss the rallies and events

they organise. I finger my one key,
   and on the poisoned field behind a fence
I grow my children and I grow them bad.

SIMON ARMITAGE

Zoom!

   It begins as a house, an end terrace
in this case
   but it will not stop there. Soon it is
an avenue
   which cambers arrogantly past the Mechanics' Institute,
turns left
   at the main road without even looking
and quickly it is
   a town with all four major clearing banks,
a daily paper
   and a football team pushing for promotion.

   On it goes, oblivious of the Planning Acts,
the green belts,
   and before we know it it is out of our hands:
city, nation,
   hemisphere, universe, hammering out in all directions
until suddenly,
   mercifully, it is drawn aside through the eye
of a black hole
   and bulleted into a neighbouring galaxy, emerging
smaller and smoother
   than a billiard ball but weighing more than Saturn.

   People stop me in the street, badger me
in the check-out queue
   and ask, "What is this, this that is so small
and so very smooth
   but whose mass is greater than the ringed planet?"
It's just words
   I assure them. But they will not have it.

Poem

And if it snowed and snow covered the drive
he took a spade and tossed it to one side.
And always tucked his daughter up at night.
And slippered her the one time that she lied.

And every week he tipped up half his wage.
And what he didn't spend each week he saved.
And praised his wife for every meal she made.
And once, for laughing, punched her in the face.

And for his mum he hired a private nurse.
And every Sunday taxied her to church.
And he blubbed when she went from bad to worse.
And twice he lifted ten quid from her purse.

Here's how they rated him when they looked back:
sometimes he did this, sometimes he did that.

Robinson's Resignation

Because I am done with this thing called work,
the paper-clips and staples of it all.
The customers and their huge excuses,
their incredulous lies and their beautiful
foul-mouthed daughters. I am swimming with it,
right up to here with it. And I am bored,
bored like the man who married a mermaid.

And I am through with the business of work.
In meetings, with the minutes, I have dreamed
and doodled, drifted away then undressed
and dressed almost every single woman,
every button, every zip and buckle.
For eighteen months in this diving-helmet
I have lived with the stench of my own breath.

So I am finished with the whole affair.
As for this friendship thing, I couldn't give
a weeping fig for those so-called brothers
who are all voltage, no current. I have
emptied my locker. I should like to leave

and to fold things now like a pair of gloves
or two clean socks, one into the other.

This is my final word. Nothing will follow.

Becoming of Age

The year the institutions would not hold.
The autumn when the convicts took their leave.
The month the radio went haywire, gargled
through the long-range forecast, and their names.
The fortnight of the curfew, and the cheese-wire
of the Klaxon slicing day from night, night
from day. The clear, unclouded ocean

of the sky. The week we met. The afternoon
we might have seen a ghost, a scarecrow
striding boldly down The Great North Road
towards us, wearing everything he owned.

The minute in the phone box with the coin,
the dialling tone, the disagreement – heads
to turn him in to the authorities, or tails
to leave him be, to let him go to ground
and keep the public footpaths trodden down,
the green lanes and the bridleways.

Then on the glass, each in its own time – one,
two, three, four, five, six fingerprints of rain.

SOPHIE HANNAH

The Good Loser

I have portrayed temptation as amusing.
Now he can either waver or abstain.
His is a superior kind of losing
And mine is an inferior brand of gain.

His sacrifice, his self-imposed restriction
Will get through this controversy intact

For his is a superior kind of fiction
And mine is an inferior brand of fact.

I have displayed my most attractive feature
And he his least, yet still the match seems odd.
For I am a superior kind of creature
And he is an inferior brand of god

And if he cuts me off without a warning
His is the book from which I'll take a leaf
For his is a superior kind of mourning
And ours a most inferior brand of grief.

My Enemies

My enemies, polished inside their caskets
My enemies sparkle behind glass doors
My enemies, curled into tilted baskets
My enemies, not yours

my enemies   You cannot steal or hire them
my enemies   You cannot loan or share
my enemies   Don't tidy or admire them
Don't even see them there

my enemies   Steer clear of the display case
My enemies try to make false amends
my enemies   The pallor of your grey face
will make them shine like friends

My enemies, proud of their faults and failings
my enemies   You take them out for tea
My enemies, beckoning through the railings
at a novice enemy

My enemies will give you proper training
My enemies shuffle up shelves for you
my enemies   The old ones are complaining
I like them better new

my   a new enemy   an equidistant
enemy showing every friend the door
politely, like a personal assistant
my enemies   One more

Two Hundred and Sixty-Five Words

I know exactly what I want to say.
I've estimated how long it will take.
I've weighed the trouble that will come my way
Against the difference saying it could make
And with no help from the mysterious They
Who ought to fight for people's right to speak,
I use my word allowance for today,
My conversation ration for the week

To talk about the baby with no manger,
The gold, myrrh, frankincense he never got,
Who was brought up for profit by a stranger
And invoiced for a rattle and a cot.
His rattle was the one thing he was fond of.
No time to say what matters most to me
Before I'm heard, before they snap the wand of
The upstart fairy on the Christmas tree.

She over-waved that wand. She used to wave it
At all bad things, hoping to make them good.
Who confiscated it? Who, later, gave it
Back to her as a heap of broken wood?
Call now with some inane response or other.
There are two phones, a black one and a white.
The right one will connect you with your brother;
The wrong one and your brother died last night.

Soon I might say *Ninety-five pounds. Nice weather*,
And call you by a name that's not your own.
You think they might put two and two together.
Sound old, sound boring and hang up the phone.
You think if we speak out then they can't touch us,
The Indiscriminately-Known-As-They
Who are responsible. Well, in as much as
I'm one of them, wave all your wands this way.

The Norbert Dentressangle Van

I heave my morning like a sack
of signs that don't appear,
say August, August, takes me back . . .
    That it was not this year . . .
say greenness, greenness, that's the link . . .
    That they were different trees
does not occur to those who think
in anniversaries.

I drive my morning like a truck
with a backsliding load,
say bastard, bastard, always stuck
    behind him on the road
(although I saw another man
    in a distinct machine
last time a Dentressangle van
was on the A14).

I draw my evening like a blind,
say darkness, darkness, that's
if not the very then the kind . . .
    That I see only slats . . .
say moonlight, moonlight, shines the same . . .
    That it's a streetlamp's glow
might be enough to take the name
from everything we know.

I sketch my evening like a plan.
I think I recognise
the Norbert Dentressangle van . . .
    That mine are clouded eyes . . .
say whiteness, whiteness, that's the shade . . .
    That paint is tins apart
might mean some progress can be made
in worlds outside the heart.

INDEX OF TITLES AND FIRST LINES

ACKNOWLEDGEMENTS

The editor and publisher gratefully acknowledges permission to reprint the following poems in this book:

SIMON ARMITAGE: "Zoom!" and "Poem" from *Zoom!* (Bloodaxe Books, 1989) by permission of the publisher; "Robinson's Resignation" from *Kid* (Faber & Faber, 1992) and "Becoming of Age" from *Book of Matches* (Faber & Faber, 1993) by permission of the publisher; JOHN ASH: "Them/There", "Poor Boy: Portrait of a Painting", "Ferns and the Night", "Desert Song" and "Following a Man" from *Selected Poems* (Carcanet Press, 1996) by permission of the publisher; JOHN ASHBERY: "How much longer will I be able to inhabit the divine sepulcher", "For John Clare", "Farm Implements and Rutabagas in a Landscape", "Pyrography", "What is Poetry", "At North Farm", "Forgotten Song" and "Hotel Lautréamont" from *Selected Poems* (Carcanet Press, 1985), *April Galleons* (Carcanet Press, 1988) and *Hotel Lautréamont* (Carcanet Press, 1992) by permission of the publisher; W. H. AUDEN: "The Wanderer", "Paysage Moralisé", "Our Hunting Fathers", "On This Island", "Lullaby", "September 1, 1939", "If I Could Tell You", "In Praise of Limestone" and "A New Year Greeting" from *Collected Poems* (Faber & Faber, 1994) by permission of the publisher; GEORGE BARKER: "Summer Song I", "Turn on your side and bear the day to me", "Morning in Norfolk" and "To Whom Else" from *Selected Poems* (Faber & Faber, 1995) by permission of the publisher; JAMES K. BAXTER: "The Bay", "Morning and Evening Calm", "Lazarus", "Thief and Samaritan", "The Buried Stream" and "Jerusalem Sonnets 36–39" from *Collected Poems* (Oxford University Press, NZ, 1979) by permission of Mrs Jacquie C. Baxter; PATRICIA BEER: "The Flood", "Middle Age", "John Milton and My Father", "Ninny's Tomb", "Ballad of the Underpass" and "Millennium" from *Collected Poems* (Carcanet Press, 1988) by permission of the publisher; JOHN BERRYMAN: "Winter Landscape", "Scholars at the Orchid Pavilion", "He Resigns" and Dream Songs 4, 8, 14, 26, 29, 61, and 255, from *Collected Poems 1937–71* (Faber & Faber, 1990) and *The Dream Songs* (Faber & Faber, 1993) by permission of the publisher; JOHN BETJEMAN: "Slough", "City", "A Shropshire Lad", "In Westminster Abbey" and "Before the Anaesthetic *or* A Real Fright" from *Collected Poems* by permission of John Murray (Publishers) Ltd; SUJATA BHATT: "Muliebrity", "A Different History", "Understanding the *Ramayana*", "White Asparagus" and "The Stinking Rose" from *Point No Point: Selected Poems* (Carcanet Press, 1997) by permission of the publisher; ELIZABETH BISHOP: "First Death in Nova Scotia", "The Fish", "Over 2,000 Illustrations and a Complete Concordance", "Questions of Travel", and "The Shampoo" from *The Complete Poems 1927–79* (Chatto & Windus, 1983) by permission of Farrar, Straus & Giroux, Inc.; EAVAN BOLAND: "The Black Lace Fan My Mother Gave Me", "The Achill Woman", "What We Lost", "Distances", "That the Science of Cartography is Limited", "Love", "The Huguenot Graveyard at the Heart of the City" and "Story" from *Collected Poems* (Carcanet Press, 1995) by permission of the publisher; KAMAU BRATHWAITE: "The Journeys", "Calypso" and "Caliban" from *Black and Blues* (New Directions, 1976, 1995), by permission of the publisher; BASIL BUNTING: "Ode 17", "Ode 37: On the Fly-Leaf of Pound's *Cantos*", "A thrush in the syringa sings" and excerpts from *Briggflatts* from *Complete Poems* (Oxford University Press, 1994) by permission of the publisher; GILLIAN CLARKE: "St Thomas's Day", "Les Grottes", "Border", "Overheard in County Sligo" and "Lament" from *Collected Poems* (Carcanet Press, 1997) by permission of the publisher; DAVID CONSTANTINE: "You are distant, you are already leaving", "Watching for Dolphins", "Lasithi" and "He arrived, towing a crowd, and slept" from *Selected Poems* (Bloodaxe Books, 1991) by permission of the publisher; WENDY COPE: "Waste Land Limericks", "On Finding an Old Photograph", "Rondeau Redoublé", "Bloody Men" and "I Worry" from *Serious Concerns* (Faber & Faber, 1992) and *Making Cocoa for Kingsley Amis* (Faber & Faber, 1997) by permission of the publisher; HART CRANE: "Forgetfulness", "Sunday Morning Apples", "Repose of Rivers", "At Melville's Tomb", "To Brooklyn Bridge" and "To the Cloud Juggler" from *Complete Poems of Hart Crane*, edited by Marc Simon, editor. Copyright 1933, © 1958, 1966 by Liveright Publishing Corporation. Copyright © 1986 by Marc Simon. Reprinted by permission of

Liveright Publishing Corporation; E. E. CUMMINGS: "in Just – ", "what if a much of a which of a wind", "a wind has blown the rain away and blown", "Poem, or Beauty Hurts Mr Vinal", and "pity this busy monster,manunkind" from *Complete Poems 1904–62* (Liveright, 1994) by permission of W. W. Norton & Company. Copyright © 1991 by the Trustees for the E. E. Cummings Trust and George James Firmage; ALLEN CURNOW: "Country School", "This Beach Can Be Dangerous", "You Get What You Pay For", "On the Road to Erewhon", "Continuum" and "Pacific 1945–1995" from *Collected Poems* (Carcanet Press, 1997) by permission of the publisher; DONALD DAVIE: "Remembering the 'Thirties", "Time Passing, Beloved", "Rodez", "Epistle", "The Fountain of Cyanë" and "The Rectitude of Their Beauty" from *Collected Poems* (Carcanet Press, 1991) by permission of the publisher; HILDA DOOLITTLE: "Evening", "The Pool", "Hippolytus Temporizes", extracts from *The Walls Do Not Fall* and *The Flowering of the Rod* from *Collected Poems* (Carcanet Press, 1997) by permission of the publisher; MARK DOTY: "The Ware Collection of Glass", "Flowers and Fruit, Harvard Museum", "A Letter from the Coast", "Homo Will Not Inherit" and "Aubade: Opal and Silver" from *My Alexandria* (University of Illinois Press, 1993) and *Atlantis* (HarperCollins, 1995) by permission of Jonathan Cape; KEITH DOUGLAS: "The Prisoner", "Egypt", "Cairo Jag", "Vergissmeinicht", "How to Kill" and "Desert Flowers" from *Complete Poems* (Oxford University Press, 1978) by permission of the publisher; CAROL ANN DUFFY: "Foreign" from *Selling Manhattan* (Anvil Press, 1987), "Girlfriends" from *The Other Country* (Anvil Press, 1990), "Small Female Skull", "The Grammar of Light" and "Prayer" from *Mean Time* (Anvil Press, 1993) by permission of the publisher; ROBERT DUNCAN: "Among my friends love is a great sorrow", "Often I am Permitted to Return to a Meadow", "Bending a Bow", "The Torso" and "The Sentinels" from *Selected Poems* (Carcanet Press, 1993) by permission of the publisher; T. S. ELIOT: "The Love Song of J. Alfred Prufrock", "La Figlia che Piange", "Sweeney Among the Nightingales", and excerpts from *The Waste Land* and *Four Quartets*, from *Collected Poems 1909–62* (Faber & Faber, 1974) by permission of the publisher; WILLIAM EMPSON: "Rolling the Lawn", "Villanelle", "Legal Fiction", "This Last Pain", "Missing Dates", "The Teasers" and "Let It Go" from Collected Poems (Chatto & Windus, 1956), by permission of the Hogarth Press; ELAINE FEINSTEIN: "At Seven a Son", "Mother Love", "The Magic Apple Tree", "Bathroom", "Getting Older", "Lazarus' Sister" and "Prayer" from *Selected Poems* (Carcanet Press, 1994), and *Daylight* (Carcanet Press, 1997) by permission of the publisher; JAMES FENTON: "A German Requiem", "The Skip" "The Possibility" and "Jerusalem" from *The Memory of War and Children in Exile: Poems 1968–83* (Penguin, 1983) and *Out of Danger* (Penguin, 1993) by permission of the Peters Fraser & Dunlop Group Ltd; ROY FISHER: "Toyland", "As He Came Near Death", "The Thing About Joe Sullivan", "The Least", "Occasional Poem 7.1.72" and "The Supposed Dancer" from *The Dow Low Drop: New and Selected Poems* (Bloodaxe Books, 1996) by permission of the publisher; VERONICA FORREST-THOMSON: "Michaelmas" and "Phrase-Book" from *Language-Games* (Leeds, 1971); "Pfarr-Schmerz (Village-Anguish)" and "Sonnet" from *On the Periphery* (Cambridge, 1976) reprinted in *Collected Poems and Translations* (London, Lewes, Berkeley, 1990). Copyright © Jonathan Culler and The Estate of Veronica Forrest-Thomson 1971, 1976, 1990. Copyright © Allardyce, Barnett, Publishers 1990. Printed by permission of Allardyce, Barnett, Publishers; ROBERT FROST: Mowing", "Mending Wall", "The Road Not Taken", "Birches", "Out, Out – ", "Stopping by Woods on a Snowy Evening", "Acquainted with the Night", "Desert Places", "Provide, Provide" and "The Gift Outright" from *The Poetry of Robert Frost* (Jonathan Cape, 1967) by permission of the Estate of Robert Frost, the editor Edward Connery Lathem and the publisher; ALLEN GINSBERG: Howl" and "Fourth Floor, Dawn, Up All Night Writing Letters" from *Collected Poems 1947–80* (Viking, 1985) © Allen Ginsberg, 1956, 1982, 1984; LOUISE GLÜCK: "The Edge", "Firstborn", "The Magi", "Nativity Poem", "The Letters", "Illuminations", "Happiness", "Hawk's Shadow", "Lamium" and "Vespers" from *The Wild Iris* (Carcanet Press, 1992) and *The First Five Books of Poems* (Carcanet Press, 1997) by permission of the publisher; JORIE GRAHAM: "Tennessee June", "History", "The Region of Unlikeness" and "The Surface" from *The Dream of the Unified Field* (Carcanet Press, 1996) by permission of the publisher; W. S. GRAHAM: "The Thermal Stair", "Imagine a Forest", and "Johann Joachim Quantz's Five Lessons" © The Estate of W. S. Graham, with acknowledgements to Faber & Faber Ltd; ROBERT GRAVES: "The Cool Web",

"Sick Love", "In Broken Images", "Warning to Children", "On Portents", "Down, Wanton, Down!", "Nobody", "The Cloak", "Recalling War", "To Evoke Posterity", "To Juan at the Winter Solstice", "The White Goddess" and "Counting the Beats" from *Complete Poems* (Carcanet Press, 1995) by permission of the publisher; THOM GUNN: "Tamer and Hawk", "The Allegory of the Wolf Boy", "In Santa Maria del Popolo", "Touch", "The Idea of Trust", "The Hug" and "The Man with Night Sweats" from *The Man with Night Sweats* (Faber & Faber, 1992) and *Collected Poems* (Faber & Faber, 1994) by permission of the publisher; IVOR GURNEY: Bach and the Sentry", "Song", "After War", "The Silent One", "Behind the Line", "Old Dreams", "The Not-Returning" and "The Mangel-Bury" from *Selected Poems* (Oxford University Press, 1990) by permission of the publisher; SOPHIE HANNAH: "The Good Loser", "My Enemies", "Two Hundred and Sixty-Five Words" and "The Norbert Dentressangle Van" by permission of the Carcanet Press Ltd; TONY HARRISON: "Heredity", "On Not Being Milton", "National Trust", "Timer", and "Art and Extinction" from *Penguin Modern Poets 5* (Penguin, 1995) by permission of Tony Harrison; GWEN HARWOOD: Carnal Knowledge II", "Andante", "Bone Scan", "Cups" and "Long After Heine" from *Collected Poems* (Oxford University Press, 1991) by permission of the publisher; SEAMUS HEANEY: "The Peninsula", "Anahorish", "Westering", "Mossbawn", "The Guttural Muse", "The Harvest Bow", "The Haw Lantern" and "Seeing Things" from *New Selected Poems* (Faber & Faber, 1990) and *Seeing Things* (Faber & Faber, 1991) by permission of the publisher; GEOFFREY HILL: Genesis", "Ovid in the Third Reich", "September Song", "The Pentecost Castle" and "Tenebrae" from *Collected Poems* (Penguin Books, 1985) © Geoffrey Hill, 1959, 1968, 1978, 1985; MICHAEL HOFMANN: "By Forced Marches", "Eclogue", "Pastorale" and "Postcard from Cuernavaca" from *Nights in the Iron Hotel* (Faber & Faber, 1983), *Acrimony* (Faber & Faber, 1986) and *Corona, Corona* (Faber & Faber, 1993) by permission of the publisher; A. D. HOPE: "The Wandering Islands", "Imperial Adam" and "On an Engraving by Casserius" from *Selected Poems* (Carcanet Press, 1986) by permission of HarperCollins Publishers; A. E. HOUSMAN: "Reveille", "Farewell to barn and stack and tree", "When I watch the living meet", "On Wenlock Edge the wood's in trouble", "Into my heart an air that kills", "Crossing alone the nighted ferry" and "Here dead we lie because we did not choose" by permission of The Society of Authors as the literary representative of the Estate of A. E. Housman; LANGSTON HUGHES: "The Negro Speaks of Rivers", "The Weary Blues", "Cross", "Old Walt" and "I, Too" from *Collected Poems* (Vintage, 1995) by permission of David Higham Associates Ltd; TED HUGHES: "Wind", "Snowdrop", "Her Husband", "Full Moon and Little Frieda", "Wodwo", "Crow and the Birds", "Crow's Last Stand", "Bones" and "That Morning" from *The Hawk in the Rain* (Faber & Faber, 1957), *Lupercal* (Faber & Faber, 1970), *Wodwo* (Faber & Faber, 1967), *Crow* (Faber & Faber, 1974), *River* (Faber & Faber, 1983) and *New Selected Poems 1957–94* (Faber & Faber, 1995) by permission of the publisher; RANDALL JARRELL: "The Island", "The Märchen", "90 North", "The Death of the Ball Turret Gunner" and "Next Day" from *Selected Poems* (Faber & Faber, 1990); ROBINSON JEFFERS: "Shine, Perishing Republic", "An Artist", "Hurt Hawks", "Return" and "The Stars Go Over the Lonely Ocean" from *Selected Poems* (Carcanet Press, 1987) by permission of the publisher; ELIZABETH JENNINGS: "Song for a Birth or a Death", "My Grandmother" and "The Resurrection" from *Growing Pains* (Carcanet Press, 1975), "After a Time" and "Christ Seen by Flemish Painters" from *Consequently I Rejoice* (Carcanet Press, 1977), "The Child's Story" from *Extending the Territory* (Carcanet Press, 1985), by permission of David Higham Associates Ltd; DAVID JONES: "A, a, a, Domine Deus" and "Angle-Land" from *The Anathemata* (Faber & Faber, 1972) and *The Sleeping Lord and Other Fragments* (Faber & Faber, 1995) by permission of the publisher; PATRICK KAVANAGH: "Shancoduff", "Stony Grey Soil", "The Long Garden", "Memory of Brother Michael", "Epic" and "Come Dance with Kitty Stobling" from *Selected Poems* (Penguin, 1996) by permission of the trustees of the Estate of Patrick Kavanagh and Peter Fallon, Literary Agent; THOMAS KINSELLA: "Soft, to your Places", "Another September", "The Laundress", "Downstream", "Brotherhood", "Talent and Friendship" and "A Portrait of the Artist" from *Selected Poems 1956–94* (Oxford University Press, 1996) by permission of Thomas Kinsella; RUDYARD KIPLING: "The Dykes", "The Broken Men", "Mesopotamia", "Epitaphs of the War 1914–1918", "Mandalay", "The Way through the Woods", and "Harp Song of the Dane Women" from *A Choice of Kipling's Verse* (Faber & Faber, 1973), by permission of A. P. Watt Ltd on behalf of The National Trust for Places of Historic Interest or Natural Beauty; R. F. LANGLEY: "Mariana" and "Jack's Pigeon" by permission of R. F. Langley; PHILIP LARKIN: "At Grass", "Deceptions", "Next, Please", "I Remember, I Remember", "Church Going", "MCMXIV", "High Windows", "The Trees" and "The Old Fools" from *Collected Poems* (Faber & Faber, 1993, with The Marvell Press) by permission of the publishers; D. H. LAWRENCE: "Discord in Childhood", "Piano", "Green", "Song of a Man Who Has Come Through", "Snake" and "Bavarian Gentians" from *The Complete Poems of D. H. Lawrence* (William Heinemann, 1957) by permission of Laurence Pollinger Ltd and the Estate of Frieda Lawrence Ravagli; GWYNETH LEWIS: "Six Poems on Nothing", "Herod's Palace" and "Walking with God" from *Parables & Faxes* (Bloodaxe Books, 1995) by permission of the publisher; ROBERT LOWELL: "Mr Edwards and the Spider", "Skunk Hour", "The Flaw", "Night Sweat", "For the Union Dead", "Waking Early Sunday Morning" and "Epilogue" from *Selected Poems* (Faber & Faber, 1965), *Near the Ocean* (Faber & Faber, 1967) and *Day by Day* (Faber & Faber, 1977) by permission of the publisher; MINA LOY: "Der Blinde Junge", "Brancusi's Golden Bird" and "On Third Avenue" from *The Last Lunar Baedeker* (Carcanet Press, 1997) by permission of the publisher; NORMAN MACCAIG: "Climbing Suilven", "Feeding Ducks", "No Consolation", "Crossing the Border", "So Many Summers" and "Toad" from Collected Poems (Chatto & Windus, 1993), by permission of the Hogarth Press; HUGH MACDIARMID: "The Bonnie Broukit Bairn", "The Watergaw", "The Innumerable Christ", "At My Father's Grave", "Of John Davidson", "Light and Shadow", "Poetry and Science" and "Crystals Like Blood" from *Complete Poems* (Carcanet Press, 1992) by permission of the publisher; SORLEY MACLEAN: "Am Buaireadh/The Turmoil", "Ban-Ghàidheal/A Highland Woman", "Ceann Loch Aoineart/Kinloch Ainort" and "Hallaig" from *Collected Poems* (Carcanet Press, 1989) by permission of the publisher; LOUIS MACNEICE: "Snow", "The Sunlight on the Garden", "Bagpipe Music", "Evening in Connecticut", "Prayer Before Birth", "House on a Cliff" and "Selva Oscura" from *Selected Poems* (Faber & Faber, 1964) by permission of David Higham Associates Ltd; DEREK MAHON: Consolations of Philosophy", "The Snow Party", "A Disused Shed in Co. Wexford", "Going Home" and "The Hunt by Night" from *Selected Poems* (Penguin/Gallery, 1990) by permission of Derek Mahon and The Gallery Press; BILL MANHIRE: "On Originality", "The Distance Between Bodies" and "Brazil" from *Milky Way Bar* (Carcanet Press, 1991) and *Sheet Music* (Carcanet Press, 1996) by permission of the publisher; GLYN MAXWELL: "Mild Citizen" and "Poisonfield" from *Tale of the Mayor's Son* (Bloodaxe, 1990) by permission of the publisher; JAMES MERRILL: "Swimming by Night", "David's Night in Veliès" and "Clearing the Title" from *Selected Poems* (Carcanet Press, 1996) by permission of the publisher; CHARLOTTE MEW: "Fame", "The Quiet House", "Not For That City" and "Rooms" from *Collected Poems* (Carcanet Press, 1981) by permission of the publisher; CHRISTOPHER MIDDLETON: "Anasphere: Le torse antique" and "Saloon with Birds" from *Selected Writings* (Carcanet Press, 1989) by permission of the publisher; EDNA ST VINCENT MILLAY: "Time does not bring relief; you all have lied", "Passer Mortuus Est", "Inland", "Wild Swans", "I being born a woman and distressed" and "On the Wide Heath" from *Selected Poems* (Carcanet Press, 1992) by permission of the publisher; ROBERT MINHINNICK: "Twenty-Five Laments for Iraq" by permission of Robert Minhinnick; MARIANNE MOORE: "The Steeple-Jack", "Poetry", "Silence", "What Are Years?", "The Paper Nautilus" and "Nevertheless" from *Complete Poems* (Faber & Faber, 1984) by permission of the publisher; EDWIN MORGAN: "Siesta of a Hungarian Snake", "A View of Things", "Columba's Song", "Itinerary", "Cinquevalli", "Sir James Murray" and "The Glass" from *Collected Poems* (Carcanet Press, 1985) by permission of the publisher; ANDREW MOTION: "Anne Frank Huis", "One Life", "Close" and "Reading the Elephant" from *The Pleasure Steamers* (Carcanet Press, 1978) by permission of the publisher; EDWIN MUIR: "Ballad of Hector in Hades", "Troy", "The Myth" and "The Late Wasp" from *Collected Poems* (Faber & Faber, 1963) by permission of the publisher; PAUL MULDOON "The Electric Orchard", "The Narrow Road to the Deep North", "Mules", "Gathering Mushrooms" and "Long Finish" from *New Weather* (Faber & Faber, 1973), *Mules and Early Poems* (Faber & Faber, 1986) and *New Selected Poems* (Faber & Faber, 1996) by permission of the publisher; LES MURRAY: "An Absolutely Ordinary Rainbow", "The Broad Bean Sermon", "The Quality of Sprawl", "Satis Passio", "It Allows a Portrait in Line Scan at

Fifteen", "Burning Want", and "The Last Hellos" from *Selected Poems* (Carcanet Press, 1986) and *Subhuman Redneck Poems* (Carcanet Press, 1996) by permission of the publisher; LORINE NIEDECKER: "Poet's Work" and "Thomas Jefferson" from *From This Condensery: The Complete Writing of Lorine Niedecker* (Jargon Society, 1985), by permission of Cid Corman; FRANK O HARA: "Animals", "Aus Einem April", "In Memory of My Feelings" and "Ave Maria" from *Selected Poems* (Carcanet Press, 1991) by permission of the publisher; CHARLES OLSON: "The Kingfishers", "At Yorktown" and "The Moon is the Number 18" from *Selected Poems* (University of California Press, 1993) by permission of the publisher; GEORGE OPPEN: "No interval of manner", "Product", "Psalm", "Penobscot" and "Confession" from *Poems of Gorge Oppen* (CLOUD, 1990) by permission of New Directions Publishing Corp.; MICHAEL PALMER: "Ninth Symmetrical Poem", "Seven Forbidden Words", "The Theory of the Flower", "Autobiography 2 (helloggodby)" and extract from *Series*, from *The Lion Bridge: Selected Poems 1972–95* by (Carcanet Press, 1998) by permission of the publisher; JOHN PECK: "Vega over the rim of the Val Verzasca", "Anti-dithyrambics", "Campagna", "End of July", "Archeus Terrae", "Monologue of the Magdalene" and "From the Viking Museum", from *The Poems and Translations of Hi-Lö* (Carcanet Press, 1991), Λ.R.G.V.R.Λ (Carcanet Press, 1993) and *Selva Morale* (Carcanet Press, 1995) by permission of the publisher; ROBERT PINSKY: "Braveries", "Shirt" and "From the Childhood of Jesus" from *The Figured Wheel: New and Collected Poems* (Carcanet Press, 1996) by permission of the publisher; SYLVIA PLATH: "Soliloquy of the Solipsist", "The Manor Garden", "Morning Song", "The Bee Meeting" and "Lady Lazarus" from *Collected Poems* (Faber & Faber, 1981) by permission of the publisher; EZRA POUND: "The Tree", "Speech for Psyche in the Golden Book of Apuleius", "The River-Merchant's Wife: A Letter", *Cantos XXX, XLV, LXXXI* and excerpts from *Hugh Selwyn Mauberley*, from *Collected Shorter Poems* (Faber & Faber, 1968) and *The Cantos* (Faber & Faber, 1987) by permission of the publisher; F. T. PRINCE: "An Epistle to a Patron", "False Bay", "For Fugitives" and "Cœur de Lion" from *Collected Poems* (Carcanet Press, 1993) by permission of the publisher; JOHN CROWE RANSOM: "Bells for John Whiteside's Daughter", "Piazza Piece", "Vision by Sweetwater" and "Dead Boy" from *Selected Poems* (Carcanet Press, 1991) by permission of the publisher; HENRY REED: A Map of Verona", "The Door and the Window" and "Philoctetes" from *Collected Poems* (Oxford University Press, 1991) by permission of the publisher; ADRIENNE RICH: "I am in Danger – Sir –" and "Burning of Paper Instead of Children" from *Collected Early Poems: 1950–70* (Norton, 1971), "Diving into the Wreck" and "Splittings" from *The Fact of a Doorframe: Poems Selected and New 1950–84* (Norton, 1984), "Delta" from *Time's Power: Poems 1985–88* (Norton, 1989), "Amends" and "Late Ghazal" from *Dark Fields of the Republic: Poems 1991–95* (Norton, 1995) by permission of the author and W. W. Norton & Company, Inc.; LAURA RIDING: "A City Seems", "The Troubles of a Book", "The Mask", "One Self", "The World and I", "The Reasons of Each", "Poet: A Lying Word", and "Divestment of Beauty" from *The Poems of Laura Riding*, by Laura (Riding) Jackson. Copyright © 1938, 1980. Reprinted by permission of Carcanet Press, Manchester, Persea Books, New York, and the author's Board of Literary Management, which, in conformity with the late author's wish, asks us to record that, in 1941, Laura (Riding) Jackson renounced, on grounds of linguistic principle, the writing of poetry: she had come to hold that "poetry obstructs general attainment to something better in our linguistic way-of-life than we have"; THEODORE ROETHKE: "The Premonition", "Mid-Country Blow", "Root Cellar", "Orchids", "Big Wind", "All the Earth, All the Air" and "Otto" from *Collected Poems* (Faber & Faber, 1985); E. J. SCOVELL: "Past Time", "The Ghosts", "Shadows of Chrysanthemums", "The River Steamer", "The Sandy Yard", "Listening to Collared Doves" and "Water Images" from *Collected Poems* (Carcanet Press, 1991) by permission of the publisher; PETER SCUPHAM: "The Nondescript", "Birthday Triptych", "The Beach", "The Key" and "Service" from *Selected Poems 1972–90* (Oxford University Press, 1990), by permission of Oxford University Press; "Pompeii: Plaster Casts" and "After Ovid, Tristia" by permission of Peter Scupham; BURNS SINGER: "Still and All", "Your Words, My Answers" and "Corner Boy's Farewell" from *Selected Poems* (Carcanet Press, 1977) by permission of the publisher; C. H. SISSON: "The Un-Red Deer", "A Letter to John Donne", "The Person", "The Usk", "The Herb-Garden", "The Red Admiral", "In Flood" and "Tristia" from *Collected Poems* (Carcanet Press, 1995) by permission of the publisher; IAIN CRICHTON SMITH: "Old Woman",

"Deer on the High Hills", "The Exiles" and "Listen" from *Collected Poems* (Carcanet Press, 1995) by permission of the publisher; STEVIE SMITH: "Dirge", "Not Waving but Drowning", "The Jungle Husband", "Tenuous and Precarious", "A House of Mercy" and "The Donkey" from *The Collected Poems of Stevie Smith* (Penguin, 1989) by permission of James MacGibbon; STEPHEN SPENDER: "My parents kept me from children who were rough", "What I expected was" and "I think continually of those who were truly great" from *Collected Poems 1928–85* (Faber & Faber, 1985) by permission of the publisher; WALLACE STEVENS: "The Snow Man", "Sunday Morning", "Thirteen Ways of Looking at a Blackbird", "The Idea of Order at Key West", "The Sun This March" and "Final Soliloquy of the Interior Paramour" from *Collected Poems* (Faber & Faber, 1955) by permission of the publisher; DYLAN THOMAS: "The Hand that Signed the Paper", "The force that through the green fuse drives the flower", "A Refusal to Mourn the Death, by Fire, of a Child in London", "Fern Hill" and "Do not go gentle into that good night" from *Dylan Thomas: The Poems* (J. M. Dent, 1978), by permission of David Higham Associates Ltd; R. S. THOMAS: "Song for Gwydion", "The Village", "In a Country Church", "Genealogy", "Period", and "Pavane" from the *Collected Poems* (Phoenix, 1995), by permission of J. M. Dent; "Taliesen 1952", "Navigation" and "Evening" by permission of R. S. Thomas; CHARLES TOMLINSON: More Foreign Cities", "Prometheus", "Against Extremity", "After a Death", "For Danton" from *Selected Poems 1995–97* (Oxford University Press, 1997) and "Weather Report" from *Jubilation* (Oxford University Press, 1995) by permission of the publisher; JEFFREY WAINWRIGHT: "Thomas Müntzer" and "The Apparent Colonnades" from *Selected Poems* (Carcanet Press, 1985) by permission of the publisher; DEREK WALCOTT: *The Schooner* Flight from *Collected Poems 1948–84* (Faber & Faber, 1992) by permission of the publisher; RICHARD WILBUR: "Parable", "Someone Talking to Himself", "Advice to a Prophet", "Leaving" and "Hamlen Brook" from *New and Collected Poems* (Faber & Faber, 1989) by permission of the publisher; WILLIAM CARLOS WILLIAMS: "Portrait of a Lady", "To the Shade of Po Chü-I", "So much depends", "Brilliant Sad Sun", "Question and Answer", "Poem", "Nantucket", "This Is Just to Say", "The New Clouds", "The Dance", *Paterson* (Book V) and "The Yellow Flower" from *Collected Poems* (Carcanet Press, 1987, 1988) by permission of the publisher; YVOR WINTERS: "The Realization", "The Slow Pacific Swell", "On a View of Pasadena from the Hills" and "Time and the Garden" from *Collected Poems* (Carcanet Press, 1978); JUDITH WRIGHT: "At Cooloolah", "Australia 1970", "Lament for Passenger Pigeons", extracts from *Notes at Edge* and *The Shadow of Fire*, from *Collected Poems* (Carcanet Press, 1992) by permission of the publisher; W. B. YEATS: "No Second Troy", "The Coming of Wisdom with Time", "September 1913", "The Magi", "An Irish Airman Foresees his Death", "The Cat and the Moon", "Easter 1916", "The Second Coming", "Sailing to Byzantium", "Leda and the Swan", "Among School Children", "Byzantium", "An Acre of Grass" and "The Circus Animals' Desertion" from *The Collected Poems of W. B. Yeats* (Macmillan, 1966) by permission of A. P. Watt Ltd on behalf of Michael B. Yeats;

Every effort has been made to obtain permission from all copyright holders whose material is included in this book, but in some cases this has not proved possible at the time of going to press. The publisher therefore wishes to thank those copyright holders who are included without acknowledgement, and would be pleased to rectify any errors or omissions in future editions. ✕